I0120513

James J. Jarves, Henry M. Whitney

History of the Hawaiian Islands

Embracing their antiquities, mythology, legends, discovery by Europeans in the

sixteenth century. Fourth Edition

James J. Jarves, Henry M. Whitney

History of the Hawaiian Islands
Embracing their antiquities, mythology, legends, discovery by Europeans in the sixteenth century. Fourth Edition

ISBN/EAN: 9783337191559

Printed in Europe, USA, Canada, Australia, Japan

Cover: Foto ©Andreas Hilbeck / pixelio.de

More available books at **www.hansebooks.com**

HISTORY

OF THE

HAWAIIAN ISLANDS:

EMBRACING

THEIR ANTIQUITIES, MYTHOLOGY, LEGENDS, DISCOVERY BY EUROPEANS IN THE SIXTEENTH CENTURY, RE-DISCOVERY BY COOK, WITH THEIR CIVIL, RELIGIOUS AND POLITICAL HISTORY, FROM THE EARLIEST TRADITIONARY PERIOD TO THE YEAR 1846.

By James Jackson Jarves.

Fourth Edition.
WITH AN APPENDIX.

HONOLULU:
HENRY M. WHITNEY, PUBLISHER.
1872.

EXTRACT

FROM PREFACE TO FIRST AND SECOND EDITIONS.

———◆———

The author deems it proper briefly to state the causes, which have led him upon venturing to place before the public, a narrative of a nation so youthful in annals, that constitute claims to the appellation of history in its most dignified sense. If he had been more ambitious of the credit of an historiographer, than desirous of presenting in their true light, the historical incidents of an interesting though humble people, a field of greater events and more storied interest would have been selected. But deeds are not always to be judged by the extent of the territories which gave them origin, or principles, by the degree of the individuals who were the means of their dissemination. Both must be tested by their relative effects. The record of the spread of moral worth and political freedom in a nation, however puny, is deserving of far more attention, than the tales of a lawless ambition, whose spirit is death, and whose path, misery and ruin. The author fain would trust that some of the interest and instruction which he, himself, has derived from studying the actual condition of heathenism as it existed among the Hawaiian nation, its providential overthrow, and the gradual and increasing ascendancy of christianity and civilization, despite many re-actions and unceasing hostility, will be imparted to his readers. The christian community have long looked with kindly interest on this experiment; their gifts, labors and prayers have nourished its growth; but to the remainder of the world, it has appeared more as an imperfectly finished picture, in which light and shade were inharmoniously blended, than as a beautiful illustration of the power of "God unto salvation." In this work, it has been attempted to trace the courses and results of the antagonistic efforts of the several influences which have been brought to impede or accelerate its progress, and also to preserve in a popular form, the records of an age which were fast disappearing. In the traditions and customs of their earlier existence, much will be found to gratify the spirit of curiosity and research; at least, they possess the merit of forming a portion in the general catalogue of human events, while without them, an additional page would be numbered among the already too numerous blanks in the history of mankind.

The author, in pursuit of health and recreation, first landed on the shores of Oahu in 1837, imbued with much of that spirit which erroneously pervades the interesting narratives of a Beechey, a Kotzebue, and others, who fancied themselves honest searchers after truth. From his course of reading and inquiries among those, whose opportunities had allowed them to form correct opinions,—had not their prejudices been too deep to be eradicated by reason,—he had formed the opinion, that the Hawaiians, though bettered in morals, were a priest-ridden people; that sectarianism and worldly aggrandizement were the

cogent motives of their spiritual teachers, and that they had succeeded in establishing a system of government, which for influence and secrecy of design might
justly be compared to the dominion of the Jesuits in South America. A close
examination, it was expected, would confirm these views. How far these opinions
have been retained the following pages will show. They are the results of
convictions derived from a nearly four years' residence at these Islands, with a
diligent study of their ancient history, and its connection with the political and
religious changes. If the writer were of the same sect as that body whose
missionary labors have been instrumental of so much good, he might be accused
of a bias toward them. But such is not the case ; he feels it a duty frankly to
bear testimony to truth, in whomsoever it may appear, and whatsover may be
its shape. Had his former views been established, they would have been as
freely proclaimed ; his earnest desire being to contribute even a mite to the
pages of history.

To the valuable labors of the Rev. William Ellis, author of "Tour Around
Hawaii," the author has been greatly indebted, and is happy to be able to verify
the general accuracy of his statements. His former position as editor of a
weekly paper at Honolulu, "The Polynesian," and his relations with all the
parties of that place, his acquaintance with the chiefs and natives, and with
others whose personal knowledge of historical events extended beyond his,
enabled him to collect much valuable information ; this, since his arrival in
Boston, has been carefully arranged and collated, with all the works of authority
relative to the Islands, including the expensive foreign editions of early voyagers.
Information has been derived from individuals who early resorted thither for
trade. Accuracy in all statements has been diligently sought, and, as all the
events are of comparatively recent occurrence, it is believed, obtained. The
translations from "Ka Mooolelo Hawaii," or History of Hawaii, written by the
scholars of the High School at Lahainaluna, were made by the Rev. Reuben
Tinker, late a missionary, and may be depended on for their fidelity.

As many of the individuals whose conduct has had an important bearing upon
Hawaiian policy and reform are still living, statements which affect them have
been made only when necessary for the exposition of political movements ; and
then only upon indisputable evidence. The history of the government is so
intimately involved with the unprincipled movements of a few characters, that to
delineate the former, it was impossible to avoid picturing the latter ; while the
natural delicacy of the unobtrusive good, prevents a more public acknowledgment of the quiet yet effective exertions of individuals whose visits or residences
have been peculiarly beneficial.

HISTORY OF THE HAWAIIAN ISLANDS.

CHAPTER I.

Sandwich Islands—True Name — Situation — Number and Extent — Harbors — General Appearance and Structure—Rain—Windward Sides—Leeward Sides —Minerals—Salt Lake—Soil—Vegetable Productions — Insects — Animals — Fishes — Climate — Winds— Storms — Diseases — Earthquakes — Phenomena of Tides—Meteoric Showers of 1825—Water Spouts.

THAT important cluster of Islands, situated in the North Pacific Ocean, commonly known as the Sandwich Islands, were so named by Captain Cook, at the date of their discovery by him, in honor of his patron, the Earl of Sandwich, then first Lord of the Admiralty. Their legitimate appellation, and the one by which they still continue to be distinguished by the aboriginal inhabitants, is "*Hawaii nei pae aina*," a collective term, synonymous with "these Hawaiian Islands." This term is derived from the largest of the group, Hawaii, whence the reigning family originated, and is gradually taking the place of the former.

The central situation of the Hawaiian Islands in the vast North Pacific, is highly favorable to their commercial growth. Their extremes of latitude are from 18° 50' to 22° 20' north, and of longitude from 154° 53' to 160° 15' west from Greenwich.

This position is nearly equi-distant from Central America, Mexico, California, and the Northwest Coast on the one side, and the Russian dominions, Japan, China, and the Phillippine Islands, on the other. When a civilized and enterprising population shall have developed the resources of those countries, these Islands will bear the same relative importance to them, in proportion to their extent, that the West Indies now do to North and South America.

Including Bird Island, which was well known to the others prior to their discovery, in 1778, the group consists of twelve.

The inhabited Islands, eight in number, are of the following extent :—

NAMES.	MILES LONG.	MILES BROAD.	SQUARE MILES.
Hawaii,	88	73	4000
Maui,	48	30	620
Oahu,	46	25	530
Kauai,	22	25	500
Molokai,	40	7	190
Lanai,	17	9	100
Niihau,	20	7	90
Kahoolawe,	11	8	60

Bird Island is a barren rock, 120 miles to the northwest of Kauai. Three of the others are equally unimportant ; Molokini, an extinct crater of but slight elevation, with one side open to the sea, lies midway between Maui and Kahoolawe ; Lehua, a mile to westward of Niihau, has an elevation of 1000 feet, some slight vegetation, and an excellent spring of water ; Kaula, seven miles southwest from Niihau, is of less extent, and, like Bird Island, abounds with wild fowl.

The whole embrace a superficial area of about sixty-one hundred miles, of which Hawaii includes two-thirds. But a small proportion of their coasts, compared with the Southern groups, is bounded by coral reefs. These are of limited extent, and extend but a short distance from the shore, forming a barrier, over which the sea rolls in sheets of foam.

There are few harbors, though numerous channels occur in the reefs, affording entrance into basins, capable of accommodating coasters. With the exception of Honolulu, on the south side of Oahu, no really good harbor exists. At Ewa, ten miles to the west of Honolulu, there is one with twelve feet at low water on the bar; the basin within is sufficiently capacious to receive the entire commerce of the Pacific; but the adjoining land is barren and forbidding. At Koolau, on the north side of Oahu, there is another harbor, with however but nine feet water in the channel. The surrounding country is verdant, well watered, and the breeze directly from the ocean. By deepening these channels, should the commerce of the kingdom ever require it, fine sites for commercial towns would be formed. Hilo Bay, on the north of Hawaii, commonly known as Byron's Bay, affords excellent anchorage; shipping are protected by a projecting reef, and the holding ground is good, but the surf breaks heavily upon the beach, and not unfrequently renders landing difficult. At all of the principal towns, with these exceptions, the roadsteads are exposed; but such is the nature of the prevailing winds, that vessels can frequent them in perfect safety during nine or ten months of the year. With good ground tackle there is little to be feared at any season. No dangers to navigation exist in the vicinity of the Islands, with the exception of a reef off the west coast of Kahoolawe. It is a little less than two miles from the shore, and with two fathoms of water on it at low tide. A few rocks, within a circumference of two hundred feet, comprise its whole extent.

The structure of the group is volcanic. On Hawaii is found the largest known active volcano, and several others of great size, partially or wholly quiescent. The mountains attain an elevation of fourteen thousand feet. They are of great extent and grandeur, and, throughout the group, present scenery of peculiar and beautiful character. To the north they slope somewhat precipitously to the sea, covered with a greensward at their base, and above with dense forests. Plains are broken by deep ravines, down whose steep sides cascades fall in bright and pretty sheets. Several of these often unite, as at Kauai, and form rivers of considerable depth and size. Palis, or precipices, in many parts, present stupendous walls of rock, from one thousand to three thousand feet perpendicular elevation, directly fronting the sea, the surging of which forms large caverns into which the sea rushes with stunning effect.

To the windward, and on the highlands, there is abundance of rain, which keeps vegetation perennially verdant. The leeward portions, during most of the year, suffer from drought, and offer a cheerless aspect. Below the region of clouds, vast and rugged masses of broken lava spread themselves over the country. Plains frequently occur with a soil formed of ashes and cinders, which, easily set in motion by violent gusts of wind, sweep over the land, and are carried to sea in dense clouds. During the winter months, when the trades are partially interrupted, showers often occur. When much rain falls the plains become covered with a species of coarse grass, which affords tolerable pasturage for cattle. Extinct volcanoes are very common. They are of every age, size and shape; at places, crowning the summits of lofty hills and mountains; elsewhere rising precipitously from plains or projecting into the ocean, they form prominent landmarks for navigators. One of the most singular and well-known, is the promontory near Honolulu, called Leahi, better known as Diamond Head, from an idea once current that precious stones were to be found there.

The minerals are few and simple, consisting of the usual variety of the lavas, from the most solid and granular to the light pumice-stone. Ledges of compact lime-stone, a good material for building, are found on several of the Islands. These being elevated considerably above the sea, have caused much speculation as to how they were formed or arrived at their present situation. The most remarkable is at Kahuku, Oahu. No metals have been discovered. Four miles to the west of Honolulu, and within a mile of the ocean, is the famous salt lake of *Alia-paakai*, elevated only a few feet above the level of the sea. It is in the heart of a crater, nearly oval in form, and about a mile in circumference. At certain seasons salt forms spontaneously and in the greatest abundance; at others but little is created, from its being overflowed by rains. Some have supposed it a mineral salt; but the general belief among the natives is, that it is formed by evaporation. The following facts favor the supposition. Its general depth is but eighteen inches; near the centre, a hole exists, five to six fathoms in circumference, which, as no bottom has been found to it, is supposed to connect with the ocean. Through this the lake is slightly affected by the tides, and at times it is crusted over with a stratum of salt sufficiently strong to bear a man's weight.

The soil of the Islands is formed of decomposed volcanic rocks, sand, mud and ashes. To be made fertile it requires constant irrigation. Valleys which receive the debris and rains of the mountains, and for ages have been accumulating deposits of vegetable mould, are exceedingly rich and productive; but they are of limited extent. The soil generally is poor, better adapted for grazing than cultivation, though with labor and skill it can be made to produce good crops. Nature yields but little spontaneously and the inhabitants have always been obliged to exercise much industry and ingenuity in their farms. The principle article of food is the well known kalo (*arum esculentum*). Great labor is necessary in raising it successfully and it requires a year or more to arrive at maturity.

The banana, yam, sweet potato, breadfruit, cocoanut, arrowroot, sugar-cane, strawberry, raspberry, *ohelo,* (a berry,) *ohia,* (a juicy, red apple, but of poor flavor,) are indigenous and plentiful. Many varieties of esculent fruits and vegetables have been successfully introduced, among which are melons, the delicious chirimoya from Peru, limes, oranges, guavas, pine-apples, grapes, peaches, figs, citrons, and tamarinds. The vegetables of the temperate region have been acclimated to a considerable extent. The uplands of Maui produce excellent "Irish potatoes." Wheat of good quality thrives in the same region.

An oil used in painting is extracted from the nut of the kukui tree (*aleurites triloba*). Sandal wood, suitable for exportation, is mostly exhausted, though the young wood is abundant.

Coffee, cotton, indigo, tobacco, sugarcane, mulberry, cocoa and most of the tropical plants can be successfully cultivated on the low grounds, while the uplands are suitable for the productions of more temperate regions.

Insects are few, though there are some of a destructive character. A species of caterpillar, the *pelua,* at certain seasons destroys vegetation to a great extent, eating even the grass to its very roots. A slug deposits its eggs in the cotton blossoms, which, when ripe, are pierced through by the young insects, and the staple entirely destroyed. Large spiders are very numerous and mischievous, weaving strong webs upon shrubs and young trees, in such quantities as to greatly injure them. A species of woodlouse, the ant-cow, is very annoying. A sooty crust, firm, hard and stiff, like strong paper, forms upon many varieties of trees and plants, covering the bark and even the leaves, giving them the singular appearance of being clothed in mourning. Rats destroy the sugarcane to a considerable extent annually. Though the Hawaiian agriculturist escapes many of the evils incidental to other tropical climes, enough exist here to make his labors no sinecure. Noxious vermin, such as mosquitoes, fleas, cockroaches, scorpions and centipedes, are a modern importation and have extensively increased. Serpents, frogs or toads have not as yet reached the Islands. A small lizard is abundant.

The forests are usually very dense, broken by deep chasms, hidden ravines and deep conical-shaped pits, which appear to have once been active craters. The trees are overgrown with masses of ferns and parasitical vines, thickly interlaced and spreading their shoots in all directions, which render it a task of great difficulty to penetrate their recesses. There are but few birds to enliven these sylvan solitudes. Wild geese are found at Hawaii; snipe, plover and wild ducks on all the Islands. A variety of the owl is very common; but nature, in the ornithological as well as the entomological tribe, has been chary of her gifts, and the traveler looks in vain for the endless varieties which the more favored intertropical countries afford. Dogs, swine, rats and domestic fowls are indigenous, and, beside the wild-fowl above mentioned, were the only varieties of animal food before the introduction of cattle.

Fish, of which there are a great variety, form one of the chief articles of diet. They consist chiefly of the albicore, bonita, flying-fish, shark, eel, and many species preserved in artificial ponds, which acquire a delicious flavor, and are highly prized. The best of these is the mullet. Edible shell-fish are also abundant, of which the pearl oyster, cuttle fish and prawn are the most palatable. Pearls are common, but of no great size or beauty. They formerly constituted a profitable branch of trade, and were monopolized by the king. The common oyster is not found.

The climate is salubrious, and possesses such remarkable evenness of temperature that the language has no word to express the general idea of weather. The tropical heat is mitigated by the trades, which blow over a wide expanse of ocean in the temperate zone. The shores on either side show but little difference in the results of the thermometer. Physiologists give a certain point of temperature as most conducive to health and longevity. The mean heat of these Islands approaches near to it, and is highly favorable to the full development and perfection of animal economy.

By visiting the interior and ascending the mountains any desirable degree of temperature can be attained. On the highest mountains snow remains during much of the year, and in exposed situations on Mauna Kea throughout the whole. Snow storms occur on the highlands of Maui during the winter months. On the upland region of Kauai, a uniform elevation of four thousand feet, both snow and hail occasionally occur. The temperature here is quite regular the year through, requiring warm garments and fires even in the month of July. The district is cold and wet, and of little value. A portion of it supports a heavy growth of timber and is frequented only by wood-cutters. The average temperature of Waimea, Hawaii, situated in the interior, at an elevation of about four thousand feet, is nearly 64° Fahrenheit—48° being the lowest extreme. This place affords an excellent retreat for those whose constitutions have become enervated by too long a residence nearer the coast. Rains are frequent at this altitude, but the dryness of the soil seldom leaves the ground damp for any length of time. At Mountain Retreat, back of Lahaina, Maui, an elevation of three thousand feet, the temperature varies from 40° to 75°; but such situations afford few comforts for the sick and their dampness renders them otherwise objectionable.

Localities can be selected on the seashore which possess advantages for invalids, particularly those affected with pulmonary complaints. Many individuals by change of residence, have prolonged their lives for years, and others who in the less favored regions of the north were perpetual sufferers, live with scarcely an admonition of their disease. Lahaina, Kailua, Ewa and Honolulu have all a good reputation in this respect. At the former, during ten years, the highest thermometrical elevation was 86°; the lowest 54°; an extreme difference of but 32°. During no day in this period was the range greater than 19°. June has the highest range—January the lowest. But little rain falls and for successive months the sun is rarely obscured by clouds.

The common range of the thermometer at Honolulu is 12° per diem. The greatest degree of heat during twelve years in the shade was 90°, and 54° for the coldest; the mean about 75°. Kailua and Ewa vary but little from the above.

At Koloa, Kauai, the thermometer varies from 50° to 88°; at Waioli, from 55° to 90°, with much rain. A change of wind affects the climate materially. During nine months of the year the northeast trade blows with great regularity and the temperature is very uniform. Oahu and Kauai are the most influenced by it; Maui, which is larger, has in a few places to the leeward, including Lahaina, the regular land and sea breeze. Hawaii, from its size and height of mountains, neutralizes its influence, and enjoys an almost uninterrupted land and sea breeze. This occurs, in some degree, even on its northeast coast where the trade is usually freshest. The winds partake of the character of the sea breeze in the day, and during the night are so modified by the influence of the land, as to vary their course from off the shore, or become very light. Where the mountain ranges are broken by steep defiles, as at Kawaihae and other bays on the west side, the wind rushes through with great violence, gathering strength as it descends until it passes off to sea in furious gusts. During the winter months the trades are interrupted, winds from the south and west often prevailing for several successive weeks;—calms are also frequent and of long duration. The south wind brings rain and is usually loaded with a briny vapor injurious to vegetation. Its effects are equally unpleasant to the human system. Headaches, catarrhs, rheumatism, and kindred diseases, prevail during its continuance. Upon foreigners its influence is very obvious, causing a compression about the head and an enervation which indisposes to mental or physical exertion; the atmosphere becomes oppressive and at times feels like the heated air of a furnace. The miasma arising from the lagoons to the southeast of Honolulu is blown back upon the land, infecting the town with an odor which but for its rarity would be insupportable. The natives call it the 'sick wind,' and with propriety. It sometimes occurs with sufficient force to destroy their frail habitations and do much damage to plantations and forests. Much of the weather at this season is however of the most delightful description; the sky becomes cloudless, the atmosphere dry, clear and bracing, and the whole system feels the invigorating influence of the change. Nothing can exceed the soft brilliancy of the moonlight nights. Thunder-storms are rare and light in their nature. No hurricanes have been known.

Epidemic diseases are few and of a light character. The mumps have prevailed very generally, and in some cases terminated fatally through mismanagement. The influenza occurs almost annually but is not often fatal unless added to other causes. The whooping-cough, a few years since, spread through the whole population, but soon entirely spent itself. Contagious diseases are scarcely known, excepting those of a cutaneous nature, which very generally prevail, owing to filthy habits and gross food. The small-pox has raged in the southern groups, but has never reached here. Vaccination is very generally practiced. The croup sometimes occurs. Hoapiliwahine, a chief woman of high rank, upwards of seventy years of age, died of this disease in January, 1842.

Powerful volcanic eruptions, attended with disastrous effects, have occurred on Hawaii several times within the memory of the present generation. Some of the largest of the craters, such as those of Mauna Haleakala, (house of the sun,) on Maui, at an elevation of eleven thousand feet, have been quiescent from a period beyond the traditions of the inhabitants. Earthquakes are chiefly confined to the largest island; the shocks felt at Maui are slight. The immense craters with which the former island abounds operate as safety-valves, by which the pent gases, generated by the vast subterranean fires, escape. Without them, the thin crusts of lava which constitute the foundation of the island, would be rent asunder, and it would become a terrific waste. Shocks are indeed frequent, but without sufficient strength to be very destructive. Trees are thrown down, rocks split, and the scene of action otherwise affected. At Hilo, in November, 1838, during the space of eight days, from forty to fifty shocks occurred. Twelve distinct ones were counted in one night. For two days and nights the earth was in a state of continual agitation; the plants and flowers trembling like frightened animals. In some cases the motion was perpendicular, like that of a ship pitching, and attended by noises and sensations similar to those produced by heavy waves striking against her sides, and some degree of nausea was felt. In others the action was lateral, easy and undulating, unaccompanied by any sounds. In April, 1841, several more powerful shocks were experienced at the

2

same place, one of which was quite severe. The houses were violently shaken, and had they not been constructed of yielding materials, would have been prostrated. The plastering was shattered, crockery-ware destroyed, milk thrown from pans, stone walls cast down, and other damage done. In March of the same year, several of a severe nature occurred at Kailua, which threw down much rock from the *pali*. These shocks were distinctly felt throughout Maui.

On the 25th of September, 1825, a shower of meteoric stones occurred at Honolulu. Reports like the firing of cannon and the repeated discharges of musketry were heard at about ten o'clock in the morning. At first the supposition was that a naval action was taking place in the immediate neighborhood; but the fall of many fragments of rock, weighing from ten to twenty pounds, accompanied by a whizzing sound, explained the nature of the noises. They struck with sufficient force to create cavities in the coral rock, and the pieces presented a greyish black exterior, with a yellowish appearance on the fractured portions.

A remarkable oscillation of the ocean was observed in 1837 throughout the group. In 1819, one on a lesser scale and unattended with any fatal consequences occurred. It was considered by the natives as prognosticating some dire event to their nation, and the death of Kamehameha, which took place soon after, was supposed to be the consummation. Upon its recurrence in 1837, the death of his son Kauikeouli or some high chief was confidently predicted; but as no national calamity ensued, this superstition was materially weakened. On the evening of the 7th of November, the commotion of the waters was first noticed at Honolulu. Neither the barometer nor thermometer indicated any unusual atmospherical changes. At five o'clock it was observed the sea was retiring. This it did with such rapidity as to cause much alarm among the foreigners, who were fearful its reaction would overwhelm the town, like the great wave which destroyed Callao in 1746; but hundreds of the native population, thoughtlessly shouting and frolicking, followed its retreat, picking up the stranded fish,

and viewing the whole as a rare piece of fun. Some, however, seemed otherwise affected, and the dismal wail which was raised in the stillness of the evening, carried the news far inland.

The first recession was the greatest, being more than eight feet; the reefs were left entirely dry, and the fishes died. The vessels, not in the deepest water, grounded; but the sea quickly returned, and in twenty-eight minutes reached the ordinary height of the highest tides: it then commenced receding again and fell six feet.[*] It rose a few inches higher on its third return and fell six and a half feet. This action continued, with a gradually diminishing force and extent, throughout that night and the forenoon of the ensuing day. The greatest rapidity with which it fell was twelve inches in thirty seconds.

On Hawaii and Maui the phenomenon was more powerful and occasioned considerable loss of property and lives. Its action increased to the windward, the northern sides of the islands being the most affected. At Maui the sea retired about twenty fathoms and returned with great speed in one immense wave, sweeping before it houses, trees, canoes and human beings. At Kahului the inhabitants, as at Honolulu, followed with rapturous delight the retreating wave, when suddenly it turned upon them, and rising like a steep wall, rushed forward to the shore, burying the natives in its foam and destroying the whole hamlet. The amphibious character of the islanders proved their safety, though they were obliged to mourn the loss of two of their number and the destruction of all their personal effects.

At Byron's Bay, Hawaii, the village was crowded with people, who had collected to attend a religious meeting. At half-past six o'clock the sea retired at the rate of five miles an hour, leaving a great portion of the harbor dry, and reducing the soundings in other places from five to three and a half fathoms. The wondering multitude, in their simplicity, eagerly rushed to the beach to witness the novel sight; quickly a gigantic wave came roaring towards them at a speed of seven to eight miles an hour,

---

[*] Hawaiian Spectator, vol. I., No 1, p. 104.

and rising twenty feet above high-water mark, dashed upon the coast with a stunning noise like a heavy crash of thunder. The people were buried in its flood; houses, canoes, fish-ponds, animals, in short, property of all kinds, were mingled in one common ruin. Cries of distress filled the air. Those in the water were struggling for their lives amid the wreck of houses or entangled among floating timber, while their relatives who had escaped the torrent, were loudly bewailing their situation. The wave which had rushed inland had in its way dashed over the deck of an English whaler at anchor in the bay. As soon as the crew recovered from the shock, they lowered their boats and through their exertions many lives were saved. Not a canoe had escaped, and numbers of the people, stunned and insensible, were floating seaward. The destruction of property was universal; even the garnered food was swept off. In two hamlets alone, sixty-six habitations were destroyed and eleven lives lost. Other portions of the sea-coast suffered in like proportion. No shocks of earthquakes or any tremor of the earth were experienced, though the action of the crater of Kilauea, the night previous, was uncommonly furious. In some spots its fires were quenched; in others, chasms were opened with violent explosions. It would appear from the simultaneousness of the commotion throughout the group, that it originated at some distance. The wave struck the several islands from apparently the same direction.

May 17th, 1841, the same scene, though on a much less violent scale, and attended with no loss of life, recurred. At twenty minutes past five o'clock, P. M., the water in the harbor of Honolulu was observed to be suddenly discolored and breaking like a tide rip. It then rushed rapidly out, leaving a portion of the harbor and all the reef bare. This occurred twice in the space of forty minutes, when it resumed its ordinary appearance. The fall was estimated at three feet. Simultaneously, at Lahaina, a distance of one hundred miles, the rise and fall of the water was several feet, and occurred frequently, at intervals of four minutes each, rushing violently and with great noise over the reefs. At about this period a similar scene was noticed on the coast of Kamschatka.

An immense water-spout broke over the harbor of Honolulu in May, 1809. The atmosphere was clear and the day calm when it was first observed. A heavy, dark cloud hung over its body, which appeared to be of the size of a stout mast. As it advanced, its bulk increased, until it attained the thickness of a hogshead. Its progress was slow, accompanied with a violent ebullition of the water at its base. Upon touching the reefs, the column broke, causing a sudden rise of the sea of three feet on the beach. Great numbers of fish were destroyed by the weight of the mass of water which fell. A few years before, one broke on the north side of the island, washed away a number of houses, and drowned several of the inhabitants.

CHAPTER II.

Early Hawaiian History—Former intercourse between the Hawaiian Islands and the Tahitian, Samoan and Marquesan groups—Superstition of "Youth-renewing Fountain"—Creation of first inhabitants—Flood —Origin of the World—of Hawaii—Traditions— Ancient Hawaiian Kings—Government — Common Law—Cruelties—Kingly power—Police—Chiefs—Retinues—Rank—How derived—Orders of nobility— Homage—Public councils and meetings—Conduct of superiors towards inferiors—Litigation—Ordeals— Praying to Death—Sorcery—Soothsayers or Magicians—Character of Religion—Notions of Future State —Hawaiian Hades—Ideas in regard to souls—Milu— Idols—Different classes of male and female—God Lono —Goddess Pele and her family—Hawaiian Centaur— Fabrication of Idols—Temples or *heiaus*—Ceremonies attending consecration—Human sacrifices—How obtained—Animal and vegetable offerings—Diviners— Priesthood—Ranks — General character — Taxes of priesthood—Remarkable privileges—Taboos—Origin and meaning of the word—Present application—Penalties attached to violation of—Cities of Refuge—Comparison between the religions and governments of the different groups.

The early history of the Hawaiian nation, like that of all savages, derived only through the uncertain medium of oral traditions, is vague, and but slightly calculated to reward the researches of the curious. Their origin is involved in an obscurity, on which their own fables, and historical and sacred *meles* or songs, are calculated to throw but little light. A certain uniformity in the earliest traditions and manners of the most savage nations exists, which would seem to indicate a common origin; or it may be the result of necessities, which, under like circumstances, adopt the same means to effect corresponding ends. This may account for customs of a common character, so frequently observed in tribes widely separated by geographical limits, and without any means of communication. The barrenness of the savage intellect affords but partial scope for observation and improvement. The same idea or necessity which would call into existence certain forms or habits of life in one latitude, would equally arise in another. Hence, but little confidence can be placed in deductions founded upon a conformity in a few isolated customs, among different barbarous communities. But, when affinities of language, physiological resemblances, corresponding manners and religious belief, and more particularly, well established traditions, pointing to a common origin, appear among tribes, which, in modern times, have lost all means of communication, the inquirer finds tenable grounds for believing in a general relationship. This appears to be the case throughout Polynesia. The language spoken in the groups so widely diffused over the Pacific Ocean, has the same common structure, with but such differences as may be resolved into dialects;—the result of long non-intercourse;—while other peculiarities are to be attributed to difference of soils, climates, governments and other local causes. The New Zealander and Hawaiian, though more than four thousand miles apart, with all the intermediate tribes, are members of one family, and require but a short period to acquire the faculty of a free exchange of ideas.

The fact that intercourse formerly existed between the various groups is tolerably well authenticated. According to traditions, voyages were of common occurrence. In those days their canoes were said to be larger and better constructed than at present. From some of the circumstances told concerning them, it is not improbable that they were the very boats, or *proas*—perhaps of Malay origin—which brought the first inhabitants to Hawaii, and which continued to be employed in keeping up intercourse with the other groups as long as they were sea-worthy. Certain it is the frail canoes of modern times are ill adapted to voyages of two and three thousand miles. The weather is often very tempestuous even within the influence of the trade winds. At the most favorable season canoes might perform the voyage in safety, by stopping at the numerous intervening coral islands for rest and refreshment. Still it would be more a matter of accident than skill. Even with better means of conveyance, and no other source of navigation than their imperfect knowledge of the stars, it is not to be wondered that these voyages should have been discontinued, as no traffic existed and curiosity or the love of relatives were the only impelling motives.

It is impossible to ascertain at what period these adventurous voyages were relinquished. Judging from the indefiniteness of the recollections concerning them, it must have been many ages since. Certain points of departure, as the southern extremities of Kahoolawe and Hawaii, were designated as the "*foreign roads.*" In Hawaiian *meles* the names of Nuuhiva and Tahuata, two islands of the Marquesan group, Upolu and Savaii, of the Samoan, and Tahiti and others in that neighborhood, frequently appear. Names of head-lands and towns in many of these are also common to others. Allusions are frequent to voyages made from Oahu to Kauai to islands far west. Tahiti or Kahiki, which are synonymous, were the names most commonly known, and appears to have been the island most visited. Popular opinion points to it as the source whence Hawaii was peopled. However, their ideas had become so vague in this respect, that it was applied to any foreign country, and to this day its actual signification answers to the English term "abroad." Bolabola, the name of an adjoining island, is usually applied to Tahiti.

The meaning thus attached to Tahiti arose, no doubt, from the circumstance, that the latest voyages were made there, and after they ceased it was the only country the knowledge of which remained among the common people. The names of the others were preserved among the priests and chiefs, though with an indistinctness that ultimately must have consigned them to oblivion. Even with the advantage of written language, the knowledge of America was lost, or but obscurely remembered by the adventurous Northmen. *Hoopahaohao* was the term used to express a different or foreign dialect.

Few only of the traditions relative to the earliest history of the islands are worthy of recital. The first inhabitants are related to have brought with them from Tahiti, a hog, a dog, and a pair of fowls. Before landing, they asked and obtained permission of the gods, then the sole denizens of this region, to remain. The arrival of a chief at Hawaii is spoken of, who finally settled on Kauai, and sent for his son. This son it seems was something of a mechanic, for he improved upon the construction of their canoes, or perhaps introduced the more recent improvements of Tahiti.

Other voyages are spoken of. One of these was made by a priest, in obedience to a communication from his god, revealing to him the existence, situation, and distance, of Tahiti, with the command to proceed thither. Obeying this injunction, he set sail from Hawaii, with forty companions, in four double canoes. After an absence of fifteen years, they returned and gave an interesting account of a country they had visited, called Haupokane, bordered with fine sandy beaches, abounding in shell-fish and delicious fruits. The inhabitants were comely and possessed much wealth.

The name of this Hawaiian Columbus was *Kamapiikai*, "a child running over the sea." He afterwards made three voyages to the same place, accompanied by numerous trains of followers, who were tempted by his glowing description of the newly discovered land, to share his fortunes. As he never returned from the fourth, he is supposed to have perished at sea.

The most remarkable feature of this tale, is what was related of the *wai-ola-loa*, "water of enduring life," a fountain or stream, said to exist in the land of Haupokane. If we may credit Kamapiikai, it possessed more marvelous properties than even the far-famed "Fountain of Youth," which Ponce De Leon vainly sought for, in Florida, in 1512. By bathing in its miraculous waters, people, however aged or infirm, deformed or ugly, maimed or diseased, were immediately restored to youth, strength, and beauty. Such being the reputation of this stream, it is no matter of surprise that Kamapiikai was able to entice numbers to brave with him the dangers of the ocean. Report does not say, whether his crews were composed only of those, whose necessities required such a bath. If they were, it will more readily account for his final loss, than his previous success. It is not altogether improbable that the Hawaiians derived this story from some of their early Spanish visitors, who had received it from the Indians of Cuba; or it may have been a superstition common to both races.

An opinion was prevalent that the first inhabitants descended from the gods, or were created on the islands. But this may be referred to a still earlier period, and different locality. Such traditions being found to exist among all nations, they evidently point to the common origin of the human species. Each nation, as it became isolated and lost knowledge of its primeval history, would naturally consider its own territory as the site of the miraculous creation, and themselves as divinely descended.

A tradition of the flood likewise exists, which states that all the land, except the summit of Mauna Kea, was overflowed by copious rains and risings of the waters. Some of the inhabitants preserved themselves in a "laau," a vessel whose height, length and breadth were equal, and which was filled with men, food and animals. This "laau," after floating awhile, finally rested upon Mauna Kea. The waters then subsided and the people went forth and again dwelt in the land. This flood is called *Kaiakahinalii*, the great deluge of *Hinalii*.

Their traditions, like those of the Hebrews, refer to a period of perpetual night, or a state of chaos, before the world existed. Nothing that now is, was then created, except some of the gods. The present state was called the "state of light," and creation was a transition from darkness to light. Any reference to existence from the earliest time was expressed thus, " from the state of confusion or darkness, until now." Hawaii was said to have been produced from a large egg, deposited by an immense bird upon the water, which bursting, formed the present island.

Maui, a superhuman being or god, is said to have laid his hand upon the sun, and arrested its course, to give his wife time to finish work, which she was anxious to complete before dark. This was certainly carrying gallantry to an extent never dreamed of by the chivalry of Europe, accustomed as they were to do brave deeds and incredible feats for their lady loves. The analogy however to be observed in this story, with the miracle of Joshua, is striking. According to Earnest Dieffenback in his recent travels in New Zealand, this Maui was a being of no little repute in that country, for to him the natives attribute the formation or fishing up of their island. They also derive their origin from countries called Hawaiki and Tawaii, in which names that author recognizes Hawaii and Kauai.] Dogs and taro were brought in the first canoes from the eastward. As further confirmation of his idea of the Hawaiian origin of the New Zealanders, he states that shrubs and trees of the same genus, though differing in species, bear similar names in both countries.*

The query, " whence the Polynesian family," has been much discussed. Dr. Lang's " View of the Origin and Migration of the Polynesian Nation," throws some light upon this perplexing question. There is no difficulty in accounting for the manner of peopling the islands; for it has been found that frail canoes and boats, either by accident or design, have performed voyages of sufficient extent to have arrived at the most remote lands in the Pacific. Japanese junks have been blown to sea, and finally stranded with their occupants upon distant islands, and have reached even the continent of America, in the 46th degree of north latitude. In December, 1832, one was

* Vol. II, p. 88, et. seq.

wrecked on Oahu, after having been tossed upon the ocean for eleven months. But four, out of a crew of nine, survived. Similar accidents, no doubt, happened centuries since. Lord North's island, a mere rock, of scarcely two miles circuit, and upwards of a thousand miles distant from any other land, has a numerous population, which must have originated from a similar casualty. Canoes, crowded with occupants of both sexes, are annually picked up at sea, far away from their places of departure, and drifting about at the mercy of the weather. The continent of Asia, owing to the numerous intervening islands, affords more facilities for reaching Polynesia in this manner, than America; though stragglers from the latter have doubtless from time to time added to the population, and thus created a mixture of customs, which, to some extent, indicate a mixed origin. The probabilities are in favor of Asia, both from affinity of language, and from striking resemblances in manners, idols, clothing, and physical conformation. But all conclusions, with the present light upon this subject, must necessarily be speculative, and of little practical utility. China was known to Egypt more than two thousand years before the birth of Christ, and a commercial intercourse maintained between the two countries. Africa was circumnavigated by the ancient Egyptian mariners; and among the relics of their high primary civilization, indications of an acquaintance with the continent of America are to be traced. Upon further development of the history of the earliest records of our race, it may be found that the geography of the world was better known than we are at present aware of —and the peopling of isolated positions and the migrations of nations, to have been performed with a definite knowledge of the general features of the globe. This, as well as their purer forms of faith, became obscured in the night of ages, when darkness and ignorance settled upon the nations of the earth. After a lapse of four thousand years, glimmerings only of the truth are revealed, in the fables of a multitude of distinct tribes of men; the general coincidence of which points to a common parentage.

Whatever may have been the origin of the Hawaiians, we find in their traditions, ground for the belief that they once possessed a simpler ritual and purer ideas of divinity than when discovered by Cook. The ideas embodied in these traditions appear to be the fragments of a faith or teachings not unlike those of the Hebrews. Perhaps like theirs, they came down to them from primeval ages, before mankind had become wholly corrupt; when the sons of God walked with the children of men. But others, and particularly several customs point to a later period, when the Israelites had become a nation under the ceremonial law. Ingenious minds may find a pleasure in tracing the parallel between customs and traditions of the Hawaiian race and the ceremonies and scripture of the Jews. But it requires further research and more proof before we can adopt the conclusion that they sprung from the lost ten tribes.

Dibble, in his History of the American Mission, favors this idea. He was intimately acquainted with all there was to be known concerning Hawaiian traditionary history and customs, and has succinctly enumerated the parallelisms. He writes:

"It is frequently remarked that every barbarous nation has some traditions more or less distinct of ancient events narrated in the Holy Scriptures, and some customs and practices also that indicate the common origin of the human race. The remark is certainly true of the inhabitants of these islands, and to such an extent that it is not difficult to imagine, that the Hawaiians are a part of the scattered tribes of the children of Israel.

"In the regular division of time and the occurrence of sacred seasons, at intervals, four times a month, there may be some trace of an ancient weekly Sabbath. There were also yearly feasts, and feasts of the new moon, which were observed with much religious ceremony.

"There is a very ancient tradition, dated back in the reign of Owaia, the second in genealogy of the Hawaiian chiefs, which may be introduced here, as it seems to bear some trace of a knowledge formerly existing, but since lost, of a superintending power above. The tradition is of a head having been seen in the heavens, which looked out of a cloud and made the following inquiry : 'Who among the kings of the earth has behaved well ?' This men here below replied, 'Kahiko, one of the kings of this lower world, was a most worthy personage, a wise man, a priest, and an astrologer, promoting the prosperity of his land, and the best interests of his people.' The head again inquired, 'What earthly king has been notoriously vicious ?' Men responded, 'His name is Owaia, an impious man, devoid of skill in divination or in war, indifferent to the prosperity of the realms and the happiness of his subjects. His every thought is absorbed in sensual pleasure, and the gratification of his avarice. He exalts himself by trampling on his subjects, whose felicity he of course fails to consult,—in a word, he pays no regard to the counsels and example of his excellent father.' Then said the voice, 'It is no wonder, truly, that the kingdom is driven to ruin, when he who holds the reins is a champion in crime.' Upon this the head disappeared.

"The *tabu* system, making sacred certain times, persons and places, and containing many restrictions and prohibitions, may easily be interpreted as a relic much changed and corrupted, from the ancient ceremonial observances of the Jews.

"The Hawaiians offered their first fruits to the gods.

"Among the Hawaiians, till the arrival of the missionaries, the practice of circumcision was common. The act was attended with religious ceremonies and performed by a priest. An uncircumcised person was considered mean and despicable. The practice did not cease till formally prohibited by Kaahumanu.

"Every person and thing that touched a dead body was considered unclean, and continued so a certain season, and till purified by religious ceremonies.

"Females after child-birth and after other periods of infirmity, were enjoined strict separation, and were subjected to ceremonies of purification similar to those of the Jews, on penalty of death.

"The Hawaiians had cities of refuge for the same purpose and under similar regulations with those of the Jews.

"Hawaiian tradition says that man was originally made of the dust of the earth by Kane and Kanaloa, two of their principal deities.

"They have the tradition of one Waikelenuiaiku, an abridged story of whom I will here introduce, that the reader may judge for himself how much it resembles the history of Joseph :

"Waikelenuiaiku was one of ten brethren, who had one sister. They were all the children of one father whose name was Waiku. Waikelenuiaiku was much beloved by his father, but his brethren hated him. On account of their hatred they carried him and cast him into a pit belonging to Holonaeole. The oldest brother had pity on him and gave charge to Holonaeole to take good care of him.

"Waikelenuiaiku escaped and fled to a country over which reigned a king whose name was Kamohoalii. There he was thrown into a dark place, a pit under ground, in which many persons were confined for various crimes.

"Whilst Waikelenuiaiku was confined in this dark place, he told his companions to dream dreams and tell them to him. The night following four of the prisoners had dreams. The first dreamed that he saw a ripe *ohia* (native apple) and his spirit ate it ; the second dreamed that he saw a ripe *banana* and his spirit ate it ; the third dreamed that he saw a hog and his spirit ate it ; and the fourth dreamed that he saw *awa*, (a native herb producing intoxicating liquor,) pressed out the juice, and his spirit drank it. The three first dreams (those pertaining to food) Waikelenuiaiku interpreted unfavorably and told the dreamers that they must prepare to die. The fourth dream (that pertaining to drink) he interpreted to signify deliverance and life.

"The three first dreamers were slain according to the interpretation and the fourth was delivered and saved.

"Afterwards, this last dreamer told Kamohoalii the king of the land how wonderful was the skill of Waikelenuiaiku in interpreting dreams, and the king sent and delivered him from prison and made him a principal chief in his kingdom.

"They have a tradition of a certain person who was swallowed by a fish and afterwards cast out upon dry land,—which may be referred to the history of Jonah.

"It may be added, that the poetry of the Hawaiians bears a greater resemblance to that of the Hebrews than to any other, that the structure of the two languages is very similar, and especially that the causative form of the Hawaiian verb is precisely the same with the Hiphil of the Hebrew. Very few words however can be found in the two languages that resemble each other."—pp. 26–28.

A genealogy of the kings of Hawaii and their wives, exists from a period long antecedent to 1778, though but few facts of an interesting nature have been preserved. Kahiko, (ancient,) the first man and Kupulanakahau, the first woman, gave birth to a son, called Wakea. Among the first settlers from abroad were Kukalaniehu, and his wife Kaku-laua, whose daughter married Wakea. This couple became the progenitors of the whole Hawaiian race. The names of seventy-seven generations of kings have been preserved in their historical *meles*, from the last of whom Kame-hameha claimed descent. Many mar-velous and absurd things are related of these men and their consorts. Papa was believed to be the mother of the islands, and to have created the kalo plant, by planting a deformed child, from which it grew. In the history of Papa is found the eastern idea of trans-migration of souls, as she is said to have inhabited different bodies by passing from one to another.

Kana was a famous warrior, and of him marvelous deeds are told. He was so tall that he could wade the ocean, and, colossus-like, stand with one foot upon Oahu and the other upon Kauai, seventy miles apart. On one occasion, the Hawaiians gave offence to the king of Tahiti, who, in revenge, deprived them of the sun. Kana, disliking the darkness, walked through the sea to Tahiti, where the maker of the sun, Kahoaalii, lived. Having obtained it, he returned and placed it where it still remains. But stories like these, origin-ating in the imaginations of the bards, or superstitions of the people, have neither interest nor value. Those given are a specimen of the better class. As a whole, they are characterized by won-der and absurdity, from which it seems impossible to extract any truth worth preserving. In their mental twilight the past assumed a dim and undefined ap-pearance, and was filled with vague shadows which became more hideous and disproportioned as their night drew on. The lives of the rulers were stained with the usual crimes of heathenism, and occupied with wars and dissensions. But one, Luamuo, retained his power and died a natural death. This was justly considered as a reward for his extraordinary virtue. Another, by the name of Puiakalani, becoming disgusted with the continued dissensions among his subjects, which he was called on to adjust, resigned his power, saying to the people, " I am tired of ruling over the land, and will no longer have care of it. It will be better for you, my subjects, to look after your own lands in a way to suit yourselves; while I take care of my own.'' The land soon fell into great confusion, and the people petitioned their prince to resume his former station, which he consented to with the proviso of ad-ditional power. To him is attributed the originating of the feudal principle, that the whole country belonged exclu-sively to the king. From his time, all lands were held in fief. The great increase of tyranny arose from the con-sideration given to the martial profes-sion. The most illustrious warriors, dreaded from their prowess and cruelty, were esteemed as superior beings, and sought after as leaders in their petty skirmishes for territory or plunder. In this manner, despotic power soon be-came the inheritance of the warlike chiefs; as for the people, they ceased to exist except as serfs, apportioned out with their lands to the favorites or de-pendents of the conquerors. New and more rigorous laws were enforced, until every vestige of former liberty was ex-tinguished.

It is probable that the political condi-tion of the country, during this period, was much the same as when first visited by Captain Cook: wars and famine, peace and plenty, alternating according to the dispositions of the ruling princes. The prevalence of such a system must effectually have checked mental or phy-sical advancement.

Before the conquest of Kamehameha, the several islands were ruled by inde-pendent kings, who were frequently at war with each other, but more often with their own subjects. As one chief acquired sufficient strength, he disputed the title of the reigning prince ; if suc-cessful, his chance of permanent power was quite as precarious as that of his predecessor. In some instances the title established by force of arms remained in the same family for several genera-tions, disturbed, however, by frequent rebellions. The rich valleys were claimed by separate tribes, whose prin-cipal occupation was to prey upon their neighbors; the highlands were arrayed against the lowlands; robbers infested all the public paths, or lurked amid the recesses of the forest. The smallest trifle of property was a sufficient temptation to murder; and no individual was safe away from the immediate precincts of his own village. The traveler of the present day hears from the lips of their descendants many a tale of horror, as they direct his notice to the haunts of these men of blood and lust. These dark features will however be found to be relieved by lighter shades, when the general character of the ancient government is explained.

It was a complete despotism, modified, to some extent, by certain customs or regulations, which had been promulgated in the early periods of their history, by the high chiefs, and which, from their general usefulness and antiquity, were considered in the light of a traditionary code. These related principally to the tenure of lands, personal security, right of property and barter. Such was the force of public sentiment upon these subjects, that the chiefs hesitated to violate the spirit of their meaning. By them the amount of taxes or labor due the chiefs from their dependants, and his duties to them, were, to some extent, regulated. This species of common law was particularly binding in regard to the means of irrigation, on which the whole value of their crops depended. It regulated, for each plantation, the amount of water which varies according to the dryness of the season. In barter, no bargain was considered as binding until the articles were exchanged and both parties expressed themselves satisfied; after which, no withdrawal was permitted, whatever might be the consequence. A common practice existed of paying workmen in advance. Should they then refuse to perform the stipulated work, their property was seized and their plantations destroyed. In criminal cases, the law of retaliation prevailed, except toward their immediate chiefs, who could commit any trespass, or even murder, at their option. In other cases, the injured party retaliated to the extent of their desires, unless they were too weak—in which event, an appeal to the king, or the chief of the district, ensured some light punish-

3

ment to the offender. Life was held in no great estimation, for murder was punished simply by banishment. Theft was more severely dealt with; those who had suffered in their houses or farms, repaired to the property of the guilty party, even if they were the strongest, and seized upon every available article. Whether there was anything approaching the form of a trial to prove the guilty party does not appear. Public opinion was however so fixed on this subject, that the whole people would sustain those who thus desired to obtain redress. This species of *lex talionis* seems in no way calculated to have improved their morals, though perhaps suited to their circumstances. In their social relations the greatest hospitality prevailed. So freely were gifts bestowed, that almost a community of property existed; and no man would refuse food to his bitterest enemy, should he enter his house. Thus the temptation to theft was much diminished, and the heinousness of the offence aggravated. If a robbery were committed on the property of a high chief, the offender was sometimes bound hand and foot, placed in a decayed canoe, and committed to the waters, to await a lingering death.

Such were the nature of some of their regulations, which, while they tended, to some extent, to create a security of property and person among the common people, in their transactions with each other, afforded but little safety against oppression on the part of their chiefs. The king could dispense with any of them, and the chiefs likewise—though an appeal to the king afforded some security against this latter abuse. The will of the monarch constituted the supreme law; consequently, the government partook of his personal character, being more or less arbitrary, according to his disposition. The general character of the chiefs, as might be expected, was such as despotic power, engrafted upon savage dispositions and sensual appetites, would be calculated to produce.

Kumalai, an ancient king of Maui, is noted in their annals for his oppression, and his memory is still preserved among the people, on account of a road of flat stones which he caused to be made around the island, part of which exists to this day. Another of these Caligulas, whose memory was universally execrated, was Huakau, a king of Hawaii. His disposition was so malicious, that if he saw the leg of a man more handsomely tatooed than his own, he immediately ordered it cut off. A good looking face or handsome hair, if unfortunate enough to attract his attention, were sufficient to cause the possessor to be beheaded; the bleeding head was brought to him, to be mangled and hacked in a most wanton manner. He was finally slain, in a conspiracy, by Umi, a rival king, and two aged men, whom he had abused.

The kingly authority extended over life, liberty and property. It was frequently delegated to the governors of the islands, or great districts, and from them to inferior officers. No chief could interfere with the tenant of another, and should he desire revenge or justice, it could only be obtained through the legitimate lord, unless he chose to risk a contest. The greatest safeguard of the people consisted in the self-interest of their masters, whose wealth and power depended chiefly on the number of their bondmen. The king was chief magistrate, and the ultimate source of appeal.

No regular police existed. The immediate attendants of the chiefs executed their orders. These attendants were very numerous, every person of rank being supplied according to his grade. A certain number were bosom friends, who always remained privileged idlers about the persons of their lords, having no voice in political affairs, but living upon his revenues: the others held different offices in the household, more or less menial, and constituted a permanent establishment. Among them were "pipe lighters," "spittoon carriers," "kahili bearers," "executioners," "purloiners," "assassins," "cooks," &c.

These retinues were formed immediately upon the birth of a chief of either sex, and were designated by titles, generally of a whimsical character, as "the fragments," "musquitoes," "umbrellas," &c. The care of the children devolved upon kahus, or nurses, who assumed the sole direction, until the child was capa-

ble of exercising its own will; a period which, as no contradiction to its caprices was allowed, soon arrived.

Rank was hereditary, and descended chiefly from the females, who frequently held the reins of government in their own right. This custom originated in the great license existing between the sexes; no child, with certainty, being able to designate his father, while no mistake could be made in regard to the mother.

Three distinct orders of nobles existed. The first embraced the kings, queens, and all branches of the royal family. It also included the chief advisers, or counselors, though of inferior birth. Governors, or chiefs of large districts, were included in the second, and the third embraced the lords of villages, priests, and those who held estates, by payment of regular taxes, which were raised by their own dependants, or those to whom they farmed lands.

Servile homage was paid to superiors, particularly to priests and chiefs of the highest rank. Neither their persons could be touched, nor their houses entered, without permission. All must prostrate themselves when they appeared. Death was the penalty of the slightest infringement of any degree of etiquette which the law required to be exercised towards them, or their rites. The people were attached to the soil, and transferred with the land, like the serfs of modern times. They had no voice in the government. The advice of the principal chiefs was taken in matters of importance by the king, though he was responsible to no one. No regular council existed, but the political deliberations were conducted with considerable diplomatic skill and secrecy. The results were promulgated to the people by heralds and messengers, whose offices were hereditary, and considered highly honorable.

Public meetings for discussing national affairs were sometimes held. Professed orators and counselors, whose offices were also hereditary, spoke on these occasions, and with a degree of natural eloquence, not uncommon among savages.

Among the chiefs a considerable degree of courtesy prevailed, with a refinement of language and demeanor which betokened conscious rank. Perhaps in nothing else was the exclusiveness of the aristocracy so strongly characterized. In every department of life a distinction was made, as if contact with the serfs, by touch, use of the same articles, houses, food or bathing places, would produce contamination. From such rules and deportment, so great a physical difference arose, that superficial observers have considered the two as distinct races. To carry this distinction to its farthest limit, the chiefs formed a conventional dialect, or court language, understood only among themselves. If any of its terms became known by the lower orders, they were immediately discarded and others substituted. Towards the common people the chiefs conducted themselves most oppressively. Respect to their persons or property was unknown, when in conflict with the whims or desires of a superior. Their security lay in avoiding them. To use the expressive language of modern Hawaiians, " their restrictions were like the poisoned tooth of a reptile." If a common man made use of any consecrated property belonging to a chief; or if a man walked in the shade of the house of a chief, with his head besmeared with clay, or with a wreath about it, with it wet, or wearing a *kihei.*—a *kapa* mantle,—or violated any one of numerous other regulations, equally whimsical and absurd, his life was the forfeit. At sea, if their canoes interrupted their progress, they were overturned ; on land, if the shadow of an individual fell upon the king, or he did not prostrate himself when anything was carried to or from him, the punishment was death. This was also the case, should any one place his hand upon his head, or be found in a more elevated position. To render this system more unjust and cruel, if it were possible, its laws were of the most varied and uncertain nature, emanating frequently from sheer caprice. Ignorance or innocence were equally unsafe, justice and humanity being of slight consideration : though, as before remarked,

the personal disposition of the sovereign greatly affected the whole system of government. The humane character of the few could afford but slight relief from the cruel and capricious desires of the many. Priestcraft lent all its adventitious aids to support this system, from which it derived its own existence. But two classes existed, the oppressor and oppressed,—those who labored, and those who reaped. Lands were held in fief. The great landlords derived them direct from the king, and in turn subdivided them among their followers, the inferior tenants being apportioned with the soil. The slightest failure of duty from one class to its immediate superior, was followed by dispossession. It was on the great chiefs that the king relied for military support, which they gladly rendered him as the title by which they retained their possessions. Not unfrequently lands were divided out to the seventh degree, and it is owing to this system that, now as the rights of each begin to be acknowledged, so much confusion in titles has arisen. Tenant, landlord, chief and king have each an interest in the same spot. Then, however, such matters were easily adjusted. The strongest took it. Nor more than one-third of the laborer's industry ever benefited him. The other two-thirds went in taxes, rents and exactions to his chiefs and to the king. Worse than this, his own third was never safe from some unforeseen exaction. If his lands were flourishing and a stock of hogs or poultry repaid his care, they were never secure from the covetous eyes of a superior. The decree had but to go forth, and house, farm and all that his labor had made his, passed irrevocably into the hands of another. Even when the good nature of one class of chiefs rendered the peasant's property comparatively secure, no reliance could be placed on its continuance. The death of a king or landlord, or even a new favoritism, caprice, or the most trivial motive, sufficed to produce a change of masters throughout. Thus one moment was no security against the next. Not to be entirely at the mercy of one man, tenants were desirous of securing small patches under several chiefs, so that when plundered by one they could repair to another. This system was an effectual bar to general improvements and the acquisition of property by the mass. It may account somewhat for their profuse hospitality, by leading every man the more willingly to bestow upon his neighbor, what he felt but slight rights of property to in himself; for food, even when prepared for the family meal, was no exception to a chief's rapacity. Beside this lion's right to property, the chief or king could assess labor upon the entire community, when and how he pleased.

In cases of litigation, some appearance of judicial forms was preserved. Both parties were generally summoned before the king or chief and heard before judgment was pronounced, the execution of which was prompt. Ordinarily, cases were left to the priests, whose examinations appealed rather to the superstitious fears of the real or fancied criminal, than to any direct evidences of guilt. Ordeals of a singular nature were practiced. One was the "*wai haalulu*," shaking water, a large dish of which was placed before the culprit, while a prayer was offered by the priest. Both hands were required to be held over the fluid, the priest gazing steadfastly upon it. If the water shook, an event, by a little legerdemain, very likely to occur, the fate of the victim was sealed.

The delusion of "praying to death" exercised a powerful influence over their minds. Chiefs and common people alike felt its force, though the former, it is to be supposed, seldom came under its baneful operation. Even to this day this superstition exists, though rapidly wearing away. Like the remembrance of goblin tales, the fear remains after the faith is destroyed. As a powerful engine of government and priesthood, it was deprecated equally by the innocent as by the guilty.

Sorcery and witchcraft were also extensively practiced, and exerted a power not inferior to the above, which may be considered as a kindred practice, depending for its success upon the same credulity and ignorance. *Kilo* was the term applied to the class that predicted future events, from the appearances of the heavens, crowing of cocks, or barking of dogs. It was analogous, and perhaps co-eval with the practice of soothsaying among the more polished nations of antiquity. The professors of practices so fatal to the people were regarded with great aversion, and seldom came to a natural end. Indeed they were looked upon rather as bad spirits than appertaining to the human race.

The priests were frequently called upon to detect those guilty of theft. The complainant was required to pay a fee, generally a pig, in advance. The following ceremonies were then enacted. Two sticks of green wood were rubbed together, until the friction produced a kind of powder, resembling snuff, sufficiently hot, upon being blown upon, to kindle dry grass into a flame. This was used to fire a pile of wood. Three *kukui* nuts were then broken, and one of the kernels thrown into the fire. While this was burning, a prayer was uttered, accompanied with an anathema, "to kill the fellow." The same ceremony was repeated until the nuts were consumed, unless the thief appeared and made restitution, which generally happened. The offence was then punished with a heavy fine. Should the culprit have neglected to appear, his fate was considered as inevitable. A proclamation was made throughout the island by the king, that theft had been committed and the guilty prayed to death. So firm was their belief in the power of these prayers to arouse the avenging deity, that the miserable victim generally pined away and fell a sacrifice to his fears. When we consider the powerful influence which the church of Rome exercised over those who acknowledged her authority, throwing, by her paper interdicts, a whole kingdom into a state of distress, scarcely conceivable in modern times, we find little to excite wonder in the "praying to death" of the untutored savage.

No spirit of benevolence pervaded their religion. It was a gloomy and fearful system, abounding in punishments for the present life and dark threatenings for the future. Among the lowest orders no distinct idea of futurity prevailed. A general opinion that there was a future state existed, and with it vague expectances of rewards and punishments. In their corrupted minds the simple truth of one all-creative power, the "Great Spirit" of the American Indians, had no being. Their traditions referred to the creation of the world, and the deluge ; but even then, according to their ideas, a multiplicity of gods existed. The knowledge of the true God was lost among many families soon after the world became peopled ; else was buried amid a mass of superstitions and heathen ceremonies, which each successive generation increased. This was emphatically the case with the Hawaiians. However simple their faith originally had been, almost all traces of truth were lost at their discovery. Every age had become more corrupt, and, at that date, the cup of heathenism was full. Savage rites and blood-loving deities, a cruel priesthood and rapacious governments, inhuman faiths and absurd superstitions, were the burdens which the people were required to believe and sustain. From the perusal of the stories of this dark era, as gathered from their own lips, it would seem as if human depravity had reached its acme, and that the people were gradually wasting away, like a mass of corruption. A religion which inculcates some degree of morality, however small, or allows latitude for the better principles of humanity, even if choked and almost destroyed by surrounding depravity, will exert an influence sufficient to temper the general evil. This was the case with the Buddhistic creed and the simple faith of the ancient Peruvians. But here no such light prevailed. The system had degenerated into unmixed evil, and the good, like that derived from government, was the result of individual action. Fortunately for humanity, the most barbarous beliefs will, at times, yield to the natural instincts of man ; and faiths, however cruel in theory, often become comparatively mild in their application. The religion of the Hawaiians, as it existed when they became known to the civilized world, incorporated no abstract principles of belief. It was rather a system of worldly despotism, better calculated to perpetuate the power of the

priests, than to direct the ideas of the people to concerns of eternal interest or temporal improvement. Deities, ceremonies and restrictions, had been indefinitely multiplied till it presented a confused mass of dark superstitions, based upon the slavish fear and ignorance of the people.

The contradictory ideas that prevailed in regard to a future state, attest the indefiniteness of their belief on this point. Their revelations were derived from dreams and pretended visions of the priests. By some, it was supposed that the souls of the departed went to Po, (place of night,) where they were annihilated, or eaten by the gods. Others considered the regions of Akea and Milu their final resting places. These were former kings of Hawaii, who, after death, went below and founded kingdoms, which became the Hades of the Hawaiian Islands. Darkness prevailed here, and lizards and butterflies were the only diet. The spirits of the departed were sometimes sent back with messages to the living. These pretended messages were expounded, greatly to their own interest, by the priests, and were received as divine commands by the people.[*] There were two gods,

[*] Hawaiians supposed they had two souls, one of which always remained with the body ; the other had the power of leaving it for good or evil ; to aid a friend or to pursue an enemy ; a belief somewhat similar to the Hebrew demonology. A class of priests were supposed to possess the power of exorcising the evil inclined spirits, and of altogether destroying them. Their souls were thought to be distinct from the body, though in near relationship ; hence, they called them *hoapili o ke kino.* "close adhering companions of the body."
In the following commencement of a "*mele*," an ode to the soul, composed by Maewa, a modern Hawaiian and a Christian, he still recognizes the old belief of two distinct yet familiar existences. The present race generally consider their souls as having the same relation to their bodies as their shadows.

> "Aloha ka uhane, ka hoapili o ke kino ;
> I pili ka ua me ka la.
> A o ke anuanu me ke koekoe,
> Aloha kuu hoa ohuniu o kahi kanaka ole.
> A o hoi na, kuu hoapili, o ka ua lanipo lua,
> Hoa ai ole o na kai ewalu,
> A me na makani cha ;
> Kuu hoa o ka maona kawalawala,
> A me ka maka poniuniu ai ole ;
> He pokakaa ka la e ni ho nei,
> A hala na makahiki cha,
> Malaila no ka halialia aloha ana mai." &c.

TRANSLATION.

"Farewell, thou soul, the body's near companion,
Companion in the rain and in the sun,
In the piercing cold, and in the chilly damp.
Farewell my soul ; we have communed together in the still retreat,
Been companions in the crowd and in the silent places.
And thou art going, my bosom friend, in the dark storm,

Library of
The ... ... of

one of whom was called *Kaonohiokala,* the eye-ball of the sun, who conducted the spirits of the chiefs to a place in the heavens, where it was supposed their rulers dwelt after death. They sometimes returned to the earth and watched over the welfare of their survivors. By this belief, it will be seen that the spiritual destinies of the nobles were well provided for by the complaisant priests, in return, probably, for favors received from them while living. Servitude was the lot of the common people in this life, and no hope enlivened their souls for the future.

Hawaiians in their gods worshiped mere physical attributes; their conceptions of divinity being limited to deeds of strength, lust and revenge, with perhaps an occasional dash of good nature. In this they differed not materially from the popular opinions of the polished Greeks and Romans. Indeed, a uniformity of ideas, though varied in application by mental cultivation and moral sentiment, is found to exist among all nations unenlightened by revelation. Man deified man. His fertile imagination peopled groves, shores, and ocean, with beings of wonderful natures; with some, the objects of fear—with others, of companionship and protection. Each individual, according to his prominent characteristic, selected his protecting deity; thus their qualities became as various as the tastes and dispositions of mankind; so that man, reversing the primeval creation, fashioned gods after his own image. In the Hawaiian mythology, little exists to interest or instruct. It is a record of depravity necessary, though painful, to examine, that a proper judgment of their aboriginal condition may be formed.

Their gods were many, and received constant additions from the most trivial circumstances. Every object of fear, or from which harm could be derived,

was worshiped. Sharks, volcanoes, and any singular appearance in the natural kingdom, had each their devotees. There were household deities, some of ludicrous and obscene character, like the Roman Penates; gods of war, the seasons, crops, and of the winds; also of precipices, or dangerous places in traveling. Images were placed on such to receive the offerings of the devout. Among the principal deities were *Lono, Ku, Kane* and *Kanuloa,* male gods. Those of the other sex were common; of which *Papa, Hukoku, Walinu* and *Kahawahine* were the most celebrated. A human origin is ascribed to all.

MALE IDOL.

The several islands had favorite idols. On Maui, *Kealoewa,* an image of wood, covered with "tapa," was much worshiped. The head, which was disfigured with an enormous mouth, was formed of fine basket-work, curiously and neatly wrought with red feathers, so as to resemble the plumage of a beautiful bird. This was surmounted by a helmet, to the crown of which long tresses of human hair were attached.

Kihu was a famous female idol of the same island, and received equal adoration with Kealoewa. On Lanai, two large stone images, personifying the deities supposed to preside over the sea, were much honored by fishermen.

FEMALE IDOL.

Mooalii, a shark, was a celebrated marine god of Molokai. Numerous temples were built on projecting headlands for his homage, and to them the first fruits of the fishermen's labors were dedicated.

Kalaipahoa, a carved, wooden image, was much feared. Its arms were extended, with spread fingers, its head

---

Who rodest with me o'er the waves of the eight seas.*
And when contending with the four winds;
My companion in rare-full meals,
And in long-fasting faintness.
While living here, the sun has onward rolled,
And four full years have past;
'Tis but a vapor of a loved remembrance," &c.
   The remainder of this ode, with an excellent translation by Rev. L. Andrews, of the Sandwich Islands Mission, will be found in the *Polynesian* for July, 1840.

   *The several channels between the islands.

decorated with human hair, and its gaping mouth ornamented with rows of shark's teeth. The wood of which this idol was made, to increase the horrid effect of its appearance, was fabled to be deadly poisonous.

One of the most popular gods of Hawaii was *Lono ;* an ancient king, who, according to the tradition, became offended with his wife, and murdered her. His contrition brought on

KALAIPAHOA—POISON GOD.

derangement, and he traveled through the islands, boxing and wrestling with all he met. Not long after, he sailed in an oddly constructed canoe for a foreign land, from which he never returned. He was deified, and annual athletic exercises held in his honor.*

This was the God for whom Cook was mistaken upon his arrival; which delusion was not altogether removed after his death.

The most fearful of all their deities was *Pele*, a goddess. Her habitation, the famous volcano of Kilauea, well accorded with her reputed character. Here, with her attendant spirits, she reveled in the flames ; the unearthly noises of the burning mass were the music of their dance, and they bathed in the red surge of the fiery billows, as it dashed against the sides of the crater. This fire-loving family is said to have emigrated from Tahiti, soon after the deluge. Their names, as given by Ellis, were characteristic of their habits, and show how readily the native intellect met-

GOD LONO.

amorphosed natural phenomena into personal qualities.

Pele was the chief goddess. Her principal followers were *Ka-ma-hu-alii*—the king of steam and vapor. *Ka-poha-i-kahi-ola*—the explosion in the palace of life. *Ke-ua-ke-po*—the rain of night. *Kane-hekili*—thundering god. *Ke-o-ahi-kama-kaua*—fire-thrusting child of war. These were brothers, and like Vulcan, two of them were deformed. *Makole-wawahi-waa*—fiery-eyed canoe breaker. *Hiaka-wawahi-lani*—heaven-dwelling cloud breaker, and several others of longer names, and similar definitions. These latter were sisters. The whole family were regarded with the greatest awe. The volcano was their principal residence, though occasionally they renovated their constitutions amid the snows of the mountains. On such occasions, their journeys were accompanied by earthquakes, eruptions, heavy thunder and lightning. All were malignant spirits, delighting in acts of vengeance and destruction. The numerous eruptions with which the island has been devastated, were ascribed to their enmity. Many tributes were assessed to avoid or appease their anger; the greater part of which went to support the numerous and wealthy priesthood and their followers, who regulated the worship of *Pele*. These were held in the highest reverence, as holding in their power the devouring fires of the all-powerful goddess. To insult them, break their taboos, or neglect to send offerings, was to call down certain destruction. At their call,

3. A man ascended the summit, and from the height thus addressed the spouse of Lono :
4. "O Kaikilani, your lover salutes you : keep this—remove that : one will still remain."
5. Lono, overhearing this artful speech, killed his wife with a hasty stroke.
6. Sorry for this rash act, he carried to a *heiau* the lifeless body of his wife, and made great wail over it.
7. He traveled through Hawaii in a state of frenzy, boxing with every one he met.
8. The people astonished, said, "Is Lono entirely mad ?" He replied, "I am frantic with my great love."
9. Having instituted games to commemorate her death, he embarked in a triangular canoe for a foreign land.
10. Ere he departed he prophesied, "I will return in after times, on an island bearing cocoanut trees, swine and dogs."—[Voyage of the *Blonde*, p. 30, where this version is ascribed to the American missionaries.]

The sacred relic from which the representation of Lono was taken, is preserved with the other idols, of which engravings have been given, in the Museum of the American Board for Foreign Missions, at their house in Pemberton Square, Boston. Lono is a slim figure, of about twelve feet in height. The male idol is a colossal image—the others are small.

† Those known as the *Makahiki*.

* The following is a translation of the *mele* composed on this event : O LONO AKUA.

1. Lono Akua (God), of Hawaii, in ancient times, resided with his wife at Kealakeakua.
2. The name of the goddess, his love, was Kaikilani Alii. They dwelt beneath the steep rock.

Pele would spout out her lava and destroy the offenders. Vast numbers of hogs, both cooked and alive, were thrown into the crater, when any fear of an eruption was entertained, or to stay the progress of one commenced. Offerings were annually made to keep her in good humor, and no traveler dared venture near her precincts without seeking her good will.

Wonderful monsters and giants abound in their traditions, showing how prevalent was the love of the marvelous. Events and people, not remarkable in themselves, in the course of time have been converted into miracles and heroes; in the nature of which the ridiculous, rather than the sublime, predominates.

Pele and her family are said to have had a contest, in which they were almost overpowered, with *Kamapuaa*, half hog and half man ; a gigantic animal, the Centaur of Hawaii. He traveled from Oahu to countries beyond the heavens, or where they supposed the sky to join the sea. In his route he visited Kilauea, and desired to pay his addresses to Pele. She rejected him with contempt, impolitely calling him "a hog, and the son of a hog." In endeavoring to drive him away, a fierce battle took place. Pele fled to her house, and her fires were nearly extinguished by great quantities of water, which *Kamapuaa* poured into the crater. The thirsty family, however, soon drank it up, and finally obtained the mastery over the demi-hog, forcing him into the sea, amidst a shower of fire and stones. This tale probably originated from an eruption, in which the lava of the volcano came in contact with the ocean. Another account states that he conquered *Pele*, and they were quietly married ; in consequence of which no more islands were formed, or extensive eruptions took place.

This same character, forgetful of his former prowess, was guilty of stealing fowls of a king of Oahu, who, to revenge himself, sent and captured him. However, he soon released himself and killed all the party but one, whom he sent back with the news of the death of his companions. This mightily enraged the monarch, and he summoned all his force for a fresh attack. Success attended this effort, and Kamapuaa, with his followers, were pent up in a narrow gorge, between two mountains, all sides of which, but the entrance, were bounded by stupendous precipices. Seeing no outlet for escape, he reared upon his hind legs, and placing his fore feet upon the summit of one of the perpendicular rocks, formed a bridge, by which his defeated army, scrambling over his back, reached the top in safety, while the monster himself, with one bound, readily surmounted the difficulty. At Hauula, where this is said to have occurred, the natives still point out the smooth channels in the rock, made by his efforts on this occasion, but which incredulous whites believe to have been water courses.

Idols were of every variety imaginable, from hideous and deformed sculptures of wood, to the utmost perfection of their art. The features of their religion were embodied in these images ; the most desired object in their manufacture being to inspire fear and horror, sentiments which, in a more refined people, would from such exhibitions have been converted into disgust. Much ceremony took place when a new idol was to be made. A great procession, headed by the highest priests and chiefs, marched in state to the tree selected for the purpose. After it was felled, a man or hog was sacrificed on its site. The rocks of a beach at Ninole, Hawaii, were in high repute among the manufacturers of stone images and adzes. They were believed to have been of different sexes, and therefore to have had the power of propagation, and were generally used in the fabrication of gods which presided over games. When a suitable stone for this design was found, it was taken to the "heiau," and certain rites performed ; after which it was properly fashioned and carried to the arena where the games were held. If the party to which it belonged were frequently successful, it was regarded as a god ; but if not, it was thrown aside. When victims were required in honor of Moa-alii, the divine shark, or it was supposed to be hungry, the priests sallied out and ensnared with a rope any one whom they could catch, who was immediately strangled, cut in pieces and thrown to the rapacious fish. Another ingenious mode of entrapping the unwary was by uttering piteous cries, like a wounded or sick individual. Those attracted to the spot were seized and sacrificed.

Temples or *heiaus* were commonly erected upon hills, or near the sea, and formed conspicuous objects in the landscapes. They were works of great labor, built of loose stones, with sufficient skill to form compact walls. Their usual shape was an irregular parallelogram. That of Kawaihae, on Hawaii, is two hundred and twenty-four feet long and one hundred feet wide, with walls twelve feet thick at the base. Its height is from eight to twenty feet, two to six feet wide at the top, which, being well paved with smooth stones, formed, when in repair, a pleasant walk. The entrance was narrow, between two high walls. The interior is divided into terraces, the upper of which is paved with flat stones. The south end constituted an inner court, and was the most sacred place. Here was placed the chief's idol, surrounded by a multitude of inferior deities. A small frame of wicker work, hollow and in the shape of an obelisk, stood in the centre of the inner court; in this the priest stationed himself when in consultation with the god. All affairs of importance were brought before him, and he, pretending divine inspiration, like the sibyls of classic mythology, answered distinctly, though ambiguously. The king and chiefs who received his responses, went outside and caused them to be proclaimed to the people. The sacrificial altar was near the entrance to this court. The high chiefs and priests only were allowed to reside within the precincts of the temple. The external walls were crowned with hideous idols of all shapes and sizes. This temple was built by Kamehameha I. previous to his conquest of the leeward islands, and dedicated to his favorite war god *Kaili*, a large wooden image richly ornamented with red feathers. On the day it was completed, eleven men were immolated on its altar, and great quantities of fruit, hogs and dogs presented. The other heiaus, the ruins of which still remain, resemble this, but were not all constructed on a scale of equal grandeur. There is one in tolerable preservation, called Kaili, in the interior of Ha-

waii, about equi-distant between the three mountains, Mauna Kea, Mauna Loa and Hualalai. It was the work of Umi, the most noted in traditionary lore of the kings of Hawaii, and imposed by him as a tribute of labor on his several conquered districts. The main building is 92 feet long by 71 wide. The walls are 6 feet 9 inches high, 7 feet thick at the top, and quite perpendicular. Adjoining it are a number of rough pyramids 18 feet high and the remains of a house said to have been built by Umi for his wife. This temple has an elevation of 5,000 feet above the sea, and is built of compact unhewn lava, without cement.*

The enclosures sacred to Lono, were built of the *ki* leaf, and four distinct houses erected for the accommodation of the idols. Fronting these was a handsomely made, high, wooden fence, called the *Anuu*, surmounted by numerous images. The *Lama* was the only timber allowed in this enclosure, except the *Ohia*, of which the idols were made. No priests except those attached to Lono, could officiate in this enclosure. This was a universal rule ; each temple being sacred to some special deity, for whose service distinct orders of priests were maintained. These orders were sub-divided into classes, each attending to some specified duty. The king alone had free access to all.

Upon the consecration of a temple, or an appointed period for worship, the day was made sacred and the most profound silence enforced. All animals that were not removed, were ordered to be confined and kept quiet ; otherwise they were seized and offered up in sacrifice. Chiefs and priests, entering the most sacred house, united in prayer for many successive hours, with their arms extended toward heaven. On important occasions, several days were spent in this manner, and were succeeded by rites of a different character. The priests went through various manœuvres, singing songs and chanting praises to their deity. Distinct sacrifices, laid upon altars and lofty scaffolds, were offered for the gods, the priests and the people. Women were not permitted to be present at these

---

* Wilkes' Voyage, vol. IV., p. 100.

4

seasons, and the restrictions were extremely severe. The two sexes were forbidden all intercourse; if they but spoke to each other, or accidentally came in contact, the penalty was death. Any infringement of the laws, however trivial, brought the same punishment. On the eighth day of the dedication the last hog reserved for this occasion, called the *puaa-hea*, or "hog to be entirely consumed," was sacrificed. If any one refused to partake of its flesh, he lost his life, as it was supposed if any portion of his body remained undevoured, the whole company would perish by some awful judgment.

Festivals of a more pleasing description were frequently held, accompanied by sports, trials of skill, dancing and other amusements.

Human sacrifices were common, and occurred previous to going to war, upon the death of any high chief, or any other occasion of importance. It is said of Umi, that being victorious in battle, he commenced sacrificing human victims to his god. After a number had been slain, the insatiate god called for more, which were granted, until none were left except Umi and the priest. In this instance, eighty victims perished. An equal number are said to have been sacrificed on other occasions. These stories show the frequency of the practice, and the prodigal waste of human life attending it. All criminals, and those who had broken any religious requirements, were slain and offered to the gods. Those who were destined for slaughter for any great event were frequently selected for months or years beforehand. They were, probably, such as were obnoxious to the priests or chiefs, whose policy prompted them thus to dispose of them, rather than by undisguised murder. Unconscious of the fate that awaited them, the victims pursued their daily avocations in apparent security, the first intimation of their danger being the fatal blow. Sometimes they were seized and carried to the temple, and there slain to avoid mangling their limbs. Their bodies were then stripped and placed on an altar before the idol, with their faces downward. If hogs were offered at the same time, they were piled at right angles upon their

bodies; after which prayers were repeated, and the whole mass left in that position to putrefy. In minor affairs, animals, fruits or vegetables only were offered. The former were slain by diviners, who observed the manner of their death, the looks of their entrails, and other signs. The face of the heavens, clouds and rainbows were also examined, and, according to their appearance, more or less favorable auguries given. It is probable, however, that the wishes of the chief had the most influence in dictating the answers.

The priesthood was hereditary, and formed a numerous and powerful body. They owned much property in people and lands, which were heavily taxed for their support. Each chief had his family priest, who followed him to battle, carried his war-god, and superintended all the sacred rites of his household. The priests took rank from their gods and chiefs; the worship of the latter usually determining the popularity of the former. The keeper of the national war-god, and the one immediately attached to the person of the most powerful ruler, was the great high priest. The power of the priest, though it partook more of a religious character, was scarcely inferior to that of the chief. Their persons were sacred, from their supposed familiarity with the gods. It sometimes happened that a chief took the sacred offices upon himself; though, perhaps, from the nature of the intimate connection existing between the two orders, the absolute power, both in politics and religion, centred in the head of the clan. When the supreme sovereignty is resolved into the whims and caprices of one individual, and is constantly changing by death or warfare, no regular system, either in government or religion, can be developed. From all that has transpired of their early history, it would appear, that while chiefs and priests maintained their power in all its absoluteness, the rites and ceremonies, and even the deities of their faith, were ever varying. The desires of the moment being the law of the land, there is, consequently, but little of permanent interest to be recorded. One fact is everywhere apparent: the spiritual, like the temporal lords of the people, amid all their vagaries, never neglected their own interests. Every ceremony or superstition was framed to aid their already overgrown power; humanity, or a regard for the rights of their inferiors, would have been received as monstrous deviations from the true policy of government. Perhaps they governed no more harshly than could have been expected from a privileged order, nursed in selfishness and brutality. Their very superiority of station and feeling, incidentally developed a slight courteousness of manner, when compared with the dark mass beneath them. Among equals, much ceremony prevailed, and an external degree of artificial politeness, which served to disguise the most odious features of their characters.

Even over the warrior-chiefs, the priests, at times, were enabled to exercise a powerful influence, and made their religious fears and blind devotion subservient to their selfish purposes. In sickness, or fear of sorcery, their aid was to be purchased only by gifts, in proportion to the rank of the applicant. Great prices were exhorted for incantations to be practiced upon enemies, or counter ceremonies, to avoid such phantoms as their imaginations had not only given birth to, but which they pretended to the exclusive power to allay.

Offerings to the gods, or, more properly, to the priests, were required at all religious ceremonies, and on every occasion the people desired their services. The wants of the priesthood regulated the amount; when the regular taxes failed in supplying their desires, the wishes of the god were called into requisition, and the coveted articles tabooed for his use. Orisons, chants and offerings were made by the priests at their meals. Even in the care of their fowls and quadrupeds, they enjoyed remarkable privileges. Hogs received alive, were dedicated to the god of the order, received his marks, and turned loose to fatten upon the plantations of the poor cultivators; none daring openly to injure or drive away the sacred animals.

The expression taboo, or, according to Hawaiian orthography, *Kapu*, which, from its usefulness, has now become incorporated into most modern tongues, requires some explanation. Originally, it meant sacred. It implies no moral quality, but is indicative of a particular distinction, or separation from common purposes, for some special design, and also expresses an unlimited restriction. Formerly, it was applied exclusively to persons or things in a sacred sense, and was strictly a religious ceremony, imposed only by the priests; but has since come into common use in the every-day concerns of life. Anciently, those chiefs who pretended to derive their descent from the gods were called *alii kapu*, sacred chiefs. A temple, exclusively devoted to the abode and worship of gods, was said to be *wahi kapu*—sacred place. Anything dedicated or reserved for the exclusive use of gods, chiefs, or priests, was considered as *kapu* for them. Certain lands and islands were *kapu*, as well as hunting grounds, fish, fruit, or whatever the sacred classes chose to reserve for themselves. These *kapus* were occasional, or permanent—particular fish, fruits and vegetables being sometimes taboo both from men and women for several successive months. The idols, temples, persons and names of their kings, and members of the royal family; persons and property of the priests; everything appertaining to the gods; religious devotees; the chiefs' bathing-places, or favorite springs of water; and everything offered in sacrifice, were strictly *kapu*. Trees of which idols were made were taboo, so whatever an individual chose as his object of worship became ever afterwards taboo to him, though it were a fish, fowl, dog or vegetable. In modern times, this magic term has become the property of all. A common man can taboo his house, lands, or make any partial restrictions, and all would respect the prohibition. Any forbidden article or action is called tabooed; hence its common use in the domestic circle, and its application to laws. A captain can taboo his ship, and none dare approach. Tabooed property is generally marked by small white flags, or other signs which are well understood. At the present time, any individual can impose such taboos as suits his necessities or convenience, provided they do not infringe personal rights or the laws of the kingdom.

Formerly a religious motive was necessary for its assignment, but as the power of the chiefs increased, its use was greatly corrupted, while its influence remained the same, and may be said to have partaken of the preternatural. The bans of the Romish church, in the proudest days of that hierarchy, were not more powerful or obligatory. Every will of a chief, however monstrous, was promulgated as a taboo, and officers were appointed to see that it was observed.

This institution, unknown elsewhere, is general with slight variations throughout the Polynesian groups. Its antiquity is co-eval with the superstitions which it so materially strengthened, and it may be regarded as one of the profoundest productions of heathen ingenuity. A more cogent principle of religious despotism, at once capable of great utility and equal abuse, could not have been devised. Its application was adapted to all wants and circumstances, and no civil or ecclesiastical government ever possessed a more refined, yet effective weapon. Its influence, among the common people, was universal and inflexible. Its exactments were of the most humiliating and troublesome description, and if anything had been wanting to complete their bondage, this, like the key-stone to an arch, was made to perfect and perpetuate their degradation. Religion like government emanating from the higher classes, fitted them loosely and easily, and could be set aside or put in motion at their option.

The penalties partook both of a temporal and supernatural character, the victims, like those of the Inquisition, being equally delivered to the terrors of the secular arm, and the judgments of offended gods. Unless powerful friends interfered, the slightest breach of any of its requisitions, however absurd or artificial, was punished with death. Some were burnt, others strangled, despatched with clubs or stones within the temples, or sacrificed in a more lingering and dreadful manner. Eyes were scooped out, limbs broken, and the most exquisite tortures inflicted for several days, before the final stroke was given.

Particular seasons were taboo; as on the sickness of a high chief, preparations for war, or the approach of important religious ceremonies. Their duration was indefinite, sometimes for a day only, then for months, and occasionally for years. Thirty to forty days was the ordinary period before Kamehameha's reign, when they were much reduced.

These taboos were either common or strict, and were proclaimed by criers or heralds. Men only were required to abstain from their common pursuits, and to attend prayers morning and evening at the heiau, during the former. But when the season of strict taboo was in force, a general gloom and silence pervaded the whole district or island. Not a fire or light was to be seen, or canoe launched; none bathed; the mouths of dogs were tied up, and fowls put under calabashes, or their heads enveloped in cloth; for no noise of man or animal must be heard. No persons, excepting those who officiated at the temple, were allowed to leave the shelter of their roofs. Were but one of these rules broken, the taboo would fail and the gods be displeased.

When the sacred chiefs appeared in public, all the common people prostrated themselves, with their faces upon the earth. The food of chiefs and priests, they being interdicted from handling anything during this taboo, was put into their mouths by their attendants.

The only feature in the religious system which can be regarded with a degree of satisfaction, and that only partially, was the *Puuhonua*, or city of refuge, which gleams amid rapidly increasing darkness, like the last faint ray of a setting sun. There were two on Hawaii; one at Waipio, the other at Honauuau. Those who fled from an enemy, the manslayer, those who had transgressed taboo, the thief, and even the vilest criminal, if they could reach their precincts, were in an inviolable sanctuary. They were free to all of every tribe, or condition, though the flying party could be pursued to their very gates, which were perpetually open. The rescued party repaired immediately to the idol, and offered a thanksgiving for his escape.

They also afforded safe retreats during war. All the non-combatants of the neighboring districts, men, women and children, flocked into them, and there awaited the issue of the struggle. To them also the vanquished fled. If they could reach a spot, a short distance outside the walls, where, during war, a white banner was displayed, they were safe. Should a victorious warrior venture further, he would be put to death by the attendant priests and their adherents. Those once within the pale of the sanctuary were under the protection of *Keawe*, the tutelar deity of the enclosure. Houses were erected for the accommodation of all within their walls. After a short period, they were permitted to return unmolested to their homes, the divine protection being supposed still to abide with them.

These places of refuge were very capacious, and built after the manner of their temples. The one at Honaunau is seven hundred and fifteen feet in length, and four hundred and four feet wide. Its walls are twelve feet high and fifteen thick, and were formerly surmounted with images, four rods apart, over their whole extent. Three large heiaus were erected within, one of which presented a solid pyramid of stone, one hundred and twenty-six feet by sixty, and ten feet high. In several parts of the wall are large masses of rock, weighing two or more tons, each raised six feet above the ground. This Puuhonua was built for Keawe, who reigned in Hawaii, two hundred and seventy years

INTERIOR VIEW OF A HEIAU, ON KAUAI, IN 1778.

ago, and destitute as the islanders were of any machinery, must have been a herculean task, requiring the labor of a vast number of people.

These sanctuaries are somewhat analogous to the Israelitish cities of refuge, and originated, doubtless, from the barbarous and sanguinary customs, common to both nations, which required a safeguard from the effects of evil passions, constantly kept in excitement by the universal prevalence of the law of retaliation, and the bloody character of their warfare.

While considerable difference in government, and certain customs, originating from local circumstances, prevailed throughout Polynesia, a general uniformity in religion existed. The earliest

traditions are strikingly similar, and the rites and priesthood are of the same sanguinary character. A more refined barbarism prevailed among the Society and Samoa islanders, the former of which have aptly been called the French of the Pacific. Still, when a general comparison is drawn, not a doubt of their common origin can be entertained. The structure of their languages, their physical characteristics, analogous religious systems, and a general conformity in all the arts and customs of life, clearly demonstrate the fact. While the Hawaiian, in certain points, appeared to more advantage than his southern brother, in religion and government he was behind him. In New Zealand, the Marquesas, Samoa and Tonga groups, an approach to republican freedom prevailed, which here found no counterpart. The power of the chiefs was more restricted, varying much in the different groups. The religion of the Tahitian, Samoan and Tongan constituted a better defined system, and was founded on certain well established traditions and maxims, handed down from their forefathers. Its effects, though disastrous in the extreme, were less conspicuously degrading. A refinement of heathenism was diffused, which served to gild the darker shades of its character, and it was not until the veil was completely stripped from the vile image, that all its deformities appeared. Many of the early voyagers formed from superficial views, favorable opinions of the savage character, which served for awhile to deceive the world with false ideas of the innocency of man, in his primeval condition. A knowledge of his sanguinary worship, and its direful effects, soon served to dissipate this belief; and now, none but those who have theoretical views to maintain give it credence. A valuable lesson is to be learned from the history of the savage tribes, so rapidly wasting away, or merging into civilized nations, inasmuch as it serves to illustrate the history of unenlightened and unevangelized man left in isolated communities to grope his way, unaided by the light of revelation. Could a result more painful to human dignity present itself? As before the flood, "the wickedness of man became great in the earth, and every imagination of the thoughts of his heart was only evil continually."

CHAPTER III.

WE now come to a consideration of the knowledge of the Hawaiians as developed in their arts, manufactures and customs. In considering these, however, it is fair to bear in mind the fact that the natural resources of their islands were extremely few, they furnishing no metals and but few minerals. When this is considered, we must award them the credit of no little ingenuity and skill in what they produced. Indeed it may be questioned whether they did not carry civilization in this point to the full extent of their feeble means. This one fact shows how important a civilized commerce has become. Without it the tribes of heathendom would still have been groping their isolated way in poverty and sensuality amid regions which required but the presence of commerce to add to them tenfold value and make them abodes for refined and intelligent beings.

The warlike weapons of the Hawaiians were few and simple. They consisted of spears, javelins, daggers and clubs, made from a tough wood, susceptible of high polish. These were their most effective weapons. They had no shields, javelins being used on the defensive as well as offensive, in the former of which they were even more expert than in the latter. Their lances were perfectly straight, flattened to a point at one end, and from twelve to twenty feet in length. Javelins were similarly constructed, barbed, and about six feet long. The *laau palau*, a species of club or halbert, several feet longer, was employed either in thrusting or striking. The *paloa*, or dagger, was from sixteen inches to two feet in length, frequently pointed at both ends, with a string attached to the handle, by which it was made fast to the wrist. Bows and arrows were rarely used, being so poorly fabricated as to be of little utility. Slings, manufactured from human hair or the elastic fibres of the cocoanut husk, were a destructive weapon. The ammunition used was small, smooth stones, which were cast with great force and precision. Small swords, or saws, the edges of which were set with sharks' teeth, were common.

Defensive armor was seldom employed. Besides the *malo*, the cloth girded about the loins, a turban was occasionally worn. The helmets and war-cloaks, although they gave their wearers an imposing and martial appearance, must have proved an incumbrance. The former being made of wicker-work, and closely fitted to the crown, were too slightly constructed to afford any security against a well directed blow. Those worn by the high chiefs resembled the Grecian casque, and were exceedingly beautiful. They were surmounted by a lofty crest, sometimes ornamented with the tail-plumage of the tropic bird, and the whole thickly wrought with glossy red and yellow feathers. With the cloaks, they were admirably adapted to set off to advantage the towering figures of the chiefs. Cloaks or capes, made exclusively of yellow feathers, were reserved for the king.

The *mamo*, or feather war-cloak of Kamehameha, occupied nine generations of kings in its fabrication, not being completed until the reign of the father of the present sovereign. Its length is four feet, with eleven and a half feet spread at the bottom. The groundwork is a fine netting. To this the feathers, which are exceedingly small and delicate, being less than an inch in length, are skillfully attached. They overlap each other, and form a perfectly smooth surface. Around the borders the feathers are reversed. The whole is of a beautifully bright yellow hue, giving it the appearance of a golden mantle. Such cloaks were rare, for savage despotism could not produce a richer or more costly garment. The birds from which the feathers are obtained are found in the mountainous parts of the islands, and caught by means of an adhesive substance smeared upon long poles, well baited, which are thickly scattered about their haunts. Alighting upon these, their feet become attached; the hunter then easily secures them, and plucks from under their wings, the two feathers—all each bird produces—which are so much coveted. These feathers are highly valued, a piece of nankeen, of the value of one dollar and a half, being the price given for five, in modern times. If the labor expended on this cloak could be estimated, its nominal worth would be found equal to that of the most costly gems in the regalia of Europe. Those of other chiefs, being alternated with red and yellow, rhomboidal figures or lines, relieved with sections of dark purple or glossy black,

were less expensive and beautiful. A smaller kind, manufactured of the same materials, was worn by those whose rank did not entitle them to the larger garment. An ornament, made from a whale's tooth, called a *palaoa*, suspended from the neck by braids of human hair, was much prized.

In their modes of warfare, they exhibited considerable address. Besides agriculture, war being a chief occupation, it was reduced to a system of which the following were the principal features.

In a war of magnitude, a universal conscription was enforced, none but those incapacitated by age or bodily infirmity, being excused from following their leaders to the field. All were drilled in the use of arms, and practiced warlike exercises, such as sham-fights, slinging stones at a mark, throwing the javelin, warding it off, or catching it in their hands, wrestling, &c. After war was declared, the king, principal warriors and priests determined the plan of attack, or the general method for its prosecution. *Lunapai*, " war-heralds," were sent through all the districts, summoning such of the chiefs and their tenants as were to bear part in its operations. Women frequently fought in the ranks, or bore refreshments to their party, through the thickest of the fray. All were required to bring their own weapons and provisions, which were generally prepared beforehand, for emergencies of this nature. Should any refuse to obey the summons, their ears were slit, and they were led into the camp with ropes around their bodies. So great was the disgrace attached to this punishment, that there was seldom occasion to resort to it.

Upon reaching the rendezvous, every chief reported the number and condition of his followers to the commander. Each division encamped around the hut of its leader, or occupied a large house by itself. No fortifications were erected, though favorable natural sites for defence were selected for camps, and pickets stationed at the several approaches. The non-combatants were sent to strongholds, or fortresses erected on steep eminences, to which, in case of defeat, the whole army retired, and defended them to the last extremity.

Unlike most savages, they appear to have been deficient in the science of strategy; seldom lying in ambush, but making their assaults openly, and generally in the day time. Their methods of attack and defence were various, according to the nature of the ground and the force of the enemy, and exhibited much ingenuity. When on an open plain, the army was drawn up in the form of a crescent. A body of spear men, forming a kind of phalanx, composed the centre, while the slingers, and those armed with javelins, were distributed throughout the line. The commander was either the highest chief, or a warrior of distinguished bravery and address. His position was in the centre, and the other chiefs were stationed about the ranks, at his discretion. When an action took place in a narrow defile, the army was formed in a single column. The first division was called *welau*, the extremity or point, and received the brunt of the onset. The strongest division, in the centre of which was the chief, was *poohiwi*, "the shoulder." Other portions were known by similarly descriptive terms. No banners were used, but idols were borne in the ranks; the priests of which, in the heat of the action, rushed forward, uttering terrific yells, and distorted their features into the most frightful forms, to spread dismay into the opposing force, and stimulate the courage of their own; the yells and grimaces being supposed to proceed from the images.

As the whole army seldom engaged at once, the battles were usually a succession of skirmishes, or but partial actions. Naval engagements, in which several hundred canoes were employed on both sides, were not unusual. Flags, called *puwalu*, were then used, and attached to the triangular sails of the canoes. Boastful shouts, yells, cries of defiance, and every noise calculated to intimidate, resounded among the combatants. The bodies of the first slain on either side, received the greatest indignities, and their mangled remains were dedicated to the gods of the victors. Sometimes a single warrior, deridingly carrying only a fan, would advance from the lines, and insult the opposite party

with the most opprobi
lenging it to begin th
singly. In reply to t
a dozen or more spea
him at once; these, b
twisting and jumpin
avoid. Occasionally,
his arm, he would
catch them in his han
back upon the foe. S
a bloody encounter ei
session of the body.
The conflicts, whic
have been very fatal
for several successiv
then terminated by
both parties, in contra
glorious civilized cust
acknowledging them
beaten. More frequer
and fled for safety to
sures, or their mounta
overtaken were massa
to the chiefs for th
Some were spared to
for future sacrifices.
was mercifully inclir
recognized the prison
safe, and could eith
own tribe, or join the
server, which they g
victors erected cairns
of their slain, leaving
vanquished to be dev
and dogs. The sub
apportioned among th
the wives and childr
being made slaves, ai
soil, to cultivate it for
who treated them wit
Branches of the *i*
banana trees, were
truce. When peace
bassadors were sent, l
bols. After arranging
the chiefs and pries
met and adjusted the
a pig was sacrificed, i
ed upon the ground—
fate of either party
wards infringe its cor
scented wreath was
leaders of both sides
a peace offering, in i
dances and public
this return of good

were sent to announce the termination of the war.

The professions of the orators and bards were hereditary and highly illustrious. The former were employed on all great occasions to plead cases, and in all national negotiations. The latter, some of whom were blind, were the repositories of the historical and sacred songs, and composers of new, which they sang in honor of their divine and temporal lords. They were handed down with great care from one generation to another; the sole occupation of the bards being their preservation, for which purpose they commenced repeating them by rote, from an early age, until they were indelibly fixed in their memories. Their language was highly figurative, often approaching the sublime; and their imagery well depicted and not without beauty. Their recitations, heightened by animated gestures and by a conciseness and euphony of language, or a wild, plaintive sadness, with local allusions, like the inspiring strains of Gælic song, swayed with startling effect the passions of their untutored hearers.

Songs and chants were common among all classes, and recited by strolling musicians as panegyrics on occasions of joy, grief or worship. Through them the knowledge of events in the lives of prominent individuals or the annals of the nation, were perpetuated.*

The Hawaiian dialect, from its great

---

* The following from Ellis' tour through Hawaii, is a specimen of their mournful poetry:

Ue, ue! ua make kuu alii,
Ua make kuu haku, kuu hoa;
Kuu hoa i ka wa o ka wi,
Kuu hoa i paa ka aina,
Kuu hoa i kuu ilihune,
Kuu hoa i ka ua me ka makani,
Kuu hoa i ka wela a ka la,
Kuu hoa i ke anu a ka mauna,
Kuu hoa i ka ino,
Kuu hoa i ka malie,
Kuu hoa i na kai awalu;
Ue, ue! ua hala kuu hoa,
Aole e hoi hou mai.

TRANSLATION.

Alas, alas! dead is my chief,
Dead is my lord and my friend;
My friend in the season of famine,
My friend in the time of drought,
My friend in poverty,
My friend in the rain and the wind,
My friend in the heat and the sun,
My friend in the cold from the mountain.
My friend in the storm,
My friend in the calm,
My friend in the eight seas;
Alas, alas! gone is my friend,
And no more will return.

5

---

smoothness and multiplicity of vowels, is admirably adapted for this kind of poetry. The chief art lay in the formation of short metrical sentences, without much regard to their rhythmical termination, though the conclusion of each, or the end of several, were made to harmonize in cadence. So popular is this form of expression, that, even to the present day, the natives repeat their lessons, orders received, or scraps of ancient songs, or extemporize in this monotonous, sing-song tone, for hours together, and in perfect concord. Monosyllables, dissyllables and trisyllables had each their distinct tune.

Analogous to this was the mournful *au-we*, uttered on occasions of calamity and death. On the decease of a great chief, the wail was commenced at his couch, and borne from one individual to another, until it spread over the island. Night and day the dismal sound was prolonged; its first notes low, gradually swelling until one full, passionate burst of grief filled the air, and resounded among the neighboring rocks and hills, whose echoes threw back the sorrowful cry. During the night its effect, as thus borne from party to party, from one valley to another, now rising into almost a shriek of bitterness, then subsiding into a low, murmuring sound, was startling and impressive. Watch-fires, surrounded by groups of both sexes, wailing and weeping violently, tearing their hair, and giving way to other barbarous demonstrations of sorrow, completed the scene.

The same expressions were also uttered on occasion of an injury, surprise, the death of a favorite animal, or even any trivial disappointment. Its signification is, "alas! to sigh or to have a deep affection." Mourners were frequently hired; and the same party could be seen one moment buried, apparently, in the deepest affliction, and, in another, reveling in boisterous mirth about their food, while their places were supplied by a fresh set.

Moku-moku, or boxing, was a favorite national game, regulated by certain laws, for the proper execution of which managers were appointed, and umpires to decide upon rival claims. A spirit of clanship inspired the champions, who usually belonged to different chiefs. The victor in one engagement paced the ring in triumph, until another antagonist appeared. The final conqueror received the highest honors. These boxing matches were often attended with fatal results. The spectators delighted in blows that brought blood, and stimulated the combatants with shouts and yells of applause, dancing and other wild expressions of delight, until, as it frequently happened, many were slain. Foot races were common; the king's messengers attained great speed, frequently making the circuit of Hawaii, three hundred miles of bad road, in eight or nine days.

Sliding down steep hills, on a smooth board, was a common amusement; but no sport afforded more delight than bathing in the surf. Young and old, high and low, of both sexes, engaged in it, and in no other way could they show greater dexterity in their aquatic exercises. Multitudes could be seen when the surf was highest, pushing boldly seaward, with their surf-board in advance, diving beneath the huge combers, as they broke in succession over them, until they reached the outer line of breakers; then laying flat upon their boards, using their arms and legs as guides, they boldly mounted the loftiest, and, borne upon its crest, rushed with the speed of a race-horse towards the shore; from being dashed upon which, seemed to a spectator impossible to be avoided. But a dexterous movement turned their course again seaward, or they nimbly slipped off their boards, which the force of the waves threw far up the rocks.

The *pahee* was a game in great vogue. It consisted in throwing, or rather glancing, heavy darts, from two to five feet in length, along a level floor, prepared with great care for this purpose. The skill consisted in the nearness to certain marks at which the darts were cast. Analogous to this was the *ulu maika*, a species of bowling, in which a circular stone, highly polished, with flat sides, was used. The *konane* was an intricate game of drafts, played with colored stones, upon a great number of

squares. The *puhenehene* consisted in secreting a stone so adroitly, in the full gaze of all present, as to deceive the watchers in their guess as to the hiding place. Five loose bundles of cloth were prepared for this design, under one of which the stone was slipped.

Hakoko, wrestling; *loulou*, a trial of strength by hooking the fingers; *honuhonu*, swimming with the hands only, the feet being fast interlocked; *uma*, a trial of the strength of the arms; *lelekawa*, leaping from precipices into water; *lelekoali*, rope swinging; *kulakalai*—wrestling in the sea—were sports in high repute. The *ume, kilu* and *papuhene* were of an impure nature, and engaged in only under veil of night.

In general, games were seldom practiced except for the purpose of gambling, to which they were inordinately addicted. In betting, every article of clothing or property was staked, and their interest only stayed by the exhaustion of their means, when violent passions were usually aroused, and fierce brawls too often ensued.

Dances (*hula*) were of various character, sometimes interspersed with chants relating to the achievements of the past

A MUSICIAN.

or present rulers, or in honor of the gods. Such was the *hula alaapapa.* The dancers were decorated with necklaces of human hair, supporting ornaments of bone, or whale's teeth. Bracelets and buskins of net-work, thickly set with the teeth of dogs or hogs, encircled their wrists and ankles. Their motions were sometimes active, sometimes slow and graceful, and in perfect time with the music of rude drums, made from large calabashes, with apertures at the top, or hollow logs tastefully carved and covered at the ends with shark's skin. The former were alternately beaten with the palms of the hands, and struck on the ground, on which cloth was laid. The gesticulations of the musicians were violent, and they also joined in the chants.

Dancing was as universal as swimming; all, of every age and character, engaging in it, though it was more commonly practiced by professional dancers in honor of the gods, or for the amusement of the chiefs. The dances of the latter consisted in a variety of uncouth motions and twistings of the body, of too lascivious a nature to bear description, and were generally preparatory to brutal revels. Their costumes were in con-

CHILDREN'S DANCE.

formity with their actions; garlands of flowers, necklaces of shells, and *leis*, beautiful wreaths, fabricated from red or yellow feathers, encircled the limbs of the females. Both sexes were tatooed, though not to such an extent as prevailed elsewhere. The dances of the youth were reported to be graceful and pleasing.

The ceremonies observed on the death of any prominent personage were extremely barbarous. The hair was shaved or cut close, teeth knocked out, and sometimes the ears were mangled. Some tatooed their tongues in a corresponding manner to the other parts of their bodies. These customs were intended to keep alive the memory of the deceased among his immediate relatives and retainers, and by many, the affection was estimated by the amount of bodily pain endured. Frequently the flesh was cut or burnt, eyes scooped out, and other even more painful per-

sonal outrages inflicted. But these usages, however shocking they may appear, were innocent, compared with the horrid saturnalia which immediately followed the death of a chief of the highest rank. Then the most unbounded license prevailed; law and restraint were cast aside, and the whole people appeared more like demons than human beings. Every vice and crime was allowed. Property was destroyed, houses fired, and old feuds revived and revenged. Gambling, thefts and murder were as open as the day; clothing was cast aside as a useless incumbrance; drunkenness and promiscuous prostitution prevailed throughout the land, no women, excepting the widows of the deceased, being exempt from the grossest violation. There was no passion, however lewd, or desire, however wicked, but could be gratified with impunity, during the continuance of this period, which, happily, from its own violence, soon spent itself. No other nation was ever witness to a custom which so entirely threw off all moral and legal restraints, and incited the evil passions to unresisted riot and wanton debauchery.

In the mechanical arts and agriculture, the Hawaiians manifested considerable ingenuity. With no better instruments than those of hard stone, shell or bone, they made large and fine canoes, the longest of which were sixty feet in length; built neat thatched houses; ingeniously carved wood and stone, and manufactured all that was necessary for their domestic purposes. The mats made from rushes or from the leaves of the pandanus, were very useful, prettily dyed, and of great size, fineness and beauty. They were used for beds, screens, partitions, and sometimes for clothing. In their cloth, manufactured from the *morus papyriferus*, equal skill was displayed. It was of every quality, from a thick, heavy article, nearly impervious to wind or water, to a more delicate and almost transparent fabric. The colors were various, some so prettily stained as to resemble printed cloths. Bowls and dishes, made from the *kou* tree, were very beautiful, and highly valued. But the most useful article, and one which can be applied to an almost endless variety of purposes, is the fruit of the cucurbita, the calabash or gourd. From it, their drinking vessels, dishes, masks and musical instruments were made. It still supplies the want of iron, glass, crockery and wooden ware. In journeys it answers for a trunk; at home for a closet. They are often prettily ornamented after the same patterns as their tapas, and are of every size, from the smallest water-cup, to the great poi-dish, capable of holding ten gallons.

WATER CALABASH.

The houses of the common orders were mere hovels, made of straw, thatched upon a light wooden frame. They were low, small and damp, and generally filthy within and without. Those of the chiefs were better and neatly kept.

There were professed trades; some men being expert in building canoes, others in carving and framing or thatching houses, &c. To finish the corners or the roofs of houses, properly and handsomely, was a difficult art, and understood but by few. Generally, every man worked at all as his wants required. When a chief ordered a dwelling to be erected, his tenants were required to take part in the labor, though to each party a distinct work was allotted. While some went to the mountains to procure the timber for the frame, others pulled grass for thatch, or made the twine with

DOUBLE CANOE WITH MASKED ROWERS.

which the frame was to be held together, and the thatch fastened on. As soon as the materials were gathered, holes were dug for the posts, the timbers of the roof grooved, and the whole frame set up. The thatchers then performed their part; and in this manner a large house could be commenced and finished within three days. The timber, which was often of great size, was brought from far in the interior. Burdens were carried on poles, supported on the shoulders of men; the friction of which frequently caused large callous swellings, greatly disfiguring the form.

The best built houses lasted from ten to twelve years; the common not more than half that time. For such a climate, they were well adapted to the wants of the population, though, having no floors, obnoxious to damp and cold. Those of the chiefs were enclosed in large yards, and were sometimes raised on a stone embankment, which rendered them much more comfortable. Around the principal house or hall, as it had but one room, were the smaller huts, which served for eating and sleeping apartments and store-houses. The whole resembled a collection of hay-ricks.

Before a new house was occupied, a number of superstitious ceremonies were performed, to exorcise such evil spirits as desired to dispute the possession with the rightful owner. Offerings were made to the gods, and presents to the priests, who, uttering prayers, and performing divers rites, for a while resided in the house; the sanctity derived from their occupancy being considered as sufficient, ever after, to baffle all attempts of malignant beings, or the incantations of sorcerers.

Clothing was of the simplest nature. With the men, it consisted of a small strip of cloth, called the *malo*, wound around the loins, and passed between the legs; that of the women was the *pau*, a garment attached to the waist, and reaching to the knee. Young children, of both sexes, went naked, as also did their parents, whenever inclination prompted.

Poi, the principal article of diet, was prepared from the kalo plant. The roots, after being baked under ground, were mashed on a large platter by a heavy stone pestle, or an instrument made of lava, resembling a stirrup, and were mixed with water, until a thick paste was formed. This is sometimes eaten in a sweet state, but generally put aside until it ferments, in which condition it is preferred. It is a highly nutricious substance, though, when solely used, has a tendency to produce acrid humors. The labor of its preparation, being too severe for females, is confined to the men.

In fishing, they were very expert, catching their prey either by hooks made from pearl shells, or in nets, some of which were of great size and fine workmanship. A vegetable poison was also used. The herb containing it being stripped of its bark, and bruised, was placed beneath stones where the fishes frequented, which soon became affected, sickened and rose to the surface. As soon as they were taken, they were cleaned, to prevent the poison from spreading. Fishes were usually eaten raw, and in the state in which they were captured.

The manners and customs of these savages are too well known to require enlarged description. If their arts were few and simple, so were their wants. The skill displayed in supplying them is sufficient to excite admiration, and exhibits mechanical abilities, which since, under better auspices, have greatly improved.

A small commerce, through the medium of barter, was maintained between some of the islands. The tapas of Oahu were exchanged for the canoes and paddles of Kauai. On Hawaii, a heavy, strong tapa, called *mamaki*, suitable for cold weather, was manufactured and supplied to the other islands. At stated periods, markets or fairs were held in various places. The most celebrated resort was the banks of the Wailuku river, in the district of Hilo, Hawaii. Here, inhabitants from all portions of the island assembled, to make exchanges of property. Certain districts were noted for the goodness of their tapas; others, for their mats, live stock, or excellence of their *poi*, or dried fish. The peddlers cried their wares, which were exhibited in piles on either side of a stream, according to certain rules. When a bargain was in negotiation, the articles were deposited on a particular rock, where they could be mutually examined in the presence of inspectors, who were appointed as arbiters in cases of dispute, and also acted as a police for the preservation of order, receiving a remuneration for their services. A toll was required from all who crossed the river.

The Hawaiian method of computation resembled the ancient Aztec. It was simple and regular, and sufficient for the wants of an unlettered race, which seldom had occasion to express any complex combination of numbers. From one to ten was as follows: *akahi, alua, akolu, aha, alima, aono, ahiku, awalu, aiwa, umi;* eleven, was ten and one, *umikumamakahi, kumama* being the conjunctive; twelve, *umikumamalua*, and so on until twenty, which was expressed by a new term, *iwakalua;* twenty-one, *iwakaluakumamakahi,* etc.; thirty was *kanakolu;* thirty-one, *kanakolukumamakahi*, etc.; forty, *kanaha;* they then commenced with one, and counted to forty again. A combination of terms were sufficient to express all numbers short of four hundred, for which a new word was required. Fifty was *kanaha me ka umi,* forty and ten; sixty, *akahi kanaha me ka iwakalua,* one forty and twenty, and so on; eighty was *elua kanaha,* two forties; one hundred was *elua kanaha me ka iwaka-*

lua, two forties and twenty; six hundred, *hookahi lau a me na kanaha elima*, one four hundred and five forties; ten thousand, *alua mano me na lau elima*, two 4000's and five 400's.*

In this system four is assumed as the lowest collection of numbers, and the basis of classification; the regular scale being graduated from four to four hundred thousand; each step multiplied by ten. Thus:

Aha kahi,	four units	made	1 kauna,	4
Umi kauna,	ten 4's	"	1 kanaha,	40
Umi kanaha,	ten 40's	"	1 lau,	400
Umi lau,	ten 400's	"	1 mano,	4,000
Umi mano,	ten 4,000's	"	1 kini,	40,000
Umi kini,	ten 40,000's	"	1 lehu,	400,000

Beyond this last number their ideas became confused; though the term *nalowale*, which means, out of sight, or lost, was sometimes employed, as expressing ten lehu, or four millions. Numbers beyond their power of reckoning or exceedingly great and indefinite, were expressed by the repetition of the words *kini* and *lehu*, as *kinikini, lehulehu*. To reduce English computation to the Hawaiian, it is only necessary to divide by four, and *vice versa*, to multiply by the same number. This ancient method is now rapidly giving way to the decimal system, introduced by the missionaries in their schools. The larger numbers are formed from the English terms; thus, one hundred accommodated to the Hawaiian idiom, is *haneri ;* thousand, *tausani ;* million, *miliona*, &c.

The knowledge and use of medicinal herbs was said to have been a gift from the gods to a man named Koleamoku, who taught them to two disciples. After their death they were deified, and to them the prayers of the doctors were addressed. The doctors were a distinct class of priests or sorcerers, who generally confined the knowledge of their art to their own families, and thus made the employment, which was lucrative, hereditary. They were called *kahuna lapaau mai*, "man or priest to heal sickness." Their practice was a compound of superstitious ceremonies, and an injudicious use of medicines and surgery. Their materia medica consisted exclusively of vegetable substances,

* Hawaiian Spectator, vol. 2, p. 91.

variously prepared
cooked, but often
stone. Their kno
cinal properties of
ble, though fatal
sued from their
feigned a knowle
orders by extern
also the power t
Healthy individua
tims to their pret
duced to take larg
compounded from
the calabash vine
powerful cathartic.
ed over ovens of h
the smoke of fires
succulent herbs.
used to mitigate n
twelve pounds wei
rolled over the afl
manual exercise
limbs they were
though more fron
but in all complic
gerous illnesses, th
than useless.

An individual,
class, was suppos
power to afflict his
diseases, and eve
also, to be enable
thor of his own
them upon the a
reasonably conjec
lieved to be capat
counteracting int
the natural fear
employed. But s
calculate results :
everything else.
plentiful employr
the largesses requ
was strongest ov
probably fear of o
them from testing
ful chiefs, who we
valuable patrons.
sult of accident,
to their agency, p
of some unpropitic

The ceremonie
rious ; the most c
that for the dis
was called *Kunia*
was used to disco

jurious incantations and sickness. None but the parties concerned were allowed to enter the house selected for the occasion. Near the invalid, a fire was kindled, and covered with stones. A dog, hog or fowl was killed, emboweled, and placed upon the heated oven. During this operation the priests muttered prayers. A small portion of the broiled meat was eaten by him, and the remainder left to be consumed. He then feigned sleep, and in visions to receive answers to his orisons, by which he informed his patient who or what occasioned his illness. Additional prayers and offerings were then required, that the disease might fasten itself upon its author, or to remove the anger of the god who sent it. If the priest said he had not been successful, and had received no revelation, he recommended another trial; which advice was commonly followed, though not always to his satisfaction; a rival being frequently sent for to exert his influence. Each had different methods, upon the degree of popularity of which their fame depended; and, like civilized quacks, they were anxious to extend the reputation of their remedies, at the expense of their less bold or skillful brethren. As might be expected, they inculcated the belief that the success of their experiments depended greatly upon the amount of offerings.

The manner of burial differed according to the rank of the deceased. The bodies of the common people were bent with the face upon the knees, arms beneath them, and the hands passed up between the legs; the heads, hands and knees were closely bound together with cord, and the corpses enveloped in coarse mats, and buried within two days of decease. Those of the priests and inferior chiefs were laid out straight, and wrapped in folds of cloth. The former were generally interred within their temples, their graves being marked by piles of stones or rough wooden enclosures. The legs, arms, bones, and sometimes the skulls, of the high chiefs whose ancestors had received the honors of deification, or who were themselves to be enrolled in the calendar of gods, were reserved, and the remainder of their bodies buried or burnt. The relics were carefully covered with crimson cloth, and either deposited in temples, for adoration, or remained in possession of the nearest relations, by whom they were held sacred; the spirits of the departed being supposed to remain with them, exercising a controlling and protecting influence over the living.

Caverns were generally selected as places of sepulture, and the remains of many successive generations deposited in the same. These were frequently embalmed by a rude method, the brains and entrails being taken out. As with the dead of the Indians of North America, their property and food were deposited with them, which were to serve them in their journeys to the world of spirits. Enclosures, surrounded by high stone walls, were also employed, each family generally possessing a distinct cemetery; though sometimes the dead of a whole town were deposited in the same cave. The floors of their own houses were used by some as graves; but a great fear prevailed of the shades of the departed, whose apparitions were supposed to hover about their final resting-places, and injure those who came within their reach. In consequence of this ghostly dread, burials were conducted in a private manner, and in the night. A portion of the bones of the worshipers of Pele were thrown into the crater, that they might continue in the society of the volcanic deities, and induce them to protect their living relatives from eruptions.

The fishermen believed to some extent in transmigration, and frequently cast their dead into the sea to be devoured by sharks. Their souls were supposed ever after to animate those fishes, and incline them to respect the bodies of the living, should accident ever throw them into their power.

The Hawaiian calendar was based upon a very superficial knowledge of astronomy; the year being divided into two seasons of six months each, summer and winter, according to the length of the days and the productiveness of the vegetable kingdom. The summer months were, *Ikiiki*, "May," *Kaaona*, *Hinaiaeleele*, *Kamahoemua*, *Kama-*

hoehope, and *Ikua*, "October:" those of the winter, *Welehu*, *Makalii*, *Kaelo*, *Kaulua*, *Nana* and *Welo*. The year commenced with *Makalii*, "December," and terminated with *Welehu*, "November." They reckoned but nine times forty nights in their years, and appear to have had no idea of the necessity of intercalary days to cause it to correspond to the true solstices. Each month contained thirty nights: the different days and nights derived their names from the varying aspects of the moon, according to her age. The first night was *Hilo*, "to twist," because the moon was then a mere thread; the next, *Hoaka*, "crescent;" then *Kukahi*, *Kulua*, &c. In the moon's first quarter, when the sharp points were lost, the night was called *Huna*, "to conceal;" the succeeding, when it became convex, *Mohalu*, "to spread out;" the next, *Hua*, "to increase;" when it was quite rotund, *Akua*, "clear;" when nearly and quite full, *Hoku*, *Mahealani*, and *Kulu*. Upon the first decrease, *Laaukukahi*, and as it continued to diminish, *Olauukulua*, *Luaupau*, *Olekukuhi*, *Olekulua*, *Olepau*, *Kaloakukahi*, *Kaloakulua*, *Kaloapau*. When it had almost disappeared, *Mauli*, "overshadowed;" when entirely gone, *Muku*, "cut off." During every month, four periods were set apart, in which the nights were consecrated, or made taboo. The duration of each varied from two to four nights, and they were called the *Kapu-ku*, "the proper taboo," *Kapu-hua*, "fruit taboo," *Kapu-kahua*, "cooking taboo," and *Kapu-kane*, "man taboo." Their astrologers were acquainted with Jupiter, Mercury, Venus, Mars and Saturn, and also had names for many fixed stars and constellations.

The only approach towards representing language, or ideas, symbolically, was in the rude scratches or carvings of lines, semi-circles, imitations of the human figure and other rough delineations, occasionally met with on rocks. These were done by travelers, and were intended to record their number, dots being used for that purpose, and rings to denote those who had circumambulated the island; if a semi-circle, it showed that the party had returned from the place where it was made. Figures of fish and fruit denoted some particular success in the supply at that spot.*

Beside these scrawls, which can scarcely be admitted as an exception, the language was strictly oral. Its chief peculiarities were the simple construction of words, predominancy of vowels, uniform termination and shortness of syllables, which were never composed of more than three letters, and generally of but two, while very many have but one. A vowel terminating every word and syllable, renders the language peculiarly soft and harmonious. Its sounds are few and simple, twelve letters only being required to represent those purely Hawaiian. Of these, when reduced to writing, the vowels received the sound peculiar to them in the principal languages of the continent of Europe, while the consonants, H, K, L, M, N, P, W, retained the English accent. It is difficult for an adult Hawaiian to pronounce two consonants without a vowel between them. Latterly, many words and sounds have been introduced, which require other letters of the English alphabet, and the language will, as intercourse with foreigners increases, become further modified. The vowel terminations are invariably retained. There are many dipthongs, though, generally, two vowels coming together retain their distinct and separate sounds. Though the letters K and L only occur in writing, in conversation K and T, or L, R and D, are synonymous. The natives of some districts using the latter, others the former; as Kauai or Tauai, Lanai or Ranai, Lono or Rono, Lii-lii, Rii-rii or Dii-dii. To this variableness in the use of these letters, is owing the difference of spelling among foreigners, of those words which have become almost incorporated with the English language—as kapu and tabu, kalo and taro, kapa and tapa, and others.

---

* Ellis' Tour through Hawaii, p. 431.

CHAPTER IV.

Physical appearance of the Hawaiians—Chiefs—Habits of—Common people—Women—Marriage—Affinities of blood—Friendships—Salutation—Cannibalism—Intemperance—Treatment of sick—Lunatics—Aged—Infanticide—Examples of—Treatment of women—Taboos of food—General character of the Hawaiians previous to contact with the whites.

HAVING in the preceding chapter sketched an outline of the original political and religious condition of the Hawaiians, it remains to speak more particularly of their social relations, before entering upon their political history. Between the higher and lower orders there existed a marked difference in stature and appearance. The former were almost invariably tall, stout and well formed, with, as age advanced, a tendency to unwieldy corpulency : the latter were, upon the average, middle sized, falling somewhat short of the European standard. Six feet and upwards were common to the stature of the chiefs of both sexes, with gigantic frames, more capable of exerting great strength than of endurance. It was said of some that they were able, by taking a man by the head and leg, to break his back across their knees. From three to four hundred pounds was not an uncommon weight. The female chiefs, when young, possessed interesting and intelligent features, which, however, soon became lost, as their bulk increased; fortunately for them, in the eyes of their lords, this but heightened their charms. When these were most matured, they became almost as helpless as the belles of the Celestial empire. The latter tottered from want of feet of sufficient size to support frames of scarcely larger proportions ; those of the former, though stout, were equally feeble to sustain the immense bulk above. Their flesh hung in deep folds about them ; their walk was a majestic stagger ; but their carriage was lofty, and betokened an innate pride of birth and rank.

No aristocracy was ever more distinctly marked by nature. As before remarked, to a superficial observer, they might, with reason, have appeared as a distinct race. The monopoly they enjoyed of the good gifts of Providence, with the greater exercise of their mental faculties, for they did most of the think-

ing for the people, served, every generation, to increase the distinction between the two classes. The great personal size was doubtless partly inherited, and partly the result of early care. The young chiefs, unless they otherwise desired, were always borne on the shoulders of attendants ;[*] their only exercises were games, sufficient to excite and amuse, without greatly fatiguing; no care or toil was theirs ; the abundance of the land and sea was at their disposal; and, from the quantity they daily consumed, particularly of that most nutritious diet, poi, it is not surprising they gave such material evidences of their training. After a surfeit—a common case—menials were always ready to do that for the system, which, otherwise, active exercise only could have effected. Servants were especially trained to *lomi-lomi*—a luxurious kneading or shampooing, and stretching and cracking the joints, exceedingly pleasant withal, and operating as a gentle and refreshing exercise. The fatter the chiefs, the more they required this operation.

Their common position was reclining upon divans of fine mats, surrounded by a retinue, devoted solely to their physical gratification. Some fanned, brushed away insects and held spittoons ; others fed them, *lomi-lomied*, or dressed their hair or persons. In short, the extremes of activity or laziness, temperance or sensuality, were wholly at their option. Ambition and apathy, superstition and avarice, love and pleasure, by turns controlled them ; and war, priestcraft and oppression, varied by occasional acts of good nature, or the ebullitions of innate benevolence, which even such an education could not wholly eradicate, were the lot of their subjects.

Among them a considerable degree of physical beauty existed, though on a less noble scale. A few might be seen who were models of active grace, but

---

[*] A favorite method of conveyance once existed, called *manele* ; a rude palanquin borne on the shoulders of four or more men. But it became unfashionable, from the following circumstance : A certain extremely corpulent chief of Kauai, remarkable for his crabbed, petulant disposition, compelled his carriers to take him up and down the steepest precipices; his amusement and satisfaction being proportionate with the difficulty of the task. However, they retorted one day, and relieved themselves of their burden by pitching him headlong over the steep, which put an end to him and the custom.

6

their general appearance was that of "hewers of wood and drawers of water." They were supple, hardy and inured to toil; yet, either from the debilitating effects of the climate, or a positive physical inferiority, the result of difference of food and living, incapable of the same endurance as the Caucasian race.

At the present epoch, the general cast of features prevailing among the whole group, is similar to that of all Polynesia, and analogous to the Malay, to which family of the human race they doubtless belong. A considerable variety in color exists, from a light olive to an almost African black; the hair is coarse and equally dissimilar, varying from the straight, long black, or dark brown, to the crispy curl peculiar to the negro. This latter is comparatively rare, though white hair among children is common. A broad, open, vulgarly good humored countenance prevails among the males, and a more pleasing and engaging look with the females, but both bespeak the predominance of animal passions. Many of the latter, when young, are not unattractive. Though farther from the equator, both sexes are some shades darker than the Tahitians, Marquesans, or Ascension islanders; all of whom excel them in personal beauty. As with them, a fullness of the nostril, without the peculiar flatness of the negro, and a general thickness of lips, prominent and broad cheek bones, and narrow, high and retreating foreheads, resembling the Asiatic, predominate.

Instances of deformity are not more common than in civilized life. Their teeth are white, firm and regular; but their eyes are generally bloodshot, which once was considered a personal attraction. The hands of the females are soft and well made, with tapering fingers. At maturity, which takes place from ten to twelve years of age, they present slight figures, which however soon disappear and are succeeded by stoutness, which in their eyes is the greater charm.

No regular marriage ceremonies existed, though, on such occasions, it was customary for the bridegroom to cast a piece of cloth on the bride, in the presence of her family. A feast was then furnished by the friends of both parties. The number of wives depended upon the inclination of the man, and his ability to support them. Though the common men usually lived with one woman, who performed household labors, no binding tie existed; each party consulting their wishes for change, joining or separating, as they agreed or disagreed. As a general thing, there was no such sentiment as chastity; sensual desires were gratified as choice prompted; their only rules being their wishes, modified by jealousy or fear. The very reverse of christian morality prevailed in this respect, for it was considered a meanness for a man or woman to refuse a solicitation for sensual gratification. Visitors of equal or greater rank than their hosts were accommodated with women, as a necessary exercise of hospitality. But the wives of the chiefs were guarded with great care, to prevent their indulging in too great license.

Some sentiments relative to connubial fidelity prevailed which may be said to have bordered on morality, or rather served in this respect to distinguish them from the mere brute. The idea connected with marriage in their minds is well indicated by the term used to express it—*hoao*—literally to try one another. After the parties had lived together awhile mutually pleased, it was considered disgraceful to separate, though it was common for those without children to do so; children being considered a strong link, not so much for fidelity as for perpetuity. Wives on the slightest suspicion of their husbands were subject to very cruel treatment, and were often severely injured. Even Kamehameha's queens formed no exception to this system of family discipline, and the highest females of the land bore marks about their persons of the jealous brutality of their lords.

Adultery, without the consent of the husband, was viewed as a crime. Kamehameha, in 1809, strangled Kanihonui, a high chief, for this offence with Kaahumanu, even at the risk of a rebellion; and later still, suspecting one of his priests of a similar practice, he laid a trap for him by which he was exposed. He was immediately executed.

Children were betrothed when quite young, and were then sacredly guarded by their parents from intercourse with others; a practice which being quite common, operated as some restraint on universal licentiousness. Common and frequent prostitution was considered in some degree disreputable, and it was enjoined by the better class of parents on their sons to avoid it.

Family alliances among the chiefs, or, more properly speaking, connections, were of the most intricate and shocking nature. Custom obliged the highest chief to marry the next in rank; consequently, brothers and sisters, full cousins, nieces and uncles, nephews and aunts, frequently exercised towards each other the relations of husband and wife. The most complex affinities arose from this unnatural law. This resulted rather from an arbitrary political custom than desire, as incest in general was considered disgraceful. In such cases the parties cohabited but seldom, and frequently the marriage was scarcely more than nominal. The highest female chiefs enjoyed the same connubial privileges as to the selection and number of those of the other sex. Sometimes father and son were husbands of the same wife.

Notwithstanding this general sexual laxity, instances of love and affection were not uncommon. The exchange of names was the strongest proof of friendship; and a partiality thus established entitled the recipients mutually to exercise the utmost freedom of persons or property. If they were chiefs, their dependents acknowledged this ideal relationship, by the same homage and services. Or, if a chief thus adopted an inferior, his influence in household matters was scarcely less than his patrons. An embrace with the noses touching, was the most affectionate mode of salutation.

Some doubt formerly existed whether cannibalism ever prevailed in the group. The natives themselves manifested a degree of shame, horror and confusion, when questioned upon the subject, that led Cook and his associates, without any direct evidence of the fact, to believe in its existence; but later voyagers disputed this conclusion. The confessions of their own historians, and the general acknowledgment of the common people, have now established it beyond a doubt; though, for some time previous to Cook's visit, it had gradually decreased, until scarcely a vestige, if any, of the horrible custom remained. This humanizing improvement, so little in accordance with their other customs, was a pleasing trait in their national character. It may have been the result of instruction and example derived from the earliest European visitors, or a self-conviction of its own abomination. Be that as it may, a public sentiment of disgust in regard to it prevailed at that period, highly creditable to them as a nation, and distinguished them from their cotemporaries of New Zealand, the Marquesas, and even from the more polished Tahitian.

Many generations gone by, it was not uncommon for them to indulge, after the close of a battle, in the fierce and bloody delight of roasting their slain enemies, and devouring their flesh like ravenous wild dogs, as the sweetest and most glorifying consummation of revenge. Later still, it was confined to certain robber chieftains, who infested mountain paths, and the recesses of forests, from which they sallied forth—the terror of the less ferocious inhabitants—slaying, plundering, and gorging, like vultures, upon the flesh of their victims. As of the ghouls, and monstrous creations of eastern tales, a superstitious dread of their haunts prevailed, which the marvelous tales spread abroad of their prowess and cruelty, served to increase. The warrior became famous who dared beard these "lions in their dens." If successful, his name, with all the eclat of the knight errant of the days of chivalry, was celebrated in song and dance for many generations.

In the use of *awa*, a liquor manufactured from the *piper methysticum*, the chiefs were exceedingly intemperate. Its effects were very pernicious, covering the body with a white scurf, or scaliness, like the scurvy, inflaming the eyes, and causing premature decrepitude. It was also taken as a medicine, and was supposed to be an effectual remedy for corpulence. No other intoxicating liquor was known.

Lunatics were occasionally treated with attention and respect, being supposed to be inspired by some god; but more commonly they shared the fate of the aged and sick, as objects of contempt, ridicule and even cruelty. Heathen charity has little respect for those unable to help themselves; hence the deformed, dependent, foolish and blind, were made the cruel sport of idlers or left to perish. Age and helplessness were frequently cast out from homes which their own hands had reared, and abandoned to die by the road-side, uncared for and unpitied by neighbor or relative. The more merciful children gave the finishing stroke at once, and left their corpses the prey of prowling dogs.

Humanity to the aged and afflicted could not be expected from those whose

"tender mercies wei own offspring. Mul destroyed before bir will not bear record permanent injury to many, perhaps, wer months and even y the light. Parents l and death over their to no one. Infantici lent among the poor rich. Whim, expe diminishing their p them were adequate their young to a barl poor destroyed many avoid the expense o them. Other classe humor, or to gratify sition. When a qu the parents, the chi sacrificed. A case waii, in regard to a age. Both parties rage ; the father sei: wrists with one hai the other, and with back across his kn mangled corpse at The child was his have interfered to Some spared two destroyed all but c times done by strar burying the innoce both parents unitin; earth over the form babe, the floor of the frequently being the indulged in such a it is said, destroyed two thirds of their credit of humanity, i it was not so preva: writers have suppo: crease was latterly women are to be fo the murder of from t children. Females less useful than ma: destroyed.

Cook, in his accou their parental affec But mere voyager: greatly in their es whom they see but 1 whom intercourse is embarrassed from ignorance of their tongue. More authentic records, and subsequent examinations, have proved infanticide, in all its horrible shades, to have been a common custom. Not perhaps to such an extent as, by itself, to occasion a great decrease of population, though joined with other causes, it produced sad results. Tenderness to the living was not to be increased by the exercise of so fell a passion. Hawaiian parents had a kind of animal affection for their offspring, which, like any instinct, not governed by reason, was as often injurious as beneficial. The ill effects of this were apparent in their education. There was no regular family discipline; a caress or blow being the only reward or punishment. It was a common practice to give away children, towards whom a community of feeling, the result of the very promiscuous intercourse of the sexes, must necessarily have existed. Children could seldom determine their real parents. Dogs and swine were quite as frequently objects of fondness, and often allowed more indulgences and better food than fell to the lot of their biped companions; their mothers' breasts giving suck to the brute in preference to the immortal being.

The cleanliness of the islanders has been much praised, but equally without reason. Frequent bathing kept their persons in tolerable order, but the same filthy clothing was worn while it would hold together. The lodgings of the common orders were shared with the brutes, and their bodies a common receptacle of vermin. All, of every age and sex, herded in common; the same mat beneath them at night, and the same tapa above. If a fly perchance alighted on their food, their delicate stomachs became sick; but the same sensitive organ found delicious morsels in the raw, uncleaned entrails of animals or fish; and the choicest of all, in vermin picked from each others hair.

Oppressive as were the laws to the men, they were far more so upon the women. Their sex was but an additional motive for insult and tyranny. The right of blood gave to the highest female the power to rule; but she,

equally with the humblest dependent, was subject to the iron law of the "taboos." Neither could eat with men; their houses and their labors were distinct; their aliment was separately prepared. A female child from birth to death was allowed no food that had touched its father's dish. The choicest of animal and vegetable products were reserved for the male child; for the female the poorest; while the use of many kinds, such as pork, turtle, shark, bananas and cocoanut, were altogether interdicted. Woman was made bitterly to feel her sexual degradation. She was excused from no labors, excepting such as were altogether too arduous for her weaker frame. Thus her lot became even worse than that of her sex generally in the southern groups.

In the preceding pages it has been my endeavor to draw a just outline of the native government, religion, manners and customs, as they existed prior to the discovery of Cook. In some points, but little change has been experienced to the present day, while in others the alteration has been total. To trace the history of the progress from its primary causes; the influences of commerce, and of civilized man in the gradual development of civilization and christianity among this benighted race; and to present, in a forcible light, the contrast between the past and present, will be the attempt of future chapters. Modern history affords no more interesting picture than this peaceful and triumphant revolution. Its action has been but partially understood and represented. Civilization and christianity have each their interested advocates, who endeavor to build up their favorite systems at mutual expense. Their influence has been generally presented as that of rival institutions; the destruction of one to be the erection of the other. Both views are equally apart from truth. The Hawaiian character in its general caste, uninfluenced by either of the above causes, may be thus summed up. From childhood no pure social affections were inculcated. Existence was due rather to accident than design. If spared by a parent's hand, a boy lived to become the victim of a priest, an offering to a blood-loving deity, or to experience a living death from preternatural fears :—a slave, not only to his own superstitions, but to the terrors and caprices of his chief. He was not to know freedom either in life or property, but in its stead a pitiless tyranny, reaping where it had not sown. To him existed no social circle to purify by kindly affections; no moral teachings enkindled a love of truth, no revelation cheered his earthly course, or brightened future hopes. Theft, lying, drunkenness, reveling, treachery, revenge, lewdness, infanticide and murder, were familiar to his youth, and too often became the practices of his manhood. Guilt was measured by success or failure. Justice was but retaliation, and the law itself arrayed each man's hand against his brother. Games and amusements were but means of gambling and sensual excitement. An individual selfishness which sought present gratification, momentary pleasure, or lasting results, regardless of unholy measures or instruments, was the all-predominating passion. The most attractive quality of the Hawaiian, it cannot be called a virtue, was a kind of easy, listless, good nature, never to be depended upon when their interests or passions were aroused. Instances of a better disposition were sometimes displayed, and occasional gleams of humanity, among which may be mentioned friendship, and a hospitality common to all rude nations, where the distinctions of property are but slightly understood, enlivened their dark characters; but these were sufficient only to redeem their title to humanity, and not make us altogether " blush and hide our heads," to own ourselves fellow-men. Individuals there were who rose above this level of degradation ; but their lives served to render more prominent the vices of the remainder. La Perouse, though fresh from the Rousseau school of innocence of savage life, thus, perhaps, a little too broadly, expressed his opinion : " The most daring rascals of Europe are less hypocritical than these natives. All their caresses were false. Their physiognomy does not express a single sentiment of truth. The object most to be suspected is he who has just received a

present, or who appears to be the most earnest in rendering a thousand little services."—Vol. 1, p. 377.

These islanders possessed a callousness to pain, wonderful to the more delicately reared white man. A like insensibility pervaded their moral system. Those who live in dangerous climates, or among alarming natural phenomena, manifest a surprising indifference to the surrounding dangers, and engage in the pleasures of life with more than ordinary zest. The native, thoughtless of the morrow, careless of results, and habituated to scenes of death, enjoyed his animal pleasures with a heartiness which vigorous health alone could give. By this many were deceived into the opinion that they were a happy, cheerful and simple race.

Their joys and griefs were equally ephemeral ; tears of sorrow could follow in quick succession peals of laughter, and both give way to an almost immovable apathy. Such happiness as a moral degradation which the world elsewhere might equal but not excel, was indeed theirs. So dark were their conceptions of one of the most pleasurable emotions of the heart, gratitude, that there was found in their language no word to express the sentiment. As far as a language affords an index of the heart of a nation, theirs presented a most deplorable picture. Prolific in epithets expressive of every degree and shade of vice and crime, copious in illustrations of the actions of the mere animal man, it was barren of words to convey correct ideas of virtue and rectitude. Their language, according to Dibble, could not even " describe a man of common faithfulness and honesty, and was incapable of expressing, without much ambiguity and confusion, the common notions of right and wrong." In losing all just conceptions of Deity, they had equally lost the power of expressing the attributes of love and goodness. So completely had the flood of iniquity which deluged the land swept away the vocabulary of moral sentiments, in their simple abstract forms, that not an uncorrupted remnant remained. Either oblivion had buried them, or corruption had so changed their nature as to leave no trace of their original brightness behind. The missionaries were put to great straits in making the truths of the gospel at all intelligible, and with all their labor, for some time the grossest notions prevailed. Besides creating terms expressive of the meaning of the gospel, they were obliged to create corresponding ideas, in Hawaiian minds, before their meaning could be rightly comprehended ; and even now, no small obstacle is presented to their success in imparting just conceptions of the revealed will of God, by the operation of the remains of that moral ignorance which the natives themselves very expressively designate as " dark-heartedness."

CHAPTER V.

Visits to the Hawaiian Islands previous to Cook—Anson's chart—Spaniards acquainted with Hawaii—Traditions of a priest—Landing of Europeans between 1535 and 1560—Shipwreck at Kealakeakua Bay—Ships seen—First appearance of Cook—His reception — Astonishment of islanders—Effects of visit—War on Maui—Cook's re-appearance—First notice of Kamehameha—Cook's arrival at Kealakeakua Bay—His deification—Remarks—Native hospitality—Thefts—Cook's desecration of the temple—Growing dislike of natives—Ships sail—Return—Succeeding events—Cook's death—Ledyard's account—Native do.—Review of proceedings—Recovery of bones—Peace—Departure of ships—Touch at Oahu—Arrive at Kauai—Wars—Attacked by natives—Visit Niihau—Final departure.

THERE are substantial reasons for believing that the Hawaiian Islands were visited by Europeans two centuries or more before the era of Cook. Among the natives the knowledge of such events has been perpetuated in numerous traditions, which coincide with so much collateral evidence as to place it beyond doubt. It is impossible to ascertain the precise time of these visits, though from the reigns to which they are referred, and the few particulars which have been preserved relative to them, they must have been long anterior to that of the English navigator. If their original discoverers were the Spaniards, as is highly probable, they were acquainted with their position previous to the seventeenth century. According to an old authority, Quiros sighted them in 1696, in a voyage from Manila to New Spain. In a chart of that period, taken by Admiral Anson from a Spanish galleon, a cluster of islands called *La Mesa, Los*

Majos, La Desgraciada, is found delineated, in the same latitude as the Hawaiian Islands, and bearing the same relative situation to Roca Partida as on modern charts, though several hundred miles farther eastward. As the Spanish charts of that time were not remarkable for accuracy, the discoveries of Quiros, Mendana and others, in the Pacific, being also placed in the same relative nearness to the coast of America, this may have been an error, either of calculation, the engravers, or of design. Lying directly in the course of their rich Manila galleons, they would have afforded a secure retreat for the buccaneers and their numerous naval enemies ; consequently it would have been a matter of policy to have confined the knowledge of their situation to their own commanders navigating these seas. As their number was small, rarely more than one ship annually following that track, it is no matter of surprise that they should have become forgotten, or perhaps the memory of them revived only at intervals, by their being seen at a distance. Their first visitors must have discovered that there were no mineral treasures to reward a conquest ; and little else in those days sufficed to tempt the Spanish hidalgo to new scenes of adventure and hardship. The name of one, *Mesa*, which means table, agrees very well with the flat appearance of Mauna Loa on Hawaii, seen at a great distance. Captain King, in approaching it, called it " table-land." The fact that no other group of islands exists in their vicinity strengthens the supposition in regard to the identity of the cluster upon the Spanish chart, with the modern Hawaiian Islands.

We must look for further proof from the aborigines themselves. Cook found in the possession of the natives of Kauai two pieces of iron ; one a portion of a hoop, and the other appeared to be part of the blade of a broadsword. The knowledge and use of iron was generally known. These relics may have been the fruit of the voyages of the natives themselves, to some of the islands more to the westward, which had been visited by Europeans, or they may have drifted ashore attached to some portion of a wreck. But it is more probable that they were left by foreigners themselves, a supposition which coincides with traditions. The long time which had elapsed since their first arrival and the small store of property brought with them, would naturally account for so little having survived the multifarious purposes, to which, from its great utility, it was applied. The value attached to these foreign articles must have led to frequent contests for their possession, which would greatly add to their chances of being lost.

Tradition states that ships were seen, many generations back, to pass the islands at a distance. They were called *moku*, " islands," a name which vessels of every description have since retained.

We have several accounts of the arrival of different parties of foreigners. In the reign of Kahoukapu a *kahuna*, " priest," arrived at Kohala, the northwest point of Hawaii. He was a white man, and brought with him a large and a small idol, which by his teachings and persuasions, were enrolled in the Hawaiian calendar of gods and a temple erected for them. Paao, such was his name, soon acquired power and influence, which he exercised in the cause of humanity, by inducing the king to spare the life of one of his sons who had been ordered to execution.

Kahoukapu reigned eighteen generations of kings previous to Kamehameha I. As few died natural deaths, their reigns were short, probably not averaging above ten to fifteen years each. If such were the case, it would bring the arrival of Paao to somewhere between the years 1530 and 1600, a period brilliant in the annals of Spanish maritime discovery in the Pacific.* From

1568 to 1595, Mendana crossed the ocean twice, and fell in with several groups. Quiros, a few years afterward, discovered Tahiti, New Hebrides and many other islands. It is not an unreasonable conjecture to suppose that some zealous friar, at his own request, was left upon Hawaii, in the hope of converting the natives to the Roman Catholic faith, or he may have been the sole survivor of a shipwreck. The idols were possibly an image and crucifix, though no traces of the latter have been discovered.

Opili, the son of Paao, succeeded him in his religious offices. During his life a party of white men are said to have landed on the southwest part of the island, and gone inland, and taken up their abode in the mountains. The natives viewed them with mysterious dread, doubtful whether they were of divine or merely human origin. Opili was sent for, and his advice asked as to the manner of opening an intercourse and propitiating them. By his directions great quantities of provisions were prepared and sent them, in solemn procession. Opili, with several others of distinction, walked at the head of the party, bearing white flags, symbolical of their peaceful intentions. The strangers seeing this, ventured from their retreat. The baked pigs and potatoes and other dainties were deposited on the ground, and the carriers retreated a short distance. When the foreigners approached, Opili spoke to them. The presents were gladly received, and a conversa-

century, to suppress journals of discoveries, or so discourage explorations that private adventurers rarely were able to enter upon them.

" The Manila ships are the only ones which have traversed this vast ocean, except a French straggler or two; and during near two ages in which this trade has been carried on, the Spaniards have with the greatest care *secreted* all accounts of their voyages."—Introduction to Anson's Voyages, page 15: London, 1748.

La Perouse is of opinion that the Coral Islands of Gaetan were the Sandwich Islands. Gaetan describes them as affording neither gold nor silver, but abounding in cocoanut trees, inhabited by a race of naked savages, and surrounded with coral reefs. This is a plausible conjecture, as he took his departure from the port of Nativity, Mexico, in 20° north latitude, and sailed *due west*, 900 leagues, which would bring him directly to the present Hawaiian Islands. The latitude of the Garden Islands is given as between nine and eleven degrees north. As there are no islands in that position to correspond with the description, and in sailing due west he would not be likely to have fallen six hundred miles to the south, it is highly probable that the latitude ascribed was a typographical, if not an intentional error. Change the degrees to the 19th and 21st, and the true latitude is found, while the distance west gives the correct longitude.

* Diego de Becerra, and Hernando de Grijalva, sailed from Mexico in 1533, and discovered an island in the South Seas, situated in 20° 30' north latitude, and *about* 100° west longitude from Paris, which they called St. Thomas Island. The latter discovered the islands now called the Revillagigedos.

Juan Gaetan, in 1542, discovered between the ninth and twentieth degrees of north latitude, and in various longitudes, several clusters of islands, which he named the Coral, Garden and Sailor Islands. It is not improbable that the Hawaiian Islands were visited during this period. The latitude in both instances agrees with their situation; but the attempt to identify them with certainty must prove futile, from the meagreness of the journals, and the great inaccuracies in longitudinal observations. It was a matter of policy with the Court at Madrid, at the end of the 16th

tion, the particulars of which unfortunately were not preserved, kept up for some time. It seems that Opili conversed freely with them, which was supposed by the natives to have been owing to a miraculous gift of language, but he probably had acquired from his father some knowledge of his tongue. The strangers were ever after regarded as gods, and treated with the utmost respect, though they did not remain on the island. Tradition states not how they embarked. The principal personage was called *malihini;* this term is still common to the Marquesan, Society and Hawaiian Islands, and is used to designate a stranger, guest or visitor.

Another, and more precise tradition, relates that a few years after the departure of the former party, another arrived at Kealakeakua Bay, on the west side of Hawaii. Their boat had no masts or sails, but was painted, and an awning was spread over the stern. They were all clad in white and yellow cloth, and one wore a plumed hat. At his side hung a long knife, "*pahi*," which term is still applied to a sword.

This party remained, and formed amicable alliances with the natives, and by their superior skill and knowledge, soon rose to be chiefs and famed warriors, and for a considerable period governed Hawaii.

In the reign of Kealiiokaloa, son of Umi, thirteen generations of kings before Cook's arrival, which, according to the previous calculation, would bring it near the year 1620, a vessel, called by the natives Konaliloha, arrived at Pale Keei, on the south side of Kealakeakua Bay, Hawaii. Here, by some accident, she was drawn into the surf and totally wrecked. The captain, Kukanaloa, and a white woman, said to be his sister, were the only persons who were saved. Upon reaching the beach, either from fear of the inhabitants, to return thanks for their safety, or perhaps from sorrow, they prostrated themselves, and remained a long time in that position. Where this took place is known at the present day by the appellation of *Kulou*, bowing down. The shipwrecked strangers were hospitably received, invited to the dwellings of the natives, and food placed

7

before them. As runs the tradition, the following question was asked, "have you ever seen this kind of food?" To which they replied, "we have it growing in our country." By what means they thus freely conversed, it is not known, though the Opili before mentioned may have again acted as interpreter. Bananas, breadfruit and ohias, "wild apples," were given them, which they ate with much satisfaction. They formed connections with the native Hawaiians, and gave birth to a mixed race, from which a number of chiefs and common people are said to have descended. Kaikioewa, the late governor of Kauai, was reputed to have been one of their descendants. It would now be a matter of much interest to know the actual fate of this, the first white woman who landed on these shores; but more than the above will probably never be known.

Another statement speaks of two vessels wrecked on the northeast coast of Hawaii, and that none of the crews were saved, being either lost in the surf or murdered as soon as they landed.*

There is a tradition extant of a ship that touched at Maui about this period, and it is possible upon further examination, the same or others were seen at the leeward islands, as one could not be visited without a knowledge being obtained of their neighbors. In clear weather, from certain points, several islands were within the range of the eye.

Though these traditions are somewhat inconsistent in a few particulars, they are quite as explicit as those that relate to their national history. The last of these visits can be referred to a period nearly a century and a half prior to Cook's arrival; a time quite sufficient to have dimmed the recollection of events and thrown a mystery over the whole. Enough has been preserved to establish the fact that centuries since, vessels visited these islands, and parties of white men landed on them and left progeny, whose descendants are distinguished

---

* Kotzebue, in his last "Voyage around the World," alludes to two anchors which were said to have been found at Hawaii, and were presumed to have belonged to one of those vessels. No other author mentions the circumstance, nor have I been able to gather any light upon the subject from the native accounts, though it is not at all improbable that such did exist, and have since been buried in the sand, or overgrown in the coral reef.

even to this day, by their lighter skin, and brown or red curly hair, called *ehu*. A party of white men called *Hea*, are said to have roamed wild in the mountains, occasionally making inroads upon the more fertile districts, much to the terror of the inhabitants, particularly the females.

The graceful form of the helmets and the elegance of the feathered mantles, so unlike the usual rude arts of the islanders, bearing as they did a striking resemblance, in form, to those formerly worn among the Spaniards, would seem to have derived their origin from visitors of that nation. If they were not originally the result of European taste, they formed a singular deviation from the general costume of Polynesia. The skill displayed in their martial manœuvres, their phalanxes of bristling spears, their well drawn up lines of battle, all savor of foreign improvement, and may be ascribed to hints received from those, who, like waifs, were cast upon their shores, and to which they were the forerunners of a civilization destined eventually to spread over the whole group. How far their influence may have extended in improving other arts, it is impossible to ascertain ; but some, particularly the good taste and pretty patterns found among their cloths, the fine polish of their wooden bowls, appear to have owed their perfection to a similar cause. That a few rude sailors or adventurers should not have been able to have revolutionized their system of religion, even if inclined, is not strange ; though doubtless their influence, compared with the bloody superstitions among which they were thus cast, was in some degree humanizing. In Paao, the priest, we perceive this principle forcibly illustrated in preventing the death of a doomed man. This individual having been the son of a king, may have been the reason of its being recorded in their traditions, while less conspicuous cases of merciful interference were forgotten in the long catalogue of succeeding cruelties and crimes.[*]

I have already alluded to the striking analogies between many of their religious customs and traditions and those of early Jewish rites and scriptures. It is impossible to say that even these were not derived from these strangers in their attempt to impress upon them a purer ritual and better faith. But the fact that we find in their traditions no traces of ideas of a triune deity, of an earth-born Saviour and of the Virgin Mary and other prominent points more likely to have been preached to savages by Roman Catholics than an observance of the ceremonies of Judaism, leads either to the conclusion that if once heard they have since been wholly forgotten, or we must refer those customs and traditions to a period which it would be vain even to hope to penetrate with the probability of arriving at any solution of so interesting an historical inquiry.

To whatever extent these islands may have been known to the Spanish navigators or stragglers across the vast Pacific, from the earlier part of the sixteenth to the middle of the seventeenth century, who from ignorance or design, left the world unacquainted with their importance, it does not detract from the credit due to the energy and ability displayed by their English successor, Captain Cook. He was probably unaware of their true position ; and if to Columbus the discovery of America is to be attributed, equally to Cook is that of the Hawaiian group. Both were simply rediscoveries ; the former owing rather to the comprehensive genius of a mind that dared to originate and soar beyond his age ; the latter, from actively pursuing the track of discovery, and infusing into its course renewed life and vigor. In following other and important designs, he was brought in contact with this valuable group.[†]

[*] A number of Hawaiian words are somewhat analogous to the Spanish, and may have been derived from them, though it is only the fact of their former intercourse that throws any probability upon this conjecture. *Pono*, good, fair or just, could without much

change have been derived from the Spanish *bueno*, or the Portuguese, *bono*, both of which have the same signification. *Poko*, short, is like the Spanish *poco*, little.

[†] It has been suggested that Cook had possession of Anson's chart, and expected, by sailing in the course he took, to fall in with land. He actually inquired of the natives of Tahiti if any islands lay to the north of them. In his journal no great surprise is evinced at discovering land in that direction, though had he been a few miles further to the west, he would have passed it unseen ; and it is natural to suppose that so distinguished a navigator had examined all charts and voyages calculated to throw any light upon the track he was pursuing. The knowledge that a group of isl-

So long a period had elapsed since the eyes of the natives had been greeted with sights foreign to their own islands, that the memory of them had become obscure, and perhaps with the generality forgotten. The appearance of Cook's ships, when he first made Niihau and Kauai, on the 19th of January, 1778, was to their unsophisticated senses, novel, fearful and interesting. Canoes filled with wondering occupants, approached, but no inducement could prevail upon them to go on board, though they were not averse to barter. Iron was the only article prized in exchange; the use of other things was unknown and even ornaments at first despised.

On the following evening, the ships came to anchor in Waimea Bay, on the south side of Kauai. As the islanders were not generally apprised of their arrival until morning, their surprise was then extreme. They asked of one another, " what is this great thing with branches?" Some replied, " it is a forest which has moved into the sea." This idea filled them with consternation. Kaneonea and Keawe, the chief rulers, sent men to examine the wonderful machines, who returned and reported abundance of iron, which gave them much joy. Their description of the persons of the seamen was after this manner: : " foreheads white, bright eyes, rough garments, their speech unknown, and their heads horned like the moon; " supposing their hats to be a part of their heads. Some conjectured them to be women. The report of the great quantity of iron seen on board the ships excited the cupidity of the chiefs, and one of their warriors volunteered to seize it, saying, " I will go and take it, as it is

my business to plunder." He went, and in the attempt was fired upon and killed.

In the account of the commencement of the intercourse between the two races, I adhere principally to the description since given by the native historians, of the sensations and singular ideas produced in the minds of their ancestors, by the novel appearance of the strangers. It is seldom, where the disparity of power and knowledge is great, that both sides are heard. In this instance, the knowledge of writing, acquired before that generation had altogether passed away, served to preserve the memory and incidents of the strange events fresh in the minds of their children, and has given to the world the opportunity to draw just inferences from mutual relations. Both dwell with emphasis upon those circumstances which to each were the most surprising; though from the greater novelty, the astonishment was far more among the natives than their visitors, and they have recorded in their simple narratives, many trifling circumstances which were not thought worthy of place in the more enlightened accounts.

Cook does not mention the death of the warrior-thief, but states that on the evening before the ships anchored, he sent some boats ashore to select a watering-place. The party, upon landing, were pressed upon by the natives, who attempted to seize their arms, oars and other articles, in consequence of which, the commanding officer gave orders to fire, which was done, and one man killed. This produced no hostility from the natives, as it accorded with their own ideas of justifiable retaliation.

Throughout all the intercourse, though the natives manifested the greatest respect and kindness toward their visitors, and both parties indulged in a lucrative trade, yet their propensity for thieving was continually manifested. Perfectly ready to yield their own property or persons to the gratification of the whites, it was but natural that, without any sense of shame or wrong, they should desire the same liberties. Theft or lying were to them no crimes. Success in either was a virtue, and it was not until several severe lessons in regard to the

---

ands did exist somewhere in the North Pacific, which he successfully sought for, is more to his credit than if accident alone occasioned the discovery; but to acknowledge no assistance from the labors of others, and to endeavor to appropriate to himself the sole honor of the adventure, is unworthy of either him or his biographers. A silence in regard to the maritime efforts of his predecessors, is observable throughout his journals. In the map of the world attached to Anson's Voyages, published in 1748, the Sandwich Islands are delineated under their Spanish appellations, correct as to latitude, and but *ten* degrees too far to the west. Another island, St. Francisco, is placed within *one* degree of the true position of Hawaii, and from its extent, corresponds well with that island. To believe that Cook was ignorant of this map, or had not read with attention so popular a work as was then known as Anson's Voyages, is to accuse him of unpardonable negligence in acquiring knowledge proper to his profession.

enormity of the former had been received, that their discretion got the better of temptation.

During the visit, which lasted but a few days, the commander manifested a laudable humanity, in endeavoring to shield the population from the evil effects which so inevitably result from connection between foreign seamen and the native females. But his efforts were vain. If the discipline of his own crew could have been strictly enforced, the eagerness of the women was not to be repressed. The native history thus accounts for its commencement, by which it will be seen that however praiseworthy the desires of the commanders of these expeditions may have been, the licentious habits of the natives themselves were sure to counteract them.

The night after the attempt of Kapupua, the warrior-thief, many guns were discharged. The noise and fire were imagined to proceed from the god *Lono*, or Cook, and they at first thought of fighting him. But this design was frustrated by the advice of a female chief, who counselled them "not to fight the god, but gratify him, that he might be propitious." Accordingly she sent her own daughter, with other women, on board, who returned with the seeds of that disease, which so soon and so fatally spread itself throughout the group.

On February 2d, the ships sailed from Niihau, where they had spent the greater portion of their stay, for the Northwest Coast of America. During this time they became acquainted with the existence of Oahu, having seen it at a distance, but received no information of the more windward islands.

This visit was auspicious of the great revolution which the islands were destined to undergo. It had commenced on the one side with theft and prostitution, which had been repaid by death and disease. Still the superior knowledge, humanity and forbearance of the whites had been seen and acknowledged, and their first moral lessons in the distinctions of property, the foundation of all commercial prosperity, received.

The wonderful news spread rapidly. It soon reached Oahu, whence one Moho, a Hawaiian, carried the particulars to Ka-

laniopuu, king of Hawaii. The strange spectacle of the vessels, with their sails, spars and flags, were minutely described. "The men," he said, "had loose skins—their clothes—angular heads, and they were gods indeed. Volcanoes belching fire, burned at their mouths—tobacco pipes—and there were doors in their sides for property,—doors which went far into their bodies—pockets—into which they thrust their hands, and drew out knives, iron, beads, cloth, nails, and everything else." In his description, which he gave second handed, he appears to have considered the ships, equally with their crews, as animated beings, or else to have so blended the two, as to have forgotten their appropriate distinctions; an error into which savages readily fall, and which accounts for the great abundance of fables and confused description which usually pervades their stories. He also mimicked their speech, representing it as rough, harsh and boisterous.

A small piece of canvas had been procured by the chief of Kauai, which he sent as a present to the king of Oahu, who gallantly gave it to his wife. She wore it in a public procession, in the most conspicuous part of her dress, where it attracted the greatest attention.

During the interval between Cook's first and last visit, a war had broken out between Hawaii and Maui, in which Kalaniopuu—the Terreoboo of Cook, and Teraiobu of Ledyard—the king of Hawaii, contested the sovereignty of the latter island with Kahekili—Titeree —the reigning prince. On this occasion, Kamehameha* accompanied him. This is the first notice we have of this celebrated man, then a mere youth; but, at that early age he gave evidence of courage and enterprise. On the 26th of November, 1778, a battle had been

---

* The orthography of native names, before the language was systematized by the American missionaries, was various and perplexing. Kamehameha was written many different ways. By Captain King, Maiha-Maiha; by others, Cameamea, Tomyhomyhaw, Hameaymea, Tomooma. Vancouver and Turnbull were the most correct: the former wrote it Tamaah-maah; the latter, Tamahama. Kalaimoku, his prime minister, Crymakoo. Kaumualii, king of Kauai, Tomorce. Any one acquainted with the nature of the true vowel sounds will readily identify the various names in their modern dress, with those given by the early voyagers, which will render it unnecessary to record their multifarious spellings.

fought between the contending parties, which proved favorable to Kalaniopuu. The victors on the eve of the same day returned to Wailuku, on the north side of Maui, to refresh their forces. When the morning dawned, the stranger "islands and gods," of which they had heard, appeared in view. Cook's vessel stood in near the shore, and commenced a traffic, which the natives entered into freely and without much surprise, though observing the port-holes, they remarked to each other, "those were the doors of the things of which we have heard, that make a great noise." Kalaniopuu sent Cook off a present of a few hogs, and on the 30th went himself in state to make a visit. Kamehameha accompanied him, and with a few attendants remained all night, much to the consternation of the people on shore, who, as the vessel stood to sea, thought he had been carried off, and bitterly bewailed his supposed loss. The following morning their young chief was safely landed, and Cook, ignorant of the rank of his visitor, sailed for Hawaii, which had been discovered the previous day.

On the 2d of December, he arrived off Kohala, where his ships created much astonishment among the simple islanders. "Gods, indeed," they exclaimed; "they eat the flesh of man—mistaking the red pulp of water-melons for human substance—and the fire burns at their mouths." However, this opinion of their divine character did not deter them from exchanging swine and fruit for pieces of iron hoop. The definition which civilized man applies to the word God, and the attributes ascribed to the Divinity, differ materially from those of the savage. With him, any object of fear, power or knowledge is a god, though it might differ not materially from his own nature. The ancients deified their illustrious dead, and as in the case of Herod, applied the title, god, to the living. In neither case can it be supposed to denote more than an acknowledged superiority, or the strongest expression of flattery. While the Hawaiians bowed in dread to powerful deities, which in their hardened understandings filled the place of the christian's God, they worshiped a multitude of inferior origin,

whom they ridiculed or reverenced, and erected or destroyed their temples, as inclination prompted. Hence their willingness at Waimea, to fight Cook or their god Lono, as they deemed him; the readiness with which they were diverted from their purpose to try more winning means to gratify him, and the alternate love, fear and hostility with which he was afterward regarded.

Cook continued his course slowly around the east end of the island, occasionally trading with the natives, whose propensity to thieving was overcome only by exhibiting the dreadful effects of fire-arms. On the 17th of January, 1779, he came to anchor in Kealakeakua Bay, in the district of Kona, the reputed spot of the landing of the Spanish adventurers two centuries before. Kalaniopuu was still engaged on Maui in preserving his conquest. At the bay it was a season of taboo, and no canoes were allowed to be afloat; but when the ships were seen, the restrictions were removed, as Lono was considered a deity, and his vessels temples.

The inhabitants went on board in great crowds, and among them Palea, a high chief, whose favorable influence was secured by a few acceptable presents. The seamen employed in caulking the vessels were called the clan of Mokualii, the god of canoe-makers, and those who smoked, for it was the first acquaintance they had with tobacco, were called Lono-volcano. As at Kauai, the women were the most assiduous visitors, though great numbers of both sexes flocked around Cook to pay him divine honors. Among them was a decrepid old man, once a famed warrior, but now a priest. He saluted Captain Cook with the greatest veneration, and threw over his shoulder a piece of red cloth. Stepping back, he offered a pig, and pronounced a long harangue. Religious ceremonies similar to this were frequently performed before the commander.

Great multitudes flocked to the bay. Ledyard computes their number at upwards of fifteen thousand, and states that three thousand canoes were counted afloat at once. The punctilious deference paid Cook when he first landed, was both painful and ludicrous. Heralds announced his approach and opened the way for his progress. A vast throng crowded about him; others more fearful, gazed from behind stone walls, from the tops of trees, or peeped from their houses. The moment he approached they hid themselves, or covered their faces with great apparent awe, while those nearer prostrated themselves on the earth in the deepest humility. As soon as he passed, all unveiled themselves, rose and followed him. As he walked fast, those before were obliged to bow down and rise as quickly as possible, but not always being sufficiently active, were trampled upon by the advancing crowd. At length the matter was compromised, and the inconvenience of being walked over avoided by adopting a sort of quadruped gait, and ten thousand half clad men, women and children were to be seen chasing or fleeing from Cook, on all fours.

On the day of his arrival, Cook was conducted to the chief heiau and presented in great form to the idols. He was taken to the most sacred part, and placed before the principal figure, immediately under an altar of wood, on which a putrid hog was deposited. This was held toward him, while the priest repeated a long and rapidly enunciated address, after which he was led to the top of a partially decayed scaffolding. Ten men, bearing a large hog, and bundles of red cloth, then entered the temple and prostrated themselves before him. The cloth was taken from them by a priest, who encircled Cook with it in numerous folds, and afterward offered the hog to him in sacrifice. Two priests, alternately and in unison, chanted praises in honor of Lono; after which they led him to the chief idol, which, following their example, he kissed.

Similar ceremonies were repeated in another portion of the heiau, where Cook, with one arm supported by the high priest, and the other by Captain King, was placed between two wooden images and anointed on his face, arms and hands with the chewed kernel of a cocoanut, wrapped in a cloth. These disgusting rites were succeeded by drinking *awa*, prepared in the mouths of attendants, and spit out into a drinking

vessel; as the last tention, he was which had been m filthy old man.

No one acquain of Polynesia could doubted that these for adoration. Ca count of this affai such may have be affects to consider dence of great re The natives say his part in this h the slightest oppos offerings, the idols he was borne, the tions and chants a have carried convi it was intended f and the whole ce deification or con If this were not respect shown by who, if he walked ence, or fell and sufficient to have sceptical mind. V be entertained of who could thus len and perpetuate the heathenism? The the expediency of erful influence ov islanders, an exped in his destruction. of his divinity las was heavily taxed of the ships, or co: cation of their offic was customary in expected. Their general jubilee w most favorable imp acter to their vis quaintance with tl ter, and their inte mon people more have appeared in result of a thoroug 19th, Captain C heiau, or more pr the priests, with th of receiving simil he disappointed. sire to depict the

PRIESTS OFFERING SWINE AND FRUIT TO COOK.

been his motives in this case, for he took an artist with him, who sketched the group. Ever afterward, on landing, a priest attended him and regulated the religious ceremonies which constantly took place in his honor; offerings, chants and addresses met him at every point. For a brief period he moved among them, an earthly deity; observed, feared and worshiped.

The islanders rendered much assistance in fitting the ships, and preparing them for their voyages, but constantly indulged in their national vice, theft. The highest chiefs were not above it, nor of using deception in trade.

On the 24th of January, Kalaniopuu arrived from Maui, on which occasion a taboo was laid upon the natives, by which they were confined to their houses. By this, the daily supply of vegetables was prevented from reaching the vessels, which annoyed their crews exceedingly, and they endeavored, by threats and promises, to induce the natives to violate the restriction. Several attempted to do so, but were restrained by a chief, who, for thus enforcing obedience among his own subjects, had a musket fired over his head from one of the ships. This intimidated him, and the people were allowed to ply their usual traffic.*

Kalaniopuu and his chiefs visited Captain Cook on the 26th, with great parade. They occupied three large double canoes, in the foremost of which were the king and his retinue. Feathered cloaks and gaudy helmets glanced in the bright sunlight, and with their long, shining lances, gave them a martial appearance. In the second came the high priest and his brethren, with their hideous idols; the third was filled with offerings of swine and fruits. After paddling around the ships to the solemn chanting of the priests, the whole party made for the shore, and landed at the observatory, where Captain Cook received them in a tent. The king threw his own cloak over the shoulders of Cook, put his helmet upon his head, and in his hand a curious fan. He also presented him with several other cloaks, all of great value and beauty. The other gifts were then bestowed, and the cere-

mony concluded
names, the greatest
The priests then ap
offerings, and wen
religious rites, inte
and responses by tl
Kamehameha w
terview. Captain
face as the most sa
its natural ugliness
a " dirty brown pa
tered over his hair
this meeting over,
ber of his chiefs we
nace to the flag-sh
received with all di
for the magnificent
Kalaniopuu a line
hanger. While th
exchanged, profour
served throughout
shore. Not a can
inhabitant to be se
lay prostrate on th
The taboo interd
from visiting the sl
the request of Cap
it related to the
could be obtained
were forbidden all
the whites; the re
precaution, either te
of venereal diseas
worked its way to
group, or of an unv
The same boun
kindness continue
resources were bro
to amuse the follov
companies or singly
try in many directic
and courtesy every
givers were amply
cious reception.
good feeling, they
fore, to pilfer; fo
were fired at the
one was flogged on
On the 2d of F
of the commander
posed to the priests
the railing which
the heiau. In this
litttle respect for tl
thology of which
spicuously, as scru

* Cook's Voyages, vol. 3, p. 16: London, 1785.

divine precepts of his own. Indeed, throughout his voyages, a spirit regardless of the rights and feelings of others, when his own were interested, is manifested, especially in the last cruise, which is a blot upon his memory. It is an unpleasant task to disturb the ashes of one whom a nation reveres; but truth demands that justice should be dispensed equally to the savage, and to the civilized man. The historian cannot so far prove false to his subject, as to shipwreck fact in the current of popular opinion. When necessary, he must stem it truthfully and manfully.

To the great surprise of the proposer, the wood was readily given, and nothing stipulated in return. In carrying it to the boats, all of the idols were taken with it. King, who from the first doubted the propriety of the request, fearing it might be considered an act of impiety, says he spoke to the high priest upon the subject, who simply desired that the central one might be restored. If we are to believe him, no open resentment was expressed for this deed, and not even opposition shown. This is highly improbable, when the usual respect entertained by the natives for their temples and divinities is considered; and in no case could their religious sentiments have been more shocked. If they were silent, it was owing to the greater fear and reverence with which they then regarded Cook.

Ledyard, who was one of the party employed to remove the fence, gives a much more credible account, and which differs so much from the other, that it is impossible to reconcile the two. King, in his narrative of this and subsequent events, manifests a strong desire to shield the memory of his commander from all blame. Consequently, he passes lightly over, or does not allude to many circumstances which were neither creditable to his judgment nor humanity.

Ledyard, in his relation, states that Cook offered two iron hatchets for the fence, which were indignantly refused, both from horror at the proposal, and the inadequate price. Upon this denial, he gave orders to his men, to break down the fence and carry it to the boats, while he cleared the way. This was

done, and the images taken off and destroyed by a few sailors, in the presence of the priests and chiefs, who had not sufficient resolution to prevent this desecration of their temple, and insult to the names of their ancestors. Cook once more offered the hatchets, and with the same result. Not liking the imputation of taking the property forcibly, he told them to take them or nothing. The priest to whom he spoke, trembled with emotion, but still refused. They were then rudely thrust into the folds of his garment, whence, not deigning to take them himself, they were taken, at his order, by one of his attendants. During this scene, a concourse of natives had assembled, and expressed their sense of the wrong in no quiet mood. Some endeavored to replace the fence and images, but they were finally got safely on board.

About this juncture, the master's mate of the Resolution had been ordered to bring off the rudder of that ship, which had been sent ashore for repairs. Being too heavy for his men, he requested the assistance of the natives. Either from sport or design, they worked confusedly and embarrassed the whites. The mate angrily struck several. A chief who was present, interposed. He was haughtily told to order his men to labor properly. This he was not disposed to do, or if he had done, his people were in no humor to comply. They hooted and mocked at the whites; stones began to fly, and the exasperated crew snatched up some treenails that laid near by, and commenced plying them vigorously about the heads and shoulders of their assailants. The fray increased, and a guard of marines was ordered out to intimidate the crowd; but they were so furiously pelted with stones, that they gladly retired, leaving the ground in possession of its owners.

Other causes were at work augmenting the dissatisfaction, which the near departure of the ships alone prompted them to conceal. Familiarity tends greatly to destroy influence even with the most powerful. Cook and his companions had become common objects, and the passions they constantly displayed, so like their own, lessened the awe

8

with which they were at first regarded. The death and burial ashore of a seaman had greatly shaken their faith in their divine origin. The most cogent reason operating to create a revulsion of feeling, was the enormous taxes with which the whole island was burthened to maintain them. Their offerings to senseless gods were comparatively few, but daily and hourly were they required for Cook and his followers. They had arrived lean and hungry—they were now fat and sleek—qualities which seemed only to increase the voracious appetites of the seamen. The natives, really alarmed at the prospect of a famine, for their supplies were never over-abundant for themselves, by expressive signs urged them to leave. The glad tidings that the day for sailing was nigh, soon spread, and the rejoicing people, at the command of their chief, prepared a farewell present of food, cloth and other articles, which in quantity and value, far exceeded any which had heretofore been received. They were all taken on board, and nothing given in recompense. The magnitude of the gifts from the savage, and the meanness of those from the white men, must excite the surprise of any one who peruses the narrative of this voyage.

As a return for the wrestling and boxing matches, the natives were entertained with a display of fire-works, which created the greatest alarm and astonishment. They very naturally considered them flying devils, or spirits, and nothing impressed them more forcibly with the great superiority of the arts and power of the white men.

On the 4th of February, the ships sailed, but were becalmed in sight of land during that and the following day, which gave Kalaniopuu a fresh occasion to exercise his hospitality, by sending off a gift of fine hogs and many vegetables. His first and last intercourse being similar acts, while his friendship, during the whole visit, was of the utmost service to the exhausted crews.

But the joy of the inhabitants was destined to be of short duration. In a gale that occurred shortly after, the foremast of the Resolution was sprung, which obliged the vessels to return.

They anchored in their former situation on the 11th of the same month, and sent the spar and necessary materials for repairing it ashore, with a small guard of marines. Their tents were pitched in the heiau formerly occupied. The priests, though friendly, expressed no great satisfaction at this event, but renewed their good services by proclaiming the place taboo. The damaged sails, with the workmen, were accommodated in a house belonging to them.

Cook's reception this time presented a striking contrast to his last. An ominous quiet everywhere prevailed.[*] Not a native appeared to bid them welcome. A boat being sent ashore to inquire the cause, returned with the information that the king was away, and had left the bay under a strict taboo. The sudden appearance of the ships had created a suspicion of their intentions. Another visit as expensive as the former, would entirely have drained their resources. Intercourse was soon renewed, but with a faintness which bespoke its insincerity. The connections formed by many of their females with the foreigners, to whom some were attached, served, so says native authority, to exasperate the men.

The former injudicious violation of the taboos, both by seamen and officers, sometimes ignorantly, and often in contempt of what appeared to them whimsical and arbitrary restrictions, had aroused the prejudices of the mass. The women in particular had been tempted, though shuddering at the expected consequences, to violate the sacred precincts of the heiau, which had been placed at the disposal of Cook for an observatory and workshop, upon the condition that no seaman should leave it after sunset, and no native be allowed to enter it by night. The immunity from supernatural punishment with which these restrictions had been broken through on both sides, at first secretly, then openly, had encouraged further disregard of their religious observances. As no attempts had been made on the part of the officers to prevent these infringements, the mutual agreement to which was considered by the chiefs in

---

* Ledyard's Life, by Sparks, p. 105.

the light of a sacred compact, they felt a natural irritation. The most sacred portion of the heiau had been used as a hospital, and for a sail-loft; with the natives, highly sacrilegious acts; and they manifested their disapprobation by burning the house which stood there, as soon as the shore party evacuated it. From these and similar causes, all amicable feeling soon came to an end. Disputes arose in traffic. The bay was again laid under taboo. Affairs went on smoothly until the afternoon of the 13th, when some chiefs ordered the natives who were employed in watering the ships, to disperse; at the same time, the natives gave indications of an attack, by arming themselves with stones. Captain King approaching with a marine, they were thrown aside, and the laborers suffered to continue their work. Cook, upon being informed of these particulars, gave orders, if the natives threw stones, or behaved insolently, to fire upon them with balls.

Soon after, muskets were discharged from the Discovery at a canoe, which was being paddled in great haste for the shore, closely pursued by one of the ship's boats. In the narrative, a bold theft is said to have been the occasion of this proceeding. The natives state it was caused by their expressing dissatisfaction on account of the women, and that the foreigners seized a canoe belonging to Palea, who, in endeavoring to recover it, was knocked down with a paddle by one of the white men. This occurred during the absence of Cook, as he, with King and a marine, had endeavored, by running along the beach, to cut off the flying canoe, but arrived too late to seize the occupants. They then followed the runaways for some miles into the country, but being constantly misled by the people, they gave over their futile chase. The narrative agrees with the native account in the other particulars. The officer in charge of the pursuing boat was on his return with the goods which had been restored, when, seeing the deserted canoe, he seized it. Palea, the owner, at the same instant arrived, and claimed his property, denying all knowledge of the robbery. The officer refused to give it up; and in

the scuffle which ensued, the chief was knocked down by one of the crew. The natives, who had hitherto looked quietly on, now interfered with showers of stones, which drove the whites into the water, where they swam to a rock out of reach of missiles. The pinnace was seized and plundered, and would soon have been destroyed, had not Palea, who had recovered from the stunning effects of the blow, exerted his authority and drove away the crowd. He then made signs to the crew to come and take the pinnace, which they did; he restored to them all the articles which could be obtained, at the same time expressing much concern at the affray. The parties separated in all apparent friendship, but mutual suspicion prevailed. Cook prepared for decisive measures, and ordered every islander to be turned out of the ships. The guards were doubled at the heiau. At midnight a sentinel fired upon a native, who was detected skulking about the walls. Palea taking advantage of the darkness, either in revenge for his blow, or avaricious of the iron fastenings, stole one of the Discovery's cutters which was moored to a buoy.

Early the ensuing morning, Sunday, the 14th, Cook determined upon a bold and hazardous step to recover the boat. It was one which he had on previous occasions successfully practiced. His intention was to secure the king or some of the royal family, and confine them on board until the cutter was restored, and as hostages for future good conduct. This could be done only by surprise or treachery. Blinded by self-confidence to the peril of the attempt, he trusted for its success to the reverence of the natives for his person. If the cutter could not be recovered by peaceable means, he gave orders to seize every canoe which should endeavor to leave the bay. Clerke, the second in command, on whom the duty devolved to lead the shore expedition, being too ill, begged Cook to take the command. The account by Ledyard of the transactions that followed, of which he was an eye-witness, being near his commander when he fell, is so explicit, and agrees so well with the statements of the natives, that I give it entire :

"Cook, previous to his landing, made some additional arrangements respecting the possible event of things, though it is certain from the appearance of the subsequent arrangements, that he guarded more against the flight of Teraiobu, or those he could wish to see, than from an attack, or even much insult. The disposition of our guards, when the movements began, was thus: Cook in his pinnace with six private marines; a corporal, sergeant and two lieutenants of marines went ahead, followed by the launch with other marines and seamen on one quarter, and the small cutter on the other, with only the crew on board. This part of the guard rowed for Kealakeakua. Our large cutter and two boats from the Discovery had orders to proceed to the mouth of the bay, form at equal distances across, and prevent any communication by water from any other part of the island to those within the bay, or from those without. Cook landed at Kiverua—Kaawaloa—about nine o'clock in the morning, with the marines in the pinnace, and went by a circuitous march to the house of Teraiobu, in order to evade the suspicion of any design. This route led through a considerable part of the town, which discovered every symptom of mischief, though Cook, blinded by some fatal cause, could not perceive it, or too self-confident, would not regard it.

"The town was evacuated by the women and children, who had retired to the circumjacent hills, and appeared almost destitute of men; but there were at that time two hundred chiefs, and more than twice that number of other men, detached and secreted in different parts of the houses nearest to Teraiobu, exclusive of unknown numbers without the skirts of the town; and those that were seen were dressed many of them in black. When the guard reached Teraiobu's house, Cook ordered the lieutenant of marines to go in and see if he was at home, and if he was, to bring him out. The lieutenant went in, and found the old man sitting with two or three old women of distinction; and when he gave Teraiobu to understand that Cook was without and wanted to see him, he discovered the greatest marks of uneasiness, but arose and accompanied the lieutenant out, holding his hand. When he came before Cook, he squatted down upon his hams as a mark of humiliation, and Cook took him by the hand from the lieutenant, and conversed with him.

"The appearance of our parade both by water and on shore, though conducted with the utmost silence, and with as little ostentation as possible, had alarmed the towns on both sides of the bay, but particularly Kiverua, where the people were in complete order for an onset; otherwise it would have been a matter of surprise, that though Cook did not see twenty men in passing through the town, yet before he had conversed ten minutes with Teraiobu, he was surrounded by three or four hundred people, and above half of them chiefs. Cook grew uneasy when he observed this, and was the more urgent to have Teraiobu to go on board, and actually persuaded the old man to go at length, and led him within a rod or two of the shore; but the just fears and conjectures of the chiefs at last interposed. They held the old man back, and one of the chiefs threatened Cook, when he attempted to make them quit Teraiobu. Some of the crowd now cried out that Cook was going to take their king from them and kill him; and there was one in particular that advanced towards Cook in an attitude that alarmed one of the guard, who presented his bayonet and opposed him, acquainting Cook in the meantime of the danger of his situation, and that the Indians in a few minutes would attack him; that he had overheard the man, whom he had just stopped from rushing in upon him, say that our boats which were out in the harbor had just killed his brother, and he would be revenged. Cook attended to what this man said, and desired him to show him the Indian that had dared to attempt a combat with him; and as soon as he was pointed out, Cook fired at him with a blank. The Indian perceiving he received no damage from the fire, rushed from without the crowd a second time, and threatened any one that should oppose him. Cook, perceiving this, fired a ball, which entering the Indian's groin, he fell, and was drawn off by the rest.

"Cook perceiving the people determined to oppose his designs, and that he should not succeed without further bloodshed, ordered the lieutenant of marines, Mr. Phillips, to withdraw his men and get them into the boats, which were then lying ready to receive them. This was effected by the sergeant; but the instant they began to retreat, Cook was hit with a stone, and perceiving the man who threw it, shot him dead. The officers in the boats observing the guard retreat, and hearing this third discharge, ordered the boats to fire. This occasioned the guard to face about and fire, and then the attack became general. Cook and Mr. Phillips were together a few paces in the rear of the guard, and perceiving a general fire without orders, quitted Teraiobu, and ran to the shore to put a stop to it; but not being able to make themselves heard, and being close pressed upon by the chiefs, they joined the guard, who fired as they retreated. Cook having at length reached the margin of the water, between the fire of the boats, waved with his hat for them to cease firing and come in; and while he was doing this, a chief from behind stabbed him with one of our iron daggers, just under the shoulder-blade, and it passed quite through his body. Cook fell with his face in the water, and immediately expired. Mr. Phillips, not being able any longer to use his fusee, drew his sword, and engaging the chief whom he saw kill Cook, soon despatched him. His guard in the meantime were all killed but two, and they had plunged into the water, and were swimming to the boats. He stood thus for some time the butt of all their force, and being as complete in the use of the sword as he was accomplished, his noble achievements struck the barbarians with awe; but being wounded, and growing faint from loss of blood and excessive action, he plunged into the sea with his sword in his hand, and swam to the boats; where, however, he was scarcely taken on board, before somebody saw one of the marines, that had swam from the shore, lying flat upon the bottom. Phillips hearing this, ran aft, threw himself in after him, and brought him up with him to the surface of the water, and both were taken in.

"The boats had hitherto kept up a very hot fire, and lying off without the reach of any weapons but stones, had received no damage, and, being fully at leisure to keep up an unremitted and uniform action, made great havoc among the Indians, particularly among the chiefs, who stood foremost in the crowd and were most exposed; but whether it was from their bravery, or ignorance of the real cause that deprived so many of them of life, that they made such a stand, may be questioned, since it is certain that they in general, if not universally, understood heretofore that it was the fire only of our arms that destroyed them. This opinion seems to be strengthened by the circumstance of the large, thick mats they were observed to wear, which were also constantly kept wet; and, furthermore, the Indian that Cook fired at with a blank discovered no fear when he found his mat unburnt, saying in their language, when he showed it to the by-standers, that no fire had touched it. This may be supposed at least to have had some influence. It is, however, certain, whether from one or both these causes, that the numbers that fell made no apparent impression on those who survived; they were immediately taken off, and had their places supplied in a constant succession.

"Lieutenant Gore, who commanded as first lieutenant under Cook in the Resolution, which lay opposite the place where this attack was made, perceiving with his glass that the guard on shore was cut off, and that Cook had fallen, immediately passed a spring upon one of the cables, and, bringing the ship's starboard guns to bear, fired two round shot over the boats into the middle of the crowd; and both the thunder of the cannon and the effects of the shot operated so powerfully, that it produced a most precipitate retreat from the shore to the town."—Sparks' Life of Ledyard.

The following, translated from Hawaiian documents, briefly recounts the particulars:

"The captain demanded that the king should obtain and restore the boat, but this could not be done, as it had been demolished by the natives for the sake of its iron. Captain Cook went on shore with a party of his armed men to fetch the king on board his ship, and detain him there till the boat should be restored. While he was endeavoring to accomplish this object, Kekuhaupio crossed the bay from Keeia to Kaawaloa, accompanied by Kalimu, another chief, in a separate canoe. They were fired upon from the ship, and Kalimu was killed, on which Kekuhaupio rowed rapidly to Kaawaloa and employed his influence to dissuade Kalaniopuu from going to the ship. On the circulation of the news of Kalimu's death, the people became

lamorous for revenge, and one with a short dagger in
his hand approached Captain Cook, who, apprehensive
of danger, fired his gun at him. The contest now became general. The captain having with his sword
struck Kalaimano-kahoowaha, a chief, he seized him
with his powerful hand in order to hold him, but with
no idea of taking his life, Lono being, as the chief supposed, a god, could not die. But on his crying out, as
he was about to fall, the chief concluded he was a
man—not a god—and therefore killed him. Then the
foreigners in the boat discharged their muskets, and
many of the natives were cut down by their fire,
against which they found the mats that were employed to shield them, a poor defence. Guns also on
board the ship were discharged, which killed others,
so that Kalaniopuu fled inland to the precipice with
his chiefs and people, taking with them the body of
Captain Cook and four of his companions who had
been slain. The king then presented the body of the
captain in sacrifice, and after the ceremony was performed, proceeded to remove the flesh from the bones,
to preserve them. The flesh was consumed with fire.
The heart was eaten by some children, who had mistaken it for that of a dog. Their names were Kupa,
Mohoole and Kaiwikokoole. Some of the bones of the
captain were afterwards returned to the ship, and the
rest preserved by the priests and worshiped."

Captain King's relation differs not materially from those given. He states that Cook, after conversing with Kalaniopuu, though he was satisfied that he was innocent of the theft, still determined to persevere in his original design. Accordingly he invited him, with his two sons, to spend the day on board the Resolution, to which they readily consented; the boys had actually embarked, when their mother, with many tears, dissuaded the party from going. He also attributes Cook's endeavors to stop the firing of the men to his humanity. The day before he had given orders to the marines to fire upon the people, if they behaved even insolently; and it is more reasonable to suppose that he had become alarmed for his own safety, and wished not farther to exasperate the natives. His look inspired consternation to the last; and it was not until his back was turned that he received his death-blow.*

Such was the fate of this celebrated navigator, who has identified his name with the islands which he made known to the world. By his own profession he is regarded as a martyr to his adventurous courage; while his self-denial, patience, skill and enterprise in carrying out his adventurous voyages, receive merited praise from all. The melan-

* This was received from an iron dagger of their own
make. Cook himself ordered their manufacture, after
the model of the native weapon, for the purposes of
trade, and his example was followed by every one who
could find sufficient iron. They were freely bartered
away. The day the Resolution put back, Kamehameha, who slept on board that night, obtained eight
from Captain Clerke in exchange for a feather cloak.

choly circumstances attending his untimely end, created at the time so deep a sympathy in the minds of not only his own countrymen, but of all maritime nations, as to entirely exclude inquiry into its causes, and to throw a veil over faults, which otherwise would have been conspicuous, and exhibited his character in a more faithful light.

While it is not my desire to detract from the fame lawfully his due, yet I cannot, with his biographers, gloss over the events which occurred at the Hawaiian Islands. Perhaps most of the errors he committed are to be attributed to his temper, which, to use the cautious words of his attached friend and companion, King, " might have been justly blamed." No one ever made the acquaintance of the aborigines of a heretofore unknown land, under more novel, yet favorable circumstances. Public feeling had been alive for many generations, with the expectation of an old and beloved king, to be restored to them, invested with the attributes of divinity. When Cook arrived, not a doubt existed that he was that god. The resources of the natives were placed at his disposal. All that kindness, devotion and superstition could effect among a barbarous people was his. No other navigator experienced a similar welcome. He had met with a hostile spirit elsewhere, but here, so warm was his welcome, and so general the joy that prevailed, that the worst features of savage nature were masked; and, in consequence, a favorable opinion formed of their domestic life and government, which later and more extended investigations have not been able to verify. Through all his intercourse, he had but one occasion of complaint, theft. Have the natives no charge to bring against him? With his influence, much might have been done toward enlightening their minds in the fundamental principles of religion; or at all events he could have done as at a later period did Vancouver—a junior officer then with him—whose justice and benevolence form a strong contrast to the course of Cook. By the former they were told of the existence of one God, the Creator alike of them and the whites. From the supposed character of the latter, his instructions would have carried with them the force of revelation, and their effect could not have been otherwise than beneficial. What his course was has been shown.* Pilfering and insolence were met with death, either dealt or ordered so to be, without the slightest attempt to distinguish between the guilty and innocent. A chief, in executing a law of his sovereign, was intimidated by the firing of a musket over his head; an abuse sufficient to aggravate the most forbearing race. The remonstrances of the men for the treatment of their women met with equal injustice. No adequate returns for the great quantity of food consumed were made. It was given at first as a tribute to their newly returned god, and ever after expected on the same terms. Yet all these aggravations did not arouse the spirit of the people to resistance; not even the contempt so openly cast upon their religion and temple, until the greatest of insults was shown, in attempting to imprison their king, and to carry him off from amid his own subjects, in utter violation of all justice. If this attempt had succeeded, it would not have promoted a hospitable reception for the next visitors. But even this might have been forgiven, had not a high chief, who was peaceably crossing the bay, ignorant of the cause for which the boats were stationed, been killed by the fire of one of them. At this wanton murder, the people could no longer restrain their passions, though Lono was in their eyes a god, and immortal.† They slew him. His body

was carried into the interior, the bones cleaned and the flesh burned, except the heart and liver which some hungry children stole in the night and ate, supposing them to belong to a dog. All will unite in deploring a result, which from far less aggravation in a civilized community, would have terminated quite as fatally; with savages, it is astonishing it did not sooner occur.

As soon as the news of the attack on Cook's party reached the other side of the bay, where were the observatory and the spars and sails of the Resolution, the natives in the vicinity commenced an assault upon the small force stationed to defend them. After being repulsed, they agreed to a truce, in which all the property belonging to the ships was carried on board. "Such was the condition of the ships, and the state of discipline, that Captain King feared for the result, if a vigorous attack had been made during the night."—Vol. 3, p. 59.

All reverence for Lono being now terminated, the natives appeared in their true character. They endeavored to allure small parties ashore, and insulted the comrades of the slain with the most contemptuous looks and gestures; at the same time displaying their clothes and arms in insolent triumph. A breastwork was also erected on the beach, and the women sent inland. Intercourse however was re-established, with the design of obtaining the corpse of Cook and the cutter. Several natives came off from time to time on the ships, declaring their innocence, and informed the commander, Clerke, of the warlike preparations ashore. Two individuals, on the night of the 15th, brought off a portion of the flesh of Captain Cook, weighing nine or ten pounds. The remainder, they said, had been burnt, and the bones were in possession of the chiefs. The next day additional insults were received, and a man, wearing

* This apathy is the more remarkable, as Kanina, a chief, whom Captain King describes as "possessing a quickness of conception and judicious curiosity rarely to be met with among these people," made many pertinent inquiries in regard to the nature of the English government, their population, manufactures, manners and customs, wars, and particularly "who was their God." It is due to Captain King to state that he appears on all occasions to have endeavored to treat the natives with justice and humanity. But his influence, with that of others who might have been disposed to join with him, was altogether neutralized by the dominant prejudices of Cook. This Kanina, who had proved himself a valuable friend, was killed in the attack. It is somewhat remarkable that in this encounter, the real friends of the English suffered far more than their enemies; a misfortune which, from the attending circumstances, could not have been avoided, as those most hostile, and those most desirous of peace, were mixed together in the crowd, and the affray more the result of accident than design.

† A sledge from the Northwest Coast, left by Cook, was worshiped by those who continued to believe in his divinity; as were his ribs and breast-bone, which

were deposited in a temple dedicated to Lono, on the east side of the island. They were annually carried in procession to several other temples, or borne around the island to collect offerings for the support of the priests of Lono. Some expected Lono would re-appear. These bones were preserved in a small wicker basket, covered over with red feathers. Their fate has never been ascertained. It is supposed they were hid, upon the abolition of idolatry, in a cave. Liholiho is said to have carried a portion of them to England, and to have presented one of the sad relics to the widow of Cook.

Cook's hat, had the audacity to approach the ships, and throw stones, in bravado. The crews not being in a temper for further forbearance, with the permission of their commander, fired some of the great guns at the natives on shore. The islanders had previously put themselves under cover, so that not much damage was done. A few were killed, and Kamehameha was slightly wounded by a blow received from a stone, which had been struck by one of the balls.

On the 17th, the boats were sent ashore, strongly manned, to water; but the annoyance experienced from the natives was so great, that the work proceeded slowly, although under the fire of the heavy guns from the ships. In all their attacks, the islanders displayed desperate bravery. Orders were at last given to fire some houses, in doing which the whole village, with the property of the friendly priests, was consumed. The sailors, imitating the revengeful passions of their opponents, perpetrated many cruelties. A man, attended by a dozen or more boys, bearing the usual insignia of peace, approached and was fired upon. This did not stop them; and when they reached the commanding officer, the herald was found to be the priest who had performed the services at the consecration of Captain Cook, and who had always showed himself a friend. He came to expostulate on the ingratitude of the treatment he and his brethren had received. The men, who had brought off the remains of Cook, had assured them, from the captains of the ships, that their property and persons should be respected. Relying upon this pledge, they had not, with the other inhabitants, removed their effects to a place of security, and from trusting to their promises had lost their all. The narrative does not state that he had received any satisfaction from those for whom he had exerted himself so much.

While the hostilities were continued between the two parties, numbers of women remained cheerfully on board the ships, exhibiting not the slightest emotion at the heads of their countrymen which were brought off, or concern for their relatives ashore. While the village was burning, they exclaimed, "a very fine sight." A fact which powerfully illustrates the deep degradation of their sex, which could thus find amusement in the sufferings of their fellows and injuries to their country.

On the evening of the 18th, messengers were sent to sue for peace; they carried with them the usual presents, which were received with the assurance that it would be granted, when the remains of Cook were restored. From them it was learned that all the bodies of the marines who fell had been burnt, except the limb-bones, which were distributed among the inferior chiefs. The hair of Captain Cook was in the possession of Kamehameha.

After dark, provisions were sent to the ships, with which were two large presents from the much injured but forgiving priest. As peace was now considered declared, the natives ceased all hostilities, and mingled freely with the whites, who however remained closely upon guard.

All of the bones of Captain Cook that could then be recovered, were brought on board the next day, neatly wrapped in fine tapa, ornamented with black and white feathers. Presents accompanied them. On the 21st, his gun, shoes, and some other trifles, were brought by one of the high chiefs, who represented Kalaniopuu and Kamehameha, as desirous of peace. He informed the commanders that six of the chiefs, some of whom were their best friends, had been killed. A difference of opinion prevailed among the natives as to the expediency of continuing hostile measures; but peace was finally agreed upon.

The remains, which had been with so much difficulty procured, were committed to the deep on the 21st, with military honors. During this scene, the bay was deserted by the natives; but the succeeding day, on the assurance that all ill-will was then buried, many visited the ships and others sent presents of eatables. In the evening the ships sailed.

On the 27th, they touched at Oahu, and a party landed on the northwest side; but meeting only a few inhabitants they sailed immediately for Kauai, and came to anchor, March 1st, off Waimea, in their old station.

Here their welcome was by no means cordial. The disease which they had introduced had occasioned many deaths and much suffering. The island presented the usual spectacle of savage contention and warfare. The goats which had been left by Cook as a gift, which might eventually have proved serviceable to the inhabitants, had increased to six, but had become a source of contention between Keawe and Kaneonea. Both parties maintained their claims by force, and a battle had been fought, in which Kaneonea was worsted. A misfortune among barbarians is more likely to beget enemies than friends, as the unfortunate chief soon experienced. The goats were destroyed, but not with them the disagreement, of which they had proved the innocent cause. Keawe having allied himself to another powerful chief, aspired to the sole sovereignty.

Cook being dead, the ships experienced such trouble as has commonly been received from the South Sea islanders, when no superstitious restraint, or knowledge of the superior power of the white race, existed. This was greatly aggravated by the absence of the principal chiefs. The men employed in watering were annoyed by crowds of natives, who pressed rudely upon them, and finally endeavored to wrench the muskets of the soldiers from their hands. They would not suffer the watering to proceed, unless a great price was given; demanding a hatchet for every cask of water. Neither had they forgotten their old trade. While some amused themselves by tripping up the sailors, pulling them backward by their clothes, and like vexatious tricks, others stole their hats, buckets, and one seized Captain King's cutlass from his side and made his escape. Gaining courage by the impunity with which they had thus far proceeded, they made more daring demonstrations. The casks, however, were filled, placed in the pinnace, and all embarked, excepting King and two others, when a shower of stones compelled them hastily to follow. The marines in the boat then fired two muskets, which wounded one man severely. This en-

raged the natives, and they prepared for a fresh attack; but the authority of some chiefs who made their appearance, drove them back.

No further disturbance was experienced. The chiefs of Keawe's party paid Captain Clerke a visit, and made him several curious and valuable presents, among which were fish hooks, made from the bones of Kalaniopuu's father, who had been killed in an unsuccessful attempt to subdue Oahu. A dagger made from iron taken from a timber that had recently floated ashore, was also brought.

On the 8th of March, the ships stood over to Niihau, where they remained but four days.

CHAPTER VI.

1779—Unfavorable opinion entertained of the islanders in consequence of the death of Cook—Death of Kalaniopuu—War of succession—Victories of Kamehameha—Kamehameha conquers Maui, Lanai and Molokai—Arrival of Captains Portlock and Dixon—Trade opened—Meare's visit—Trade—La Perouse visits Maui, 1786—Maui, Lanai and Molokai rebel—Arrival of the Eleanora—Capture of boat and murder of a sailor—Metcalf's bloody revenge—Fair American captured—John Young and Isaac Davis made prisoners—Difficulties between traders and the islanders—Kamehameha's indignation at the capture of the Fair American—Treatment of prisoners—Kaiana's ambitious views—Attempts on vessels—Vancouver's arrival—First notice of Kaumualii—Dædalus arrives at Oahu—Massacre of Lieutenant Hergest and Mr. Gooch—Avarice of chiefs—Intercourse with Vancouver—Kaahumanu—Princely hospitality—Jealousy of other chiefs—Cattle first introduced at Hawaii—Discipline of ships—Orders of the king—Widow of Kalaniopuu—Sham battle—Present to King George III.—Transactions at Maui—Murderers executed at Oahu—Festival of Makahiki—Benevolent efforts of Vancouver—Theatrical entertainments—Cession of Hawaii—Departure of Vancouver—1794.

THE news of the disastrous events recorded in the last chapter, produced an unfavorable impression in Europe and America, of the character of the islanders. Without fully comprehending the causes, they were judged to be a cruel race, and disposed to commit atrocities upon ships. For a number of years none ventured to touch at their shores. The aged Kalaniopuu died at Kau, Hawaii, in April, 1782, after a reign of thirty years, and bequeathed his dominions to Kiwalao, his son, jointly with Kamehameha, who was to be subordinate to him. Kamehameha was the reputed nephew of Kalaniopuu, by his brother Keoua, but Kahekili, king of

Maui, claimed his paternity. By this new arrangement, Kau, Puna and Hilo, the most fertile districts, fell to Kiwalao; and Kona, Kohala and Hamakua to Kamehameha. No sooner was the will made known than intrigues to defeat it were set in motion. In July following, after the season of mourning had ended, the Hilo chiefs being anxious to obtain the district of Kona, on the east side of Hawaii, on account of the calmness of the bordering sea, which made it a better fishing-ground, endeavored to excite their new ruler to wrest it from Kamehameha. Having gained him over to their design, it was determined to execute it under the guise of paying funeral honors to his deceased father. A number of warriors, taking the corpse of Kalaniopuu with them, embarked in a war-canoe for Kona. On their way, Keeaumoku, a tried chieftain of Kamehameha, met them, and going on board, joined in the wail for the dead. From the appearance of the party, his suspicions were aroused, and he inquired where it was their intention to inter the body. They replied, at Kailua, the chief town of Kona. From this answer and the extraordinary haste they manifested, he suspected they designed surprising that place.

HOUSE OF KEAWE—TOMB OF THE KINGS OF HAWAII, AT HONAUNAU.

While off Honaunau, the place of sepulture of the ancient kings of Hawaii, they were overtaken by a violent rain-squall, which obliged them to land. The body was there deposited in the ancestral tomb of the kings of Hawaii, the house of Keawe, from whom all chiefs of pretensions to high nobility endeavor to trace their descent. Keeaumoku secretly left the party and hastened to Kamehameha to inform him of his suspicions. Kiwalao and his followers remained to concert further measures, as it was their intention to conquer and apportion all Hawaii among themselves. In the meantime information of their arrival and plans had been conveyed to Kamehameha, who immediately advanced to the camp of Kiwalao, and in an interview the two became apparently reconciled. Kiwalao endeavored to satisfy the rapacity of his chiefs, by dividing his own territories among them, but Keoua, his uncle, either not receiving a share proportionate to his desires, or being neglected in the apportionment, became enraged and marched off with his retainers, determined on war and plunder. Entering the territories of Kamehameha, he committed considerable devastation by cutting down cocoanut trees. In a skirmish several were killed on each side. The war having thus commenced, Kiwalao, unable further to resist the solicitations of his followers, joined Keoua, with all his forces, and a general engagement took place at Keei between the two rivals for Hawaii, which was continued for eight days with no decided advantage to either party. Ka-

9

mehameha being next in rank and influence to Kiwalao, was heir to the entire island upon the death of his cousin; consequently, the struggle was obstinate and bloody. Keeaumoku, the chief who had discovered the designs of Kiwalao to Kamehameha, was seized by two of the warriors of the former, and badly wounded; one smiting him with a spear, and the other with a dagger, both exclaiming, in derision, "the weapon strikes the yellow-back crab." The anxiety of his enemies to secure as a trophy, a highly valued ornament made of a whale's tooth, which he wore about his neck, preserved his life. Kamehameha perceiving the danger of his favorite warrior, rallied the boldest of his troops and furiously charged the enemy. In the melee, Kiwalao was knocked down by a stone. Keeaumoku, enabled to rise, rushed upon the fallen king, and with a shark's-teeth sword despatched him. The fate of their leader so dispirited his followers, that they were entirely routed. Some fled to the place of refuge at Honaunau, and others to the mountains, or sought safety by flight in canoes. Kamehameha was thus left master of the field, and lord of Hawaii.

Further opposition awaited him. Keoua and Keawemauhili, the principal instigators of the war, had fled to the mountains. The former obtained possession of Kau, and the latter the fine districts of Hilo and Puna. Three districts only sided with Kamehameha. The rebel chiefs, however, were disturbed in their own domains, by commotions excited by dissatisfied subjects; one of whom being unsuccessful, went over, with all his retainers, to Kamehameha, and by his persuasions induced him to renew the war. An engagement, which, from the obstinacy with which it was fought, received the name of Kauaawa—bitter contest—took place on a mountain in Kau. Neither party were able to claim the victory. Kamehameha actively followed up the contest, and marched upon Hilo, where in a skirmish he received a blow on his forehead from a paddle, which well nigh terminated his career.

Kahekili, who had made himself master of Molokai, Lanai, Oahu and Maui, and was allied to Kaeo, sovereign of Kauai, in revenge for a fancied affront, sent succor to the enemies of Kamehameha; who, in retaliation, made a descent upon Maui, about the year 1790, while Kahekili was at Oahu. His son, a youth, encountered the invader at Wailuku, and was totally defeated. In this battle Kamehameha displayed much skill. His active mind turned every mistake of his enemy to his own advantage, and seized upon the most favorable moments for a charge or retreat. The prodigious strength for which he was remarkable, joined with great personal courage, which had already established for him a reputation for prowess throughout the group, availed his troops much. When his bodily exertions were not needed, he remained quiet, issuing his orders with coolness and sagacity; if the line of battle wavered, he rushed to the thickest of the fight, encouraging his men with his deep-toned voice. Both parties fought with bravery; the engagement being in a narrow defile there was little room for flight. The carnage was dreadful; many were killed by being hustled off precipices; the waters of Iao, a small stream, were damned by the bodies of the routed foe, and the engagement was ever after known as the Kepaniwai (stopping the water.) Kalanikupule, the prince, made his escape to Oahu.

While the war was thus prosecuted on Maui, Keoua quarreled with his friend, the ruler of Hilo, and slew him. Infatuated by his growing power, he again ravaged Kamehameha's provinces, and was opposed by Kaiana, one of his generals, a distinguished warrior of Kauai, who had been taken from that island by Captain Meares, in an English vessel, in 1787, and carried to Canton, where he attracted much attention by his shrewdness, elegance of form and demeanor. He was six feet five inches high, well proportioned, and of a handsome countenance. The following year he returned in the Iphigenia, Captain Douglass, and not daring to land on Kauai, where, since his departure, his brother, influenced by a priest, had become inimical to him, he proceeded to Hawaii, and at the request of Kamehameha, settled there. This was in January, 1789. His active mind and warlike disposition, with the store of European articles, including fire-arms and ammunition, which he possessed, made him a valuable acquisition. The more firmly to attach him to his interests, Kamehameha conferred upon him high rank and extensive possessions.

Before tracing the conquests of Kamehameha further, it is necessary to record the arrival of the first ships since the demise of Cook. They reached Kealakeakua Bay before the king left on his Maui expedition. By the natives they were called *o Lo*, and were noted by them for bringing the first beads.* They were the King George and Queen Charlotte, trading vessels from London, commanded by Captains Portlock and Dixon ; the former of whom had made the last voyage with Captain Cook. On the 25th of May, 1786, they made Hawaii, and were soon surrounded by canoes, bringing off hogs and fruit, which were gladly exchanged for bits of iron. The next day they came to anchor, and were visited by a great number of natives, whose bearing was insolent and troublesome. No chief appeared to keep them in order, and the captains were obliged to drive them from the vessels. The character which the bay bore made them very cautious, and on the 27th, their fears had so far increased, that after firing several guns to frighten away the natives, they unmoored and made sail. Standing along the coast, they continued to traffic for swine and water ; nails and buttons being given in exchange for calabashes of the latter.

June 1st, they anchored off the east end of Oahu, and supplied the natives with iron and trinkets. The islanders at this time appear to have been so well acquainted with the whites, as to manifest only a natural curiosity at what was novel. A party from the ships discovered Waikiki Bay, which, from not being exposed to the violence of the trade winds, soon became the favorite anchoring ground. Leaving Oahu, they again anchored at Waimea Bay, Kauai, where they remained until the 13th.

* Voyage Round the World, by N. Portlock, Quarto, London, 1789.

No difficulty was experienced on either island ; the natives had acquired a fondness for foreign articles, for which they gladly exchanged their own manufactures, with a fairness which proves that they had begun to comprehend the old, though to them, new adage, " honesty is the best policy."

In the autumn, the same ships returned, and visited Hawaii and Maui, off which island a canoe with four men, completely exhausted with fatigue, were picked up. They were treated with great kindness, loaded with gifts, and sent ashore entirely recovered, to tell of the humanity of the white men.

The ships having arrived at Oahu, anchored in their former situation. Kahekili, the king, who was then a stout, well-made man of fifty years of age, went on board, and made inquiries in regard to his rival of Hawaii. While they lay there he was hospitable and attentive, but an old priest, who came frequently on board, informed Captain Portlock that there was a plot brewing to cut off both vessels. As no other evidence of such a design transpired, it was either a false report, or effectually checked by the vigilance constantly displayed by their crews, and dread of firearms ; the effect of which the king, at his request, had been shown. In December they visited Kauai, and there met with Kaiana, brother to Kaeo, the chief ruler. Both showed them much kindness, and supplied them liberally with provisions.

In October, 1787, Captain Portlock again touched at Kauai, and his intercourse was as friendly as before. In his voyage he speaks feelingly of the oppression of the chiefs to the common people, of which he was a witness, and endeavored to influence the former, though without success, to treat their inferiors more humanely. The poorer classes were accustomed to come in their canoes to the ships from long distances, bringing their little store of provisions, which they would barter for iron or trinkets. No sooner, however, had they got them into their possession, than they would be rifled by some lazy chief who had been waiting the opportunity. This was submitted to without repining, as it was the custom of the country.

In August, 1787,* Captain Meares, in the Nootka, arrived at the islands, and after experiencing a pleasant reception, took away with him Kaiana, who was desirous of visiting Britain. Douglass, the partner of Meares, touched at several of the islands in the ship Iphigenia, many times in that and the two succeeding years. He saluted the chiefs with heavy guns ; it being first done with seven at Kawaihae Bay, for Kamehameha, who was highly delighted with the novel honor. The chief endeavored to procure a carpenter from him, and was successful in obtaining a swivel, some smaller fire-arms, and ammunition. In July, 1789, a number of chiefs in Hawaii, conspired to seize the Iphigenia, but the friendly Kaiana, her late passenger, disclosed the plot. Kamehameha asserted his innocence of the design, though in the risings of his ambition, before his plans were matured, and his policy formed, the temptation to make himself master of a foreign ship may have been awakened. But no such idea was ever manifested; his sagacious mind early perceived the greater advantages to be derived from securing the friendship of his commercial visitors.

About this period, numerous vessels, mostly English and American, visited the islands, and commenced a trade, which has ever since been actively pursued. Several, among which was the Lady Washington, were fitted out by the merchants of Boston in 1785. Their reception varied according to the whims or policy of the contending chiefs. None were much molested, though some were annoyed by theft and the vexatious tricks of the natives. Prices varied according to the caprice of the rulers. The more important articles of warfare were in demand, and abundantly supplied by thoughtless traders, who in some cases found them turned upon themselves. A taste for ardent spirits, which at first were exceedingly offensive, was gradually excited among the chiefs. Interest annually carried more vessels to their shores, and the same motive impelled a more judicious treatment of their visitors.

* Meares' Voyages, 2 volumes, London, 1790.

The much lamented La Perouse came to anchor, with his exploring frigates, at the leeward side of Maui, near the present town of Lahaina, on the 28th of May, 1786, a few days only after Portlock and Dixon reached Hawaii. He speaks favorably of the kind disposition of the inhabitants, and attributes the shrewdness manifested in their petty barter, to former communication with Spaniards. Frenchmen were the first Europeans of modern times who landed at Maui. Their stay was limited to two days, in which their intercourse with the inhabitants was very slight.

While the true state and value of this group were becoming known by these visits, and an interest in them gradually awakened, which led to a more extended intercourse, the wars of supremacy among the rival chiefs were vigorously prosecuted. The possession of fire-arms made their contests more bloody, but sooner decided.

During the contest which Kaiana sustained against Keoua, while his chief was on Maui, a most singular interposition of natural phenomena enabled him to triumph over his active opponent. At that period, it had a great effect over the minds of the natives, who, from that moment, considered their goddess Pele a favorer of the rising fortunes of Kamehameha. The army of Keoua had separated into three divisions, marching at some distance from each other, and were descending from the volcano by three distinct paths, not greatly apart, and which running parallel with each other, led towards the habitable portion of Kau. The first division had not far advanced, when a heavy earthquake and eruption from the volcano took place. The ground shook so violently as to render it impossible either to stand still or proceed, and they reeled to and fro like drunken men. The noise accompanying this motion was awful, far exceeding thunder in loudness, while the sky, which hitherto had been unclouded, was filled with a shower of cinders and ashes, extending for many miles around. Owing to the height to which they were first cast by the action of the crater, they cooled in their descent and did no injury, though a strong sulphurous gas was evolved, producing a suffocating sensation in the party exposed. However, they escaped with the loss of a few of their number scorched to death, and as soon as practicable hurried from the spot.

The rear party experienced a similar motion, accompanied by the like noises and showers, which quickly passed over. They then hastened to rejoin their comrades, but were met by an appalling sight. The central division lay stiffened in death; but so natural were the postures of many, that they did not discover that life was extinct until they had closely examined them. Some were lying in apparent slumber, while others were sitting upright. with their wives and children firmly locked in their embrace and noses pressed together, as in the act of salutation. Out of four hundred human beings, not one was alive. A hog, belonging to one of the families, alone had been able to resist the effects of the sulphurous vapor, and was quietly rooting about them.

Kamehameha having returned from Molokai—1791—joined forces with Kaiana, and easily routed the army of Keoua, dispirited by so sad an event. Their leader was driven for shelter into the further part of Kau, and there remained a fugitive, until, having become wearied of his erratic life, he determined to surrender himself to the clemency of the conqueror. Accordingly, he went to the seaside, passing with the permission of Kaiana through his camp. He received much attention from the people some of whom foreboded his fate, and embarked with his most faithful followers and their effects for Kawaihae Bay, where Kamehameha was encamped. The energy and ambition of Keoua having been prolific sources of trouble to him, that chief determined to rid himself of one who had proved so valiant a competitor, and whose claims to the supreme power, from his relationship to Kiwalao, would always be adverse to his own. Accordingly, secret instructions were issued to Keeaumoku, who having enticed Keoua to the land, assassinated him as he stepped from his canoe. Seven of his friends shared the same fate. The corpse was then taken

to the neighboring heiau, and offered in sacrifice. This occurred in 1793. Some say that he was treacherously slain, against the wishes of Kamehameha; but as it was done in his presence, the statement is improbable. The whole island of Hawaii was now his by conquest; but his successes here were counterbalanced by reverses elsewhere. Maui, Lanai and Molokai, which had been but partially subdued, threw off the yoke, and again acknowledged Kahekili as their liege lord.

In the autumn of 1789, the American snow Eleanor, commanded by one Metcalf,* arrived at Hawaii, and remained there trading during most of the succeeding winter. In the month of February, 1790, she anchored at Honuaula, Maui. Two of the chiefs of a neighboring place, called Oloalu, having heard of her arrival, went to Honuaula, and in the night stole her boat, which was moored under her stern. A watchman was in it, but had fallen asleep. So adroit were they, that he did not awake until they were near the shore. He then attempted to give the alarm, but was unheard. Before he could cry out again, one of the thieves killed him. The boat was taken ashore, and broken up for the sake of the iron, which was manufactured into awls and fish hooks. The chiefs returned to their own village, and for a while Honuaula was made to bear the brunt of a revengeful attack. One man was killed, and two made prisoners; one of whom being from Oloalu, gave information of the real criminals. Metcalf weighed anchor, and proceeded thither.

At the time of his arrival a taboo existed, which prevented any individual from putting off in a canoe under pain of being burnt to death. The bones of the murdered seaman, and the remains of the boat, for which a reward was offered, had been delivered up; and the natives supposing the anger of the captain appeased by the attack he had already made, innocently asked for the promised reward. This he said they should have. As soon as the taboo was annulled, multitudes of people from all

---

* Vancouver's Voyages, 21 volume: London, 1798. Also, Ka Moolelo Hawaii, Lahaiualuna, 1838.

parts of the island flocked to the ship to trade. They were all ordered to lie with their canoes on the starboard side, which they did, not perceiving the means preparing for their destruction. If any lay off the bows or stern, they were pelted with stones, until they took the prescribed situation. The ports, which had been closed, were then hauled up, and the battery, charged with musket balls and nails, and depressed to bear into the thickest of the fleet, run out and fired among them. Metcalf stood in the gangway to witness the awful effect, and directed the volleys of musketry and small arms which were poured in to complete the destruction. One hundred individuals were said to have been killed outright, and vast numbers wounded. The natives dragged for their bodies with fish hooks, and collected the mangled masses upon the beach, where, to use their own expression, "their brains flowed out of their broken skulls."

After this horrible massacre of innocent wretches, Metcalf sailed for Hawaii, where, owing to the hostility which existed between the two islands, he was well received. But there was retribution in store for him.

In connection with the Eleanor, was a small schooner of twenty-six tons—the Fair American—a tender, manned with only five seamen, and commanded by Metcalf's son, a lad of eighteen years of age. This vessel arrived off Kawaihae Bay in March, but did not fall in with her mate, which was a little farther to the westward. Kameeimoku, a high chief, who, for some trifling cause, had received a flogging from the elder Metcalf, while on board of his vessel, had resolved to revenge the insult upon the first whites that came within his reach. The smallness of the schooner, and the inexperience of her commander, afforded too favorable an opportunity to be overlooked. Without the powerful motive which actuated his mind, she would have proved an almost irresistible temptation to the cupidity of savages, when away from her consort. Accordingly, with a number of his people, he boarded her, and carried many presents. While the attention of the youth and crew were occupied in receiving them, and in

hearing news of his father, the savages pressed on board. Suddenly, the chief seized young Metcalf and threw him overboard, where he soon perished. The rest were massacred, except Isaac Davis, whose life was spared by one of the party, who bound up his wounds. He was then taken ashore, where he was kindly treated. The schooner was stranded and plundered.

John Young, boatswain of the Eleanor, had gone ashore on the 17th, but to his surprise, upon attempting to leave, was forbidden by Kamehameha, and in the evening learned of the capture of the schooner. The snow remained two days off Kealakekua Bay, firing guns for Young to return. This the king, after he heard of the massacre, would not permit, nor would he allow a canoe to go alongside, lest Metcalf should revenge himself, as at Maui; consequently he sailed without hearing of his loss.

While a general warfare raged through the group, and individual chieftains sought to add to their power by gaining possession of the more destructive weapons of the whites, it is to be supposed that serious misunderstandings would often arise. From the known treachery and avarice of savages, it cannot be doubted that the provocations sometimes originated with them. Some of the foreign commanders were men of little or no principle; the discipline preserved on board of their vessels corrupted their own crews, and excited the cupidity and dislike of the natives. Disturbances arose in consequence, and the captains seeking justice, and oftener mere retaliation, for real or fancied wrongs, too frequently, without due inquiry, vented their rage in deeds, scarcely inferior in wanton barbarity, or abuse of power and confidence, to the customs of the savages themselves. Men there were of that day, and the race is not altogether extinct, whose characters could be resolved into two principles—lust and gain. To accomplish their desires, no action was too base or cruel. Such may be properly termed pirates; for their selfishness spared neither friend nor foe; the useful servant nor profitable ally; all were equally their victims. Captain William Sturgis, an American ship-master, and good authority in this matter, having traded extensively both with the Hawaiians and the Indians on the Northwest Coast soon after this period, says, in a published lecture, that the loss of life and disasters which have occurred in voyages among these savages, were owing chiefly " to the bad faith and deceitfulness of the white man."

But the tales of the natives themselves, of injuries done them, when not well authenticated, are to be received with limitation. In the few years ensuing between Portlock's visit and Kamehameha's complete ascendency, some cases occurred where commanders of vessels fired upon the natives; or, acting upon the exigencies of the time, thoughtlessly did deeds which in their cooler moments would have been disapproved. The rapid growth of trade, and the general and increasing good will that prevailed, is sufficient evidence that the islanders appreciated the value of foreign commerce.

The two prisoners, Young and Davis, though rude and ignorant seamen, in moral education and religious knowledge, were far in advance of the most enlightened of those who held them in bondage. Kamehameha found in them tried and faithful servants, who more than repaid his protection, and the oppressed serf ever had reason to bless the humane influence they exerted over the mind of their arbitrary master. Equal consideration is due them from their own countrymen, and the mariners of other nations, who traded to their shores. They both rose to be chiefs of consequence, possessing to the last the confidence of high and low, and their history, particularly that of Young, will be found to be closely interwoven with that of their royal guardian. There were other white men on the islands at this time, runaways from ships, but chiefly of bad characters. Their influence, however, was greatly modified by the superior address and intelligence of these prisoners, and by the comparison which the natives necessarily drew between the two, which gave them their first definite notions of morality.

Kamehameha was highly indignant at the outrage committed by Kameeimoku, but his authority was not sufficiently established to authorize him to punish this violation of his policy. He rebuked him severely, and took possession of the schooner, which he caused to be hauled up and carefully preserved, to be returned to her owner, should he re-appear. Isaac Davis was immediately provided for, and treated with a degree of attention, which fully proved the sincerity of his sentiments. While reprimanding Kameeimoku, he is said to have shed tears.

The two seamen were immediately taken into the confidence of their patron, and both from him and other high chiefs, received valuable presents of estates on the sea-side. They made themselves so beloved, that popular opinion would not have permitted their departure had the king been inclined to let them go. They were carefully guarded whenever a vessel appeared in sight, and never suffered to go afloat; and if any one had been detected in carrying any correspondence for them on board a vessel, he would have been put to death; one was held responsible for the other, and their mutual fidelity deserves high praise. They made a joint but vain attempt to escape to Captain Colnett's ship, and had it not been for the active exertions of Kamehameha, who vigorously defended them, their lives would have been forfeited. After this, they became more contented in their new relations. Kaiana, who had lately become ambitious and turbulent, and had lost all sense of gratitude for the favors he had received from the whites, was their enemy, and conspired to take their lives; but the friendship of the other chiefs rendered the plot abortive. The attentions which he had received abroad, had given him a great opinion of his own consequence. Possessing a stock of fire-arms and ammunition, he was desirous of seizing upon any traders that might come within his reach. Had Kamehameha coincided with his views, trade would have been ruined, and the Hawaiians would have acquired the character of pirates. But his plans were constantly overruled by the greater influence of his superior and his counselors. In one instance, it was nearly decided to attempt the capture of the Spanish sloop Princess Royal; the chief argument used for its legality was that she had been captured from the English; consequently there could be no harm in their taking her from the Spaniards. A sophism very agreeable to their covetous dispositions, and which at first met with little opposition. The pacific policy carried the point, however, even against so cogent a reason.

Before Captain Metcalf sailed for Maui in 1789, Kaiana nearly accomplished the capture of the Eleanor. It was proposed to the king by his party, to seize the snow, and put to death all of her crew, except a few who should be reserved to navigate the vessel. By so powerful an addition to his navy, the conquest of the other islands would be made sure. The plan was to seize the opportunity when the crew laid aloft to loose the sails; those on deck were to be murdered, and the remainder kept in the rigging, until possession of the vessel had been secured. The project, though so much in accordance with his ambition, was rejected with indignation. Notwithstanding the opposition of their sovereign, the chiefs determined upon the attempt, and went on board for that purpose. News of their assembling having been conveyed to Kamehameha, he hurried off, and ordered them out of the vessel. Fearing that he would disclose the plot to Captain Metcalf, they obeyed, and the ship sailed without the divulgement of the design. The safety of many vessels, and the lives of their crews, about this period, were owing to the active interference of Kamehameha, and intercourse was continued in ignorance of the dangers to which they had been exposed.

Vancouver, after Cook, the most celebrated of modern English voyagers, arrived at Kealakeakua Bay March 3d, 1792. As his visits exercised so powerful and lasting an influence upon the islanders, it will be necessary to enter into their details. He had with him two surveying vessels, the Discovery and Chatham. Kaiana came on board, and from the favorable opinions expressed of him in Meares' voyages, was received with courtesy and attention. One of his first acts was to exaggerate his own im-

portance, and misrepresent that of the king, with whom he stated that he equally shared the government. On his departure he was saluted with four guns, but was chagrined at not being able to add to his stock of foreign weapons. In the evening a canoe came alongside with a young native, who spoke English tolerably well. He had been to the United States with Captain Ingraham, of Boston, and had recently returned. As Vancouver sailed slowly along the coast he was visited by several chiefs, to whom he gave garden seeds and other productions likely to become serviceable.

On the 7th of March, he anchored at Waikiki Bay, Oahu, and was visited by many of the natives. The knowledge of the character of the vessels having spread abroad, those who went ashore were treated with a coolness which argued great indifference to visitors who came for other purposes than trade. On the 9th the ships came to anchor at Waimea, Kauai. Their reception was neither hearty nor friendly. Gain was the all-impelling motive of the inhabitants; and as it was not to be acquired to the extent of their desires by trade, they strove to excite the sensual desires of the crews, by a display of gross wantonness, which tended rather to disgust than please.

Kaumualii—the eldest son of Kaeo, who was then at Maui—a boy of twelve years of age, visited the ships, and from his affability and cheerfulness created a favorable impression. The features of the young prince were expressive of vivacity and intelligence, and his inquiries and observations were considered as uncommon for a lad of his years. His conduct was indicative of a desire to please and to acquire information. But before either he or his guardian would venture on board, hostages were demanded for their safe return; and in all their transactions, an honesty of purpose manifested, with a discreet caution, which showed that the principles of trade had become well understood. A number of whites resided on the island, who made themselves useful to both parties.

The depopulation throughout the group, caused by the constant internal dissensions since Vancouver's first visit in 1778, struck him painfully. The town of Waimea had been reduced two-thirds, and of all the chiefs then living, with whom he had been intimately ac-quainted, Kamehameha alone survived.

At this time attention was first drawn toward sandal wood, as an article of ex-port. Two men had been left from a Boston brig by Captain Kendrick, on Kauai, to contract for several cargoes, and also to gather pearls; but it was not until many years afterward that the former was made an important branch of trade.

On the 11th of May, the same year, the Dœdalus, an English national store-ship, appeared on the north side of Oahu. The natives unaccustomed to the sight, greeted her appearance with many excla-mations of affright and surprise. Some ran inland, and reported that " coral rocks were floating thither; " others vo-ciferated, "prodigious, prodigious." The vessel lay off Waimea, while a party went ashore to procure water. It being brackish near the sea-side, they were obliged to roll the casks some distance up the stream, where it was pure. Hav-ing filled them, they made preparations to return, when a dispute arose between the seamen and natives, which termi-nated in the death of a Portuguese sailor. Lieut. Hergest, the commander of the shore expedition, with Mr. Gouch, the astronomer, unaware of the difficulty, had incautiously wandered from the party, and were surrounded by many of the islanders, who, hearing of the affray, immediately attacked these gentlemen. The further account of this melancholy affair, I give literally from the native historian, by which it will be seen that from their own confession, it was a wan-ton murder.

"Kapaleiuka cast a stone against the chin of one of the foreigners, which knocked him down. When the natives on the other bank saw that one had fallen, they came to join in the fray. The white man cried out with the pain inflicted, on which the natives said— ' They cry, indeed—they are men per-haps,—we thought them gods, their eyes were so bright.' One remonstrated, ' Be not in haste to kill the god Lonoikaou-

alii,—for great Lono having been slain at Hawaii, this one remained, the great and powerful Pekeku this—he is a god.' This remonstrance was vain. The com-pany in the boat returned and obtained their guns, and lay upon their oars. Those on board the vessel perceiving that some of their number had been slain, worked the vessel inland and fired on shore. The natives exclaimed, ' What is this whizzing?' One replied, ' Don't you know it is burning sand—powder— a deadly thing; it will burn perhaps this day and destroy our land. Perhaps we shall escape inasmuch as we have killed the two gods; had they lived among us, we had all been dead men!' The firing continued till evening, when the vessel took her departure."

The perpetrators of this cruel act were a lawless band, owing allegiance to no particular chief. The kings of the sev-eral islands, occupied with their wars of conquest, paid little attention to the af-fairs of the distant portions of their king-doms, consequently a general license prevailed; and petty squabbles, robberies and murders were of frequent occur-rence.

Vancouver returned from the North-west Coast of America, and anchored off Kawaihae, Hawaii, February 14, 1793. A taboo then existed, by which the in-habitants were restricted from trading with any vessels, except for arms and ammunition. Through his firmness in refusing to purchase supplies with these articles, the taboo was remitted. Reli-gious taboos were now of frequent oc-currence, lasting for periods of several days each, during which, as in the holi-days of the Roman Church, no business could be transacted. However, when the inconvenience attending them was great, the highest chiefs exercised an authority similar to the Pope's, and granted dispensations for their own ben-efit and that of their favorites. On the 19th, with the assistance of Kalaimoku, one of Kamehameha's chief counselors, he landed a bull and cow, which were all that remained of several cattle, which he had brought from California, with the benevolent design of introducing the breed of these valuable animals. The cow died soon after landing. The op-

10

position which Kalaimoku made to aiding him in the landing, though he well knew they were a gift which would largely benefit the islanders, forcibly illustrates the avaricious spirit which pervaded all classes, and to which Kamehameha alone was superior. He objected to granting the use of his canoe, which was large and commodious, until a sufficient bribe was offered him ; and this was subsequent to receiving presents suitable to his rank.

So greatly had trade increased, and the desire of the useful superseded the passion for ornaments, that trinkets no longer were of value, unless they were of a novel description. Woolen cloth, printed cottons, linen, hardware, and the staple articles of traffic, were in great demand. The islanders suffered in some instances from the shameless dishonesty of the civilized trader, who deceived them in the quantity and quality of goods. Muskets were sold, which burst upon the first fire, and often produced dangerous wounds. But these vile practices recoiled upon the heads of the offenders, for the natives soon learned to appreciate an honest man, and to distinguish the good article from the bad, and were not long in becoming as keen in their mercantile transactions, as the shrewdest of their teachers. Vancouver also speaks in terms of just reprobation of some of their visitors, who after being supplied with provisions by the chiefs, departed without making any return.*

While cruising slowly along the western side of Hawaii, Kamehameha came off to the Discovery, bringing Young with him. Vancouver was agreeably disappointed in the change which a few years had made in the countenance of this celebrated warrior. The savage look which Captain King ascribed to him, had lost much of its expression of

stern ferocity, while it retained its natural dignity and firmness. His carriage was majestic, and every action bespoke a mind which, under any circumstances, would have distinguished its possessor. His eyes were dark and piercing ; in the words of one who not long after was well acquainted with him, he seemed capable of penetrating the designs and reading the thoughts of those about him ; before his glance the most courageous quailed. His general deportment was frank, cheerful and generous. In form and stature a herculean savage; in abilities and character, a man that a more advanced country might have been proud to acknowledge as her son.

His sagacious mind seized upon every opportunity of improvement and aggrandizement. While the benevolent counsels of Vancouver could not repress the latter, they confirmed him in his peaceful and protecting policy toward foreigners. His bias, both from intellect and interest, lay toward them, and no other barbarian was more feared and respected by all classes, strangers and subjects, than this wonderful man. Cook's narrative presented him as a wonderful savage, ambitious, brave and resolute ; Vancouver's intercourse showed him in the dawn of a ripened intellect, as possessing all the latter qualities, yet humane and hospitable. His character will be gradually pictured in the subsequent events of his active career ; and the reader can then judge if this description do him justice.

Soon after his arrival on board, Kaahumanu, his favorite queen, with several of her relatives, followed him. This is the first notice we have of this woman, who afterwards proved herself a consort worthy of the greatest and best of her nation. She was then but sixteen, beautiful and pleasing. The ship was soon crowded with well-behaved visitors of high rank, among whom presents were distributed, which gave much satisfaction. Kamehameha received a scarlet coat, trimmed with gold lace, in which he promenaded the deck to the great admiration of his subjects.

February 22d, Vancouver anchored at Kealakeakua Bay. Kamehameha immediately put off in great state. He was

* The traffic of the islands, at this period, was confined mostly to the purchasing of supplies, for which object vessels of the principal maritime nations frequented them, but particularly those of the United States, engaged in the fur trade on the Northwest Coast of America, and the Canton business; of which many interesting particulars will be found in Greenhow's memoir of the Oregon. The most noted of these were the Hope, Captain Ingraham, the Eleanor, and Hancock; of the English, besides those already mentioned, the Princess Royal, and Argonaut, under the direction of Captain Colnett. The islanders were frequently employed as seamen, and for other purposes on shipboard, in which they gave general satisfaction.

dressed in a printed linen gown, given by Cook to Kalaniopuu, over which a magnificent feather cloak was thrown, which trailed upon the ground. His head was surmounted by an elegant helmet. Eleven large canoes, arranged so as to form two sides of an obtuse angle, formed his squadron. The largest, in which he was, had eighteen paddles on each side, and headed the procession. It was a little in advance of the others, which followed its motions with the utmost precision, being guided by the orders of the king, who regulated the manoeuvres with great skill. The fleet paddled around the vessel in a slow and solemn manner. The ten canoes were then ordered to form in a line under the stern, while his own was paddled with the utmost exertions of the crew, to the starboard side. When abreast of the gangway, notwithstanding the great speed with which it was shooting ahead, it was instantly stopped by a skillful back dip of the paddles.

Kamehameha then ascended the side, and taking the hand of Vancouver, inquired if he were sincerely a friend, and if the king of Great Britain were amicably disposed. These questions being satisfactorily answered, he saluted him by touching noses. Four helmets of beautiful fabrication, were then presented, and the ten canoes ordered alongside. Each of them contained nine of the largest sized swine, which, with a prodigious quantity of fruits and vegetables, 'brought by a fleet of smaller canoes, were deposited on the decks of both vessels. Although the quantity was more than could be used, nothing was allowed to be returned.

Five cows, with some sheep, were carried ashore as a present to the king, who personally attended to their care. In addition to the princely gift he had already sent, he had prepared a large quantity of cloth, mats, and other articles of their manufacture, which, as there was not room on board for them, he ordered to be stored on shore, under the charge of an agent, who was made responsible for their final delivery.

The presentation of all the large cattle to Kamehameha created some jealousy among the other chiefs. Kaiana coming on board, Kamehameha received him with a look of sullen gloom and austerity, indicative of the growing dissatisfaction between them. Both were equally ambitious. Kaiana sought to obtain his ends by violence and bloodshed. In his former patron he had found a steady opponent, and neither could brook an equal; though for the present, policy prevented an open rupture.

Kaiana was civilly received and a handsome present accepted, though it could not be taken on board. Keeaumoku, the slayer of Keoua, who was present, was angry at this, as his present had been unconditionally declined. The king who had sat silent, with considerable warmth declared that there was no occasion to accept the present of any other chief besides himself, as he was fully capable of supplying all their wants. Vancouver, anxious to conciliate all, determined to regulate his conduct to these jealous chiefs according to their rank; treating the inferior with due respect and attention, while he paid principal court to Kamehameha, as one who, if he did not then possess absolute authority, would soon secure it from his superior force and abilities.

As it was necessary to erect an observatory ashore, and in the intercourse which would necessarily ensue in a long visit, there would be temptations to pilfer, and difficulties might arise from lack of discipline on one side, and the aggressions of evil disposed natives on the other, enemies to his government, or retainers of chiefs, over whom he had no positive control, Kamehameha desired that certain rules should be strictly observed. In promulgating them, he seems to have had forcibly in his mind, the sad results of the unrestrained license of Cook's crews, and the want of prudence and injudicious harshness of their commander. On the part of Vancouver, he urged that the strictest discipline should be observed; that no individuals should be permitted to infringe upon their sacred observances, or in any way violate their places of religion; that none should stray about the country; and none but the principal chiefs be allowed to visit the vessels. In the day time, he would frequently come on board, and his presence would prevent any lawless conduct. If any of the whites desired to travel, he would be responsible for their safety, and would supply them with confidential attendants, who should provide for all their wants, and regulate their conduct that it might not unintentionally offend. Should any theft or irregularities be committed, he would see that the offenders were severely punished. Orders were issued to all subjects requiring of them the strictest obedience to all the rules prescribing their intercourse with the whites. Vancouver with a cordiality that reflects credit upon his judgment, heartily co-operated with these reasonable desires ; from the mutual respect of which may be reckoned the increase of good will, which rendered the visit so beneficial, and the departure so sad to both.

Kamehameha soon had occasion to prove his sincerity, by restoring some goods stolen by women who had been permitted to sleep on board.

Kekupuohe, one of the widows of Kalaniopuu, visited Vancouver. It had been her fortune to witness in the wars that followed his death, the extirpation of almost all her race. She was then in honorable captivity, supported according to her rank by the conquerors of her family. He had once saved her life from the fury of some of his own revengeful relations, who in a public commotion had sought her destruction, and that of all her adherents.*

* She died at Kailua, in February, 1836, at a very advanced age, being upwards of ninety, and was buried in a cave at Kealakeakua. In 1825, she joined the Protestant church, and, notwithstanding the feeble condition of her eyes, learned to read. To her death she was an indefatigable student of the Bible. She was a poetess, even in the decline of life, and not long before her death composed a song, of which the following extract, translated by the Rev. H. Bingham, will give an idea of her powers :

" Once only hath that appeared which is glorious,
It is wonderful, it is altogether holy ;
It is a blooming glory ; its nature is unwithering,
Rare is its stock, most singular, unrivaled,
One only true vine. It is the Lord," &c.

Another, composed in 1830, entitled " A Mele on the Creation," exhibits much beauty, force and simplicity of diction.

" God breathed into the empty space,
And widely spread his power forth,
The spirit flying, hovered o'er ;

" His power grasped the movable, it was fast,
The earth became embodied,
The islands also rose.

" God made this wide extended heaven,
He made the heavens long, long ago ;
He dwelt alone, Jehovah by himself,
The spirit with him.

On the 4th of March, Kamehameha entertained the officers of the ships with a sham battle, between one hundred and fifty of the best of his warriors. They were divided into three parties, to represent the armies of his rivals, Kahekili and Kaeo, and his own. Their spears were blunted, and as the parties approached, taunts, menaces and vaunting speeches were uttered on either side to excite fury. The battle commenced by a discharge of spears, and was continued without any regard to order, each individual advancing or retreating at his will. Some of the most expert defied the whole body of their adversaries, fending with the spear they held in their left hand, those thrown at them, or catching them in their right and launching them back upon their opponents. In this exercise, none excelled the king ; six spears were hurled at him at once ; three he caught, two were parried, and the sixth nimbly avoided by a trifling inclination of his body.

The skirmish was succeeded by an engagement of a more military character, in which the chiefs bore a conspicuous part. Each was attended by a body guard, armed with long sharp lances or with barbed javelins. Their ranks were formed into corps or phalanxes. Both parties previous to the fight sat upon the ground with their lances pointed at each other, while their leaders argued with much energy for war or peace. Not being able to agree upon the conditions of the latter, both parties arose, closed their ranks, and in serried columns slowly advanced. Their movements were made with much caution, each guarding with the greatest circumspection against any advantage which the other might seek ; the wings were engaged with slings and other missiles, but the action depended upon the fate of one of the phalanxes. The ground was firmly disputed and the mutual lunges warded with great dexterity. Some of Kahekili's troops fell ; upon which the opposing party with shouts rushed impetuously forward, and in the charge

" He fixed the sun his place,
But the islands moved, moved the islands,
With sudden, noiseless, silent speed ;
We see not his skillful work,
God is the great support that holds the earth."
Haw. Spect., vol. 2, page 80.

broke through the opposing ranks and gained the victory. Those who were supposed to be slain, were dragged by the heels over the beach, to be presented to the king; thence to the heiau, where they underwent a feigned sacrifice. Vancouver strenuously exerted himself to bring about peace between the Hawaiians and the inhabitants of the leeward islands. The chiefs of the former listened deferentially to his arguments, but they produced but little real impression upon their minds, bent upon conquest, and strengthened in their views by the very attentions he had paid them. In return, they requested his assistance in bringing all the islands under their dominion, which was the true policy; for one effective government established over the group, would effectually stop the hostilities which petty and independent chieftains ever wage with each other.

Kamehameha made another valuable present to Vancouver on the eve of his departure for the leeward, and as the most valuable relic the island afforded, sent his own war-cloak, pierced with spear-holes, as a present to George III., with the injunction, that as it had been worn by no other person but himself, it must honor no other shoulders than those of His Britannic Majesty. Vancouver presented him with many useful articles, among which were carpenters' and agricultural tools. Other chiefs also received abundant evidence of his liberal spirit. Kamehameha made a final attempt to procure some of the coveted fire-arms, by observing that his canoe, which had been fitted by the sail-maker with a full suit of canvas sails, would look better if she had a few swivels mounted. But the magic "taboo King George," stopped all further hints.

On the 8th of March, the vessels left for Maui, and anchored in Lahaina roads on the 12th. Here the intercourse was amicable, and in an interview with the aged and infirm Kahekili and Kaeo, his arguments for peace produced more effect. They had been great losers in the contest; their dominions were almost in a state of anarchy, and Maui had been so ravaged that it was necessary to bring food from Oahu and Kauai for the sup-

port of their armies of observation, which were stationed on the east, to repel the anticipated invasion. Their poverty prevented them from making the usual presents; but this did not hinder Vancouver from treating them with the consideration due their station. Kaeo produced a lock of his hair which he had given him in token of amity, while with Cook at Kauai. He was then a fine looking young man, but the use of *awa*, as with most of the chiefs, had brought on premature decay.

These chiefs satisfied Vancouver of their innocence in regard to the murders at Oahu. By their orders, three men had already been executed; and they were disposed to do all that lay in their power to bring the remainder to condign punishment. Vancouver manifested a determination to chastise the guilty, with a proper discrimination of the innocent, which effectually convinced the natives that such deeds could not be done with impunity; that if the whites were the aggressors, they must suffer the consequences; and that impartial justice should be dealt to all. In his discourse with the leading men, he endeavored to convince them of the distinction between the whites, governed by principles of honesty and humanity, and those reckless traders whose pecuniary interests were pursued regardless of the cost of blood and suffering to others. The dire evils which such men have produced among savage tribes, are sufficient to make humanity weep, but should not blind us to the less conspicuous, but beneficial influence of others. Unfortunately, savage nature affords too fruitful a soil for the vices and diseases of civilization; grafted upon their own, were it not for the remedies which so closely follow in their train, they would speedily depopulate the fairest country and convert a blooming garden into a dreary waste.

Kalanikupule ruled over Oahu for his father. Upon the arrival of the vessels, three men were brought on board by his orders, and delivered up as those actively engaged in the death of Lieutenant Hergest, Mr. Gooch, and the seaman, with the request that they might be immediately executed. All possible care was evinced to ascertain the guilt of the prisoners; and though the evidence was not so complete as the importance of such a case demanded, yet the concurrent testimony of the natives themselves, pointed them out as the real criminals. After commenting upon the enormity of the crime, the evidence of their guilt, and the design of the punishment, they were delivered to their chiefs, one of whom, in the presence of a large concourse, having placed them in a double canoe, a short distance from the vessel, blew out their brains with a pistol. Their sentence was executed at Waikiki, on the 22d of March.* Some doubt has since existed as to these men being the real murderers; and it has been asserted that they were sacrificed by their chiefs to appease the anger of Vancouver, and that another man, who was really guilty, was afterwards shot at Honolulu, by the mate of a vessel; the natives viewing the act with indifference, esteeming it to be just retaliation. Even if this be true, Vancouver must be exonerated from acting prematurely. The evidence against them was strong; and if there be criminality in their execution, it lies on the heads of their own countrymen, and shows a baseness which few would be willing to attribute even to savages.

Vancouver having caused this salutary example to be made, next proceeded to Kauai. When midway between the two islands, they fell in with the finest canoe which they had yet seen. It was sixty-one and a half feet long, with a proportionate depth and width, and finished off in a most workmanlike manner. It was made from an American pine log, which had drifted ashore in a perfectly sound condition on Kauai, where it had remained unwrought for some time; the islanders hoping a mate of equal dimensions might arrive, in which case they would have constructed a double canoe, which would have been their boast, and the terror of their enemies. Their patience becoming exhausted, they made the present one, which, from its buoyancy, was an admirable sea-boat, and was appropriated to carrying despatches to and from Kaeo, while he remained at

* Vancouver, page 204, vol. 2.

the windward. Its size considerably exceeded the largest canoe made from native timber, but was not uncommon for pine trees on the banks of the Columbia river, where, according to Douglass, they are to be met with from two hundred and fifty to three hundred feet in height.

In the canoe were messengers hastening to inform their absent ruler of a rebellion that had arisen, but had been fortunately quelled, with the loss on the part of the conspirators, of two chiefs and five men killed, and several wounded. As trophies of their success, they had the leg-bones of the chiefs, with a portion of the flesh adhering to them. A number of smaller canoes followed, filled with prisoners, whose fate was to be decided by Kaeo in person.

Upon his arrival off Kauai, the young prince Kaumualii again visited him. Vancouver remained two days, during which he was mostly employed in securing comfortable residences for two young girls, who had been carried from Niihau in an English vessel, some time before. At the request of the master, he had brought them from the American coast, and being much pleased with their beauty and amiability, exerted himself successfully to procure a favorable reception for them, from the chiefs of Kauai. But the wealth they carried ashore, he feared would prove too great a temptation to the cupidity of their countrymen, for them to dwell there long in safety. On the 30th of March, the ships sailed.

They returned for the last time in January, 1794, and arrived on the 9th off Hilo Bay, Hawaii, which, owing to unfavorable weather, he did not enter. Kamehameha, who was then residing there, went on board. At the urgent solicitations of Vancouver, he with his train remained until the ships arrived at their old station at Kealakekua. In doing this, he trenched upon one of their religious customs, to the strict observance of which he was strongly wedded. It was the festival of the New Year, and in the ceremonies he always bore a conspicuous part. It was called the "Makahiki," the name of the first day in their year, and lasted a long while, generally a month, being a sort of Saturnalia.

The people amused themselves with games, dances, theatrical performances and sham-fights. It belonged to the highest chief to open the festival. Dressing himself in his richest armor, he embarked in a canoe at early light, and coasted the shore until sunrise, when he was obliged to land. The most expert and valiant of his warriors was stationed to receive him. As soon as he touched the beach, he threw three heavy spears at him in quick succession, at the distance of thirty paces. There was no jesting in this. Either one, if not avoided, would have killed him outright, or severely wounded him. The first was to be caught in his hand; with this he warded off the others, and then carried it into the heiau, with the point downwards. His entrance was the signal for the assembled multitude to commence their sports. During their continuance, all punishments were remitted, wars discontinued, and no person could leave the place where he commenced the holidays, until their expiration. Kamehameha, in after years, was advised to abolish a custom so dangerous to his person, but he answered, that "he was as able to catch a spear, as any one to throw it."*

A MELO-DRAMATIC DANCE.

On this occasion, he urged that it was necessary for him to obtain the sanction of the priests to his absence, but the arguments of his counselors, joined with those of the commander, who stated that there would be no opposition to his wishes, and the more cogent reason of further confirming his importance in the eyes of the other chiefs, by this opportunity of showing his intimacy with Vancouver, overcame his religious scruples. During the passage, numbers of his subjects came off and were surprised to find him on board, but were satisfied when he made known it was his own choice. The same boundless liberality of provisions and presents was shown as before. Kamehameha considered them as his guests, and everything was apportioned on a princely scale. The strictest attention to the customs and wants of the whites was required of all his subjects. Some of his own train could not overcome their propensity to pilfer, and five knives were missing when they went on shore; but upon representation to the king, he, much chagrined at the theft, compelled their restitution.

An instance of the cruel effects of the law of retaliation, occurred while the ships were at the island. In a spear exercise between a common man and the son of a chief, the former had the misfortune to wound the young noble, for which he was seized, his eyes scooped

* Lisiansky's Voyage, p. 119: London, 1814.

out, and at the expiration of two days he was put to death.

On February 1st, the keel of the first vessel built at the islands was laid. She was thirty-six feet long, with nine feet and a half beam, five feet hold, and was named the Britannia. The carpenters of the ships were employed upon it, in conjunction with one Boid, in the pay of the king, and the services rendered by Vancouver in building and rigging her, were intended as some return for the hospitality so abundantly received from the kingly savage. Nor were Vancouver's good offices confined to this act. Through the influence of inimical chiefs, Kamehameha had been estranged and separated from his favorite Kaahumanu for a long time, on account of an alleged intimacy with Kaiana. Vancouver invited her on board, and by an artifice, induced the king to come off also; the parties met; Vancouver placed the queen's hand in his; his stern heart, softened at the distress of his wife, resisted no longer. Reconciliation, tears and a warm embrace ensued, but before leaving, the queen persuaded the captain to induce Kamehameha to promise upon their return to forego beating her. He also gave him useful hints for the discipline of his soldiers. By his counsel, trained bands, armed with muskets, were formed, which were to constitute a special body-guard, divided into regular watches for the day and night. These were drilled by his officers, until they constituted for the islands, an invincible force, devoted to the service of their chief. He recommended his countrymen, John Young and Isaac Davis, to his confidence, being convinced from their good conduct, that they were worthy. He desired them to use every endeavor to establish peace, and to infuse a humane spirit into the domestic habits, warfare and government of the nation; above all, to devote themselves to the service of their benefactor, and to counteract the malicious designs of interested foreigners, who might be disposed to promote bloodshed, or defraud the natives of their lands. He wished to confine the number of white settlers to these two, or such others whom they could trust; but Kamehameha and the other chiefs, knew

too well the value of foreign auxiliaries to be induced to banish them. There were but few on Hawaii, and those mostly of the better sort. Among them was one Howell, once a clergyman of the Church of England; afterward supercargo of a Boston brig, which he left at this island. Vancouver, with judgment that reflected much honor, while he did nothing to offend their idolatrous system, which would have at once ruined his influence, endeavored to direct Kamehameha's religious views into the true channel. He told him of the one true God, Creator, Ruler and Judge of all races; that their earthly deities were vain and foolish; their taboo system tyrannical and injudicious; and that if he desired it, he would request the king of England to send him a teacher of the true religion. His instructions seem to have made little impression upon the heart of the king, who, either from conviction or policy, was strongly attached to the idolatry of his country. Among his subjects he was considered favored of their gods, and he repaid their imaginary aid by a respect to their rites, which brought the priesthood into high repute. The early part of his reign may be considered as their happiest period. Church and State were in perfect harmony, acknowledging one head. Foreign influence, as yet, was not sufficient to create any general infidelity; the little that did exist made priestcraft more tenacious and active, and gave it a more powerful hold in the minds of the mass.

To confirm the general good-will and establish an amnesty for past troubles, Palea, the chief who stole the cutter of the Resolution, was allowed to visit the vessels; Kameeimoku, the murderer of young Metcalf and his crew, having humbled himself, and urged in justification of his revenge, the harsh treatment he had received from the father, obtained permission to come on board. He arrived at the bay in great state, attended by a thousand men. This act does not appear consistent with Vancouver's previous inflexibility in obtaining justice upon the death of his countrymen, at Oahu. In this instance the property was American, and the principal actor a high chief, whom it would have been difficult to secure, and whose death would have caused a hostility which would have led to dire revenge. Impunity for crime where wealth and rank are engaged, is not peculiar to the savage.

He was present at a feast given by Vancouver, when an incident transpired which shows how liable is the slightest misconception in the minds of savages to lead to fatal results. The Hawaiians were accustomed to obtain revenge by the means of powerful vegetable poisons, in the preparation of which a certain class, called poisoners, were skilled, and whose art was confined to themselves. During the feast, liquor was freely passed about; Kamehameha accustomed to its use maintained his reason, but Kameeimoku was soon overpowered, and in its first effect, raved that the English chief had poisoned him. His followers were much excited, and one who had concealed an iron dagger, handled it nervously, while the deadliest passions gleamed from his visage. But Kamehameha, understanding the real cause, ordered the drunken chief to be carried out; he was soon relieved, and returned in perfectly good humor. Had any accident befallen him under the operation, the whites would have been charged with his murder.

A large concourse of people appeared at the bay, but the guards preserved admirable order. Dramatic entertainments were given in the open air, to an audience of four thousand people, all gaily appareled, and in excellent humor. At the commencement of the exhibition, a girl dressed in figured tapa, gathered about her waist, and spreading downwards after the fashion of a hoop petticoat, with slow illustrative gestures, recited a poem. After she concluded, some females of high rank, similarly dressed, with garlands of leaves on their heads and shoulders, appeared, attended by their customary retinues. The most profound respect was shown them. The music consisted of rude drums, beaten with great vehemence, to the noise of which their actions corresponded. They were at first highly graceful and spirited; their recitation was a compound of speaking and singing, in honor of the

princess Keopuolani, who was in captivity, some sixty miles distant. At each mention of her name, she being the female of highest rank living, every spectator was required to strip to the waist. The scene concluded with a libidinous and disgusting dance.

Before leaving, Vancouver was convinced of the futility of his efforts to secure peace. The people of Maui made a descent upon Hawaii, but were driven off. He obtained from the king a taboo on the cattle landed, that none should be destroyed for ten years. This was rigidly observed, though they increased so rapidly and acquired such wildness as to become troublesome; destroying food, breaking down inclosures, and on one occasion, goring four natives to death. They were finally driven to the mountains. The women were to be allowed to eat of their flesh, though only on the same condition as dogs; the animal of which the men ate was to be entirely tabooed from them.

On the 21st of February, a great meeting of the chiefs was held on board the Discovery, for the purpose, as Vancouver writes, of ceding Hawaii to His Britannic Majesty, but as the natives, with more justice, state, " to request the king to protect our country." The conduct of Vancouver had done away all the bad impressions of Cook; the chiefs felt grateful for his kindness and the interest he manifested in their welfare. They had also been led to believe that other countries looked with envious eyes upon their domains and trouble would ensue, unless protection was offered by the greatest naval power. But the prominent motive with them was selfishness; in return for the compliment they expected to derive real advantages; that England would aid them in uniting all the islands under the power of Hawaii and a consequence be imparted to them in the eyes of the world be imparted to them. Speeches were made on the occasion by Kamehameha, Kaiana, Kalaimoku, Keeaumoku and others, in which these expected advantages were set forth; the chief topic was the necessity of chastising their contumacious enemies. The chiefs, as if apprehensive of yielding more than they intended, expressly reserved to

11

themselves the right of sovereignty, and the entire regulation of their domestic concerns. In case of disturbance from other powers, they were to be considered nominally as subjects of Great Britain. The English evidently exceeded the right granted them; Mr. Puget went ashore, hoisted the English colors and took *possession* of the island in the name of His Britannic Majesty, leaving an inscription on copper to that effect in the house of the king.* A salute was then fired, and the natives shouted "Kanaka no Beritane,"—we are men of Britain.

Kamehameha, Kaahumanu, Young and Davis staid on board the Discovery with Vancouver to the last moment, and manifested much emotion at his departure. The English seamen, although they now had it at their option to depart, chose to return on shore and remain. The wealth, distinctions and families which they possessed, joined with the sincere friendship of their munificent patron and preserver of their lives, were more powerful inducements than the love of their native land, where a sailor's hard lot would have awaited them.

The visit of Vancouver was beneficial

DANCE OF FEMALES.

to both races. With his own countrymen, it placed the character of the natives in a better light, and made the rising genius of their chief known to the world. The knowledge that a powerful nation felt a deep interest in them, was a check both upon any malpractices they might be disposed to commit, and the evil designs of the whites. It enlightened the policy of Kamehameha, strengthened his resources, and rendered his remaining conquests easier and more readily secured. Foreigners in his successes felt their own interests to be promoted, and what under other circumstances would have been looked upon as a violent usurpation, came to be viewed as a matter of expediency and advantage, and even of real utility to the islanders themselves.

Before leaving, he learned of an attempt of the natives of Kauai, instigated by a few renegade seamen, to get possession of the brig Hancock, of Boston. It was to have been done by scuttling her, and before she sunk, to haul her upon the reef, under the pretence of saving the cargo, which was to have been plundered. The design was frustrated. The natives of the leewardmost island, unrestrained by the power of any dominant chief, had become more bold

* "On the 25th of February, 1794, Kamahamaaha, king of Owhyhee, in council with the principal chiefs of the island, assembled on board His Britannic Majesty's sloop Discovery, in Karakakooa Bay, and in the presence of George Vancouver, commander of said sloop, Lieutenant Peter Puget, commander of his said Majesty's tender Chatham, and the other officers of the Discovery, after due consideration, unanimously ceded the said island of Owhyhee to His Britannic Majesty, and acknowledged themselves subjects of Great Britain."—*Vancouver, 3d vol.*

in their villainy. The dissensions continuing to increase, Captain Brown, of the Butterworth, a London ship trading at the islands, took Kahekili to Kauai in his vessel. By his assistance, Kahekili was enabled to place affairs in a more favorable situation.

Vancouver touched again at Kauai, and was entertained by a dance, in which six hundred women, dressed in figured tapas, took a part. Their voices were pleasing, motions graceful, and not of that licentious description he had witnessed at Hawaii. The recitations were varied and harmonious. On the middle of March, 1794, he took his final departure.

Vancouver left behind him a character which the most distinguished of his profession might be proud of possessing. Had the intercourse of those of his countrymen who succeeded him been conducted upon the same benevolent principles, the natives of the Hawaiian Islands would have been unalterably bound to English interests and feelings. His memory is still dear to those who knew him. Many chiefs, long after his departure, looked for his revisit, which he had given them reason to suppose would take place. As the attachment was mutual, it is probable that his untimely death alone terminated his intentions. He promised the chiefs to return, accompanied by missionaries to teach them a better religion, and artisans to aid them in civilization. A high rank was to have been his, and he would have resided among them, either a resident with authority from his government to protect and promote their interests, or by his own judgment to direct their councils. His plan appears to have been, to have christianized and civilized them, fostered and protected in his relations by the English ministry. The result would have proved beneficial, and civilization been advanced twenty years. The islanders might then have been confirmed in their English predilections, and the wish of Meares eventually fulfilled, that " one day, half a million of human beings inhabiting these islands may be ranked among the civilized subjects of the British empire."

CHAPTER VII.

ON the departure of Vancouver, warlike operations were resumed; the superior discipline and equipments of Kamehameha's forces, led by chiefs of tried courage and military skill, assisted by foreigners, and headed by the best general of the group, gave the invaders a decided advantage.

Kaeo and Kahekili united their forces at Oahu, and sailed with a large number of canoes for Hawaii. The naval force of Kamehameha, the flag-ship of which was the schooner Britannia, armed with three brass cannon taken from the Fair American, met them off Kohala, and in an engagement destroyed or dispersed the combined fleet. The vanquished chiefs fled to Maui. Kahekili, worn down with age and misfortunes, foreseeing the ultimate triumph of his foe, pleaded for a truce. In a message to Kamehameha, in reply to a challenge to battle, " Wait till the black tapa covers me," said he, "and my kingdom shall be yours." His death soon took place. Kaeo of Kauai, unmindful of their common enemy, and exasperated by a plot to assassinate him, laid claim to his dominions, in defiance of the legal rights of his nephew, Kalanikupule. Kaeo at first met with some success, and several foreigners in the service of Kalanikupule were slain. But the latter, with the assistance of Mr. Brown and his crew, was ultimately victorious, and slew him in an engagement at Kalauao in 1794. Brown was master of the English ship Butterworth. The same year he discovered and surveyed the harbor of

Honolulu, which he called Fairhaven. It was first entered by the schooner Jackall, tender to that ship. On the 1st of January, of the ensuing year, 1795, Brown was in this harbor with two vessels, the Jackall and Prince Le Boo; the Butterworth had sailed for England. The American sloop Lady Washington, Captain Kendrick, was lying in the harbor at the same time. Captain Brown on his return to Honolulu from fighting in the ranks of Kalanikupule, fired a salute in honor of his victory. A wad from one of his guns entered the cabin of the Lady Washington and killed Captain Kendrick, who was at dinner. Captain Kendrick was buried on shore, and the funeral service at his interment was the first Christian rite of the kind witnessed by Hawaiians. They looked upon the ceremony as sorcery to compass the death of Captain Brown. The grave was rifled the same night to procure the winding sheet. The Lady Washington sailed soon after, leaving Captain Brown at Honolulu, who furnished Kalanikupule with fire-arms and contracted a great intimacy with him.* From the assistance he had rendered Kalanikupule, and the general good feeling which a long intercourse had engendered, he felt secure from any treachery on his part, and abode with him in an unguarded manner. A petty chief suggested to Kalanikupule a plot to cut off Captain Brown and his vessels. At first he opposed the treachery, but finally consented, and a plan was concerted to capture both vessels. On the anniversary of the new year, the crews were ashore, engaged in pleasure, and in preparing stores for their voyage. Taking advantage of the defenceless condition of the vessels, the natives flocked off. Brown, and Gardner the other commander, were instantly murdered; one by being precipitated through the hatch with sufficient force to dislocate his neck; the few remaining individuals were wounded, and the possession of the decks secured. The pirates then took the vessels out of the harbor, into Waikiki Bay. The seamen ashore receiving intelligence of their capture, assembled and pushed off in their boats;

by a vigorous attack, the natives were overpowered, and driven overboard; having regained possession of the vessels, the survivors of the crews sailed without delay for China. It is remarkable that these piratical attempts should have been committed within two miles of the spot of, and not long after the execution of the murderers of Lieutenant Hergest and Mr. Gooch.

Kamehameha supported in his ambitious desires by the last words of Kahekili, set out with all his disposable force, said to have amounted to sixteen thousand men, to subjugate the neighboring islands. Young, Davis and a few other foreigners, expert in the use of fire-arms, accompanied him. Maui, Lanai and Molokai were quickly overrun, suffered all the horrors of savage warfare, and were effectually subdued. Oahu, to which the heir of Kahekili had retired, was his next aim. In February, 1795, he prepared for this expedition, and landed upon that island with one detachment of his army, leaving the remainder under the command of Kaiana, with orders to follow without delay. His arrival was impatiently awaited, that an attack might be made upon the enemy, who had made preparations for a vigorous defence. Kaiana, thinking this a favorable opportunity to crush his rival, embarked for Oahu; and avoiding the camp of his king, deserted with all his forces to Kalanikupule. He was aware that if Kamehameha could be destroyed by their combined exertions, there would be no chief left of sufficient energy and resources to compete with him, and the authority to which Kamehameha aspired would be his. But his treachery proved his ruin. Kamehameha, nothing dispirited by the news of his defection, marched to the valley of Nuuanu, where the two chiefs were encamped. Their position was on the steep side of a hill, about three miles in the rear of the present town of Honolulu: a stone wall protected them in front, and the steepness of the ground availed them against an assault. Believing themselves secure, they defied their enemies with insulting gestures and bravados. A field-piece, which Young had brought to bear upon them, knocked the stones about their

* Dibble, pages 68 and 69.

heads, killed Kaiana, and so disordered their ranks that they broke and fled. The forces of Kamehameha charged; in the onslaught many of the Oahuans were slain, and the rest pursued with great slaughter, until they were driven to the end of the valley, which terminates in a precipice of six hundred feet, nearly perpendicular height, forming a bold and narrow gorge between two forest-clad mountains. A few made their escape; some were driven headlong over its brink, and tumbled, mangled and lifeless corpses, on the rocks and trees beneath; others fought with desperation and met a warrior's death, among whom was Kalanikupule, who gallantly contested his inheritance to the last. The bodies of the slain were sacrificed, and their heads impaled upon the walls of the heiau at Waikiki. Three hundred perished in the fight; but numbers escaped to Kauai, among whom were two high chiefs. This decisive victory put the conqueror in possession of all the group, except Kauai and Niihau. These he prepared to attack, and embarked for that purpose; but a violent wind drove him back, and obliged him to suspend his designs.

In January, 1796, Capt. Broughton,[*] commanding H. B. M. sloop Providence, of sixteen guns, anchored at Kealakeakua Bay, where he remained three weeks in amicable intercourse with the natives. His wants were liberally supplied by the lieutenants of Kamehameha. Leaving this place, he spent a few days at Lahaina, where the same hospitality awaited him. He then anchored at Waikiki Bay, where he received a message from Kamehameha, inquiring if he should salute the ship with his heavy guns. Provisions were abundantly sent on board, and the usual presents of feathered cloaks. His next visit was to Kauai, where he saw Kaumualii, who was endeavoring to suppress an insurrection, and urgently solicited a supply of powder. Broughton exerted himself, though vainly, to appease the hostile parties. In July, after a cruise to the north, he returned to Hawaii; and being in want of water, was obliged to pay at

the rate of one hundred nails the hogshead, it being brought five miles in calabashes, from a scanty source. He found the cattle and poultry left by Vancouver had increased rapidly. This was the period of the rebellion of Namakeha, brother of Kaiana, who had overrun a part of the island, and was fast gaining ground. In one battle a European was killed. The officers of Kamehameha were in great trepidation, but vigorously endeavored to stem the efforts of the traitorous chief, while they sent despatches to inform their king of the unexpected revolt. At the same time, Broughton sailed for Oahu, where he arrived on the 25th of July. The island was suffering all the miseries of protracted warfare; provisions were exceedingly scarce; many natives had starved to death, and some had been burnt alive by their chiefs for stealing food to supply their famishing families. Kamehameha was said to have already lost six thousand of his troops; the losses of the enemy had been far greater. Probably at no period had depopulation been going on at a more rapid rate, especially at the leeward islands. War, famine, pestilence and oppression, with all the attending evils of an unsettled community, bore heavily upon the nation.

At Kauai all provisions were tabooed, except for powder. Broughton finding it impossible to obtain supplies from the larger islands, sailed, July 28th, for Niihau, to procure yams. On the 30th, he sent a party ashore in a cutter, with only two armed marines. The crew being incautious, were suddenly attacked; the marines killed for the sake of their accoutrements; the botanist knocked down, and, with the remainder, narrowly escaped being murdered. Their situation being seen from the ship, assistance was sent. The detachment fired upon the natives, without, however, harming any. Having landed, they burned all the houses within their reach, and destroyed sixteen canoes. Not being able to obtain further satisfaction, the ship sailed on the 21st. This is the last of the wanton murders which stain the earlier Hawaiian annals. It was Kamehameha's desire, after completing the conquest of Kauai and its tributary island, to have sailed for Tahiti, and carried his arms to the south of the equator. This scheme was suggested by some natives of that island with him. It would indeed have been a singular spectacle, to have witnessed this triumphant chieftain embarking the flower of his forces on board of his fleet of canoes, or tiny vessels, chartering perhaps some of a larger size, for an expedition against scarcely known lands, thousands of miles distant. The design was worthy of his ambition; and had he been able to have extended his conquests over the boundaries of Polynesia, he might have sighed for " new worlds to conquer," and the petty leader of a barbarian tribe have become master of the Pacific. But his destiny was to found a less extended, though better consolidated power.

News of the reverses in Hawaii having reached him, he promptly embarked for that island, where his presence soon decided the contest. Namakeha, the head of the conspiracy, was slain, and his followers subdued.

This was the last war in which he was actively engaged ; all opposition to his authority was now over. His original territory was Halaula, a large district on the northeast coast of Hawaii, which he inherited from his parents. During the lifetime of Kalaniopuu, he acquired a portion of Kona ; and it was the war which arose in consequence of the attempts of his cousin to dispossess him, that developed his martial energies, and step by step, led him on until he was master of the group. His talents were no less conspicuous in establishing his power, than in acquiring it. Towards the conquered families he practiced no unnecessary severity; the principal, by alliances or gifts, were firmly bound to his interests. He espoused Keopuolani, grand-daughter of Kalaniopuu, who became his prisoner at the conquest of Maui. As she was a lineal descendant of the ancient kings of Maui and Hawaii, this marriage strengthened his title to the throne. Kalaimoku, now his trusty counselor, had fought in the ranks of Keoua at Keei, was made a prisoner and owed his life to his clemency. Although allied to the royal family of Maui, he became strongly attached to him. The descendants of Kahekili were liberally cared for. The beneficence and humanity of the conqueror, left chiefs and people nothing to regret in the change of masters. He had the faculty of inspiring those about him with generous sentiments, and creating in them a resolution and energy of purpose, second only to his own. An almost intuitive perception of character, enabled him to secure the affection and co-operation of the best of his countrymen.

The nominal submission of the king of Kauai contented his ambition as to the dependencies of that chief, though he never lost sight of their ultimate conquest. He remained at Hawaii four years, and afterward spent much time at Lahaina, occupied in establishing his power on a permanent basis. The political axiom upon which his legislation was framed, was that all the lands in the group were his. This principle had been before acknowledged, though not in so complete a sense. To their old custom, he added the cogent argument of conquest, in right of which he claimed to be the sole lord and proprietor of the soil. This was apportioned among his followers according to their rank and deserts ; they holding it on the feudal tenure of rendering military services, and a proportion of its revenue. It was generally confirmed to their heirs, but this depended upon the will of the king. His authority was absolute ; dispensing with his own regulations as his interests dictated. But such an event was rare ; and under his reign the ancient traditionary laws of the kingdoms were so arranged and executed as to have all the force of a written code. Each island or cluster, had a governor ; he, with the approval of the king, appointed chiefs of districts ; head men, who presided over villages ; tax gatherers, and other petty officers. Beside the general proprietorship of the soil, the king held certain districts which were his private property, and under no authority except his own. Favorite chiefs sometimes received lands in this way, independent of the governors. No regular amount of taxes was enforced. The governors were accountable to the king for the amounts apportioned to them; they regulated theirs, by their desires or the resources of the people; the chiefs required another, and the lesser officials left but little to the poor tenants. Lands were sometimes leased upon regular agreements as to the amounts of the crops. Those who were deficient in their rents, were turned from the land, and their property transferred to others. The districts were divided into towns or villages, and these subdivided into farms or plantations; to which a definite portion of mountain land, valley and sea shore, with right of forest and fisheries, were attached. The tax gatherers, though without a knowledge of writing, kept true records of the various lands, their resources, and the amount of taxes rendered, by lines of cordage of several hundred fathoms in length. The several districts were distinguished by knots, loops and tufts of various sizes, shapes and colors. The different taxable articles and their rates were marked upon it, in an equally ingenious manner. Beside the stipulated rents, presents of the first fruits of agriculture or the fisheries, were required to be made to the chiefs. Certain lands, the gift of favoritism or the reward of distinguished services, were held free from all rents or taxes, although it was customary to make presents; the value and frequency of which were optional with the giver. From the most faithful of his warriors, his governors or counselors were selected, and he seldom decided upon an important measure without their advice. A certain number constituted a regular cabinet, and enjoyed his full confidence. Merit, more than rank, was the passport to his favor. Keeaumoku, a chieftain of prodigious personal strength, who had rendered distinguished services, was at the head of his council. He was the father of a son of the same name, heir to his titles, afterward known as Governor Cox, and of Kaahumanu, Piia, Kuakini and Kekauluohi, the late premier. Kalaimoku, Manawa and Kameeiamoku, were also particularly distinguished. Besides these, he had a number of "wise men," who assisted him in the organization of laws, and regulating the minor affairs of his kingdom. So perfect was the order preserved by his agents, that the anarchy which had laid waste lands and destroyed people, was entirely checked. Peace was everywhere firmly established. Laws were enacted prohibiting murders, theft, oppression and the usual crimes of a disturbed country. So complete a change was effected, that old and young, the innocent and helpless, abode in comparative security. Contrasted with former disorder, it may with propriety be termed a golden age. Kamehameha permitted no crimes but his own, when his interests were not too deeply involved. To consider actions sanctioned by their customs from time immemorial, a blot upon his character, would be unjust, however arbitrary they may appear to those whose lot has been placed in a land of freedom. They were merciful in comparison with what the islanders had undergone. No penalty could reach an individual screened by the favor of his chief, and the favorites of Kamehameha enjoyed the exemption common to successful courtiers.

Those chiefs, whose ambitious views he feared might disturb his newly acquired power, were retained about his person, and obliged to follow in his train wherever he went. By this means they were kept from their hereditary domains, where they might have excited discontent, and were always under the observation of faithful attendants, by whom any symptom of dissatisfaction would have been detected. The most powerful provinces were placed under the charge of those whose fidelity was undoubted. Young, who was not liable to become involved in the intrigues of the native princes, was left in charge of Hawaii, a station which he filled for many years, to the satisfaction of the king, foreigners and natives. Davis remained about the person of the sovereign and enjoyed extensive possessions, free from taxation. They both accommodated their modes of living to the manners of the natives, and from their humanity and usefulness became deservedly popular. As his power grew more firmly established, the king affected greater state; consequently the people had less access to his person. The foolish and arbitrary customs of the ancient kings of Hawaii were rigidly enforced, with such additional ceremony as was calculated to increase the awe of his own subjects, and his importance in the eyes of foreigners. Whenever he passed, heads and shoulders were to be uncovered; the same was required on approaching his residence, or any house which he had honored with his presence. When his food was carried to or from him, every person within hearing of the cry uttered by the menials, was obliged to uncover and seat himself after the native manner, by squatting on his hams.

Before any article could be touched, the attendants were obliged to strip to the malo. Neither the shadow of the king nor of his house could be crossed. His drinking water was brought from particular springs, many miles inland, reserved for his use; and as the carriers ran past, the same humbling ceremony as for his food, was required. To be above him, was the highest crime. Not a subject dared appear on the part of the deck of a vessel under which he by chance might be. The etiquette required from chiefs varied according to their rank, but was of the most obsequious character.

The attention required to religious duties was equally rigid. By this system of uniform despotism, of which he formed the sole head, the condition of the people was greatly ameliorated, for it broke the power of the petty lords who heretofore, like locusts, consumed all that the storm had spared. Chiefs were provided with retinues suitable to their stations. Laws, regulating the fisheries and agriculture, were promulgated; in these pursuits he set a laudable example of industry, by working with his own hands. By suitable rewards, he encouraged the skillful in the various handicrafts. No object, however trivial, was beneath his notice, provided it added to his wealth and resources. His vessels were free to his subjects, and on the whole, taxes were not onerous. His soldiers were well disciplined, and were divided into various bodies; some of whom were his

body guard, while others were appointed for his wives; principally as checks upon illicit intercourse. If they failed in their duty, they were punished with death. His partial native biographers thus feelingly sum up his excellencies, the more prominent from the contrast with earlier and subsequent reigns; and they illustrate the nature of the extortions too often practiced. " He did not become involved in debt, nor exact much silver from his subjects; he did not cut from a division of land on this side and that, till only a circular and centre piece of the original field remained; he did not by petty taxation collect all the hens, ducks and turkeys; nor appoint days in which his subjects were all to labor for his exclusive benefit; his measures were generous and constant, not fickle and oppressive."

In his foreign relations his acts were characterized by equal liberality. In the infancy of his power he was in the habit of procuring from commanders testimonials of his honest and hospitable conduct; but this was relinquished as soon as his reputation became established. No chief was better acquainted with the real character of foreigners, and the purposes for which they visited his dominions. To the war-ships, or those that came for scientific purposes, he showed himself the hospitable prince; to traders, a merchant not excelled in sagacity by the keenest, nor in reputation by the most honorable. He made himself well acquainted with weights, measures, currencies and proportionate values, and monopolized the most profitable sources of trade. His equitable regulations induced ships to visit his shores; while his extended power insured them an equally welcome reception in all portions of his kingdom. No port in the Pacific was better known than Honolulu. By his energies, a petty fleet of foreign built vessels was collected; soldiers were drilled, equipped, and dressed in a motley uniform; batteries of heavy guns mounted; rude forts erected; and a corps of foreign artisans and sailors, received into his service, well treated, freed from the vexatious etiquette required from the highest of his own race, but compelled to preserve order, and render due obedience to the authority which supported them. His own subjects, by his encouragement, manifested an aptness in acquiring civilized arts, that alarmed many of these foreign mercenaries; even Isaac Davis, with an illiberality that dishonors his general good conduct, sought to prevent the extension of knowledge among them; observing, "they will soon know more than ourselves."* All his subjects were required to keep their weapons in perfect order, so as to be ready for war at the shortest notice.

His observations of foreign manufactures and customs denoted an inquiring, intelligent mind. No idea or circumstance that could be made serviceable escaped his notice. He took great delight in visiting fine specimens of naval architecture. His arrival was sometimes announced in form, and the visit conducted with ceremony; but friendship once formed, artificial restraint was thrown aside, and he would put off by himself in a canoe, and go on board in the most unceremonious manner. In 1801, a fine Boston clipper-built ship, commanded by Capt. William Sturgis, was lying in his principal harbor, and as she was engaged in the Indian trade, martial order was preserved on board. Kamehameha coming off alone, was repulsed by the sentinel, who did not recognize his person. He then gave his name, and with the permission of the officer of the deck, was admitted. So far from feeling chagrined at this want of respect, he complimented the captain upon his excellent discipline, and called the sentinel a "worthy fellow."

In 1801, Kamehameha returned to Oahu, to prepare for the conquest of Kauai. This occupied him two years. He raised seven thousand warriors and fifty whites, mostly armed with muskets. Beside these, he had forty swivels, six mortars and abundance of ammunition. A fleet of twenty-one schooners, from ten to fifty tons each, some of which carried guns, and were commanded by Europeans, and a vast number of war-canoes, were prepared to convey this force, against which the Kauaians could have offered but faint resistance. At

this time—1804—he added to his navy the American ship Lilybird, mounting twenty guns. She had got ashore, and he purchased her by exchanging one of his schooners, and paying the difference in dollars. Before he could embark his forces, an epidemic broke out among them, of a peculiar character, which spread over the island and proved very fatal. Multitudes perished; among them some of his chief counselors. Three hundred dead bodies are said to have been carried out to sea from Waikiki in one day. He was himself attacked, but recovered. The sons of the deceased chiefs succeeded to the offices of their fathers, but never acquired as much influence as those who had shared all his perils.

Kaeo, king of Kauai, had been succeeded by Kaumualii, his son. The bright parts and generous spirits noticed by Vancouver, had been fully sustained. His subjects were devotedly attached to him, as were also a number of foreigners, who had enlisted in his service. Like his rival of Oahu, he was friendly to strangers, and encouraged trade; possessing equal humanity and intelligence, he was deficient in the martial talent and iron will which characterized Kamehameha. Fear and courage alternated; supported by the generous devotion of his people, he had energetically prepared to resist attack. His warriors were well armed, and a store of European arms and ammunition had been provided, sufficient to have protracted his fate, if he had vigorously opposed the invader. With the capricious spirit of one of his disposition, encouraged by the long delay which had attended Kamehameha's operations, he sent him repeated messages of defiance, and finally threatened to invade Oahu. But this bravado was not borne out; for fully appreciating the great resources opposed to him, he caused the mechanics in his pay to prepare a vessel, in which, as a last resource, he with his family, could fly the island, and abandoning themselves to the wide Pacific, find such a home as the winds and waves might provide them. This was an idea worthy of his genius, in the composition of which, much that was chivalrous entered. Without a

* Campbell's Voyages, page 141.

12

knowledge of navigation, but possessing the compass, he could easily have carried his fortunes to some of the groups further to the leeward, and there founded a new dynasty.

The vastness of Kamehameha's preparations showed his opinion of the importance of the conquest, and argued considerable respect for the military skill and resources of Kaumualii. The disease which destroyed the flower of his troops, did not check his ardor. Turnbull, who arrived at this juncture in an English ship, was importuned by Kamehameha to take him, and an officer of his army, to Kauai, that they might themselves see the condition of the island. This bold request was refused. An American captain then in port, whose interests would have been greatly jeopardized by the war, volunteered to sail for Kauai, and induce Kaumualii to return with him, and enter into negotiations at Oahu. As the presence of Kamehameha was necessary at Hawaii, where a deficiency in the revenue had occurred, he consented to this measure. The captain sailed for Waimea, and by leaving his mate as a hostage for the safe return of their king, a measure, without which his subjects would not have permitted his departure, Kaumualii embarked. In the word of his enemy, pledged for his safety, he had entire confidence; so greatly was Kamehameha respected by those to whom treachery had, not long before, been far more common than truth. He was received and entertained with princely greeting; festivity, shows, and every profession of friendship attested the good disposition of his royal entertainer. Won over, he ceded to Kamehameha his kingdom; this was generously relinquished, and an agreement made, by which the leeward king was to hold his islands in fief from Kamehameha, retaining all that was legitimately his own, and in addition receiving the protection of the greater power. In this manner the islands were nominally united under one sovereignty, while each king ruled in his appropriate sphere; the treaty thus peaceably agreed upon, gave mutual satisfaction, and was faithfully respected during the lifetime of Kamehameha.

Some of his enemies give a different, but highly improbable version of this negotiation. They state that the death of Kaumualii was designed; and that the welcome he received was intended to allay suspicion. The time of his fate was fixed, but the American captain getting wind of it, went on shore, brought the king off, and sailed immediately for Kauai. If this were true, the friendship which afterward existed between the two is unaccountable, and is sufficient to disprove the statement. A more probable version is that his assassination was proposed to Kamehameha by some of his petty chiefs, or if that failed, by means of sorcery. Kamehameha in his indignation slew the proposed sorcerer. The chiefs then plotted secretly to kill him, but Isaac Davis hearing of it, informed Kaumualii, who immediately went on board. This occurred in 1809. Davis dying in April, 1810, his death was attributed to poison administered by the disappointed assassins.

Kaumualii's wife, Kapuli, better known by her baptismal name, Deborah, then young and attractive, exercised great influence over his mind. This occasionally gave umbrage to the government at Oahu, and word was sent him to put her away; but paying no heed to it, she was suffered to remain without further remonstrance. The chiefs were usually very strict with their females; but Kaumualii in his easy nature allowed Kapuli all the latitude with his friends, that the most ardent disposition could desire. Kamehameha put to death a near relative, for taking improper liberties with his favorite, Kaahumanu.

In June, 1804, Lisiansky, in the Russian discovery ship Neva, arrived at Hawaii. Young was then governor, and showed him many civilities. In his intercourse with the natives, he had occasion to perceive the extent to which the king undertook to regulate trade. Certain necessary articles could only be obtained by giving in exchange bar-iron, of which he was greatly in want. By such restrictions he was enabled to provide himself with many useful things, which the whites would not otherwise have sold. Lisiansky found the knowledge of prices and the art of bargaining

ng all classes, but
their honesty and
he value of dollars
d trade generally
e character of reg-
ictions. Lisiansky
ing Kamehameha.
irchant vessels that
nds at this period,
ike the savages of
st, the islanders
generally as Bos-
l them with great
of January, 1803,
ided from a Boston
nd beauty created
lmiration; but the
in California, not
a soon cease to be
Kamehameha be-
ossessor of several,
playing his horse-

tempt was made to
truth of the Chris-
tening to the argu-
unately, were not
so arranged as to
vorable light to his
plied, " by faith in
iything can be ac-
Christian will be
larm. If so, cast
yonder precipice,
red, I will believe."
y convicts having
o Oahu, were re-
e of the king, and
nd given them, on
gar-cane, and con-
acture ardent spir-
, riots and quarrels
nehameha at first
m, but his leniency
They finally mal-
when he sent them
lext drinking and
d be present. This
once. It was from
of whites that the
eatest injury.

useful articles of
such as cloths and
re greatly in de-
accordance with

jes, vol. 1, p. 229.

the spirit of the day, traded in rum.
Fortunately for the nation, it was in
general monopolized by the king, who
would occasionally join in a revel with
his wives and favorites. The disputes
which arose, in consequence of too great
indulgence among the women, afforded
the chiefs whose heads were more potent, much amusement. Kamehameha
was quite regular, though not intemperate in his potations. His subjects
acquired a fondness for its use, which,
however, during his reign, was duly restrained. Peace being now universal,
munitions of war had lost their former
value.

Kamehameha was desirous of procuring an anvil which he had noticed on
board of a ship. It was given him, upon
condition of his divers bringing it up
from ten fathoms water. To this he
agreed; the anvil was thrown overboard,
and the divers descended; but its weight
proved too great for their utmost exertions. Unwilling to abandon the prize,
they rolled it along, at the bottom of the
harbor, rising occasionally for breath, and
alternately relieving each other, until it
reached the beach half a mile distant.

So favorable an opinion had been
formed of the character and capabilities
of the islanders, and of the good influence exerted by comparatively uncultivated white settlers, that Turnbull,* as
early as 1803, suggested the speedy establishment of missionaries among them.
He judged the situation and advantages

* John Turnbull was supercargo to an English ship,
which voyaged extensively in the Pacific, between 1800
and 1804, visiting chiefly the Society and Hawaiian
groups; an interesting account of which is to be found
in his "Voyage around the World," published at London, and reprinted at Philadelphia in 1810. He was a
man of enlarged and humane views. Some of his opinions have since been so amply fulfilled, as to now appear almost prophetical. Of the Americans he writes,
"they will do more than any others to exalt them
the Hawaiian Islands—to a singular degree of civilization." Page 125.
He foresaw the evils which would originate from the
introduction of ardent spirits, and thus strongly expresses himself: "I know no sufficient punishment
that the wretch would merit who should import a cargo
of spirituous liquors into the Sandwich or Society Islands; it would in every respect be tantamount to the
willful administration of an equal quantity of poison."
Page 148. A bold and ingenuous sentiment at an
epoch when the baneful trade was not only legalized,
but encouraged by all classes. Kamehameha was so
fully persuaded of the evil, that, although he permitted
its importation, and allowed it to be used to a certain
extent by his followers, he tabooed, shortly before his
death, all stills within his own kingdom. Not a drop
of any kind was allowed to be manufactured; and any
infringement of this law was visited by a forfeiture or
destruction of the delinquent's property.

as infinitely superior to the field occupied by his countrymen at Tahiti. The suggestion, however, fell upon unwilling ears, and America was left afterward to reap the rich reward of disinterested benevolence. The number of natives who had been in foreign countries, acquired the English tongue, and had become partially weaned from their superstitions, rendered the enterprise most favorable. The greatest obstacle would have been the strong religious tendencies of Kamehameha himself; but could these have been rightly directed, as there is little doubt they might have been, they would have exerted an activity in the cause which would even have surpassed the late efforts of Kaahumanu, who gave it an impetus which revolutionized the nation. As it was, he continued his devotions to his idols to the last, though acknowledging their worthlessness. He doubtless viewed the system as a powerful engine of government, and more of politics than piety mingled in his later views. His stern bigotry did not always get the better of his humanity. A boy whom he loved, was doomed for sacrifice by a priest, when very low, and expected to die on a day sacred to his god. A crime so heinous could only be obviated by an earlier death. The priest told this to Kamehameha, but he sternly ordered him to bring the youth to him. By his care he recovered, and ever after was one of his family.

The saliva of the king was carefully preserved in a spittoon, around the edges of which were set the teeth of his ancestors. If his enemies got possession of any of it, they were supposed to have the power to occasion his death by sorcery and prayer.

In 1809, a Russian ship arrived at Honolulu, having on board Archibald Campbell, a sailor who had been shipwrecked at Sannack. At his wish he was taken into the service of the king, in which he remained upwards of a year, and was treated with much kindness, and had a farm given him. His narrative* was subsequently published, and contains many interesting particulars of the domestic life of Kamehameha,

related with an artlessness which attests their truth. He speaks in grateful terms of the friendship received "from all ranks, from my much honored master, the king, down to the lowest native." He states that Kamehameha generally conformed to the customs of his own country in regard to food, adopting only such articles of foreign dress as were suitable to the climate ; although on some occasions he wore a uniform, of which he had a number of beautiful suits. The whites about him were served more in accordance with their civilized habits, being provided with plates, knives and forks. In March, 1810, Campbell left for England in the whaler Duke of Portland, Captain Spence, by whom Kamehameha sent a feather cloak to the king of England, with a dictated letter, in which he reminded him of a promise received from Vancouver, that a man-of-war, with an armament of brass pieces, and loaded with articles of European manufacture, should be sent him. He expressed his regret that the distance prevented him from rendering service to him in his wars, and assured him of his regard. Although Kamehameha learned to converse in English with tolerable fluency, he never acquired the art of writing.

Don Francisco de Paula Marin, a Spaniard, had settled many years before, at Oahu, and made himself useful by the attention he paid to agriculture and cattle. He introduced many plants, fruits and vegetables, and at one time he was in the confidence of the king, being employed as interpreter. In 1810, the number of whites on Oahu alone amounted to sixty ; some of whom were sober and industrious, and much respected by the chiefs ; but the generality were idle and dissolute, held in restraint only by the authority of the king. The number of half-breeds was considerable. This unfortunate class received little attention from their parents, and grew up in vicious ignorance. Many of the natives had become tolerable carpenters, coopers, blacksmiths and tailors.

Kamehameha by his trade in sandalwood and pearls, and various monopolies, acquired considerable wealth. His stores of European, American and Chi-

* Voyage Round the World, from 1806 to 1812, by Archibald Campbell. 12mo. Edinburgh : 1816.

nese goods were extensive and valuable. Arms and ammunition he possessed in great abundance, and his coffers were well filled with dollars. A number of small houses, erected after the European manner, had been built for him, but he preferred the straw habitations of his country.

Two queens composed his legitimate wives; of these Kaahumanu remained the favorite, no one except her husband daring to enter her presence uncovered.

She was inordinately fond of ardent spirits, and frequently drank to excess. A daughter was born to him in 1809, and the event announced by a salute of sixteen guns from the battery in front of his residence. On this occasion, the queen in accordance with their customs, retired to a house in the forest for ten days.

Kamehameha consorted with Kaahumanu from affection and with Keopuolani from policy. The latter might be

KAAHUMANU, WIFE OF KAMEHAMEHA I.

termed his official wife. The custom of the country relative to the royal family, required him to visit her monthly, immediately after her purification, of which she gave him notice. In marriages of this political character, the royal parties usually lived apart, both being furnished with partners of choice, who abode constantly with them. In this sense Hoapili was the husband of Keopuolani, by consent of Kamehameha. When he visited her it was in great state, and if by water, in a canoe, the paddlers of which were dressed in a rude uniform, made by winding completely around their bodies cloth similar to that of their malos. Ka-

mehameha always treated Keopuolani with superior deference, as of the most exalted rank in the kingdom. Her children, and not Kaahumanu's, are heirs to the throne. When the queen was in labor, the king's own idol was brought immediately into the room, in the presence of which the child was required to be delivered. Should it not arrive in season, the navel-string remained uncut until it was brought in, which done, the child was considered as the legitimate heir.

Kekauluohi, daughter of Kaiana, the late premier, was one of the wives of Kamehameha, having been educated for him when a child, as a royal virgin, in the greatest seclusion and care. After their quasi marriage she was sedulously restrained from all society, and diligently taught the genealogies and ancient lore of the country. Upon his death she became the wife of his son, who, however, provided another husband for her.

Liholiho, his eldest son, was born of Keopuolani, on Hawaii, in 1797. Kamehameha, to establish the succession in his family, in 1809 invested him with royal honors, by which he became entitled to the same etiquette as himself, but the government continued in its customary routine. The prince was an indolent, pleasure-loving youth, of a frank and humane disposition. His manners were generally dignified and agreeable ; his mind inquisitive and memory retentive. Circumstances might have made him worthy of his parentage, but his high station, and freedom from care, made him reckless and dissipated. He was fond of liquor, but, until his accession to the throne, was under the same powerful influence which held all, from the highest to the lowest, in complete thraldom.

Kamehameha remained at Oahu nine years ; he then embarked with his suite on board of some foreign vessels, and accompanied by a large fleet of small craft and canoes, sailed for Hawaii, touching at Lahaina, Molokai and other places, to dispose of sandal-wood and other products, which had been collected by Keeaumoku, governor of that portion of his dominions. Kalaimoku was left in charge of Oahu. The king lived at Hawaii, principally about Kailua and Kealakeakua, until his death. In his hereditary possessions he was greatly revered. During a famine, he labored for his own food, and compelled his followers to work likewise. The spot of land which he tilled is pointed out to this day as a mark of his benevolence. With a providence unusual to his nation, he allowed none of the young sandal-wood to be cut, observing that such wood was to be preserved for his successors. Neither would he permit the birds which were caught for their feathers to be killed ; but ordered them to be set free, after they were plucked of the few that were wanted. The bird-catchers, with native logic, inquired "who will possess the birds set free? you are an old man." He replied, new feathers would replace those plucked, and the birds would again be useful.

Like civilized conquerors, he delighted equally in overcoming obstacles of nature as of men. Undertakings which had been considered impracticable he accomplished. Some of the most conspicuous and extensive heiaus, fish-ponds, and other public works, were erected by him. At Halaula, his patrimonial district, he dug through a ledge of stone from a perpendicular height of one hundred feet, making a good road with a gradual descent to the sea-side. At another spot, he endeavored to procure pure water, by digging through the several strata of lava ; after penetrating to considerable depth, through compact rock, he was obliged to relinquish the enterprise, from want of gunpowder and suitable tools. At Kiholo is another monument of his enterprise, in a fish-pond two miles in circumference, formed by a strong stone wall built across a small bay. It is half a mile long, six feet high in parts, and twenty wide. Several arches, closely guarded by strong wooden stakes, allow egress to the water, but prevent the fish from escaping.

In 1814, a ship owned by Baranoff, the governor of the Russian colony at Sitka, was wrecked at Waimea, Kauai ; the principal part of the cargo was saved, and entrusted to the care of Kaumualii for the owners. In 1815, the Russian governor sent a German physician, by the name of Scheffer, to take possession of the wrecked property. He arrived at Kailua in the American ship Isabella, Captain Tyler, bringing with him a quantity of powder and clothing. Kamehameha received him in a friendly manner, and sent orders to Kaumualii to deliver the property into his charge. After a few weeks stay at Hawaii, he sailed for Waimea, Kauai, landed his goods, built a house, and commenced trading. Kaumualii purchased the powder, and some other articles, for sandal-wood. Soon after, a Russian ship, Discovery, arrived with thirty Kodiack Indians, a part of whom were females,

ful search for a seal
·ders of the governor
dians were left with
the vessel returned.
two Russian vessels,
Captain Long, and a
rican captain, arrived
eir crews numbered
They immediately
ig a block-house near
which they mounted
splayed a flag. This
f the natives and the
:rs, and word was im-
ed to Kamehameha.
such a suspicious act
ign power, was char-
vhich has ever since
t Kalaimoku to Oahu
g judicious orders :
the conduct of the
low to oppose them.
rage upon the people,
to bear it patiently.
with forbearance, but
standing, in case of
to make a firm resist-
ly upon Kalaimoku's
s sailed for Kauai,
a captain having quar-
r, who was agent for
trom the command.
·rdered to the Bay of
rth side of the island,
ed during the winter.
a slight fort on a cliff
, and had a few can-
; anxious to secure his
tending the building
Vaimea, gave him the
inalei and other valu-
excited his cupidity,
secure the whole isl-
ed a schooner, with
s, to the king, and in
btained a lease of the
long period. The fort
ompleted to mount a
n one side ; a maga-
d a flag-staff erected,
sian colors were occa-

: natives, Scheffer laid
iumualii and his chief
which he had invited

them. The American captain revealed it to the king, who, however, attended, with the precaution of a guard sufficient to prevent any nefarious attempt. Nothing transpired to confirm the report. Scheffer made himself obnoxious by his arbitrary conduct, and reports were carried to Kamehameha that the Russians were preparing to invade his dominions, and had already obtained possession of Kauai. Much alarmed, he sent word to Kaumualii to drive them away. Accordingly, Scheffer was compelled to embark with his Indians without delay, on board of the brig, which was at Waimea. The next day his property was taken off to him. He then sailed for Hanalei, rejoined the ship, and both left for Honolulu. Upon arriving here he was requested to depart, which he did, but the Myrtle proving unseaworthy obliged him to put back. She was condemned at Honolulu, and the Russians allowed to remain until an opportunity offered for leaving.*

The acts of Scheffer, which seem to have had no other origin than a desire for his own aggrandizement, with the hope of being ultimately supported by the Russian governor, or perhaps the government, created a very unfavorable opinion towards the Russians throughout the group. Apprehensive of further attempts, the king caused guards to be stationed along the coast of Hawaii, with directions to resist any attempt at landing. The Diana, a Russian sloop-of-war, arrived soon after at Waimea, made some inquiries concerning Scheffer, purchased supplies, and then left.

Captain Kotzebue, in the Russian discovery ship Rurick, arrived off Hawaii, November 21, 1816. He soon learned of the hostile feeling towards his countrymen, which at first placed him in some jeopardy. He assured the islanders of the kind intentions of his emperor, and that Scheffer's conduct was the result of his own private ambition, and was neither countenanced nor approved

* Robert Greenhow, in his historical memoir, gives a most singular and erroneous account of this affair, but does not name his authority. He states that one hundred Aleutians, sent by Baranoff, under the command of Dr. Scheffer, *ravaged* the island of Kauai for one year, without subduing it; they were then obliged to leave for Hawaii, where they entered the service of some American whalers, &c. Page 149. For the correct particulars, see Hawaiian Spectator, vol. 1, p. 219.

by his government. These representations satisfied Kamehameha, and when the Rurick anchored at Kealakeakua, he received him with his customary courtesy and hospitality. He excused himself from visiting on board, by alleging the fears of his subjects, whose apprehensions were not entirely allayed.

Kotzebue visited him at his palace, and there met with Liholiho and Kaahumanu, who made many inquiries after Vancouver. He remarked the general use of tobacco, which was carried to such excess, from inhaling its fumes, as to produce partial derangement, intoxication, and often death. Even young children indulged in the pernicious practice.

The Rurick was supplied with stores and refreshments gratuitously; in acknowledgment for which, Kotzebue gave Kamehameha two brass field-pieces, wire, and iron bars, which were highly acceptable. He then sailed for Honolulu, and the Rurick was the first man-of-war that entered that harbor. Considerable excitement existed in regard to his intentions, which, however, subsided when Kalaimoku made known the king's commands. Two fine vessels bore the national flag, which had been adopted shortly before; they displayed the English union, with seven alternated red, white and blue stripes, emblematic of the principal islands. One was a ship, newly purchased, destined for China, with a cargo of sandal-wood, and the other a war-brig, the Kaahumanu, of eighteen guns, commanded by an Englishman, of the name of Adams. Wishing to survey the harbor, Kotzebue placed flags upon several different stations; the sight of them reminded the natives of Scheffer's acts, when he hoisted the Russian flag, and these were supposed to have been planted with a like intention. A commotion arose which would have proved dangerous to the surveying party, had not Young, who then lived on the island, overseeing the erection of the present fort, explained the cause, and substituted brooms for the obnoxious ensigns. Clothes were much in demand at this time among the chiefs, and their costume presented the same ludicrous mixture of barbarism

and civilization that exists among the poorer classes at the present time. A lance fight was exhibited for the gratification of Kotzebue, which terminated in dangerous wounds to some of the party. The passions of the combatants, so long unexercised in war, on these occasions were apt to become exasperated, and the mock battles to terminate in furious and bloody encounters. Kamehameha seldom allowed them to take place, and then only under a guard of soldiers armed with muskets. On the 14th of December, the Rurick sailed; she was the first national ship that exchanged salutes with the batteries of Honolulu.

An attempt was made to cement an alliance between the royal families of Hawaii and Tahiti, by a double marriage. Gifts and friendly messages had been frequently exchanged between Pomare I. and Kamehameha, and finally it was agreed that a son of each should marry a daughter of the other. Kekauluohi was selected for Pomare, but his death broke off the matches, and the project was never resumed. Earlier than this, Kaumualii sent an agent to Tahiti, in a foreign ship, to negotiate with the reigning family for a wife for himself; but the man proved unfaithful to his trust, and seduced by the well favored beauties of that island, settled there.

On March 17th, 1814, Kauikeaouli, the present king, was born. Nahienaena, the princess, was born about two years later of the same mother, Keopuolani; so that their rank, and that of Liholiho, was derived equally from the past and reigning dynasties; consequently, by descent and conquest, they were heirs to the throne of the united kingdom.

Kamehameha had made some overtures toward opening a direct trade with the governor of the Russian settlements, in the early part of his reign. However, but little resulted from them. Sandal-wood had now become the great article of export, amounting in one year to near four hundred thousand dollars. While it lasted, it was a mine of wealth to the chiefs; but it engendered luxury and extravagance; and many rich cargoes were purchased at the cost of great labor and heavy taxation. They were frequently stored in unsuitable buildings, and there perished from neglect. Kamehameha, learning of the great profits derived by the merchants from their sales in China, determined to prosecute the business on his own account; accordingly he fitted up the ship before mentioned, loaded her with the wood, and under the direction of English officers, and a native supercargo, Kapihe, despatched her for Canton; the first foreign port in which the Hawaiian flag was displayed. Extravagant port charges, and the dissipation of the captain and supercargo, ran away with the proceeds of the sales. She returned safely, but in lieu of the riches of the Celestial empire, the king found himself three thousand dollars in debt. The chief items of charges were pilotage, anchorage, and custom-house dues. This suggested to him the idea of raising a revenue in the same manner, and from that time harbor fees were established.

Though, toward the latter period of Kamehameha's reign, a general laxness in regard to the taboos began to prevail, yet every open transgression was severely punished. A woman was put to death for entering the eating house of her husband, though at the time she was tipsy. As late as 1818, three men were sacrificed at Kealakeakua; one for putting on the *malo* of a chief, another for eating a forbidden article, and the third for leaving a house that was taboo and entering one that was not.

Kamehameha resided at Kailua seven years. The changes which had occurred at Tahiti, by the final triumph of the Christian religion, aroused his attention, and he made many inquiries in regard to the causes and results. He desired to be instructed in the doctrines, and to learn of the nature of the Supreme Being the foreigners worshiped. Unfortunately, the whites around him were little calculated to explain the sublime truths, or to tell him of the heavenly tidings of the Gospel.

On the 8th of May, 1819, at the age of sixty-six, he died as he had lived, in the faith of his country. It was his misfortune not to have come in contact with men who could have rightly influenced

13

his religious aspirations. Judged by his advantages, and compared with the most eminent of his countrymen, he may be justly styled not only great, but good. To this day his memory warms the heart and elevates the national feelings of Hawaiians. They are proud of their old warrior-king; they love his name; his deeds form their historical age; and an enthusiasm everywhere prevails, shared even by foreigners who knew his worth, that constitutes the firmest pillar of the throne of his son.

In lieu of human victims, a sacrifice of three hundred dogs attended his obsequies; no mean holocaust, when their national value is considered. The bones of Kamehameha, after being kept for a while, were so carefully concealed that all knowledge of their final resting place is now lost. There was a proverb current among the common people that the bones of a cruel king could not be hid; they made fish-hooks and arrows of them, upon which in using them they vented their abhorrence of his memory in bitter execrations.

The native historians relate the circumstances of his death with a feeling and minuteness, which so well illustrates many of their customs, that the reader will pardon the insertion.

"When Kamehameha was dangerously sick and the priests were unable to cure him, they said, ' Be of good courage, and build a house for the god, that thou mayest recover.' The chiefs corroborated this advice of the priests, and a place of worship was prepared for Kukailimoku, and consecrated in the evening. They proposed also to the king, with a view to prolong his life, that human victims should be sacrificed to his deity; upon which the greater part of the people absconded through fear of death, and concealed themselves in hiding places till the kapu, in which destruction impended, was past. It is doubtful whether Kamehameha approved of the plan of the chiefs and priests to sacrifice men, as he was known to say, ' The men are sacred for the king;' meaning that they were for the service of his successor. This information was derived from his son, Liholiho.

"After this, his sickness increased to such a degree that he had not strength to turn himself in his bed. When another season, consecrated for worship at the new temple—heiau—arrived, he said to his son Liholiho, ' Go thou and make supplication to thy god; I am not able to go and will offer my prayers at home.' When his devotions to his feathered god, Kukailimoku, were concluded, a certain religiously disposed individual, who had a bird god, suggested to induce that through its influence his sickness might be removed. The name of this god was Pua; its body was of a bird, now eaten by the Hawaiians, and called in their language *alae*. Kamehameha was willing that a trial should be made, and two houses were constructed to facilitate the experiment; but while dwelling in them, he became so very weak as not to receive food. After lying there three days, his wives, children, and chiefs, perceiving that he was very low, returned him to his own house. In the evening he was carried to the eating house, where he took a little food in his mouth, which he did not swallow; also a cup of water. The chiefs requested him to give them his counsel. But he made no reply, and was carried back to the dwelling house; but when near midnight, ten o'clock, perhaps, he was carried again to the place to eat; but, as before, he merely tasted of what was presented to him. Then Kaikioewa addressed him thus: 'Here we all are, your younger brethren, your son, Liholiho, and your foreigner: impart to us your dying charge, that Liholiho and Kaahumanu may hear.' Then Kamehameha inquired, 'What do you say?' Kaikioewa repeated, 'Your counsels for us.' He then said, 'Move on in my good way, and——.' He could proceed no further. The foreigner—Mr. Young—embraced and kissed him. Hoapili also embraced him, whispering something in his ear, after which he was taken back to the house. About twelve, he was carried once more to the house for eating, into which his head entered, while his body was in the dwelling house immediately adjoining. It should be remarked, that this frequent carrying of a sick king to and fro from one house to another, resulted from the taboo system then in force. There were at that time six houses connected with an establishment; one was for worship, one for the men to eat in, another for the women, a dormitory, a house in which to beat kapa, and one where at certain intervals the women might dwell in seclusion.

"The sick king was once more taken to his house, when he expired; this was at two o'clock—a circumstance from which Leleiohoku derived his name. As he breathed his last Kalaimoku came to the eating house to order those in it to go out. There were two aged persons thus directed to depart; one went, the other remained on account of love to the king, by whom he had formerly been kindly sustained. The children also were sent away. Then Kalaimoku came to the house, and the chiefs had a consultation. One of them spoke thus: 'This is my thought, we will eat him raw.' Kaahumanu replied, 'Perhaps his body is not at our disposal; that is more properly with his successor. Our part in him—the breath—has departed; his remains will be disposed of by Liholiho.'

"After this conversation, the body was taken into the consecrated house for the performance of the proper rites by the priest and the king. The name of this ceremony is *uko*; and when the sacred hog was baked, the priest offered it to the dead body and it became a god, the king at the same time repeating the customary prayers.

"Then the priest addressing himself to the king and chiefs, said, 'I will now make known to you the rules to be observed respecting persons to be sacrificed on the burial of this body. If you obtain one man before the corpse is removed, one will be sufficient; but after it leaves this house four will be required. If delayed until we carry the corpse to the grave, there must be ten; but after it is deposited in the grave, there must be fifteen. To-morrow morning there will be a taboo, and if the sacrifice be delayed until that time, forty men must die.'

"Then the high priest Hewahewa, inquired of the chiefs, 'Where shall be the residence of King Liholiho?' They replied, 'Where, indeed! you of all men ought to know.' Then the priest observed, 'There are two suitable places; one is Kau, the other, Kohala.' The chiefs preferred the latter, as it was more thickly inhabited. The priest added, 'These are proper places for the king's residence, but he must not remain in Kona, for it is polluted.' This was agreed to. It was now break of day. As he was being carried to the place of burial, the people perceived that their king was dead, and they wailed. When the corpse was removed from the house to the tomb, a distance of one chain, the procession was met by a certain man who was ardently attached to the deceased. He leaped upon the chiefs who were carrying the king's body; he desired to die with him, on account of his love. The chiefs drove him away. He persisted in making numerous attempts, which were unavailing. His name was Keamahulihia. Kalaimoku also had it in his heart to die with him, but was prevented by Hookio.

"The morning following Kamehameha's death, Liholiho and his train departed for Kohala according to the suggestions of the priest, to avoid the defilement occasioned by the dead. At this time, if a chief died the land was polluted, and the heirs sought a residence in another part of the country, until the corpse was dissected and the bones tied in a bundle, which being done, the season of defilement terminated. If the deceased were not a chief, the house only was defiled, which became pure again on the burial of the body. Such were the laws on this subject.

"On the morning in which Liholiho sailed in his canoe for Kohala, the chiefs and people mourned after their manner on occasion of a chief's death, conducting like madmen, and like beasts. Their conduct was such as to forbid description. The priests, also, put into action the sorcery apparatus, that the person who had prayed the king to death might die; for it was not believed that Kamehameha's departure was the effect either of sickness or old age. When the sorcerers set up by their fire-places sticks with a strip of kapa flying at the top, the chief Keeaumoku, Kaahumanu's brother, came, in a state of intoxication, and broke the flag-staff of the sorcerers, from which it was inferred that Kaahumanu and her friends had been instrumental in the death of Kamehameha. On this account they were subjected to abuse."—*Hawaiian Spectator, vol. 2, p. 227.*

CHAPTER VIII.

By the death of Kamehameha, the key-stone, which had continued firmly to unite the rites of heathenism with the policy of government, was removed, and the fabric gave evidence of speedy ruin. The scepticism which pervaded all ranks became manifest; none had a more hearty desire to be rid of the absurd restraints of their pagan ceremonies than the new king, Liholiho. The foreigners, whom he had gathered in his train, had succeeded in infusing their infidelity into his mind, without giving him any correct principles for the foundation of a new belief. In his love of sensual gratification, disregard of customs and traditions sanctioned by usage immemorial, desire yet fear of change, and ignorance of the means of accomplishment, he embodied the general spirit of his nation. The utter worthlessness of their old system and consequent evils were apparent to all, and its downfall ardently desired.

This condition of the public sentiment necessarily resulted from their commercial relations with foreigners. Those who railed at the doctrines of Christianity, were not wholly devoid of its spirit in their acts. Exposed as they were in manhood to the pernicious influences of a licentious heathenism and unfettered by a public moral sentiment, they too frequently fell in with the gross practices about them, and gave free rein to their lusts and avarice. Yet even with such, the good seed implanted by parents' counsels and the habits of Christian lands occasionally took root, and threw out blossoms which in contrast with the general fruit of paganism were sweet and attractive.

From what has been exhibited of native character previous to the commencement of intercourse with whites, it will readily be admitted that it was degraded in the extreme. Consequently the contact of a better race must necessarily cause some moral improvement. That this was the case, the condition of the Hawaiian nation at this epoch, plainly shows. The influence operating upon them had been directly commercial, dictated by the keenest self-interest; yet religious ideas and a desire for knowledge had been incidentally developed, by example or advice of benevolent individuals. The very fruits of civilization displayed to their covetous eyes in the superior knowledge, and above all in the property of the whites, begot in them a respect and desire for the faith which to their minds teemed so rich in temporal blessings. Example, expostulation and judicious reproof did much for the Hawaiians; the many cases where the direct influence of foreigners was exerted to ameliorate the lot of savages, and to implant a desire of civilization, cannot be all recorded. Much as was accomplished in this way, it must be acknowledged the result was small, compared with the greater influence of a selfishness, which cherished order and enterprise as the best means of promoting its own interests.

The example of the southern groups, in the destruction of their idols, added to the spreading disbelief. Incontestible evidences of the falsity of their oracles, together with the increasing inconvenience of their absurd rites, confirmed the scepticism. Those interested in the continuance of paganism, redoubled their efforts; threats, prophecies and promises were freely uttered, and as freely falsified by their own failure. Like Laocoon and his offspring in the folds of the serpent, heathenism writhed and gasped, each moment growing weaker in the strangling embrace of public opinion. It was noticed that foreigners conformed to none of their rites, yet they lived and prospered; their own countrymen who had gone abroad, lived in equal disregard of their ritual, and with like impunity. Individually, their memories convicted them of frequently breaking taboos, yet no evil overtook them, while they were unknown to the priests. Men and women had eaten together, and of forbidden food; the predicted judgments slept; their priests must be as the foreigners described them, liars, and the taboo system altogether foolish and contemptible. Drunken chiefs had often violated the most sacred injunctions; no divine vengeance pursued them; the female rulers had of late broken through all restrictions, yet prosperity and health were still theirs. Female influence went far to induce scepticism among the men. Having broken through the taboos themselves, they encouraged others to do the same; and in this way the conviction of the folly of supporting an oppressive and corrupt faith for the benefit of a few, daily strengthened.

The young prince Kauikeaouli, induced by his mother, and countenanced by his brother, broke the taboo by eating with Keopuolani. Liholiho perceiving no evil to ensue, remarked, "It is well to renounce taboos, and for husbands and wives to eat and dwell together, there will be less unfaithfulness and fraud." He was yet undecided, though Kaahumanu urged him "to disregard the restraint of taboo." On the very day of Kamehameha's death, a woman eat a cocoanut with impunity, and certain families displayed their contempt for these laws by feasting in common.

Liholiho remained ten days at Kohala, while the body of his father was being dissected. He then returned to Kailua, and on the second day after his arrival, the chiefs and inhabitants were collected to witness his induction into office.* He appeared in great state, dressed in rich clothing, with a feather mantle over his shoulders, and surrounded by a brilliant

* A list of the principal chiefs comprising the court of Kamehameha II., with their respective ranks, is necessary clearly to understand their relative situations and the stations they ultimately filled.

Kamehameha II. (Liholiho) king of all the group.
Kauikeaouli, his younger brother,
Nahienaena, his sister,
} Keopuolani, queen mother.

Kaahumanu (second in authority), dowager queen, and guardian of the kingdom.
Kalakua (Hoapili wahine), Namahana, } also former wives of Kamehameha I.
Kamamalu,
Kinau,
Kekauluohi, or Auhea,
Pauahi,
Kekauonohi,
} queens of Liholiho. The first two were daughters of his father by Kalakua.
Kaumualii, king of Kauai and Niihau.
Kealiiahonui, his son.
Kapuli, queen of Kauai.
Kalaimoku (William Pitt), originally of minor rank, but from his abilities promoted to fill the highest stations. He was prime minister, and, next to the king, the most influential man in the kingdom, though in authority subordinate to Kaahumanu.
Leleiohoku, his son.
Kaikioewa, guardian of the prince.
Keaweamahi, his wife.
Hoapili, guardian of Nahienaena.
Naihe, hereditary counsellor and national orator.
Kapiolani, his wife.

Kuakini (John Adams), governor of Hawaii. } These two were sons of Kamehameha's famous warrior and counsellor Keeaumoku, brothers also of Kaahumanu, Kalakua and Namahana; all descended from the royal family of Maui.
Keeaumoku (Cox), governor of Maui and its dependencies }

Boki, governor of Oahu, brother of Kalaimoku.
Liliha, his wife.
Wahinepio, sister of Kalaimoku, mother of the queen Kekauonohi.
Kahalaia, her son, and nephew of Kamehameha I.
Kapihe, commander of the king's vessels.
Kekuanaoa, superintendent of sandal-wood, and treasurer to the king.
Kakio, Kahokili, } brothers descended from the last king of Maui, and said to have Spanish blood in their veins.
Ii, Laanui, Puaa, Kalaikoa, } all of these were "punahele," or bosom companions of the king.

Beside these names the chiefs had a multitude of others, which answered for titles. They were frequently changed or assumed for trifling circumstances. The English appellations were bestowed by visitors. The Hawaiian names are highly figurative, and generally derived from some particular event which they were desirous of commemorating. Kamehameha signified "the lonely one;" Keopuolani, "the gathering of the clouds of the heavens;" Kauikeaouli, "hanging in the blue sky;" Kamamalu, "the shade of the lonely one;"—a name assumed after the death of her father; Hoapili, "close adhering companion," from the friendship which existed between the old king and himself; Kaahumanu, "the feather mantle;" Liliha, "the fat of hogs;" Auhea, literally "where," from her mournful repetition of this word, after the decease of Kamehameha; Kapiolani, "the captive of heaven;" Kalakua, "the way of the gods;" Kahekili, "thunder;" Paalua, a name of Kalaimoku's, "twice blind," expressing his grief by saying, he had lost his eyes for the deaths of Kamehameha and a favorite wife. Many of these nobles were remarkable for their corpulency. Some weighed from three hundred to four hundred pounds. Others were of herculean stature and strength, and well proportioned.

retinue. The kingdom was transferred to him by Kaahumanu, with the injunction of Kamehameha, that if he should not conduct himself worthily, the supreme power should devolve upon her. She also proclaimed it as the will of the late king, that he should share the administration with her, to which he assented. This haughty queen dowager had always retained her influence over her husband, and she had taken the precaution to secure to herself an authority equal to the king's, to the exclusion of the more legitimate rights of Keopuolani. As this assumption of power was universally acquiesced in, it must have been considered the true exposition of the commands of the deceased sovereign. This singular feature of a double executive has been retained, though modified, to this day, and the powers and limitations of both defined by written law. Neither could act officially without the other; each in turn being a check or support as the policy of the government required; and no act was valid without the sanction of both. This is an anomaly in governments, but the principle is so well understood and recognized by the Hawaiians, that the harmony of the kingdom has never been endangered. By interest and blood, these personages are closely allied, and mutual convenience cements the tie. The king is the lawful ruler and proprietor of all the islands, the negotiator in foreign relations; the premier is at the head of the internal policy, chief counselor, and in the king's absence, or death, acts as guardian for the heir, and becomes the responsible agent. This office originated in the affection of Kamehameha for his favorite queen, and the necessity of a check upon the heedless passions of his son. Liholiho was crowned, and received the title of Kamehameha II.

After the mourning for his father had terminated, the new monarch went to reside at Kawaihae, in deference to a superstition, which considered a place defiled by the death of a king. Sceptical as to the religion of his youth, yet wavering between old and new desires, he was undecided as to his course. On the one hand the priests exerted themselves to restore his credulity, while {alaimoku influenced ral policy. The latter iled, and Keopuolani :o eat in violation of the example herself. ering, temporarily re- rites and assisted at a ulging with his train, unkenness. He also ı to his god at Hono-

, the French corvette cinet commander, ar- ed a few days. Ka- : as he was familiarly minister, was induced of baptism, at Hono- the formula of the 'hurch. His brother, example; neither had ınsion of its meaning oth, after exchanging ɔycinet, returned to ɔus practices. Unin- is ceremony to them, ɔ their minds for fur- Kaahumanu, deter- ɔsition to the priests, re measures. In No- ord to the king, that t Kailua, she should To this he made no his retainers pushed ı the shore, and re- ter two days, indulg- revel. Kaahumanu le canoe for him, in ıght to Kailua. Be- rs were arranged for ment of their designs. ıd drank with the fe- st was prepared, after ɔ country, with sepa- sexes. A number of ertained at the king's. their seats, he delib- ked to the place re- ɔen, and seated him- To complete the 'ents of paganism, he te in freely partaking ıred for them, direct- do likewise; but he t which showed that ɔested himself of the ıd of habitual repug-

nance. This act however was sufficient. The highest had set an example, which all rejoiced to follow. The joyful shout arose, "the taboo is broken! the taboo is broken!" Feasts were provided for all, at which both sexes indiscriminately indulged. Orders were issued to demolish the heiaus, and destroy the idols; temples, images, sacred property, and the relics of ages, were consumed in the flames. The high priest, Hewahewa, having resigned his office, was the first to apply the torch. Without his coöperation the attempt to destroy the old system would have been ineffectual. Numbers of his profession, joining in the enthusiasm, followed his example. Kaumualii having given his sanction, idolatry was forever abolished by law; and the smoke of heathen sanctuaries arose from Hawaii to Kauai. All the islands uniting in a jubilee at their deliverance, presented the singular spectacle of a nation without a religion.

The character of the people at this period was peculiar. Superstition had been stripped of many of its terrors, and the general standard of morality had increased. Perhaps it is more correct to say that a knowledge rather than a practice of purer precepts existed. The most repulsive trait was the universal licentiousness; not greater than existed a century before, but was made a shameless traffic. Although the majority of the idols were destroyed, yet some were secretly preserved and worshiped. Centuries of spiritual degradation were not to be removed by the excitement of a day, or the edict of a ruler. Its interested advocates prepared for a fierce struggle. Availing themselves of their influence, they aroused the fears of multitudes; defection arose in the court, and some of its prominent members deserted Liholiho and joined Kekuokalani, a nephew of Kamehameha, who next in priestly rank to Hewahewa, had been incited to erect the standard of revolt with the promise of the crown if successful. The priests, fearing for their occupation and influence, urged him to the struggle by quoting a common proverb among them, "A religious chief shall possess a kingdom, but wicked chiefs shall always be poor." Said they, "of all the wicked deeds of wicked kings in past ages for which they lost their kingdoms, none was equal to this of Liholiho." Those who feared innovation and desired "to resist and turn back the tide of *free eating* which was threatening to deluge the land," and those who were dissatisfied with the existing government, gathered about him, and he soon became popular, as the defender of their ancient faith, and the protector of the oppressed. His mother endeavored to induce him to return to loyalty, but urged on by his partisans, who had committed themselves too far to retract, he turned a deaf ear to her entreaties.

In the first skirmish the loyalists were worsted. The news reaching the king, a consultation was held, in which Kalaimoku urged an immediate attack with all their force upon Kaawaloa, the headquarters of the enemy, and by a decisive blow to crush the insurrection before it had become formidable. It was determined, however, first to attempt conciliatory measures. Hoapili and Naihe were appointed ambassadors, and Keopuolani volunteered to accompany them. They reached the camp of Kekuokalani the same evening, and used every endeavor to effect an amicable settlement. Hoapili urged his relationship, for he was his uncle, and offered to leave the heathen worship optional with his partisans; but such was the rage and excitement of the rebels, that the ambassadors considered themselves fortunate to escape with their lives. Kekuokalani's forces marched that night on Kailua, with the intention of surprising it. The royal army, aware of the expected attack, prepared for action under the command of Kalaimoku. The armies met at Kuamoo; the engagement commenced in favor of the rebels, and had their fire-arms been equal to those of their adversaries, the day would have been decided in their favor; but a charge of the royal troops drove them with considerable slaughter toward the sea-side, where, under cover of a stone wall, they made for some time a successful resistance. A squadron of double canoes, in one of which was a mounted swivel, under the charge of a foreigner, sailed along the coast, and

their shot enfilading the rebels, did considerable execution, and created disorder in their ranks. This fleet was under the command of Kaahumanu and Kalakua; the women then, as anciently, engaging freely in battle.

Kekuokalani, though early wounded, gallantly continued the contest, and several times rallied his flying soldiers, but was at last struck down by a musket ball. Manona, his wife, during the whole action, courageously fought by his side; seeing him fall, she was in the act of calling for quarter to Kalaimoku and his sister, who were approaching, when a ball struck her on the temple, and she fell and expired upon the body of her husband. After this, the idolaters made but feeble resistance, though the action continued ten hours, until all the rebels had fled or surrendered. Most of the leaders perished. The victors carried their arms to Waimea, where another body of insurgents had taken the field. They were quickly subdued, and the king used his success with such moderation, that the whole island returned to its allegiance. About fifty of the rebels and ten of the royalists were killed in these engagements. The reaction against the tide of "free eating" in consequence of this victory was past. The chiefs who had so warmly sustained the priests, turned upon them and slew Kuawa, who was the chief agent in so fatally misleading Kekuokalani. They next attacked their idols, throwing them into the sea, using them for fuel, and otherwise expressing their rage and contempt for their pretended sanctity. "There is no power in the gods," said they, "they are a vanity and a lie. The army with idols was weak; the army without idols was strong and victorious."

Before the news of these remarkable events reached the United States, an interest had been awakened in the religious public, for the purpose of conveying to these islands the knowledge of the Holy Scriptures. Some Hawaiian youths, who had spent several years in that country, and ardently desired to carry the blessings of Christianity to their countrymen, increased this interest. Among them was George Kaumualii, son of the ruler of Kauai, who had been sent when a mere lad to the United States, to secure an education. The sea-captain who had him in charge died suddenly, and the funds provided for his expenses were lost. George thus cast upon his own resources, led an erratic life, and finally shipped on board of a United States' vessel, served during the war, and in 1814 was discharged at Charlestown. Here he was recognized by some benevolent individuals, who sent him to school, where he made respectable progress. His father had often expressed a wish for the arrival of teachers to instruct his people, in which desire he had been joined by several other chiefs; and he had expected good results from the education of his son. A letter had been received from him, written at school, in which he adjured his parents to renounce idolatry.

On the 30th of March, 1820, the first missionaries arrived at Hawaii. The cheering intelligence of the abolition of idolatry, and the favorable condition of the nation for the reception of a new religion, reached them that evening. They were kindly received, and Kalaimoku and the two dowager queens, on the first of April, made them a visit on board their vessel, the Thaddeus. On this occasion they were neatly dressed in foreign costume, and their urbanity made a favorable impression on the missionaries. April 4th, the brig anchored at Kailua; they met with a hospitable reception from Kuakini, who spoke English, and who seemed pleased at their arrival. Hewahewa* was cordial in his welcome to his "brother priests," as he called them. He possessed an uncommon liberality of mind; five months before he had counseled the king to destroy the idols, publicly renounced heathenism himself and ac-

knowledged his belief in one Supreme Being. "I knew," said he, "that the wooden images of our deities, carved by our own hands, were incapable of supplying our wants, but I worshiped them because it was the custom of our fathers; they made not the *kalo* to grow, nor sent us rain; neither did they bestow life or health. My thought has always been, 'Akahi wale no Akua nui iloko o ka lani'—there is 'one only Great God dwelling in the heavens.'"

By an old regulation, no foreigner was allowed permanently to remain without the consent of the king and his council. The former sovereign would not permit a foreigner to build a house on the islands except for himself. The missionaries made no attempt to settle on shore, until the free consent of the government had been formally obtained. Prejudices had been imbibed in regard to their intentions from evil disposed persons, who had represented that the Government of England would be displeased if missionaries from America were received; and that they intended eventually to monopolize both trade and political power. In a full meeting of the principal chiefs, these objections were overruled, and the missionaries, after a detention on board the brig of two weeks, were allowed to settle among the islands for one year, with the understanding that if they proved unworthy, they were to be sent away. Their chief patrons were Kaahumanu and Kalaimoku; the king, though friendly, was considerably influenced by vicious whites in his train, who foresaw that as knowledge increased, their importance and occupations would cease. The principal of these intriguers was John Rives, a low Frenchman, who filled the offices of cook, boot-black, secretary and boon companion, as the inclination of the king permitted. This man had the address, assisted by the influence of certain Englishmen, who were jealous of the Americans, to procure an edict for the expulsion of all residents of that nation. They were ordered to leave the islands by the first vessel, and the missionaries were expected to follow at the end of their year of probation. At this period the chiefs were fearful of giving umbrage to Eng-

* In a conversation with a gentleman, then on board the Thaddeus, Hewahewa related the method by which the king and himself came to understand each other relative to the destruction of the idols and their rites. So great was the fear that then existed upon the subject, that although each suspected the desires of the other, neither dared openly avow them. The conversation opened as follows: "What do you think of the taboos?" The reply was a similar interrogatory. King: "Do you think it well to break them?" Priest: "That lies with you." King, again: "It is as you say." And in this manner, endeavoring to penetrate each other's sentiments, they were led to the true expression of their thoughts.

land by showing favor to Americans in allowing them to settle, and they seem to have imbibed the idea that their sovereignty would be endangered by them. Mr. Young was ordered to write to England to inform the government that American missionaries had come there to reside to teach the people. The missionaries were forbidden to send for others, for fear they might be burdensome or dangerous.

In their interest for the spiritual welfare of the Hawaiians, the friends of the mission had not been unmindful of their physical improvement. Among the number of the first band, were a mechanic, physician, farmer and printer; also three clergymen, Messrs. Bingham, Thurston and Ruggles. All brought families, and their wives were the first civilized women who landed on these islands; much was expected from their exertions in setting examples of well regulated households, the pleasures of domestic life, and the beneficent influence of Christianity, particularly in ameliorating and elevating their sex.* Notwithstanding the licentious dispositions of the islanders, but one instance of an insult to a white female ever occurred. This happened at Kailua, soon after their arrival, where a native, smitten by the charms of one of their number, behaved with a rudeness which caused alarm. Liholiho, by the advice of the foreigners present, determined to put the fellow to death, but at the intercession of the husband of the insulted lady, spared his life. Mr. Thurston remained at this place. Mr. Bingham, with several others, proceeded to Honolulu, and there met with a kind reception from the foreigners and Governor Boki. Messrs. Ruggles and Whitney sailed for Kauai, with George Kaumualii. When the intelligence of

his arrival reached the king, he fired a salute of twenty-one guns, and manifested the utmost joy at once again embracing his son. He expressed great pleasure at the arrival of the missionaries, and engaged to provide liberally for them. From this time to his death, he remained their steadfast friend. To the captain of the brig he made valuable presents; on George he conferred the second station of importance in his island, besides giving him chests of clothing, the fort at Waimea, and finally a large and fertile valley. These distinctions elated the youth, though he continued disposed to serve his friends, and lived after a civilized manner. His father, to induce the settlement of all the missionaries with him, offered to build houses for them, for schools and for places of worship, and to use his authority in causing his people to respect the Sabbath, and attend their teachings. Messrs. Whitney and Ruggles, in July, took up their residence on Kauai. It is not an uninteresting event to record that the interpreter of Kaumualii, middle-aged native, had dined with General Washington in New York, who gave him clothes and treated him with much kindness as a native of the islands where Cook was killed.

At Oahu, the foreigners subscribed six hundred dollars for a school fund for orphan children; several manifested kindness and attention to the wants of the missionaries, a desire to aid them in their labors, and made laudable exertions for the education of their families.

The chiefs made many requests for artisans to instruct their people, with offers to support them handsomely.— Their applications were forwarded to the United States. The zeal of the king for instruction was truly royal; none of the common people were at first permitted to learn to read. In accordance with their ideas, knowledge, with the other good things of life, were the birth-right of rank. The progress of several of the chiefs was rapid. In July, Liholiho could read intelligibly; in November four schools, containing one hundred pupils, were established.

In the autumn of the year, Liholiho removed with his court to Lahaina, on

* The islanders thus expressed their opinions of the females: "They are white, and have hats with a spout; their faces are round and far in; their necks are long; they look well." They were called the "ai ocoe,"—long necked. In their curiosity, they followed them about in crowds, peering under their bonnets, and taking many liberties in handling their dress, which was permitted, as no offence was intended. When the missionaries first engaged in prayer, closing their eyes according to custom, the natives fled, imagining them to be sorcerers, engaged in praying them to death. The Holy Trinity was considered as three distinct Gods, to whom they gave the names of Kane, Kanaloa and Maui; and their first conceptions of the doctrines of Christianity were exceedingly rude, and imbued with the gross ideas of their old theology.

he island of Maui. He soon paid but ittle attention to his studies, and spent nost of his time in revelry, though he earnt rapidly, and his knowledge of eography, the customs, productions and overnments of other countries was respectable. The vagabond whites about im, taking advantage of his inquisitiveness, corrupted his mind by teaching im the basest phrases of their own language. By them he was freely supplied vith rum, and encouraged in gambling. At times he would spend many hours at is desk; and when not under the effects f liquor, was kind and affable. But his issipation lead to ruinous debts; the ich stores and treasures of his father vere squandered on favorites, and the nonopoly of the sandal-wood trade carried to such an extent as to produce the nost disastrous consequences. His favorites, availing themselves of his easy ;ood nature, in moments of conviviality btained orders for their personal benfit, which the people were obliged to xecute. Days were spent in drunkenless and debauchery. While intoxiated, the king purchased largely of oreigners, and profusely bestowed gifts f broadcloths, richest silks and satins, ind other costly goods upon his retainrs. Vessels were bought on credit, for arge sums; $80,000 in sandal-wood was aid for the Cleopatra's Barge, a yacht ent out by a Boston house at an exense of $30,000. $40,000 were given or the brig Thaddeus, $16,000 for a mall schooner, and their cargoes purhased at corresponding rates. Through uch extravagances heavy debts were ontracted, and to pay them monopolies reated and taxation carried to its utnost bounds; not a fowl or vegetable ould be sold without a premium paid o the chiefs. Vast quantities of sandalvood were collected and sold, but debts ugmented. The uniform and equalized system of Kamehameha I. was set aside, ind instead of one humane task-master, a thousand tyrants sprung into existence; he confusion which prevailed in court, spread elsewhere; the avarice, wants ind dissipation of the chiefs increased, as their resources diminished, and taxation, exposure and tyranny daily carried disease and death into the house-

holds of the tenantry. The infatuation prevailed during Liholiho's reign and did not cease until the conversion of some of the principal chiefs to the Christian religion. In the figurative tongue of Hawaii, rum was a "poison god," and debt, "a moth" which consumed the islands.

No sooner was the influence of the missionaries felt than vigorous efforts to counteract it were manifested. Some of the natives were influenced by the misrepresentations and calumnies of certain foreigners, but as a body they respected their motives and character. Every allowance that charity can permit should be made for those who by circumstances beyond their own control or by fortuitous events, have been exposed to unusual temptations. To youth ardent in the first impulses of manhood, unfixed by principle and unfortified by habit, no situations can be more alluring than those which while they give them a real or nominal superiority freely acknowledged by those around them, leave them full scope in the indulgence of their selfish desires. Such was emphatically the case here at this period and much later. The native women were but too proud to form connections with white men; the white men were equally free in the gratification of their sensual appetites. The temperance reformation was then in its infancy. The Pacific was notorious for its facilities for dissipation and its lack of moral restraint. Self-interest had led the whites here, and that gratified, nothing remained but physical pleasures. Had there been opportunities for moral and intellectual excitement and the amenities of social life, few even of those men would have gone the lengths they did in the indulgence of their passions. But as it was, history obliges us to record the fact that the whites settled on the islands were, with exceptions, it is true, a dissolute race, fostering in the natives the very habits they were too prone to indulge in by nature and custom, but which the missionary steadily frowned upon as at variance with the morality of the gospel. Under such circumstances, the whites could not but feel reproved by their example, and irritated by their preaching. Hence arose an enmity towards the mis-

14

sion, confined, at its commencement, to that class whose depraved appetites, or selfish interests, were affected by the increase of virtue and knowledge. The presence of pure domestic circles, while they reminded them of the homes they had left, contrasted widely with their loose lives even in the eyes of natives With some perhaps the novel restraint of an incipient public opinion gave an additional zest to their illicit pleasures. Hence we find a contest early commenced between certain of the whites and the missionaries; the one endeavoring to secure as mistresses the young half caste females of most promise in mind and body, and the other to provide for them permanently in schools where they would be rigidly secluded from vice and instructed in the knowledge and virtues of domestic life. But as might have been expected, the allurements of dress and an indolent life, corresponded too well with previous impressions and desires, to enable them in every instance to cleave to their white sisters, by whom they would have been taught habits of household industry, naturally repugnant to them. Beside the contests which arose from this rivalry between virtue and vice, others more directly appealing to the self-interest of the traders speedily operated to widen the breach between missionary and resident. It was unavoidable that the former in preaching to the chiefs should reprobate their extravagance and urge a more rational expenditure and husbanding the national resources.— Anxious as the missionaries were to avoid collision with their fellow-countrymen, exiles like themselves, though from far different motives, yet it was impossible for them not to proscribe to their converts, and indeed it was their duty, the wicked waste of merchandise which characterized the nation, and particularly to declaim against the use of ardent spirits. They came also to impart knowledge. As that knowledge increased among the people, they inquired the cost of foreign merchandise, and drew comparisons between it and the prices of the traders. The result went naturally to diminish extravagant desires and to lessen the chances of ex-

travagant profits. Some of the residents had the manliness and perception to foresee the true results, and cultivated an amity which was mutually beneficial. Respect was shown to the Sabbath, and the moral requirements of religion gradually observed; in the progress of civilization and Christianity they perceived real advantages, even to worldly pursuits, and they could not fail to respect virtues which though they might judge them ascetic, they knew to be sincere. But there were many who could ill brook to hear vice called by its legitimate name.

At an annual entertainment given in honor of his deceased father, at Kailua, in 1820, Liholiho invited all the mission family, and at his request, a Christian blessing was invoked. Kaumualii and his wife commenced their studies. In April, 1821, desirous of opening a friendly intercourse with Pomare, to witness for himself the results of missionary enterprise, and to procure valuable and useful exotics for his island, he planned a voyage to Tahiti in a fine brig belonging to him, lying at Waimea. At his request, two of the missionaries were to be in his suite. The calumnies of a few foreigners, who represented the Tahitian missionaries as great hypocrites and wholly unworthy of credit, and that the port charges would be ten thousand dollars, induced him to relinquish the undertaking. It is an ungrateful task to be obliged to recur to facts like these, but it is the duty of the historian to state the truth when necessary to his subject. Much of the earlier portion of Hawaiian history will be found pregnant with details highly discreditable to parties, who from the time their pleasures or interests came in conflict with the purer objects of the missionaries or the welfare of the people, maintained against both a bitter and reckless hostility. Enmity on one side was sometimes opposed by error on the other, and it will be my object to state faithfully whatever is requisite, but nothing more, for the clear understanding of the means and principles brought to bear on either side, by which the nation has laboriously worked its way into something like a regular and efficient government.

There will be found throughout the prolonged contest, a conservative, civilized and moral principle on the one hand; on the other an opposition, active, persevering and unsystematic; bound by no tie of a common purpose, except so far as interested views or factious dispositions knit men together. At this juncture commenced the struggle between the two parties; the one to uphold morality, strengthen the nation, and implant civilization on the basis of the word of God; the other, with no avowed purpose of opposing these views, but with maintaining an influence favorable to their own less rigid principles, and friendly to their personal desires. Good and evil will be found mixed in both. Without condemning in full all who chose to range themselves under the anti-mission banner, for among them were men who, though they erred perhaps in theory, yet in practice were often just, generous and serviceable, the most consistent friends of the nation will be found on the other side; not that they were always wise in their policy, or unselfish in their desires, but the principles they professed have been such as to secure the confidence of the people and preserve them through many periods of trial. At this date, however, they were suspicious of the designs of foreigners generally, a state of feeling kept alive by national prejudices, operating on the ill-informed minds of the natives. At Honolulu, uneasiness was expressed on account of a cellar that was being dug for Mr. Bingham's house, which had been sent out from America in frame. It was reported to be designed for a secret magazine of arms, and that a conspiracy was intended, in which the royal family were to be slaughtered. But stories so preposterous recoiled upon their authors. Before the expiration of the year, the chiefs were satisfied with the designs and intentions of the mission, and requested them to send for a reinforcement. The missionaries, desirous of securing still further the favor of the king, offered to have built for him a similar house, which was then considered, in comparison with the thatched huts, a grand affair.

Two Russian ships of war entered Honolulu harbor, April 2d, 1821. The officers were entertained on board "The Pride of Hawaii," his majesty's flag ship; late the "Cleopatra's Barge." In return, the king dined with the commodore, receiving the honors of his rank.

In July, Liholiho made the voyage to Kauai in an open boat. Having become jealous of Kaumualii, on account of a letter received from George, in which he was addressed simply as "king of the windward islands," he determined to visit him. Without disclosing his intention, he left Honolulu for Ewa on the 21st, with Boki, Naihe, and about thirty attendants, including two women. Having arrived off that place, the wind being fair, he ordered the helmsman to steer for Kauai. The chiefs expostulated, but to no purpose; the boatmen were frightened; they had neither water, provisions, chart nor compass; the island was one hundred miles distant; the channel rough, and the wind strong; moreover, Kaumualii might prove hostile, and crush their little party. But he was not to be dissuaded. The whim had seized him when half intoxicated, and, reckless of consequences, he sternly ordered them to proceed. Although he had never been at Kauai, he had a correct idea of its position; and spreading out his fingers, to represent the different points of the compass, naming them in broken English, he directed the course of the boat. Twice was it nearly capsized, and ready to sink. His attendants begged him to put back. "No," said the resolute king; "bail out the water, and go on; if you return with the boat, I will swim to Kauai." By vigorously plying their calabashes they kept it free from water, and continued their course, steering well to the northward. Just before dark the island was discovered, being several points on the lee bow. Putting their craft before the wind, they ran for it, though at considerable hazard from the sea, which continually broke over them. Early the next morning, exhausted with hunger and fatigue, they came to off the coast. As soon as Kaumualii was apprised of the circumstances, he hurried on board, and welcomed him to his dominions. A commodious house was prepared for him, and a brig and schooner despatched to Oahu to relieve the apprehensions of his subjects, and to bring two of his wives, with their retinues. Liliha, Boki's wife, arrived on the 23d, with four attendants, having made the voyage in a small canoe, in the management of which the natives are much more skilful than of boats, easily righting and freeing them from water when upset. The king was highly delighted with her adventurous courage.

The forbearance of Kaumualii when Liholiho was so completely in his power, is remarkable. Instead of making it an occasion of demanding the acknowledgment of his independence, or other confirmation of his present authority, with a spirit faithful to the very letter of his agreement with Kamehameha I., he voluntarily proposed a formal surrender of his kingdom to his guest. With much emotion, he addressed him in the following terms: "King Liholiho, hear! When your father was alive, I acknowledged him as my superior. Since his death, I have considered you, his rightful successor, and, according to his appointment, king. I have many muskets and men, and much powder; these, with my vessels, the fort, guns, and the island, all are yours. Do with them as you please. Send me where you please. Place what chief you please as governor here."* Naihe next addressed the assembled chiefs, and confirmed the dependence of Kaumualii to Kamehameha I. A deep silence prevailed, and all awaited with anxiety the reply of the monarch. With a mildness and suavity that deceived every one, he spoke as follows: "I did not come to take away your island. I do not wish to place any one over it. Keep your island, and take care of it just as you have done, and do what you please with your vessels." A shout of approbation resounded on all sides, and the magnanimity of both was highly lauded. After this scene Liholiho indulged in a debauch. Kaumualii was assiduous in his endeavors to please his royal visitor, whose insincerity and real designs were soon manifested. His beautiful vessel, "Haaheo o Hawaii,"—pride of Hawaii,—having arrived with the expected chiefs, Kaumualii was invited on board. While unsuspiciously seated in

* Vol. 18, Missionary Herald, p. 244.

the cabin, orders were secretly issued to make sail, and the generous and faithful chief was made a state prisoner, and borne from his dominions, which were entrusted to the guardianship of Keeaumoku. On the arrival of the royal parties at Honolulu, Kaumualii was compelled to part from his favorite Kapuli, and marry the imperious Kaahumanu. His title was continued to him, but with it no authority. After this dishonorable transaction, Liholiho proceeded to Hawaii. Kaahumanu also took to husband, Kealiiahonui, the son and heir of Kaumualii, thus holding father and son in her chains, which, at that period, were not altogether silken.

August 15, 1821, the first building—a small thatched edifice—erected on the islands for the service of Christianity, was dedicated at Honolulu.

Liholiho continued in his profligacy, occasionally manifesting a desire for better things. To the arguments of a missionary, who urged him to reform, he replied, "five years more and I will become a good man." Throwing off all restraint he became more reckless and dissipated than ever, spending his time in carousals in different parts of his dominions as humor prompted. In a fit of jealousy he beheaded a chief. A native who had stolen a few pieces of calico from him, he ordered to be ironed and thrown overboard.

As the sandal-wood diminished, or became more difficult to be procured, new means of extortion were contrived, one of which, from its singularity, deserves record. Whenever a chief erected a house of better appearance than common, no one was allowed to enter it, without a gift adequate to the rank and wealth of the visitor. The chiefs on such an occasion, would present the king with from fifty to a hundred dollars each; foreigners from twenty to thirty, and all other classes, to the lowest menial of his household, a proportionate sum. By this means, the king occasionally raised several thousand dollars—governors and chiefs lesser sums. The gross habits of the ruler infected the whole nation; female chiefs of the highest ranks boarded ships in a state of entire nudity, and not unfrequently visited the ladies of the mission in that condition, in the presence of the other sex. The saturnalian practices of all orders were too vile even to be alluded to; all the variety and indecency that lewdness and drunkenness could accomplish, were to be seen. At the present day, it is almost impossible to credit that such was ever the case; but the testimony is undoubted.

The first experiment in printing was made on the 7th of January, 1822. Keeaumoku was present. He assisted in setting up the types, and in taking a few impressions of the first sheet of the Hawaiian spelling-book. The king, chiefs and foreigners generally, took a deep interest in the success of this enterprise. The missionaries employed themselves assiduously during the first part of this year, in forming the Hawaiian alphabet upon the basis of a plan furnished them by the Hon. John Pickering, of Boston. The vowel sounds were the same as those employed in his alphabet of Indian languages. Printing gave a new impulse to the desire of knowledge among the chiefs. Kuakini, Kamamalu, Keeaumoku, and others, applied themselves diligently to learn to read and write. Liholiho again enlisted himself as a regular pupil; his brother and sister also became scholars. Even Kaahumanu shared in the general enthusiasm, and laid aside her cards for her alphabet. Others of lesser note followed the example of the royal family, and the schools flourished. The king was able in a few months to write legibly. In September, five hundred pupils were receiving instruction.

The arrival at Oahu in April, of Messrs. Tyerman and Bennet, deputized by the London Mission Society to visit all missionary stations, and the Rev. W. Ellis, a Tahitian missionary, with Auna, a converted chief of that nation, and his train, proved of much service to the American mission. By their efforts, the misunderstanding of their objects, which had been so industriously cultivated by inimical persons, was counteracted. Intelligent and influential Englishmen were found who countenanced its objects, which they would not have done, were they apprehensive of any sinister designs upon the islands by a rival nation. The people themselves could not believe that those who came with their families, indulged in ambitious or hostile views. Warlike designs and operations received no encouragement from the presence of females. At the joint request of the American mission and the chiefs, Mr. Ellis consented to return with his family and remain one year. By this act, the last lingerings of jealousy were dissipated, as it was seen that the benevolent of both nations united in laboring for their welfare. The sentiment that England was their protector, and exercised a species of guardianship over their country, still extensively prevailed, and was kept alive by acts of national courtesy, and the interested views of English traders, who wished to secure a superiority over other nations in mercantile transactions. The chiefs themselves, from their regard for Vancouver, and a desire of increasing their national importance, were not averse to an alliance, even if it implied some degree of vassalage; though their disposition to acknowledge themselves solely and wholly British subjects, was doubtless exaggerated. Their intercourse, from the commencement of the century, had been mostly with Americans, and their predilections toward that nation gradually increasing. When the deputation arrived, they found forty ships at anchor at Hawaii and Oahu, nearly all whalers from the United States.

The English government uniformly manifested a courtesy toward the islanders that was highly honorable. Without asserting a claim to the Islands, they recognized their nationality by numerous acts of courtesy, and encouragement toward civilization. On the first of May of this year, Captain Kent presented to Liholiho, in the name of His Britannic Majesty, a schooner of seventy tons, called the Prince Regent, fully rigged and coppered, with an armament of six guns. This was the long-promised vessel of Vancouver to Kamehameha; a gift which unfortunately neither he nor his royal friend had the satisfaction of seeing accomplished.

On Sunday, May 6th, Liholiho celebrated his accession to office, with a mixture of barbaric pomp and attention to civilized customs, which showed how rapidly the latter were becoming naturalized. Salutes were fired from ships and batteries, and national flags displayed from all the vessels in port. Great quantities of clothing were distributed, in which the soldiers and attendants made a respectable, though incongruous spectacle. Gaudily colored uniforms, richly bedizened with gold lace; chapeaux, boots, plumes, silk stockings, satins, velvets, broadcloths, *tapas* and calicoes; gold watches, canes and jewelry; feather cloaks, helmets and *kahilis*, were seen in the throng. Some wore dresses fashioned by foreign artisans; others, a mixture of the past and present costumes. Brilliant silks, wrapped in many folds, encircled the waists of portly dames, while flower wreaths, or hair necklaces, negligently rested upon their exposed bosoms. A dinner was prepared and served in European style; and throughout the whole, notwithstanding the quantity of ardent spirit consumed, an unusual decorum prevailed. Eighty dogs formed a portion of the viands. The common orders indulged in excesses of the vilest description.

The anniversary of the national independence of the United States of North America, was celebrated on the fourth of July, in a more rational manner. An oration was delivered in the mission chapel, by J. C. Jones, Esq., acting American consul, and a poem recited by Mr. Bingham. A prayer was also offered and a psalm sung. After which the company adjourned to a public dinner, the king with the principal foreign residents being present.

The first Christian marriage was celebrated, August 11, between two converted natives. On the 13th, Kaumualii and Kaahumanu, with a retinue of nearly twelve hundred people, sailed for Kauai. Four small vessels conveyed this multitude, which crowded their decks, and even occupied the chains, tops and bowsprits. Previous to their departure Kaahumanu issued a general ordinance against drunkenness, which was proclaimed by public criers throughout the town of Honolulu. The object of the voyage was to collect the annual tribute of sandal-wood. While they were on the island, the wife of the governor, Keeaumoku, died. Though none of the prin-

cipal chiefs joined in the ceremonies, the heathen customs of sacrifices of animals, with chants and prayers, were practiced for several successive days. In December following they returned. A few days afterward a young member of the royal family died, and at the request of his relatives received a Christian burial. It is necessary to notice many events of little interest by themselves, but proper to record, that the gradual development of the spirit of Christianity, with its frequent fluctuations, may be clearly traced.

Upon the departure of the English deputation, Captain Kent, with whom they sailed, was charged with the following letter to the King of England. Though it bears the signature of Liholiho, it was not written by him, but was supposed to convey his real sentiments. Towards the ship's company he behaved with a liberality worthy of his father.

"*Oahu, Sandwich Islands, August* 21, 1822.
"MAY IT PLEASE YOUR MAJESTY:
"In answer to your Majesty's letter from Governor Macquarrie, I beg to return your Majesty my most grateful thanks for your handsome present of the schooner, Prince Regent, which I have received at the hands of Mr. J. R. Kent.
"I avail myself of this opportunity of acquainting your Majesty of the death of my father, Kamehameha, who departed this life the 8th of May, 1819, much lamented by his subjects; and, having appointed me his successor, I have enjoyed a happy reign ever since that period; and I assure your Majesty it is my sincere wish to be thought as worthy your attention as my father had the happiness to be during the visit of Captain Vancouver. The whole of these islands having been conquered by my father, I have succeeded to the government of them, and beg leave to place them all under the protection of your most excellent Majesty; wishing to observe peace with all nations, and to be thought worthy the confidence I place in your Majesty's wisdom and judgment.
"The former idolatrous system has been abolished in these Islands, as we wish the Protestant religion of your Majesty's dominions to be practiced here. I hope your Majesty may deem it fit to answer this as soon as convenient; and your Majesty's counsel and advice will be most thankfully received by your Majesty's most obedient and devoted servant,
"KAMEHAMEHA II.,
"King of the Sandwich Islands.
"To GEORGE IV., King of England."

Notwithstanding efforts made to induce the king entirely to abandon his studies, and give himself up once more to debauchery, he persevered and succeeded in acquiring the elements of instruction, while the truths of Christianity were acknowledged by his intellect, though set at nought by his conduct. Of their requirements he was not wholly ignorant before the arrival of the missionaries. When one of his wives, soon after the Thaddeus anchored at Kailua, urged their being permitted to remain, he jocosely observed, "If I do, I shall be obliged to put you away, for their religion allows but one wife." The interest of the other chiefs daily became more apparent. In February, 1823, they proclaimed a law for the public observance of the Sabbath, and imposed a fine of one dollar upon all who should be guilty of laboring upon that day. This was the dawning of that legislation which was afterwards so violently opposed by foreigners, and finally resulted in bringing the chiefs and missionaries into intimate relations. It will be seen that it bore the arbitrary impress of the old. It was natural for them to suppose that by the simple promulgation of their will the natives could be compelled to observe the new doctrines. Externally it proved the case. Many became convinced of their truth and utility, though clinging to past license; the flesh pots of Egypt were not to be forgotten in a day; with a few, they produced a thorough reformation. Among the most prominent was a blind bard, of the name of Puaaiki, who afterward received the baptismal name of Bartimeus. His memory was prodigious. Versed in all their former history, he became an equal adept in the instructions of the new teachers. Not a thought was uttered, or advice given, but he treasured it up. He soon became a valuable acquisition to the mission, and qualified to impart wisdom to others. To his death he could repeat sermons delivered by the earliest missionaries, and his life gave evidence of the sincerity of his conversion.

In March, 1823, Hoapili was sent with Keopuolani, whom he had married, to Maui, as governor. Puaaiki was received into their family as a domestic chaplain. Previous to this, on the 27th of April, the ship Thames arrived from America, bringing a large missionary reinforcement. They were cordially welcomed; some of the chiefs were really desirous of securing them in their families as religious teachers, while all received them as public benefactors. The utility of writing, by the knowledge of which their orders were transmitted with so much ease and accuracy, with other useful arts derived from the mission, had created a powerful revolution in

their favor. All the distrust which had been so signally manifested in 1820, was now removed. Liholiho, notwithstanding his constant strait for money, remitted the harbor fees, amounting to one hundred and sixty dollars, both to the vessel that brought Mr. Ellis, and the Thames. To the captain of the latter he addressed a letter, of which the following is a literal translation:

"To Captain Clasby:
"Love to you. This is my communication to you. You have done well in bringing hither the new teachers. You shall pay nothing on account of the harbor —no, nothing at all.
"Grateful affection to you,
"LIHOLIHO IOLANI."*

On the 26th of the same month his majesty held his annual festival in celebration of the death of Kamehameha I. On this occasion he provided a dinner in a rural bower, for two hundred individuals. The missionaries and all respectable foreigners were present; the dresses were an improvement upon the costumes of the preceding year. Black was the court color, and every individual was required to be clothed in its sombre hue. Kamamalu appeared greatly to advantage. The company were all liberally provided for by her attentions, and even a party of sailors, to the number of two hundred, who were looking on with wistful eyes, were served with refreshments. While at the table, a procession of four hundred natives appeared in single file, clad in white, and deposited their taxes at the feet of the king. The festival was prolonged for several days, and was concluded by a procession in honor of his five queens. Its ceremonies were striking and interesting; the more so as being the last national exhibition of their most ancient customs, combined with the splendor derived from commerce, and arranged by their taste. Kamamalu was the most conspicuous personage in the ranks.† She was seated in a whale-boat, placed upon a frame of wicker-work, borne on the shoulders of seventy men. The boat and the platform, which was thirty feet long by twelve wide, were overspread by costly broadcloth, relieved by the richest colored and most beautiful tapas. The carriers marched in a solid phalanx, the outer ranks of which wore

* A favorite name of his.   † Stewart's Journal, p 91.

a uniform of yellow and scarlet feather cloaks, and superb helmets of the same material. The queen's dress was a scarlet silk mantle, and a feather coronet. An immense Chinese umbrella, richly gilded and decorated with tassels and fringes of the same gaudy color, supported by a chief, wearing a helmet, screened her from the sun. Kalaimoku and Naihe stood behind her on either quarter of the boat, both with *malos*, or girdles of scarlet-colored silk, and lofty helmets. Each bore a *kahili*, the staff of royalty; these were nearly thirty feet high, the upper part being arranged so as to form a column or plume of scarlet feathers of a foot and a half in diameter, and from twelve to fourteen feet long; the handles were surrounded with alternate ivory and tortoise-shell rings, beautifully wrought and highly polished. More magnificent insignia of rank, conveying at once the ideas of grandeur, state and beauty, as they towered and gracefully nodded above the multitude, were never devised by barbarians.

Kinau and Kekauonohi, appeared in similar pomp, and in lieu of a boat, were mounted upon double canoes. The prince and princess wore simply the native costume; the *malo* and *pau*, made from scarlet silk. Their carriage consisted of four Chinese field bedsteads, fastened together, covered with handsome native cloth, and surmounted with canopies and drapery of yellow figured moreen. Hoapili and Kaikioewa, the one bearing a dish of baked dog, the other a calabash of poi, and another of raw fish, the prime articles of Hawaiian diet, followed them as servants; this was indicative of their comparative relations to the royal children, notwithstanding their own proud lineage, and high offices; the former being their step-father, and the latter their guardian.

The dresses of the queens-dowager were remarkable for their size and expense. Seventy-two yards of cassimere of double fold, half orange and half scarlet, were wrapped around the figure of one, till her arms were sustained by the mass in a horizontal position, while the remainder, forming an extensive train, was supported by a retinue selected for that purpose.

Pauahi, when an infant, experienced a narrow escape from being burnt to death, from an accidental ignition of gunpowder, by which five men were killed, her house destroyed, and she badly injured. Hence her name, *pau*, completed, and *ahi*, fire. To commemorate this event, after performing her part in the procession, she alighted from her couch, and set it on fire, with all its expensive decorations; reserving only a handkerchief, as an apology for a covering, she threw all of her dress into the flames; her attendants imitated her example, and a valuable amount of cloth, both native and foreign, was consumed.

The richness and variety of the dresses and colors, and the exhibition of the wealth and power of the chiefs, their hereditary symbols of rank, the stately *kahilis*, splendid cloaks and helmets, and necklaces of feathers, intermingled with the brilliant hues and deep green of the flowers and wreaths, from their native forests, rendered the spectacle at once unique and attractive. Groups of dancers and singers, to the number of several hundred, accompanied the procession, enthusiastically shouting their adulations in the willing ears of their chiefs. The beating of drums and other rude music, swelled the wild notes of their songs, and the acclamations of thousands of voices, with the heavy tramp of their feet, broke in upon the deep-toned choruses and thrilling responses. Amid the throng the king, with his suite, excited by the revelry of a week's duration, mounted upon saddleless horses, rode recklessly about; a body-guard of fifty men, dressed in shabby uniform, followed by a multitude, shouting and cheering, endeavored to keep pace with the royal troop.

In September, Keopuolani was taken ill; all the principal chiefs assembled at Lahaina and wailed around her couch. As her disease gained ground, the utmost affection and grief were manifested by all classes. Among the people, alarm for the consequences of her death prevailed. Being the highest female chief, the usual excesses were expected to ensue. Many natives fled to the mountains; the foreigners prepared to retreat to the shipping, and urged the missionaries to follow their example. For a year previous, Keopuolani had expressed a deep interest in the instructions of the missionaries, and her deportment gave evidence of a decided change of character. Having given sincere proofs of her conversion, the rites of baptism were administered. Her dying counsel was directed to the religious welfare of her relatives and people. She strove to influence the king to abandon his cups, and for a few weeks he continued perfectly sober. She enjoined, and her wishes were proclaimed as laws by Liholiho and Kalaimoku, that no heathen rites should be observed at her death. So public an example, from the highest authority, of the breaking down of usages, sanctioned by the custom of centuries, proved their death blow. Once abrogated, few could regret the attendant disorder, debauchery and crime. On the 16th she died. Her remains were interred in accordance with her desires; but the deep wailings of the people were not to be suppressed, though the rites of Christian sepulture were hers. The corpse, covered with a rich pall, was borne by the five queens of Liholiho and the wife of Boki; around it were the family as principal mourners. Chiefs and people, foreigners and missionaries, joined in the procession, bearing badges of mourning, while the tolling of the bell, and the firing of minute guns proclaimed its solemn progress, until it reached the stone tomb prepared for its reception. As was customary, the relatives erected little booths in its vicinity, in which they dwelt for a season. The people of the district were employed in removing the stones of a dilapidated heiau, to form a wall around her burial place. All the chiefs, except the king and Hoapili, assisted in this labor with their own hands; and the singular spectacle was presented of the portly Kaahumanu, and her almost bulky husband carrying large stones, while stout men walked lazily beside them, bearing nothing but light feathered staffs, the badges of their authority.

Keopuolani was born in 1778; she had given birth to eleven children, of whom Liholiho was the second. He, with that young prince and princess were all that survived.

15

In proportion as the mission flourished, and the doctrines of Christianity began to have a perceptible influence upon the acts of the government and the character of the nation, in like manner did the opposition increase. No artifice was too low, nor falsehood too gross, for its purposes. In most cases, the vileness of the one, and the shallowness of the other, defeated their design. As the narrative proceeds, the nature and design of the enmity to the spread of Christianity will be more clearly seen. Originating, as has been shown, in a few vagabonds, the contamination gradually spread to persons, if not of better principles, of more knowledge; and the falsities so diligently uttered by the former, found their way into journals and reviews, whose editors would have shrunk from contact with their authors, as from plague-spots, had they but known them. In no place has the triumph of the cross been more signal than at the Hawaiian Islands; in none other has enmity been more bitterly manifested. Instead of adducing arguments against supposed faults of the system, or affording any tangible ground on which to base an attack, the characters of its advocates were assailed by the grossest calumnies, and the faith and resolution of its converts, by the most artful designs. Those who so prominently figured in these attempts, had the satisfaction occasionally to witness the instructions of the benevolent made abortive, and grief, misery and shame carried into families which else would have continued in well-doing. While the death-bed scene remained fresh in the memory of the king, his conduct was that of a reclaimed man; but in an evil hour, he listened to the desires of some whites, who persuaded him to visit a vessel, under the pretence of showing him some new goods. Several dinner parties had been provided for him previously on the Sabbath, which he had uniformly declined attending. But in this instance, suspecting no sinister object, he went on board. The favorite liquors were proffered, which he refused. A bottle of cherry-brandy was then produced, an article he had never seen, and which, being told it would not intoxicate, he tasted. The insatiable thirst was aroused, and his entertainers plied the glasses until the king, requesting some to carry ashore, prepared for a revel. Not content with this, the sacred forms of religion were made a scorn and by-word. One chief was taught to call his fellow, as a nickname, Jehovah. A foreigner engaged in mock prayer before Kuakini, while another wrote the vilest words of the English language for his perusal.

Hoapili set an example of further innovation upon their customs. Instead of selecting a number of wives as soon as the corpse of his consort was removed, to be changed at will, he waited more than a month, and then was joined in matrimony to Kalakua, who took the name of Hoapiliwahine. The ceremony was performed October 19th, in church, by the Rev. Wm. Richards. This was the more to his credit, as there were five candidates for his household from among the highest females.

About this time, Liholiho began to entertain a design of visiting England and the United States. Beside the natural curiosity for viewing foreign lands, he was desirous of an interview with the governments, and entering into formal relations with them. In October, a council was held at Lahaina, in which, after a full discussion, it was decided that he should embark in the English ship L'Aigle, Captain Starbuck. Kamamalu, his favorite wife, Boki and Liliha, Kapihe and Kekuanaoa, with a steward and a few male servants, were to accompany him. It was the wish of the king and the chiefs, that Mr. Ellis should go with him to act as interpreter and counselor. A large sum was offered for his passage. Captain Starbuck alledging his inability to provide accommodations for his family, he was compelled to remain. Kauikeouli was appointed successor to the throne in case the king never returned, and was also made heir to his private lands. The government was to be administered by the chiefs in council, the regency being invested in Kaahumanu, with Kalaimoku as prime minister. November 18th, the royal train went on board the L'Aigle, and under a salute from all the shipping and batteries, sailed in company with ten other vessels for Oahu. On the 27th, the L'Aigle left Honolulu, amid the sad forebodings of the people. Kamamalu remained on shore to the last, mingling her tears with those of her attendants, to whom her amiability and attention to domestic concerns had greatly endeared her. Before stepping into the boat, after the manner of her forefathers, she thus chanted her farewell: "O! heaven; O! earth; O! mountains; O! sea; O! my counselors and my subjects, farewell. O! thou land for which my father suffered, the object of toil which my father sought. We now leave thy soil; I follow thy command; I will never disregard thy voice; I will walk by the command which thou hast given me." Salutes were fired, and the ship soon disappeared before a favorable breeze.

While preparations for sailing were being made, Rives, the Frenchman, endeavored to persuade his royal master to permit him to join the train. Not wishing to disgrace his retinue by such an appendage, he refused; but Rives managed to convey himself aboard by stealth, and after the vessel was underway, baggageless as he was, contrived to secure permission to remain. Boki, though of inferior talents to his brother, was as good a specimen of the chiefs, as Kamamalu of the beauties of her native islands. She was then twenty-six years of age.

Upon the first arrival of the mission families, they suffered from the thieving propensities of the natives, who did not consider it disgraceful to pilfer from the whites, as they had so much property; even the chiefs indulged in the practice, and kept professed thieves. But as they became convinced of its dishonesty, they exerted themselves to eradicate the habit. The most decisive measure for its suppression, was performed in December of this year by the young prince. His Kahu, to whom he was strongly attached, and who had borne him in his arms since his birth, was detected in stealing. The prince immediately expelled him from his household and gave the office to another petty chief.

At Kailua, Kuakini built a house of worship within the inclosure of a ruined temple, at which the average attendance on the Sabbath was eight hundred.— Other chiefs united with him in enforcing the observance of the day. Kapiolani dismissed all of her husbands but Naihe; became temperate, and to her death. in 1841, was a sincere believer. No other female adopted more thoroughly the habits of civilized life. Her house was tastefully arranged and furnished, and she was excelled by none in neatness, and attention to all her duties.

Keeaumoku, governor of Kauai, died on March 23d, 1824. On the 26th of the following May, the ex-king of Kauai breathed his last. No chief had won more upon the affections of the missionaries. He had been an intelligent convert, and, toward the latter part of his life, was active in exhorting his countrymen to cast aside their vain superstitions and embrace the truth. He was remarkable for his personal beauty and dignified and gentlemanly manners.— His dominions were bequeathed to Liholiho, to be held in trust by Kaahumanu and Kalaimoku. According to his last request, his remains were carried to Lahaina, and deposited by the side of Keopuolani, to whom he had been closely united in friendship.

On the 30th, the chapel at Honolulu was destroyed by an incendiary; Kalaimoku, in a few weeks, caused another and more spacious one to be erected.

When the news of the death of Kaumualii reached Kauai, the people broke through all restraint and renewed their heathen practices. Riot, pillage, licentiousness, knocking out of teeth, and mutilation of limbs, spread over the island. During this general anarchy they prepared for war, as it was thought a favorable time to throw off the yoke. The nephew of Kalaimoku, Kahalaia, a cruel and weak man, had been appointed governor. No sooner had he landed than the Kauaians manifested their detestation of him by the destruction of public property and other acts of insubordination. In two weeks, Kalaimoku, accompanied by Kekauluohi, arrived to receive the submission of the chiefs, arrange the affairs of the island and look after the wreck of the *Pride of Hawaii*. On landing at Hanalei, they narrowly escaped seizure and assassination. In a council at Waimea, the Kauai chiefs demanded a new division of lands and property, which Kalaimoku, in obedience to the will of Kaumualii, refused.

George Kaumualii, or Humehume, as he was called by his countrymen, had rapidly degenerated in character since his arrival. Elated by the honors conferred upon him, he aspired to greater consequence. Upon the arrival of Kalaimoku at Waimea, he with other chiefs hastened to tender their gifts. Kiaimakani, the most active of the dissatisfied chiefs, meeting them, proposed to proclaim Humehume their ruler.—" Come with us—you shall be our king; the islands are yours, as they were your father's. Much will we fight for you." He immediately joined their party. On the 8th of August Humehume, at the head of a numerous but undisciplined band, attacked the fort at Waimea. The rebels suddenly entering the gates, got possession of the magazine and armory. Instead of following up their success by quietly putting to death the few soldiers that were mostly sleeping or but half armed, the principal part of the garrison being encamped outside with Kalaimoku, they vain-gloriously fired their guns. This aroused the main body, who joining those inside the fort, after some sharp fighting, and losing six of their number, drove the rebels out, with the loss of ten. In this attack, Kalaimoku narrowly escaped with his life. Among the killed on his side were two Englishmen. Messrs. Bingham and Whitney, with their families, resided in a house near the walls, and were repeatedly endangered by the balls of both parties. As soon as the fight terminated, Kalaimoku sent for them, knowing that they would be exposed to the fury of the disappointed chiefs who were mostly pagans. As he was still closely besieged in the fort, he advised them to take passage in the schooner which he was on the point of despatching for Oahu with news of the insurrection. Accordingly they embarked; with them went a fine looking young chief, who had been made prisoner. Knowing the fate that awaited him, he requested to be shot, but was carried on board and confined. When midway between the two islands, he was sent for; "I know what you want," he replied, as he manfully ascended the companion-ladder. Hardly had his feet touched the deck, when a knife was passed through him, and his body immediately thrown overboard. A number of lesser note were served in the same manner; a method of disposing of state prisoners which had been adopted in lieu of the former sacrifices.

Had the widow of Kaumualii, the repudiated Kapule, who was greatly beloved, joined the rebels, the consequences would have been much more serious. Her loyalty and firmness preserved many true to the will of their late king; and her exertions, though poorly repaid, were considered as highly serviceable. The news of the war created a great excitement at the windward islands. When the intelligence reached Oahu, the enthusiasm was so great that the people rushed to the fort and demanded arms, that they might embark immediately for Kauai. Runners spread the cry of "rebellion" over the island. The vessels in the harbor were quickly filled with warriors, who embarked in such haste as almost to neglect arming themselves, and without provisions of any kind, they sailed without delay for the seat of war. One was detained to carry arms and munitions. The chiefs prepared energetically to crush the insurrection, but the people, in many places left to themselves, indulged in riot and dissipation. A thousand warriors, headed by Hoapili, Kahekili and Kaikioewa, reinforced Kalaimoku. A skirmish ensued between the hostile parties at Wahiawa; the numbers and ardor of the government troops soon dispersed the rebels, and they fled in all directions, leaving the ground strewn with slain, among whom was Kiaimakani. In the action and pursuit one hundred and thirty were slaughtered; of the loyalists but one fell. George Kaumualii fled to the mountains, where after enduring great misery and privation for two months, he was captured. Kalaimoku had issued the most positive orders, that he should be taken alive and unharmed, even if he made resistance to the attacking party. After his capture, his

kindness to him was unremitting, both for the sake of his old friend the late king, and a feeling of compassion for the folly and indiscretion of George, who had been made a mere tool in the hands of the conspirators. He kept him near his person, and allowed him only to eat of the food prepared for himself, for there were many who desired to take his life, and would not have hesitated at treachery when force was found unavailing. Kalaimoku shortly after sent him to Honolulu, where he continued in honorable captivity until his death, which happened not long after.

After the first resentment had subsided, the victors treated the conquered with a moderation before unknown in their contests. This was owing to the advice of the missionaries, who on this occasion openly counseled them "to proceed with confidence and courage—that a just God would give them the victory since the blame was evidently on the side of the enemy." Kaahumanu and the other principal chiefs arriving at Kauai, a grand council was held for the final settlement of the island. It was formally annexed to the kingdom of Liholiho, and Kaikioewa appointed governor. The disaffected chiefs and their tenants were distributed among the other islands, where it would be impossible for them to combine in another conspiracy. Their lands were divided among the loyal favorites and chiefs, who filled the minor offices with their creatures. The poor serfs were looked upon in the contemptuous light of conquered rebels, and for many years groaned under the heavy exactions of their new lords.

The desire of education daily grew more popular. Before the expiration of the year, two thousand had learned to read, and fifty natives were qualified as elementary teachers. At a public examination of schools, Kaahumanu was the first pupil examined. A feeble attempt was made, by a few individuals of rank, whose desires yearned toward the old deeds of revelry, to revive dances and other idolatrous practices. The young princess was persuaded to engage in a heathen sacrifice. Wahinepio, sister to Kalaimoku, was the most active of this party, which originated from a lingering faith in the superstition of "praying to death." Whatever belonged to a chief was carefully disposed of, to prevent any one inimical from obtaining an article which would give them the power of causing a mortal illness. A portion of the wardrobe of the princess which had been cast aside, was secretly buried in the sea; but one of the dresses, it was supposed, had been stolen by a sorcerer, and her attendants prevailed upon her to offer a sacrifice, as the only means of averting the evil. This was covertly done at a village eight miles from Lahaina; that place being supposed to be too much under the influence of Jehovah to ensure success. This is only worthy of note as being the last heathen rite of this character, sanctioned by the authority of a high chief.

The principal rulers not only were now favorers of the mission, but sincere converts to Christianity. Old as were many, they acquired the art of writing, and wrote letters of gratitude to the patrons of the mission in America. That fierce warrior and sagacious statesman, Kalaimoku, gave the last hours of his active life to the support of its doctrines. By example, he exhibited their beneficial effects, and by authority, brought their influence to bear upon the nation. But no brighter change was seen, than in Kaahumanu. In the days of her heathenism, she was a cruel, haughty, imperious woman; the glance of her angry eye carried terror to all her obsequious and crouching vassals; not a subject, however high his station, dared face her frown. Many suffered death in her moments of irritation: her carriage was pride itself; for among those who held rank in the greatest estimation, she was the proudest. Though friendly at first to the missionaries, her deportment was lofty and disdainful. Their courtesies were met with an averted eye, and her little finger simply extended to a proffered hand. Her decision, energy and ability, united as they were in harmony with the experience and good judgment of Kalaimoku, extricated the nation from difficulties into which it was frequently involved, by the follies and extravagance of the king. Their sternness humbled the most rebellious, and preserved order amid many trying scenes. By them the designs of evil-minded foreigners were nipped in the bud; their cunning and temptations availing little against the superior penetration of these chiefs.

After her conversion, her violent passions were checked; the cold and contemptuous behavior gave way before the strong, natural flow of affection. To the missionaries she became warmly attached; and among her own people, and even foreigners, her character was so entirely altered, her deportment so consistent with the principles of her faith, that none could doubt its sincerity. "The new and good Kaahumanu," passed into a proverb.

The same activity and firmness which were infused into all her former acts, became united with real desires for the welfare of her subjects. Close attention was given to all affairs of government. Idols were ferreted out and destroyed; the people exhorted to forsake their vices, and schools encouraged. The machinery of the old system, which centered all power in the hands of the chiefs, in whom, it may with propriety be said the nation was individualized, was brought to aid the moral reform. The will of the rulers being the will of the populace, the revolution that followed was not surprising. As the weathercock is affected by the wind, so was public opinion at this era, by the example of the chiefs. Providentially, they had become Christians. Its pure doctrines were manifested in the lives of a few of all degrees, but with the mass it was an external habit, like the clothes borrowed from civilization. For centuries the temporal and spiritual governments had been closely united. As it was impossible to enlighten the minds of the chiefs in the same ratio as their morals, or at once to infuse into monarchists the democratic tendencies of the age, this same principle was incorporated with all their new acts. So habituated had they become to swaying the public by simple expressions of will, that in their zeal for the diffusion of Christianity, they blindly pursued the same course. In moral degradation, the minds of all had heretofore been upon a level, and it was as easy to agitate the mass by an edict or example, as to stir the waters of a calm lake by the casting of a stone. But there now existed a wide difference. The gale in its violence may flatten the sea, but when it lulls, the commotion becomes deeper and stronger than before. It will be perceived that, whenever the powerful arm of government was manifested, vice and corruption cowed their heads and pursued their ends covertly; a great apparent moral revolution occurred, which the missionaries, not rightly understanding, were led to exaggerate.

At this time commenced the cry against the missionaries, that they meddled in government affairs. So far as their influence affected the chiefs this was true. That they gave advice in emergencies, when asked, is evident from the humane influence they exerted, and the encouragement they afforded the loyal chiefs in the late rebellion at Kauai. It may be that they were not always sufficiently frank and open in it, and shrunk unnecessarily from encountering boldly the opposition when their assistance would have been serviceable to the chiefs; or they rendered it in too cautious and non-committal a manner for it to avail much at a crisis, though it effected much in the general issue. The charge was raised by the same class of individuals who as actively endeavored to corrupt the chiefs. They had perseveringly tried to influence the government to continue in vice; yet with an inconsistency to which they seem to have been entirely blind, they charged those whose lives and instructions were devoted to removing evil, with endeavoring unworthily to effect what they were themselves pursuing. In the struggle, religion prevailed, and the discomfitted assailants at once exclaimed, church and state; by-words well calculated to impress those ignorant of the nature of the Hawaiian policy, with the idea that the missionaries sought to incorporate the two, and fatten upon both. They found them united by the alliance of ages; it is not politic, even if possible, for man rudely to sweep away the prejudices of a nation. It will be found that, although the missionaries erred in

judgment in some points, the general influence of their body, as it increased, was to widen these distinctions and enlarge the liberty of the subject. In the early stage of their career, the strong attachment of the rulers to their teachers, and the inseparable policy of the government with the religion it fostered, caused its precepts to be felt in every political movement; the missionaries were truly and rightfully the active causes; but with the authorities lay the errors of execution.

No more positive proof exists, of the hold which the mission was acquiring in the affections of the government, and their appreciation of its motives, than the liberal aid furnished in furtherance of their views, and in securing suitable accommodations for their families. In March, 1825, the whaler Almira arrived, bringing supplies gratuitously for the mission. As soon as this fact was made known to Kalaimoku, he remitted one half the customary harbor fees. She also brought intelligence of the deaths of Liholiho and Kamamalu. Kaahumanu and Kalaimoku immediately proposed to address prayers to Almighty God; they wrote also to the governors of the different islands, to unite in humbling themselves before Heaven, to preserve order among their people, and to await the summons for a general council. The letters were signed by Kauikeouli, who, in his official acts, assumed the title of Kamehameha III. The will of the late king in regard to the succession, which delivered the kingdom in trust to Kaahumanu and Kalaimoku, for the young prince, being well understood, was quietly acquiesced in.

On the 16th of April, Richard Charlton, Esq., with his lady and her sister, arrived at Honolulu. They were the first European women who became residents. He immediately assumed the duties of his office of Consul for the Hawaiian and Society groups, to which he had been appointed by the government of England.

CHAPTER IX.

THE motives which occasioned the refusal of Captain Starbuck to allow the passage of Mr. Ellis, were soon apparent. The king had placed on board twenty-five thousand dollars in specie to pay his expenses; the regulating of which the captain wished to secure to himself. Assisted by Rives, whom the historian of the voyage describes as possessing a " low, cunning, and profligate nature," Liholiho was allured to his old practices of gambling and intoxication. The ship put into Rio Janeiro for a short period. The consul-general of England gave a ball for the entertainment of their Hawaiian majesties, and the Emperor, Don Pedro, treated them with distinguished attention. On the 22d of May, 1824, Captain Starbuck landed his passengers at Portsmouth, England, without making any provision for their comfort. The government were apprised of their arrival through the kindness of the owners of the ship. The Hon. F. Byng immediately received the appointment of guardian to the royal cortege, and quarters were provided for them at Osborne's hotel, London. Their cash chests were forwarded to the Bank of England. On being opened, but ten thousand dollars were found; of the remainder, no account was given by the captain, except a bill of three thousand dollars for expenses incurred at Rio.*

The appearance of the royal travelers, before suitable dresses were provided, was, for London something novel. Kamamalu exhibited herself in loose trowsers, and a long bed-gown of colored velveteen; Liliha, in a similar costume. However, the tailors soon fitted the males to the newest cut; and Parisian modistes clothed the ladies in accordance with the court fashion of the day. Corsets for the first time encircled their ample waists;

and the London fair, in their rage for the strangers, sought patterns of the turban that graced the brow of the queen. The contrast between the simple *malo* of their deceased father, and the splendid habiliments with which his children were clothed, must have excited curious reflections in the minds of their attendants. They behaved, however, with propriety; though on one occasion one of the party seeing a mullet, which resembled the species found in their island waters, seized it with avidity, and hurried home, where the impatience of the royal guests would not await its dressing. It was devoured raw, and no doubt was the most savory morsel they tasted while abroad.

Rives was dismissed from his office of interpreter, on account of repeated ill-behavior, and James Young, a son of the favorite of Kamehameha I., was appointed in his place. The nobility bestowed many flattering attentions upon the party. Their pictures were to be found in every shop window, and the lions of the moment were the savage king and queen of the islands discovered by Cook. They were feasted and flattered; taken to the shows and sights of the metropolis, and hurried from one route to another with an activity which their ensouciant dispositions and tropical constitutions were poorly calculated to sustain. The chapel of Henry VII., the burial-place of England's sovereigns, Liholiho could not be prevailed upon to enter, esteeming it too sacred to be profaned by the foot of even a brother monarch.

. On the 12th of June, Manui, the steward was attacked by the measles; the next day, the king sickened, and by the 19th, all of the party were afflicted with the same disease. Dr. Holland attended them; but in a few days the queen became dangerously ill, and a consultation of physicians was held. Boki and Kekuanaoa rapidly recovered, and Kapihe soon grew better. On the 4th of July, Liholiho was sufficiently well to give an audience to the newly appointed consul to his dominions. By the 8th, no hopes of the queen were entertained. The mutual grief of the royal couple was affecting. They held each other in a warm and protracted embrace, while the thought of dying so early in her career, so far from her loved islands and friends, caused the tears to gush freely. In the evening she died. This sad event so affected the depressed spirits of the king, that although hopes of his recovery had been entertained, he sank rapidly, and on the 14th, after much severe suffering, breathed his last. Previous to his death he drew up a rough memorandum, in which he expressed his wish to have his body and that of his consort conveyed to their native land; his personal effects he distributed among his retinue.

KAMAMALU.

The survivors received much kindness, and were taken to such places as were calculated to enlighten their minds, and give them favorable impressions of the power and civilization of England. On the 11th of September, George IV. granted them an interview at Windsor, in which he received them courteously, and promised protection, should any power manifest a disposition to encroach upon the sovereignty of their islands.

Canning, also, was friendly, and held frequent conversations with the party. All their expenses were provided for by government, and the money lodged in the bank of England, returned to them, which they expended in presents for their friends at home.

The frigate Blonde, commanded by Lord Byron, was ordered to convey to Oahu, the remains of the sovereigns, which had been deposited in lead coffins, enclosed in wood, covered with crimson velvet, and richly ornamented. Suitable inscriptions in English and Hawaiian, gave the rank and age of the deceased. Boki and his followers, embarked at Portsmouth, on the 28th of September. On their voyage they had an opportunity of observing several other countries. The frigate touched at Rio, St. Catherines and at Valparaiso, where Kapihe died; also, at Callao and the Galapagos; thence they sailed to Lahaina, Maui. Before their arrival, Liliha and Kekuanaoa, were baptized, at their request, by the chaplain, Lord Byron standing sponsor.

On the 4th of May, 1825, the Blonde came in sight of Lahaina. A boat put off from the frigate, containing Boki and his consort, and their suite. The cry spread through the village, "it is Boki, it is Boki;" and thousands thronged the shore to await his landing.' Some began to wail; Hoapili, the father of Liliha, took a seat upon the beach. As she approached the crowd opened a passage for her into the centere of the circle. The wailing gradually increased, until her venerable parent rose from his chair, and, in the words of an eye witness, "with a *roar* which scarcely resembled the human voice," embraced his daughter. The princess Nahienaena then threw herself into Liliha's arms. Hoapili, unable longer to restrain his emotion, cast himself on the dirt at Boki's feet, literally scouring his face in the sand. His example was followed by all the veterans of the court, and the assembled multitude broke forth into a wail, which drowning the roar of the surf, echoed over the hills and carried the tidings far and wide.

Boki was the first to speak; he inquired, "where shall we pray." As soon as the chiefs joined in devotion, the wailing ceased. Boki, after writing to his brother, at Oahu, to apprise him of his arrival, spoke of the voyage and of the kindness he had received from the English nation. He repeated to the people King George's words, "if you wish to have me for your friend, you and your people must all learn to read and write. If you do not attend to instruction, I shall not be your friend." He also told them that when he inquired of him, "whether it was wise to encourage the teachers of religion," he replied, "yes, they are a people to make others good. I always have some of them by me;" and spoke of the former barbarous state of Britain, referring to its present condition, as an instance of what Christianity and civilization could accomplish.*

The Blonde arrived at Honolulu on the 6th and fired a salute which was promptly returned. Boki and his party were received at the landing by all the chiefs, dressed in deep mourning. Files of soldiers kept the crowd at a respectful distance. Kaahumanu led the way to the barges, accompanied by her two sisters and the widows of the deceased monarch. When the parties were sufficiently near to recognize each other, the queens gave expression to their sorrow and wept aloud. Boki's barge stopped when within a little distance of the shore; all the near relatives indulged in violent paroxysms of grief, wringing their hands, while the air was filled by the clamorous lamentations of the populace and the gloomy roar of the minute guns. The mourners disembarked and embraced. After a short interview, they hastened to the house of Kalaimoku, who was too unwell to be out; thence to the chapel, where divine services were held; after which, Boki made an address, recommending attention to "letters and religion."

On the succeeding day, the chiefs gave an audience to Lord Byron and his officers, at which the gifts of George IV. to the heads of the nation, were presented. The young king was clothed to his great satisfaction, in a rich suit of Windsor uniform, with chapeau and sword. Kaahumanu and Kalaimoku also received testimonials suitable to their station.

The funeral obsequies were performed on the 11th, with a mixture of barbaric pomp and civilized customs, which accorded well with the transition state of the nation. Twenty men in the native mourning habit, some with rich feathered cloaks, bearing, by couples, the immense feathered staffs of state, waving heavily to and fro in the wind, headed the procession. Double lines of soldiers extended on both sides of the road from the fort to the chapel, a distance of half a mile. The marines, band and officers of the Blonde, with all the foreigners, walked in regular files. The coffins were placed on two cars, surmounted by rich canopies of black, and each drawn by forty of the inferior chiefs, clad in mourning. The king and his sister, with Lord Byron and Mr. Charlton came immediately after; the chiefs two by two, according to their respective ranks; a hundred seamen of the frigate in uniform, closed the procession. The church was hung in black. After the religious services, the procession marched to the residence of Kalaimoku, which had been prepared for the reception of the officers. Here this venerable chieftain, the tears starting down his care-worn countenance, despite the convulsive effort of manliness to suppress them, received the remains of those who, through life, had been to him as his own offspring. Strange reflections thickened upon his memory. He had fought against their father, to his humanity owed his own life. In war he had shared his perils, and in council and at the domestic board his confidence and love. It was amid the obscene memorials and unholy rites of a now obsolete faith that he had closed the eyes of the old king. The throne had come to the son in the conflict between the votaries of heathenism and the advocates of license rather than reform. Kalaimoku looked in vain in that crowd for his old companions in arms, Kamehameha's veteran counselors. They had died as their master, heathens. He alone connected the past with the present. That new and holy faith which, like the grain of mustard seed, in noiseless increase, had swelled and flourished in his own heart, appeared too late for them to share its blessings; and now amid the passing away of the old, the pomp and decorum of civilization, and the sacred symbols of Christianity, he beheld the ashes of the children of his benefactor consigned to their last resting-place, enveloped in more splendid cerements, than within his memory, the wealth of the kingdom could have furnished.

On the 6th of June, the grand council assembled for settling the succession, and regulating other governmental affairs. Beside the chiefs, Lord Byron, the English Consul and Mr. Bingham were present. Naihe opened the business, by stating they had met to confirm the crown to Kauikeouli, and establish suitable laws for the state. The young prince was unanimously proclaimed king. Kalaimoku then addressed the chiefs, setting forth the defects of many of their laws and customs, particularly the reversion of lands to the king on the death of their occupants. Kamehameha had partially introduced a hereditary succession, based upon feudal tenure, which confirmed predial servitude among the common orders. A powerful aristocracy had arisen in consequence, which his superiority alone could keep in due subjection. His successor, either fearing their overgrown power, or avaricious of their wealth, revived the more ancient custom. Kalaimoku proposed that Kamehameha's policy should become the established law of the kingdom, and that the lands of the chiefs should be unalienable in their families. except in cases of treason. A proposal so greatly to their advantage, was adopted by acclamation, and the result has been to leave very little landed property in the actual possession of the king and people.

Boki informed the chiefs of the results of his interview with George IV. in which he had consented to watch over the kingdom, and protect it from foreign invasion. He also repeated the advice in regard to the missionaries; paid a just tribute to the English for their hospitality, and concluded by expressing his deep loyalty to the young king.

Kuakini proposed that Kauikeouli should receive a Christian education, and be separated as much as possible from those of his subjects, whose influence would lead him to the vices which had stained the character of his brother. This met with the approbation of all.

Kapiolani then stated her endeavors on Hawaii to diminish the prominent vices of the nation, and that she had promulgated laws prohibiting murder, infanticide, theft and debauchery. Kaahumanu, in a short speech, expressed her approval of such measures, proposed their universal adoption, and that instruction should be given to the people at large.

Lord Byron gave some useful hints for their domestic polity, in which he urged a uniform taxation, the abolition of villanage, and protection of life to the common people. He also approved of the labors and designs of the mission; its principles being primarily explained in an address by Mr. Bingham, who stated that their instructions expressly forbade any interference in the political concerns of the nation. The recognition of their existence by the English government, as a free and independent people, was fully assured them, and that in no wise would that power dictate or interfere in their domestic affairs. By his recommendation the exorbitant port duties were much reduced, and regulations for the seizure and delivery of deserters from ships agreed upon. These were reduced to writing, signed, sealed and promulgated by Kalaimoku. It was the first official written document of their legislation. Kaahumanu was continued in the regency during the minority of the king, with Kalaimoku as her prime minister. The council then broke up. To show gratitude to the English government for the attention received in England, Boki proposed that sites for the English consulate and consular residence should be bestowed upon the consul, for himself and successors in office. With the approbation of Kaahumanu, this was done by verbal grant, and Charlton received the spot of land since known as Beretane, as his residence, and a smaller lot near the fort for his office. These spontaneous gifts to the English nation were afterwards made by Charlton a most fruitful source of vexation and injustice to the chiefs.

The Blonde sailed for Hawaii, having Kaahumanu and suite on board. Grateful for the attentions and kindness of Lord Byron, the chiefs vied in their semi-barbaric hospitality to do honor to the guest of the nation. At Kealakekua, Lord Byron erected a humble monument to the memory of Cook, on the spot where his body was burnt. It consisted of an oaken cross, into which a copper plate was inserted, bearing an inscription, ascribing to Captain James Cook, the discovery of these islands. Byron shares with Vancouver, the affectionate remembrance of the chiefs.

The immediate region about the crater of Kilauea, Hawaii, being remote from all the mission stations, remained for several years much under the influence of the priesthood of Pele. It was seldom visited by the ruling chiefs, and its inhabitants living within the circuit of the former devastations of the volcano, and in sight of its terrific action, were more deeply imbued with heathen superstitions, than those whose idols had been destroyed, and whose faith had been yearly weakened by an increased foreign intercourse. Here, apart from their fellows, they existed an almost distinct race. Sacrifices were daily offered to Pele, and occasionally her prophets wandered into the more civilized districts, denouncing awful retribution for the general apostacy. But these denunciations had been too frequent and faithless to excite anything but ridicule among the better informed, while the chiefs remonstrated with these self-deluded agents on their folly, or sternly ordered them to renounce their claims to inspiration. Gradually a spirit of inquiry was awakened even here. The first blow given to this dominant belief was in the summer of 1823, when a party of missionaries visited the crater. In defiance of the threats of the priests and the fears of the people, they partook of the sacred fruit, and boldly invaded her very fires. The impunity with which this was done, astonished the natives; but they attributed it to the superiority of Jehovah to their goddess, rather than to an entire absence of the supernatural.

But early in the year 1825, their credulity was staggered by the boldness of Kapiolani, who, with a daring which, when her previous associations are considered, does her infinite credit, determined to convince its votaries of the falsity of their oracles. She visited the wonderful phenomenon; reproved the idolatry of its worshippers, and neglected every rite and observance which they had been taught to consider as necessary for their welfare. In vain the priests launched their anathemas, and denounced upon her the vengeance of the offended deity. She replied she feared them not; the fires of the volcano were the work of the God she worshiped; she would abide the test of daring Pele in the recesses of her domains. Venturing to the brink of the abyss, she descended several hundred feet toward the liquid lava, and after casting the sacred berries into the flames, an act than which none more sacrilegious, according to their ideas, could have been done, she composedly praised Jehovah amid one of the most sublime and terrible of his works. The sincerity of her faith could not have been put to a severer test.

The island of Hawaii affords specimens of at once the grandest, most picturesque, and sternest of nature's works. Raised from the sea, by volcanic action, at a date never to be ascertained by man, it has accumulated layer upon layer of lava rock, piled in every shape that so fearful and powerful an agency can give them, until it has shot up mountains more than two and a half miles high. Mauna Kea on the north, and Mauna Loa on the south, with the lesser mountain, Hualalai, to the west, divide the island between them. Mauna Kea rises to an elevation of 13,950 feet. Mauna Loa 13,760 feet. Both are vast in their proportions, though differing widely in their natural features. Mauna Kea is a succession of craters long extinct, which have risen one above another, heaping up stones, ashes, sand and cinders, long enough quiescent to form soil and clothe its flanks with vegetation. To all appearance it has had a much longer respite from internal fires than its neighbor. But, judging from the late eruptions, all of Hawaii must be a mere crust raised upon a vast globe of fire. Mauna Loa forms an immense dome with a base of 120 miles, and a horizon at the top of 27, covered with a gigantic crater through nearly its entire extent. Nothing can exceed the cold sterility of this region, or the fury of the blasts that sweep over it. At long intervals its gigantic crater heaves with internal fires, throwing its boiling lava over its crest, and bursting vents for it lower down its sides, from which it spreads in fiery currents to the plains beneath, consuming before it every living thing. On the eastern flank of this mountain, some 10,000 feet down, at an elevation of 3,970 feet above the sea, is situated that vast pit six miles in circumference, and from 400 to 1,000 feet deep, according to the activity of its fires, called Kilauea, the fabled residence of the goddess Pele. No region on the globe affords greater attraction to the lover of volcanic phenomena than this. Stupendous in their scale, always active, though varying greatly in intensity, they never fail to impress the traveler with wonder, interest and fear. Vesuvius sinks into insignificance in comparison. The visitor must not, however, expect to find a huge pit, two miles in diameter, filled to overflowing with fluid lava, as the imagination readily suggests at the idea of a crater. Kilauea more frequently presents the appearance of a smoking ruin, sunken deep into mother earth, flashing with light and flame, heavy with smoke, and stunning with detonations and angry noises. Occasionally the black crust or mass beneath heaves and is rent asunder; rivers of viscid, boiling lava arise, spouting blood-red jets far into the air; or they spread into a lake which sends its heavy waves against its sides with the noise and fury of the surf on a precipice bound shore.

To the eastward, Kilauea, by the lateral pressure of its lava, has thrown out a series of smaller mouths or craters, reaching to the sea-side, from which it ejects its superfluous masses, before accumulating sufficiently to overflow its own banks. These operate as safety valves, and preserve the country in the immediate vicinity, which is fertile and forest-clad, from devastation.

The greater portion of Hawaii has re-mained to this day comparatively dark and benighted. It has afforded a retreat to the few remaining votaries of the past, and has been the field whence have sprung wild beliefs, which, under more favorable circumstances, might have ripended into fanatical creeds. The character of the inhabitants seems to partake of the natural wildness about them, and their imaginations to be ripened amid the blackness of desolation which marks the action of the volcano. Here arose a system of theology, some years since, remarkable for its ingenious combination of Christianity and heathenism. A few young men promulgated that there were three gods: Jehovah, Jesus Christ, and Hapu, a former prophetess, whose bones had been disinterred, adorned after the manner of their idols, and deposited in a certain enclosure, denominated the place of refuge. They traveled through the island, exhorting all to flee within its bounds, as the heavens and the earth were about to meet, and all not there assembled would be destroyed. Multitudes obeyed; a temple was erected and they continued worshipping day and night; but the destruction not taking place at the appointed time, hunger compelled many to leave. The appearance of a missionary, who expostulated with them upon their folly, decided the remainder, and, after firing the temple, they quietly dispersed.

No restriction excited the anger of the enemies of the mission more than the taboo, which prevented women from frequenting ships. Since the discovery of the islands, this practice had been carried on openly and without restraint. Masters of vessels frequently hired young girls to perform voyages with them. So universal had been licentiousness, that the first appearance of any restraint appeared to be viewed by its advocates as an infraction of their natural rights. It is on record that vicious whites, previous to the arrival of the missionaries, inculcated licentiousness as a virtue, by telling the natives that it was right for them to prostitute their women. This species of hospitality was freely proffered the missionaries, and the natives were at first greatly surprised at their refusal, and the doctrines of purity they preached, quoting against them the opposite sayings of their first teachers. In the fall of 1825, the chiefs were induced to forbid the traffic in lewdness The good sense of the majority of foreigners approved of the reform, but the violence of others was unpardonable.

In October, the British whaler Daniel, Baptain Buckle, arrived at Lahaina, where this law was in force. Some of the crew charged Mr. Richards with being its author, and demanded that he should procure its repeal. He informed them that the law emanated from the chiefs, who acted in this respect in accordance with the word of God. They withdrew; others came up and threatened the destruction of his property and lives of his family. After they retired, the natives kept guard, and allowed no seamen to approach the premises. The next day Captain Buckle sent word to Mr. Richards, that all his crew were ashore, and were determined not to return without women; and if he gave his consent, all would be "peace and quietness." An attack was made by the armed crew upon the house, which was repulsed by the guard. The chiefs were vainly solicited by the infuriated seamen to repeal the law.

On the 14th of January, 1826, the U. S. schooner Dolphin, Lieut. John Percival, arrival at Honolulu. This commander expressed his regret at the existence of such a statute, and interested himself, and with partial success, in procuring the release of some women who were confined for immoral offences. Violent menaces were circulated against the missionaries, to whose influence the regulation was rightfully attributed. The evening of the 26th of February, being the Sabbath, Mr. Bingham went to hold divine worship at the house of Kalaimoku, who was lying ill on his couch. Several of the Dolphin's crew entered, armed with clubs, and demanded the abolition of the law; in case of refusal, they threatened to destroy the building. Before they could be ejected, all the front windows were broken in. Driven from this quarter, and having received a reinforcement of shipmates, they directed their course to the residence of Mr. Bingham. Seeing this, he endeavored to reach the house first, but falling in with them, was immediately seized, and threatened with further violence. The natives now interfered, and in the melee Mr. Bingham was released, fortunately escaping a blow aimed with a club, and the stab of a knife. These rioters were secured, but another gang reached the house and broke in a window. Two attempted to force the door, when one unexpectedly turned upon the other, and without any apparent provocation, with a sudden blow, laid him senseless. Another was dangerously wounded by a sabre, in the hands of a native. Through the authority of the chiefs who were present, no further injury was received, although one seaman owed his preservation to the interposition of a missionary.*

In the evening, Percival waited upon the chiefs, and declared his intention not to leave the island until the prohibition was repealed. Awed by threats, and wearied by importunity, some of them gave a tacit consent. Numbers of women immediately went on board, and when the first boat load pushed off, a shout of triumph rang through the shipping. The delinquent chiefs were severely reprimanded by Kalaimoku; but the prestige of the taboo had been overborne by a national vessel of a powerful nation, and it was not until there was more moral sentiment to sustain it that it could be reestablished. Lieut. Percival expressed his gratification at the result, and his further determination to compel the recision of the edict at the windward islands, where it still continued in force. His vessel remained at Honolulu ten weeks, in the full enjoyment of the immorality for which he had so successfully interfered. So odious was the example that his vessel has ever since borne the soubriquet of the "mischief-making man-of-war."

With such a precedent, it is no matter of surprise that lawless captains should incite their crews to equally overt acts. At Lahaina, some mouths after, where through the firmness of Hoapili, the law was rigidly enforced, the seamen of several ships lying in the roads, declared their determination to murder Mr. Richards. He was then absent; but they

*Tracy's History of Missions, p. 181. Boston, 1842.

proceeded to his house with the intention of demolishing it. A guard of natives drove them off; they continued for several days, to destroy the property of the inhabitants, and committed many excesses. Hoapili was also absent, and had left the place in charge of a female chief, who, at the commencement of the difficulties, ordered all the females to retire to the mountains.

A year afterward, another and more aggravated assault was made by the crew of the John Palmer, an English whaler, commanded by an American, of the name of Clark. Several women had succeeded in getting on board, whom the captain declined giving up. Hoapili refused to allow Clark, who happened to be ashore, to return to his vessel until the delinquents were landed. Word was carried to the crew of the detention of their captain, and they prepared to fire upon the town. Upon the promise of Clark to return the females, he was released; before, however, the intelligence of his liberation reached the crew, they had discharged five cannon balls in the direction of the mission-house, none of which, though they passed near it, proved destructive. The next morning Clark, violating his pledge, sailed for Oahu, taking the women with him.

Outrages from similar causes, of more or less virulence, were not uncommon at this period. The forbearance of the islanders, and the inflexible courage of the missionaries, contrast forcibly with the malignity of disappointed sensualism. Thomas Ap Catesby Jones, Esq., commanding the U. S. ship Peacock, arrived at Honolulu in October, 1826, and remained three months. During this time transpired an event, to understand the occasion of which, it will be necessary to trace its cause. Two parties then existed; one composed of the powerful chiefs who were under the religious influence of the mission; their polity bore deeply the impress of their new ideas; and the whole force of government was employed to crush the licentious spirit of the nation, and compel the people to receive instruction. To their teachers they looked with strong affection; although the principles of the latter forbade any direct political assumption, yet their pupils

zealously endeavored to implant in their legislation the direct influences derived from the simple commandments of the Gospel. So far as the missionaries were faithful to their cause, they became identified with government; for it was only to them, and the transient visitors of intelligence at the islands, that the chiefs could safely apply for disinterested advice. This was frequently given, but in its execution the old Kamehameha policy was adhered to. And in the then existing state of the nation, when everything was in a state of transition, nothing short of absolute authority could effectually keep in check the efforts at misrule. The external sentiment of the nation fell in with the power and patronage of the chiefs; and while their power remained unshaken, their decrees were observed with a rigidness which annoyed those whose interests and pleasures lay more in unrestricted freedom. It must not be supposed that the outward compliance with the new laws, so generally prevalent, was a safe criterion of the moral condition of the nation. As under their old taboos, fear of the chiefs was the main cause of a compliance with regulations foreign to the dispositions of the masses; but it must be acknowledged that at this time a moral discrimination had arisen, favorable to the cause of virtue. The consistent piety of the chiefs, put to the blush the conduct of civilized men, who had formerly shared in their revels, and consequently acquired an influence in their councils, which had been supplanted by the mission. Hence arose an enmity, which gradually settled into a systematic hostility to every act of government: all its acts of a moral tendency were ascribed to the mission, and the party thus formed, vigorously assaulted the motives of its supporters, and endeavored, by secretly undermining the good effected, corrupting the converts, or by availing themselves of the mass of vileness, which, like a spent volcano, lay concealed in the nation, and needed but an opening to cause it to rage strongly and fiercely, utterly to destroy the missionaries from the land. Foiled in their endeavors, they had ventured to assail their personal characters, and circulated cunningly devised falsehoods and the basest calumnies, some of which poisoned the minds of worthy men, who thought they saw objectionable features in mission operations generally, and eagerly caught at what, coming from the same field, was supposed, with all their exaggerations, to originate in truth. By such causes were the intelligent minds of men like Kotzebue, Beechey, and others circumvented; men whose fault lay in not examining candidly for themselves, but giving a too willing and credulous ear to specious charges. Supported by them, some of the popular reviewers and writers fell into most egregious errors, which have since been amply refuted.

Farther to give evidence to their statements, a letter was published in the London Quarterly Review, which the editor pledged to be a genuine production of Boki, in which they were confirmed, and the thrice told tale of the power passing into the hands of the missionaries, fully re-echoed.* Unfortunately for the party, it no sooner appeared than it was proved a forgery, and by it the real character of those who resorted to such fabrications to support a sinking cause, was disclosed. If the opponents of the mission had taken the stand that the influence of governmental matters was gradually passing into their hands, and the policy of the nation was perceptibly assuming their hue, they might have been sustained by facts. But they undertook to prove too much when they accused the missionaries of aiming to build up an ecclesiastical polity, centering all power and wealth in themselves, after the manner of the Jesuits of Paraguay. The weapons they employed against them were foul in themselves. Consequently the evil they intended recoiled on their own heads, and rendered their testimony even upon other matters dubious.

It must not be supposed that all who were not of the mission were in the ranks of their enemies. There were many men who honestly differed from them, but respected their cause, and who could see errors in practice or persons without passing wholesale condemnation upon a creed or sect. The venerable John Young expressed his surprise and pleasure at the reform; foreign settlers there were who lent aid by counsel and example. But those low men, who formerly held unlimited influence over the chiefs, of whom Rives was the principal, formed the nucleus of the party. About them gathered the degraded in moral sentiment of all classes; men whose interests or sensuality were curtailed by the increasing knowledge. At their head now appeared the English and American consuls. In the selection of the former individual, the government, for its own credit, had been most unfortunate. So popular had Vancouver and Lord Byron made that nation, that an official agent of generous sentiments and general intelligence, might have secured an influence which would have hastened the progress of civilization, and conferred honor upon himself. But this man unfortunately was, by temperament, habits and abilities, inadequate to such usefulness. His character for mendacity soon became proverbial throughout the nation, and he was considered a reproach to his own countrymen by those who had an opportunity of knowing him.* He was often kind and courteous to the American missionaries, but was jealous of their superior influence, and feared that the tone of the people would tend towards that nation. As American commerce and settlers were by far the most numerous, and both yearly increasing, English influence would gradually be absorbed, and in time the islands become an appendage to the great republic. This was a sufficient motive for an attempt to frustrate their growing prosperity. Availing himself of the discordant elements about him, he managed, by exciting their cupidity, sensualism and fear of religious intoleration, to combine into one party the classes before described. Several Americans, circumvented by his artifice, and imbibing an almost equal hostility towards their countrymen, impolitically condescended to serve under his banner, under the persuasion that they were opposing liberal principles to fanatical rule. On a small scale it was the gay cavalier against the zealous round-head. Whichever party secured the state proved as-

---

*Appendix to Stewart's Residence in the Sandwich Islands,—see letter 6.

* See Nautical Magazine, Vol. III., page 511: 1834.

cendant. By turns Charlton flattered and bullied the chiefs; and at all times endeavored to convince them that they were the subjects of the British empire, and under some sort of guardianship to him. But the assurance of Lord Byron, and the terms of his own commission, by which he received his appointment to a friendly and independent nation, gave the lie to those assertions. Failing in defeating the progress of the American mission, at this period he proclaimed it his intention to divide the nation and create a rival religion, by the introduction of English Roman Catholic priests. Such was the state of affairs at the visit of Captain Jones.

In the management of their foreign relations, the chiefs depended greatly upon the advice of the highest foreign officers who touched at their islands. Either party felt strengthened according to the course such pursued. The conduct of Percival was a triumph to the liberal party, as they considered themselves; that of Jones strengthened the confidence of the government in the honor of his nation, and served fully to expose the malicious designs of their defamers. He arrived imbued with many of the prejudices common at that era; numbers zealously hastened to confirm them. The excitement became so great that the mission issued a circular, stating the course they had pursued, denying the charges, and challenging an investigation. The residents accepted it, and appointed a meeting, at which both parties could appear and be heard. Captain Jones and his officers were to be witnesses. At the appointed time all assembled; Mr. Charlton repeated the substance of the usual complaints; that he was dissatisfied with the management of the mission; that the people were growing worse; that no chief dared testify against a missionary, &c.; but he refused to commit any of these charges to writing, or render himself liable for the proof. He said he came to hear what the mission had to prove. Their circular was read, and the accusers were requested to bring forward some special charge or testimony of evil, if there were such. Not being able to adduce any, the meeting was adjourned. Before his departure, Captain Jones, hav-

ing made himself acquainted with the facts and statements of both sides, wrote to the mission, bearing testimony to the good results of their labors, and their readiness to submit to an investigation of any charges derogatory to their system or character.*

On the 2d of March, 1827, the nation sustained a loss in the death of their venerated chieftain, Kalaimoku, who died at Kailua, Hawaii, of the dropsy; a complaint from which he had long suffered. By his countrymen he was significantly termed the "iron cable" of Hawaii.† Boki, whose influence and abilities were no ways equal to his brother's, was continued governor of Oahu, and was vested by Kaahumanu with the guardianship of the young king, a measure which she soon had cause to regret. He was of an easy temperament, and frequently duped by designing foreigners. For a considerable period he faithfully discharged his duties, acting in harmony with Kaahumanu, but was finally seduced into a course which distracted the nation, and brought ruin upon himself.‡

---

* Captain Jones' account of the result of this meeting is curious and interesting. In a letter, under date of 1835 he writes:

"I own I trembled for the cause of Christianity and for the poor benighted islander, when I saw on the one hand the British Consul, backed by the most wealthy and hitherto influential foreign residents and shipmasters, in formidable array, and prepared, as I supposed, to testify against some half dozen meek and humble servants of the Lord, calmly seated on the other; ready and even anxious to be tried by their bitterest enemies, who on this occasion occupied the *quadruple station of judge, jury, witness and prosecutor.* Thus situated, what could the friends of the mission hope for or expect? But what, in reality, was the result of this portentious meeting, which was to overthrow the missionaries and uproot the seeds of civilization and Christianity, so extensively and prosperously sown by them in every direction, while in their stead idolatry and heathenism were to ride triumphantly through all coming time? Such was the object and such were the hopes of many of the foreign residents at the Sandwich Islands in 1826. What, I again ask, was the issue of this great trial? The *most perfect, full, complete and triumphant victory* for the missionaries that could have been asked by their most devoted friends. Not one *jot* or *tittle,* not one *iota* derogatory to their characters as *men,* as *ministers of the Gospel* of the strictest order, or as *missionaries,* could be made to appear by the *united efforts of all* who conspired against them."

† At his death his stone house, the best built and most costly in the island, was dismantled in accordance with a superstition that still lingered among them. Upon the death of a high chief, it was not uncommon even at so late a period, to destroy much of his property, that none other might possess it; and valuable loads of satins, velvets, broadcloths and other rich goods were taken to the sea-side, cut into small pieces, and cast into the surf.

‡ An attempt has lately been made by the advocates of Romanism—see anonymous pamphlet, published at Honolulu, 1840, entitled "Supplement to the Sandwich Island Mirror"—to exaggerate the authority of Boki, and destroy that of Kaahumanu, who is represented as an usurping old woman, led by the American mission. No

When it was found that exposure attended the criminal practices and violence of those captains who insulted the native authorities, and heaped abuse and violence upon the unoffending heads of their teachers—for it was at this date that the public press was first made use of as a check to those whose lawlessness was meted only by fear of public disgrace—the virulence of the party that supported them, knew no bounds. In their rage, they desired the deaths of those who had been active in creating the moral sentiment which placed a bar to their intemperate passions. Charlton blusteringly demanded satisfaction for the detention of Clark at Lahaina. Such deportment rendered the chiefs more attached, as they saw an attempt to visit the hostility to their acts upon the mission. During the month of December, it was thought necessary to establish a

military guard for the protection of the most obnoxious. The fortifications at Lahaina were made capable of resisting any attack from whale ships; though it is improbable that the threats would have been put into execution. Foiled thus on every side, their enmity settled into a subtle malignity, which sought expression by poisoning the minds of visitors, and creating prejudices which they hoped would result in the final overthrow of the mission, and the chiefs that gave it support. Dibble quotes from a journal kept by a native, an account of a noted occurrence at this period, which, as illustrative of the peculiar relative position of the different parties, and the policy of each, is worth giving in this connection.

"The excitement became very great, and some foreigners who had formerly been favorable to the mission, were gained over to take part in it; and certain unstable chiefs also, particularly Boki and Manuia, joined with the opposers, saying it was wrong for Mr. Richards to make known in America the conduct of foreigners which took place at these islands. Certain chiefs of Oahu wrote to chiefs on Maui, to this effect: 'Chiefs of Maui, if Captain Buckle and Captain Clark and the English Consul demand your teacher, do you take care of yourselves and not refuse to give him up; let a foreigner contest the matter with foreigners, and intermeddle not yourselves lest you become guilty.'

"This sentiment gaining ground and causing great confusion, Kaahumanu called a council of all the chiefs, to determine whether it was right to give up Mr. Richards to the rage of the foreigners, or whether it was their duty to protect him.

"Mr. Richards to sail to Oahu on Wednesday evening, and on the afternoon he preached to his people at Lahaina, from the parting address of Paul to the Ephesian Church. The congregation were in tears, for they had heard the opinion of many chiefs not to protect him, and supposed they should never again hear his voice.

"The chiefs met, and were in council two days without coming to a decision, for Boki and even Mr. Young, the companion of the old king Kamehameha, said it was wrong for Mr. Richards to write to America.

"On the third day, David Malo and Kanaina entered within one of the doors of the council room, and Kaahumanu, having much confidence in David Malo as a teacher, beckoned him to sit down. She then said to him with tears: 'What can we do for our teacher? for even Mr. Young and Boki say that he was very guilty in writing to America.' David said: 'The foreigners certainly are very inconsistent, for they say it is very foolish to pray, but very well to learn to read and write, and now they condemn Mr. Richards, not for praying, but for writing a letter. But,' said he, 'let us look at this case; if some of your most valuable property should be stolen, and you should be grieved for the loss of it, and some one should give you information of the thief, so that you could regain your property, whom would you blame, the informer or the thief?' 'The thief, surely,' said she. David said: 'Kanihonui was guilty of improper conduct with one of the wives of Kamehameha, and Luluhe was knowing to the fact and gave him information, which of the two did Kamehameha cause to be slain?' She said, 'Kanihonui.' David said: 'In what country is it the practice to condemn the man who gives true information of crimes committed, and let the criminal go uncensured and unpunished?' 'No where,' said she. 'Why then,' replied David, 'should we condemn Mr. Richards, who has sent home to his country true information, and justify these foreigners whose riotous conduct is known to all of us?' Kaahumanu replied: 'The case indeed is very plain; Mr. Richards is the just one; we chiefs are very ignorant.' Kaahumanu then conferred with the well-

historical fact can be more clear than that the supreme power devolved solely upon her after the death of Kalaimoku, until the king became of age. Previous to that, by the universal testimony of the king, chiefs and natives, Kalaimoku though perhaps more often in contact with the whites than herself, derived his authority from her, and was her "Kanaka"—agent or business man—doing nothing without consultation and her assent. Kalaimoku has been called regent, but he was regent only in the sense that the premier, according to the Hawaiian constitution, can be considered as king. He acts with the authority of the king, for him. As the favored wife of Kamehameha, Kaahumanu was second only in power to him in his lifetime. Before his death she was appointed guardian of, or more properly a constitutional check upon Liholiho, whose father feared the result of his erratic habits, and at his accession was confirmed by him in this office. On his departure, the kingdom was left jointly to her care, and that of Kalaimoku, as before explained. This government was again confirmed at the national council on the 6th of June, 1825. After the death of the latter, the sole authority reverted to Kaahumanu, both by virtue of rank and previous appointment. It was not till a later period that Boki, instigated by foreigners, aspired to greater power. Both Kaahumanu and Boki filled their respective offices without collision, and with the approbation of the other chiefs. The limits of each were well understood. Kaahumanu was the political guardian of the kingdom, the executive power, repeatedly recognized by national councils and edicts, also by the officers and war-ships of foreign powers.

Boki was governor of Oahu, and the *personal* guardian of the king. Like that of the princess, it was an important office, but not of a political character. It had been previously filled, and was at a later period, by chiefs of equal rank with Boki, who never assumed other political importance in consequence.

Next to the children of Keopuolani, Kaahumanu, by descent, was entitled to the chief power, being the daughter of her husband's most noted warrior, Keeaumoku, and second only to him in military rank. The importance of his family is shown by the offices they filled even in the lifetime of Kamehameha I. The daughters were his queens, of which Kaahumanu was chief. Two sons, Kuakini, governor of Hawaii, and Keeaumoku, governor of Maui, Lanai and Molokai, afterward placed in an office of still greater responsibility by Liholiho, the governorship of Kauai. No other family was of like importance, though the service and fidelity of Kalaimoku entitled him to equal consideration, and it is upon the rank that he filled—derived not so much from descent as from the friendship and confidence of two kings—that the defamers of Kaahumanu endeavored to establish his brother.

17

disposed chiefs, and came to a decided resolution to protect Mr. Richards.

"The next morning came the British Consul in his official dress, with Capt. Buckle, Boki, Manuia and several
merchants, and with an air of confidence and importance entered into the hall of the council, and insisted that
Mr. Richards should be punished. But Kaahumanu had
made up her mind, and she told them her decision; and
all knew, foreigners, as well as natives, that whatever
they might afterwards say would be like the beating of
the sea against a rock. The matter, of course, was ended."

At a general council, held by order of
government, it was proposed to reduce
the edicts, which had been hitherto issued according to the will of the individual governors, into a species of national
code, which should embrace penalties,
based upon the principles of civilized
lands. As they were to include the
selling of ardent spirits, and restrictions
upon certain liberties which heretofore
had been free as the winds, the opposition was strong. The vengeance of the
British government was threatened by
the English consul, if they dared to leg-
islate for themselves. He prevailed so
far as to defer the execution to an indefinite period, of all the laws enacted,
except those for murder, theft and adultery. The whole were printed and distributed for the information of the people.

Two years before, an attempt had
been made to introduce a municipal code
of a similar character. The regents had
invited some of the missionaries to be
present at the council at which the several clauses were to be discussed. It
was rumored that the Decalogue was to
be the basis of the new regulations.
Some of the foreigners, irritated at these
measures, broke in upon the meeting,
and by their violence and menaces, intimidated the chiefs from then accom-
plishing their purposes.[*]

CHAPTER X.

1827—Arrival of Roman Catholic Priests—Their history
—Reception—Policy—Opinion of chiefs—Foreigners—
Spread of Protestantism—Boki's rebellion—1829—Conduct of the King—Legislation—Hostility of foreigners—
Causes of—Visit of U. S. ship Vincennes—Fatal expedition of Boki—Persecution of Papists—Liliha's attempt
at revolution—Removal from office—Kuakini appointed
Governor of Oahu—Jesuits sent away—Death of Kaahumanu, 1832—Succeeded by Kinau—Kauikeouli assumes the government—His abolition of taboos—Effects
—Reaction—1834.

THE year 1827 is memorable for the
introduction of the Romish mission, and
the commencement of the fulfillment of

* Stewart's Visit to the South Seas, vol. 2, p. 149.

the desire of Mr. Charlton, the founding
of a rival faith ; though, could he have
foreseen in its results, the establishment
of a French interest, which well nigh
led to the supremacy of that rival nation, his jealousy would doubtless have
created a coldness towards it, as great
as at first his apparent cordiality. Its
origin was as low as the measures to
establish it were base and deceptive.
After the departure of Boki from London, Rives, who had been dismissed
from the royal train, went to France;
there, by fictitious representations of
his wealth and importance at the Hawaiian Islands, of the real condition of
which the French were ignorant, having
no intercourse at that time, he acquired
notoriety, the greater, as it was supposed
he had held a responsible office about
the person of the sovereign. This he
turned to his advantage, contracting for
a large quantity of goods, which he was
to pay for upon arrival at Oahu. Artisans and priests were advertised for, to
go out under his patronage, and laborers to work upon his plantations. In
July, 1826, Rev. John Alexius Bachelot was appointed Apostolic Prefect of
the Sandwich Islands, by Pope Leo
XII. Messrs. Armand and Short, with
four mechanics, were to accompany him.
Church ornaments, to the amount of
several thousand dollars, were engaged,
which, with the passage money, were
to be paid for by Rives, at Honolulu.
He took passage in another ship for
the Pacific, and instead of going to the
islands, landed upon the western coast
of America, where he soon squandered
his money and lost his credit. His fate
is not known, but he never ventured to
appear before the chiefs, by whom he
had been discarded, or to meet his unfortunate countrymen, whom he had
been the means of deluding into exile.

The ship Comet, Captain Plassard,
sailed from Bordeaux, with the goods
and missionaries, in the early part of
1827 ; arrived at Honolulu July 7th,
and anchored outside the reef. No person appeared to receive the property, or
welcome the priests. Plassard, unable
to sell his cargo, unceremoniously landed his passengers, in violation of a law
which required permission first to be ob-

tained. He was informed by the governor of the statute, and ordered to take them away. Being beyond the range of the batteries, he determined not to comply, alleging that he " had had trouble enough with them ; " and expense also, for no passage money was paid. The priests were thus left dependent upon their own exertions for a subsistence. They procured a house from an American, and lived in company with the mechanics, in an humble manner. By the natives they were treated in the same way as other foreigners.

Boki, by command of the regent, had been bearer of the order for their expulsion. He understood the general distinctions between the Roman and Protestant systems of theology, and professed his willingness to treat them kindly while they remained; but as the islanders had already received one set of teachers, with whom they were perfectly satisfied, discordant doctrines would create unpleasant dissensions, in so small and rude a nation. In powerful and enlightened countries, like the United States and England, he remarked, when discussing the propriety of their remaining, numerous denominations could exist in comparative harmony; but with them, difference in their present condition would beget contention, and it was better that they should leave. The opinion of Boki obtains to the present day, and the king has repeatedly said, that had the Protestants sought a footing after Roman Catholicism had been established, they would have met with a similar repulse.

The priests, ignorant of the language and customs of the Hawaiians, easily became the dupes of foreigners, who desired to use them as an additional resource for overturning the existing order of things. By false representations they had been seduced to leave France, and by the same system of deception were they allured to remain. Bachelot and Short—Armand having been lost overboard on the passage—appear to have been men of simple and pious habits, and desirous of effecting good in accordance with the mandates of their church. Had they been dropped among an entirely heathen tribe, their zeal, instruc-

tions and purity of lives would have won respect, and success crowned their labors.

Deluded into the belief that the islanders groaned under the tyranny of priest-ridden chiefs, and that numbers, if they dared, would hail with joy their presence, these men pertinaciously determined to remain at every hazard. That they had ever received permission from government, they never claimed. Bachelot, in a letter published in the "Annals of the Propagation of Faith," writes, " we had never obtained the formal *yes* in relation to our remaining on these islands; " and a little later, he says, " it never came into my mind to ask for it, till it was too late." They well knew that their stay was in violation of the express orders of the government and the general wishes of the nation; yet, with an effrontery that shows a sad want of moral principle, they elsewhere relate the pitiful subterfuges which they employed to deceive the chiefs. These accorded with the spirit of fanaticism, but are a sad comment upon the candor and boldness of the evangelist by whose authority their church claims ecclesiastical supremacy. The kindness and forbearance of the chiefs to them at this era, deserve notice. Unwilling to do them injury, they suffered them to remain and commence their labors, thinking that they would voluntarily obey the injunction for departure so soon as means could be provided.

On the 14th of July, they celebrated their first mass ; a small chapel for worship was opened in January, 1828. Through the kindness of the American mission, they were furnished with copies of their works in the Hawaiian tongue, to enable them to prosecute their studies. A small congregation was gathered, principally of those foreigners who conformed to their communion. To them, their religious services were valuable ; and no one can doubt the justice of allowing all to worship God according to the dictates of conscience. Of this, the government seemed to have been aware, and offered no molestation. Curiosity attracted some natives to witness the ceremonies ; they speedily reported that images were worshiped. This excited much surprise, and drew many of the chiefs to the chapel; among them the young king. He afterwards confessed he could scarcely avoid laughing at the absurdity of worshiping a lifeless stock.* This led to an investigation of the new rites; the popish doctrines of veneration of holy relics, use of images, fasts and feasts, were found strikingly analogous to their previous idolatry. To use the words of the chiefs, " this new religion was all about worshiping images and dead men's bones, and taboo on meat." Any one who has examined the external forms of the two systems, will perceive that this was a natural conclusion to their uninstructed minds. How far this similarity may have originated in the teachings of their early Spanish visitors, it would be an interesting query to determine. The usual objection will be urged, that the pictures and images were representations and memorials of divine things, and not in themselves objects of worship. The distinction between the idols and the spiritual essences, of which they were merely intended to convey the outward ideas, was equally as well understood by the priests and chiefs, as the difference between the images of the Roman church and the holy personages whose impress they bore, is by enlightened Romanists. But by the mass of ignorant worshipers of either faith, this distinction was either altogether lost, or little borne in remembrance. The chiefs and common orders universally recognized the identity of forms, and were fearful that the predictions of those foreigners who favored its increase, would prove true. The destruction of their old faith had brought civil war; the introduction of another, which from its many points of semblance was supposed would spread rapidly among the discontented, and those who looked back with desiring eyes to the era when " the tide of free-eating " had not spread over the land and its good gifts were the birthright of the priestly favored few. This was the more to be feared, as it had the active support of the British consul and his partisans. From these circumstances originated the hostility of the government to its

* Manuscript letter to William IV.

introduction; with them it was a political question, as well as one of religious welfare. The strong connection which the idolatry of their old system and the rites of the Roman church bore in their minds, was pointedly expressed by Kaahumanu, some time afterward, in her reply to Mr. Bingham, who remonstrated with her upon the punishment of the converts to that faith. " You have no law," said he, " that will apply." She immediately referred him to the edict against idolatry, promulgated in 1819, replying, " for their worship is like that which we have forsaken."

Such were the natural inferences of native intellect; other causes tended to strengthen their impressions. Boki's bias, both from conviction and prejudice, imbibed while in England, was then decidedly Protestant; it has been seen how his opinions influenced the chiefs in their first decisions, before an acquaintance had been formed with these new rites. Foreigners, whose principles of the faith in which they had been instructed, had not been swallowed up in hostility to all religion, or whose impressions of Romanism had been derived mostly from Spanish America, strongly urged upon the government the impolicy of allowing its introduction. Some with more zeal than propriety, taught them of the long and bloody persecutions of Europe, the inquisition, crusades, papal supremacy, and all the iniquities of its most corrupt age. These sunk deep into their minds, and their fears, magnified by ignorance of history, conjectured like evils for their dominions. The continued disreregard of the priests to their injunctions, confirmed these sentiments.

As the proselytism of natives slowly progressed, and the Romish mission gave indications of permanency, the Protestant missionaries, by force of argument, teaching, and all the influence they could lawfully employ, endeavored to arrest its progress. The minds of the chiefs were sufficiently established; the variable disposition of the mass was feared. Sermons, defending the theology of Protestantism, and attacking the dogmas of the hostile church, were uttered from every pulpit; tracts gave further circulation to their opinions, and a war of discussion was commenced and actively pursued. Government lent its aid, and unfortunately for the principle, though necessarily for its support, church and state were more closely united than ever. In the American missionaries, the chiefs saw friends, who had triumphed over every prejudice, and proved their sincerity and devotedness by years of toil and usefulness. In the Frenchmen, lawless intruders, tools of a violent faction, that assailed both with equal acrimony. Consequently, the nation became confirmed in friendship toward the former, and more inimical to the latter. The American missionaries were charged with originating all the acts of the government, prejudicial to the priests and their neophytes. So far as their influence created an opposition to their tenets, this was true; it was due to their own principles, and to the requests of the chiefs and the desires of the people, that the errors of Romanism should be refuted; the more vigorous the attack, the more powerful the defence; yet there were found Protestants who reviled them, for not welcoming those whose success would have proved their destruction; and some even of their own number have felt a disposition to gloss over their efforts to oppose its establishment, as if ashamed of their zeal. So far as it may have exceeded the bounds of truth or charity, and in polemical contests, words and arguments are not always sufficiently weighed, they may hang their heads. Multitudes can attest their views to have been derived from their teachings, but the government openly avowed its acts to be its own.

Every additional band of American missionaries was welcomed by the chiefs. Under their tuition, instruction rapidly spread; a greater interest was manifested in religious exercises, though the outward show of morality was far greater than its real progress.

The greatest obstacle to the advancement of Christianity, was the relapse of Boki and his wife, carrying with them a large number of adherents, who soon formed a dangerous party in the state. The rigidness of the chiefs more imme-

diately under the influence of the missionaries, was averse to the dispositions of these rulers; and the seductions of pleasure, and the unceasing importunities of foreign advisers, finally overcame their better resolutions. They abandoned themselves to intemperance; contracted debts, and squandered the resources which had been collected for extinguishing those of Liholiho. On a smaller scale, the general license of his reign was repeated, and the island of Oahu groaned under renewed exactions. Boki was induced to aim at the regency; the party that had led him astray, as easily bound him to the interests of the papists, and for a while he was their steady friend, while they identified themselves with him, a conspirator against the government. "The two consuls, English and American, were particularly attached to him."[*] The chief hindrance which the government has received even to this day in the establishment of law and order has been from the hostile attitude and machinations of foreign officials, who, forgetful of their duty, have been more bent upon engendering discontent and embarrassing the rulers, both in their internal and external relations, than in attending to their legitimate offices. The young king, likewise, fell into dissipation, and his example rendered this party the more dangerous. The life of Kaahumanu was endangered and a revolution meditated. An attempt was made to corrupt many of the chiefs; largesses of lands were distributed, and numbers were drawn over to Boki, until he found himself at the head of a formidable conspiracy. Arms were prepared, and both sides expected some decisive movement. Boki encamped at Waikiki, Oahu, menacing the town of Honolulu. Kekuanaoa, his fellow-voyager to England, went alone to his camp, and by his persuasions finally induced him to give over any overt designs, and be reconciled with government. He resumed his offices, though still disaffected. Under his easy administration, the grosser practices of the inhabitants were in some degree revived, although no positive difficulties were experienced. Kaahumanu and the

---

[*] Annals of the Propagation of the Faith, vol. 6, p. 94.

king made the tour of Oahu, and afterwards sailed for Maui, where Hoapili and Nahienaena joined them in a progress around all the windward islands, by which the kingdom became quieted.

This year, 1829, the king began to take an active part in the affairs of government. He was now nearly sixteen years of age, and had improved much under the instruction of his teachers. On the 3d of July, a thatched meeting-house, one hundred and sixty-nine feet in length by sixty-one in breadth, built by order of government, at Honolulu, was solemnly dedicated. Most of the high chiefs were present; the king appeared, dressed in his rich Windsor uniform; and his sister, superbly attired, sat beside him, on a sofa in front of the pulpit. Four thousand natives were assembled. Before the religious exercises commenced, the king arose and addressed the congregation, saying that "he had built this house, and he now publicly gave it to God," and declared his wish that "his subjects would serve His laws and learn His word." After the services were closed, the princess made a similar address, and the king concluded by publicly engaging in prayer.

Complaint has been made against the Hawaiian rulers, that they too literally based their government upon the strictest moral principles of the Scriptures. It was fit that powerful remedies should be used for violent diseases. Besides they knew no other course. The crimes so prevalent, were seen to violate the letter of the divine injunctions; consequently the simple rules deduced from them were applied with a vigor and rigidness, which formed a powerful contrast to the saturnalia of former years. As usual, the faults of execution were attributed to the missionaries, and they were charged with endeavoring to crush the free spirit of the nation, and substituting long prayers, fasting and preaching for innocent recreations and commercial pursuits. It is perhaps true that some of the Protestant preaching has had an effect to deaden industry by an unwise prohibition of the ornaments of dress and person, which could be procured only by money, and money only by labor. Savages require a strong stimulus to work, and habits of industry are better commenced this way than not at all. It would have been found that one want would beget another, so that not only the desires but tastes of civilized life would have been hastened.

The inconsistency of expecting from untutored rulers, who were feeling their way toward civilization, the perfection of legislation which centuries of experience had accumulated in more favored countries, never influenced a liberality of sentiment with their defamers. Those who had lived so long away from moral restraint, were restless under its spread. That savages, on whose sensuality they had gloated, and from whose resources wealth had been created, should dare to bring them within the pale of law, was an insult beyond endurance. As the folds of a better public opinion gathered around them, the more bitter but useless were their struggles.

On the 7th of October, the king issued a proclamation in his own name, and that of the regent and the high chiefs, in which he declared that the laws of his kingdom forbade murder, theft, licentiousness, retailing ardent spirits, sabbath-breaking and gambling, and that these laws would be equally enforced on subject and foreigner. This was the more necessary, as cases of collision not unfrequently occurred, which if not brought within the reach of government, would eventually lead to retaliation and revenge.

Previous to this enactment, it had been promulgated, that "Christian marriage was proper for man and woman," and to put an end to the polygamy and polyandry of the natives, as well as to draw a veil over the dissoluteness of foreigners, penalties were enforced for the violation of the statute. All who continued to live with one partner, after a certain date, were to be considered legally man and wife. An act like this had become necessary to check the most prominent sin of the nation, and to enforce the sanctity of that relation upon which, above all others, the well-being of society depends.

Strange as it may appear at this day, although the most vicious could but acquiesce in its propriety, opposition was aroused to even this salutary law. Mr. Charlton, with pompous words, strove to bully the chiefs; he declared it necessary for all laws passed by them, to receive the sanction of the king of England: five hundred men were said to be under his control, and it was boasted that he had sufficient force to oppose the regent, remove the governors, take possession of the forts, and imprison the royal family. His own creatures were to be appointed to office. But his threats were unheeded. Unawed by the menaces of opposition, they steadily pursued a policy which had become necessary for the preservation of order. Those who now stood at the head of the nation had once been drunkards, and none were better qualified to judge of the evils arising from the use of ardent spirits. They were well acquainted with the strength of the acquired taste which prevailed among their people; and were convinced that restriction alone could prevent its increase. On no point had a greater effort of principle been shown. The policy then established has been, with occasional relapses, steadily pursued to the present time. Boki let land at Oahu for sugar plantations, the produce of which was to be converted into rum. Kaahumanu at once rescinded the lease; and from that period it has been the condition on which all lands are leased, that no ardent spirits are to be manufactured or sold on them.

The arrival of the United States ship Vincennes, Captain Finch, soon after these attempts at establishing a polity, which should embrace all classes and misdemeanors, confirmed the resolution of the chiefs. The government of the United States had sent gifts to the king and principal chiefs, which were presented in form; also a letter, congratulating them on the progress of civilization and religion in his dominions, and recommending earnest attention to "the religion of the Christian's Bible." It also added, "the President also anxiously hopes that peace and kindness and justice will prevail between your people and those citizens of the United States who visit your islands, and that the regulations of your government will be such as to enforce them upon all. Our citizens who violate your laws, or interfere with your regulations, violate at the same time their duty to their own government and country, and merit censure and punishment." Here was a positive condemnation of the conduct of the crew of the Dolphin, and ample sanction to the new legislation. The rage of those whose assertions were so speedily and unexpectedly disproved, was extreme, and vented in a protest of singular nature to the American government. The advice bestowed by Captain Finch was of the most judicious character, and his whole intercourse of eminent utility to the best interests of the nation and his countrymen. Through his negotiations, debts to Americans to the amount of fifty thousand dollars were acknowledged, with a pledge of speedy liquidation. The payment was to be made in sandalwood, and the several islands were assessed their respective amounts. After the departure of the Vincennes, its collection was industriously enforced.

In November, a vessel arrived at Honolulu, from which it was communicated to Boki, that some where in the South Pacific, an island abounding in sandal-wood had been fallen in with. Its situation was a secret, known only to few; one of the number proposed to the governor to fit out an expedition and take possession of it. The prospect of so speedily acquiring wealth, and the desire of wiping out his debts and retrieving his credit, were too tempting to be resisted. The beautiful man-of-war brig Kamehameha, and a smaller one, were selected. Each was well provided with arms and ammunition and stores for colonizing. Including soldiers, sailors and attendants, nearly five hundred people embarked, among whom were the flower of the youth of Oahu. Ten foreigners also were enlisted for the navigation of the vessels. The command of the smaller vessel, the Becket, was given to Manui, a confidential agent of the governor's, and who had made the voyage to England with him. Although of but one hundred tons, one hundred and seventy-nine individuals were crowded on board for a long voyage through the tropics. With Boki, the press was even greater. Hastily equipped and insufficiently manned, they sailed on the 2d of December, against the advice and remonstrances of many of the merchants, who endeavored to induce Boki to abandon the undertaking. The infatuation which pervaded the minds of the youths, was equal to the lust of gold which led thousands of Spanish hidalgos, in earlier days, from homes of comfort and happiness, to scenes of toil, famine and death. Women wailed the departure of their husbands, sons and brothers, as if the grave had closed upon them. Previous to his departure, Boki thus addressed his people : "Attend, my friends, hear what I have to say; you know my sin is great; it smells from Hawaii to Kauai; it is enormous, and it is my own, and not another's. I am about to take a voyage to extinguish the debt of the king, and not for unworthy purposes."

The expedition first touched at the island of Rotuma, one of the New Hebrides. Here discontent from the hardships of the voyage began to arise. Boki treated the inhabitants of that little isle with the rapacity of a conqueror, and finally compelled a number to work in cutting sandal-wood. Erromanga, the island to which they were bound, was distant but a few days' sail. Boki having completed his preparations, sailed ten days in advance of the Becket. His fate has never been with certainty ascertained. But from the careless habits of the natives with their pipes, and the quantity of powder on deck, it is conjectured that the brig was blown up, though not a fragment, which could be identified, has ever been found. The Becket arrived at Erromanga, and not meeting her consort, her disastrous end could only be surmised. Manui remained there five weeks, committing outrages on the natives, which led to frequent hostilities. The object of the expedition was entirely defeated. A distemper broke out which destroyed many; among them Manui. The Becket then sailed for Oahu, and a scene of horror ensued, which baffles description. Crowded with the sick, the dying and the dead, the vessel became a floating charnel-house. The sufferings of the living were aggravated by famine; they lay under a burn-

ing sun, enduring agonies of thirst, and were destitute of medicines or medical skill; feebler and fainter, day by day arose the groans of the suffering passengens and the wails of the almost equally helpless crew. The slow progress of the brig was tracked by corpses. The conduct of the foreigners, who seem to have been wrapt in the selfishness of despair, was barbarous, and its remembrance inflames the resentment of relatives to this day. The dying, as well as the dead, were reported to have been cast overboard. In addition to their original numbers, forty-seven natives of Rotuma were on board; and out of the two hundred and twenty-six souls that composed the brig's company, but twenty returned, and of these eight were foreigners. Twenty natives had been left at Rotuma, on their way, some of whom afterwards found their way back. On the 3d of August, 1830, the Becket arrived at Honolulu, and as the news of the disaster spread, the voice of weeping and wailing was heard by night and by day. The loss of so many active, intelligent men, was a severe blow to the nation. Kaahumanu was on Kauai when the expedition was fitted out; had she been present, it is supposed she would have prevented its departure.

Oahu had been left in charge of Liliha, and Kaikioewa resumed the guardianship of the king. Previous to his departure, Boki seemed desirous of regaining the esteem of his fellow chiefs. He had issued an order, August 8th, at the command of Kaahumanu, forbidding the natives to attend the religious services of the papists. It was found that their proselytes refused to attend schools or receive the rudiments of instruction; and that through their influence, the party hostile to the chiefs was increasing. However, permission was granted for the continuance of their labors among foreigners, but they were enjoined not to allow natives to enter their chapel. Despite of this injunction, numbers received instruction; force was then used to compel their absence, and at this time commenced what has been called "the persecution." Religious intolerance cannot be justified; but the question arises, how far the policy of the government partook of that character? When the manner of the introduction of the priests is considered, and the contumely they exhibited toward the government, persevering in remaining against the wishes of the rulers, who were disinclined to employ force, its leniency was remarkable: especially when the imperious Kaahumanu held the reins of state. It is true that Boki favored them, but only when in rebellion against the legitimate authorities, and in connection with the enemies of the nation. Leaning on him, and duped by the party headed by the English consul, they and their converts, who were very few, unfortunately became identified with them.

Political views, quite as much as religious, occupied their attention; and it was to Boki that they gave their support, as the aspirant for the highest office in the kingdom. A complete revolution was to attend his success. It was the desire of license that influenced the mass of his partisans; creeds, whether papal or protestant, were of little consequence in their eyes, though they were glad to strengthen their cause by such valuable auxiliaries as bigots or sincere converts to novel doctrines invariably make. The government unwisely imposed fines and imprisonment upon the latter. Too powerless to have disturbed the peace of the state, it would have been a more merciful and wiser policy to have let them alone; but it is not surprising that rulers just emerging from the grossest despotism, should employ more of physical force than charity. Expostulation, entreaties and advice were first used; and it was not until the chiefs were defied that they were confined, and set to work in making stone walls, repairing roads and fabricating mats—labors to which they had been accustomed from their infancy, but now aggravated by filthy lodgings, bad food, and the contempt and rudeness common to the lowest orders, particularly of natives, with whom malevolence to the unfortunate had always been an active principle. They were punished for idolatry; and they who repeated the offence five times, either by worshiping at the chapel, or indulging in their old rites, were obliged to remove the filth of

the fort with their hands. Instead of the inhumanity of these acts being attributed to the American missionaries, their mildness, in comparison with the bloody executions which would have awaited these offenders but a few years before, is owing to the humanizing spirit of the Christianity they had introduced. Nine years of instruction had sufficed to produce the change. What might not have been hoped for in as many to come. But individuals, too prejudiced and narrow-minded to acknowledge or ascertain the truth, charged those whose labors had been emphatically turned toward extinguishing the barbarism of the olden regime with the sole responsibility of these unwise acts. The American missionaries would have rejoiced to have seen Romanism driven from the land through the intervention of enlightened public sentiment; but not one proof can be shown that they ever advocated cruelty. Individual instances there were of those whose minds, illiberalized by sectarianism, looked on with reprehensible apathy; but the spirit of the body was far different.

Romanists, to the number of thirty, men and women, were incorporated in the ranks of common malefactors, and from time to time for several years, made liable to similar punishments. But their sufferings have been greatly exaggerated.

In ten years from the commencement of the mission, nine hundred schools, taught by native teachers, were established, and forty-four thousand eight hundred and ninety-five learners brought under their influence. Rude and ignorant as were the former, they proved useful to the latter, by aiding in forming correct habits, and withdrawing them from scenes of doubtful good.

In May, 1830, the king and Kaahumanu visited the windward islands, the government of Oahu remaining in the hands of Liliha and her partisans. During their absence the laws of 1829 were suffered to fall into disuse; immorality again abounded; and gaming and drunkenness were unpunished. Liliha prepared to maintain her supremacy by an appeal to arms, as it had been rumored that she was to be removed. The sym-

18

pathies of a large body of foreigners were with her, and much excitement prevailed. The king publicly committed the charge of affairs to Kaahumanu, who immediately appointed her brother, Kuakini, governor of Oahu. Naihe was left in charge of Hawaii. No chief was more capable in an exigency of this nature than Kuakini; to the stern spirit of his father, he joined the intelligence derived from superior advantages. He spoke English well, and was considered the shrewdest of the chieftains. Troops were landed secretly, and at several points, at once, on Oahu; the forts and military stores secured; the revolutionary party completely overawed, and its leaders supplanted in office. Kuakini entered upon the duties of his station with a determination of enforcing the very letter of the law; this was done with a rigor which gave cause of offence to many foreigners, but his sternness quelled every appearance of insubordination. He was fully equal to the task of subduing the impertinence of lawless whites, and compelling them to keep within their proper spheres. At the same time his officers, with a rudeness which was inexcusable, entered private houses, and carried liquor from tables. Horses were seized from their owners for violating the law respecting the Sabbath, but were eventually released. The violence with which the statutes were now enforced, contrasted forcibly with the laxity of the previous rule. Armed bands paraded the streets; grog-shops, gaming-houses and haunts of dissipation were suppressed; even quiet riding on Sundays was forbidden. But the strong arm of government was not capable of infusing order and sobriety into a dissolute population; though outward decorum prevailed, far preferable to the former laxity, secret means of indulgence were sought out; all his measures met at first a strong opposition, and many continued to be evaded. It was proposed to sell rum to foreigners only; Kuakini replied, "to horses, cattle and hogs you may sell rum; but to real men you must not on these shores." A national temperance society was formed, in the objects of which the chiefs cordially united.

Entirely to suppress all opposition to government, Kuakini next determined to send away the Romish priests; on the 2d of April, 1831, they were summoned to the fort, and ordered to leave the islands in three months. As they manifested no disposition to comply, this order was repeated twice afterward. The course of the priests is somewhat remarkable, and sufficiently obstinate and deceptive to have caused harsher measures in a more civilized nation.[*] Meanwhile, they continued their labors, and among the disappointed adherents of Liliha, gained some new converts; the most noted of whom was an aged sister of Kalanikupule, the late king of Oahu, who perished at the battle of Nuuanu, but whose family, though deprived of all political influence, was by the clemency of Kamehameha allowed to retain many of the advantages of their former rank. She died in 1837. The duplicity of the priests being now too manifest to be longer disregarded, if the government wished to retain even the shadow of power within their own kingdom, it was decided "to send them away at the public expense. It is evident throughout all the transactions of the priests and their partisans, that they wished to irritate the chiefs to measures,

---

[*] "That we might appear to yield in some degree to the demands of the chiefs, and to avoid irritating them, we took care, when any vessel was about to depart, to request, in writing, of the captain, a gratuitous passage. We did this in respect to several; and as they knew our intentions, they answered us, also in writing, and absolutely refused to grant our request; for no captain was willing to engage in executing the sentence pronounced against us.

"A short time afterward a Prussian vessel arrived, the captain of which brought presents from the king of Prussia to the young king of the Sandwich Islands. The arrival of this vessel furnished an occasion for a new attempt to compel us to leave the archipelago. The governor of Hawaii re-appeared. 'Here,' said he to me, 'is a ship from near your own country. It will conduct you to your own land.' 'What you say is reasonable,' I replied, 'but who will pay my passage? I came here with nothing but my body and the word of God; my heart has not been upon the things of this world; I have amassed no money.' 'Perhaps he will take you for nothing.' 'It is possible: but ask him yourself, and you shall see.' Kuakini retired with this answer. The captain came to see us; I explained to him our situation; i.e obligingly offered to receive us on board of his vessel, if we wished to depart; but if not, he told us to make an application to him in writing, and to dictate the answer which we wished him to make: which was done. The governor of Hawaii also went to see him, and urged him to take charge of us. The Prussian captain answered him that he would do it with pleasure, but that before M. Patrick and I could come on board, he must be paid five thousand dollars, (more than twenty-five thousand francs.) The poor governor had a great desire to rid himself of us, but he was still more anxious to keep his money. He was therefore obliged to abandon his project."—*Annals of the Propagation of the Faith, vol. 10, p. 370.*

which, exaggerated and distorted by their representations, should wear the appearance of religious persecution, and being an apparent breach of the laws of nations, involve them with their respective governments. Unfortunately, they succeeded but too well, and the undesired presence of these papists, with the equally unprovoked insults of their supporters, were at last crowned by the unjust interference of France.

Letters had been received from the prefect of the Roman Catholic missions in California, inviting the priests to their aid, as their services were greatly needed. It was determined to land them in that country; accordingly a native brig, the Waverly, was fitted out for that service, at an expense of one thousand dollars. On the 7th of December, Kaahumanu issued a proclamation, in which she stated the reasons for thus sending them off; that they had remained in defiance of their orders, and by them some of the people had been led into seditious practices; that their plea for not leaving before had been, " We have no vessel to go in : " " therefore we put them on board our vessel, to carry them to a place where the service is like their own." Certainly, for barbarians, a humane consideration to be exercised toward such obstinate contemners of their laws.

On the 24th they were embarked ; and on the 28th of January, 1832, were landed at San Pedro, California, where they were welcomed into the mission of San Gabriel, without incurring further hardship than is incidental to all travelers in those parts. The mechanics of the mission were suffered to remain. Kaahumanu* died the 5th of June following, in the 58th year of her age.

* The faith she entertained of a happy immortality was simple and yet effective. On the night of the 4th, when her end was expected, she remarked—referring to the custom of her nation, which requires new houses to be erected in whatever part of her territories the royal family were to visit—" The way that I am going the *house* is prepared—send the thoughts thither rejoicing." Her attachment to the members of the mission was of the most devoted nature, mingled with gratitude for the change they had been instrumental in effecting. When the life of one of their number was threatened at Lahaina, and fears were entertained that violence would be attempted by certain foreigners, she sent for him to come to Honolulu. Upon landing, taking him by the hand, she led him through the fort, and showed him her magazines of arms, and her soldiers. " These," said she. " are all mine, and both they and I shall perish before harm reaches you."

She was a firm and conscientious Christian to the last; beloved by those who intimately knew her, and universally respected for her abilities. Her remains were deposited in the royal tomb at Honolulu, beside those of Liholiho and Kamamalu.

After the death of Naihe, which occurred in December, 1831, Kuakini returned to his proper government of Hawaii, where his efforts for the forcible suppression of vice were as vigorous as at Oahu, in which Kapiolani, with more gentleness and judgment, joined.

In August, 1832, the United States frigate Potomac, Commodore Downes, arrived at Honolulu. That distinguished commander exerted himself to enlighten the minds of the chiefs, while he treated them with the courtesy due to their station. To those unacquainted with the peculiar condition of Hawaiian society, it may seem puerile to mention the frequent visits of men-of-war. But they should consider that the deportment of their commanders had an important influence either to sustain the chiefs in their attempts at exercising their just jurisdiction, and the missionaries in their labors, or to encourage the contemners of the one and the opposers of the other.

In the early part of 1833, Kauikeouli assumed the responsibilities of government, Kinau holding the same relative situation to him, under the title of Kaahumanu II., that her step-mother did to Liholiho. The character and capabilities of Kinau were very similar to those of her predecessor; before her conversion she was haughty, cruel and dissolute ; afterward, firm, conscientious and temperate. The king had acquired a great fondness for nautical affairs, and as most of their fine vessels had been wrecked, desired to purchase a brig at an expense of twelve thousand dollars. This Kinau and the other chiefs opposed, upon the ground of the impolicy of incurring further debts, while their old were undischarged. The king reluctantly yielded ; he had been an apt scholar, and had given, thus far, proofs of an amiable disposition, and a desire to rule with sobriety. But power and youthful passions are strong temptations; of themselves they might have been sufficient to have led him into a course of dissipation, in which the affairs of government would have been relaxed. But the endeavors of certain foreigners were unwearied to wean him from all religious obligations, and to render him an easy tool in their hands. The power of Boki's faction was too far gone to allow of hope in that quarter; but by pandering to the low tastes of a semi-savage monarch, he might be won. Accordingly he was plied with tempting wines and liquors, until his better resolutions were overpowered, and he acquired a thirst as strong as that of his predecessor, though his indulgence was by no means equal. Seduced by such characters, he avoided his counselors, and sought the society of young, unprincipled men. It was urged upon him to take off all taboos; the real desires of the natives and the hopelessness of the labors of the missionaries would then be apparent. The generally moral condition was declared to be entirely owing to the absolutism of the chiefs; and if they turned, the nation would follow. That this was partly true, no missionary could deny. They numbered but few real converts, though they justly claimed the amelioration of manners, the desire of instruction, and much of the gradual change for the better, to be the result of their labors. Still following the example of the rulers, it had become fashionable to be of their belief; all important offices were in their hands; and interest more than intelligence conspired to produce an outward conformity to morality. While numbers, to the best of their abilities, were Christians, thousands joined their ranks from unworthy motives. Perhaps in no instances have the united cunning and mendacity of the Hawaiian character been more strikingly displayed than in their stratagems to deceive their religious teachers. By fraud, by even giving up much loved sins, and by ready knowledge of the Scriptures, many managed to become church members, because by it their importance was increased, and their chances of political preferment better. This is too *Christian* a practice for civilized men to wonder at. Deceived by appearances, the friends of the mission exaggerated their success. Now

was thought the opportunity of putting it to the test.

The principles of the king had become loosened, and he longed to indulge in the forbidden pleasures of his race. The moment was opportune; he was persuaded, and finally gave the signal. Hoapili hastened to Honolulu to endeavor to arrest the torrent, and persuade the king to retire with him to Lahaina. But he had gone too far to retract. He immediately issued a proclamation, centring in himself all legal authority, the power of life and death, and taking off all penalties of the laws, excepting those for murder, theft and adultery; the latter at any time was almost a dead letter. Foreigners were to be protected in their persons and property. The consequences of the sweeping away of moral restraint and municipal regulations in a well-ordered community, can be imagined; how far worse the consequences among a dissolute population, ripe for crime, lust, debauchery and revenge. The scene that followed beggars description. Some remained faithful to their instructions, and had the amount of missionary good been confined to those few, their labors would have been amply repaid. The worst scenes were enacted at Honolulu, but a general civil and moral anarchy prevailed throughout the group. Schools were deserted, teachers relapsed, congregations were thinned, excesses abounded, and in some places, especially in the district of Hilo, Hawaii, idolatrous worship was again performed. Several churches were burned and some lives lost. Groggeries were opened, and distilleries set in motion. The wild orgies of heathenism rioted over the land; men left their wives, wives their husbands; parents, brothers, sisters and relatives united, like beasts, in common prostitution; they gambled, they fought, for old grudges were then scored off; they drank and they reveled. Kinau, surrounded by a faithful few, dared not venture without the walls of the fort: her person would have been as common as the lowest female. Kaikioewa, and some of the old warriors, wished, by force of arms, to compel the king to put a stop to such a course; but more peaceful counsels prevailed, and it was thought best to let the passions of the mass exhaust themselves. The king retired to the west part of Honolulu, and there, countenanced by Charlton, who boasted that the American missionaries would be sent off on the arrival of the next English armed vessel, and attended by bottle companions, indulged in continuous debauchery. Several times was he visited by Mr. Bingham, who endeavored to reclaim him by kindly but forcible monitions. He was treated with respect, and his remonstrances had an effect the king was unwilling to acknowledge. The princess, though almost equally giddy and volatile, became alarmed, and was incessant in affectionate endeavors to reclaim her brother. Urged by pernicious counsels, he had determined to remove Kinau from the regency and substitute Liliha. The partisans of the latter assembled round him, and were clamorous for the event. It was to have been done publicly ; the chiefs were present ; the revocation was on his lips, when he unexpectedly turned to Kinau and solemnly confirmed her in office. The effect was electric ; all perceived the days of misrule were numbered. When expostulated with for not carrying out his intention, he gave the significant reply, " very strong is the kingdom of God."

In their relation of this reaction, the Roman Catholics, though they appear to rejoice in its effects so far as it was injurious to Protestantism, yet are obliged to confess, that even among their converts, the " piety of some appeared to grow cold."

For awhile the king wavered between two courses ; sometimes dissolute, at others respectful and attending divine worship. Multitudes, wearied by their excesses, or disgusted with scenes which had long been given over, returned to their teachers, and confessed they had had enough; they were satisfied that law and order were better ; the experiment of unrestrained license had been tried, and demonstrated as vicious. The contrast between such times, when neither life nor property were safe ; when sensuality became palsied with excess ; when revenge rioted unchecked, and gambling begat insatiable desires ; and

the peaceful systems of education, commercial pursuits and united households, was made so apparent to the advantage of the latter, that it would have been found difficult to have again renewed the former. It was the final effort of the disorganizers to bring about a revolution; and it cannot be doubted that some among their ranks shrunk in affright from the foul phantom they had conjured up. Its effects were long felt, especially by individuals ; families were forever separated; healths ruined; limbs bruised or broken ; and much property squandered or destroyed. No foreigner suffered, except in the interruption of business and anxiety for the results.

In 1834, the reaction of the previous year began to be conspicuous. The king gave sanction to the laws, and the traffic in ardent spirits was mostly suppressed, except at Oahu. Efficient aid to the cause of temperance was afforded by shipmasters, who had long experienced evils from the use of ardent spirits among their crews, and were anxious to see its sale altogether discontinued. At Honolulu it was finally put under certain restrictions, which, while they prevented much of the former disorder, gave the king an annual revenue from the licenses issued for the privilege of retailing.

CHAPTER XI.

A NEW era was now dawning. The missionaries had carried forward the nation to a certain point, when it became necessary for new influences to operate, that their work of civilizing as well as evangelizing might be completed. The religious movement in one sense had fulfilled its task. Sixteen years had elapsed since the idols were overthrown. In that time, Christianity had made rapid progress, until the entire nation owned its sway. Pulpits, schools and mission stations were scattered over the land. Idolatry, infanticide, licentiousness, intoxication, murder, the worst features of heathenism, which, by its standard, half partook of the character of virtues, had been successively vanquished. The strenuous opposition to the progress of the Gospel was gradually changing its character, and settling into a political animosity to the chiefs. Laws, people and government partook of the puritanical caste of their religious teachers. Without exaggeration, the nation may now be said to have been Christianized; that is, their faith was fixed in Jehovah, and the principles of the revealed Gospel were their professed guide. To advance further, the religious reformation must operate on individuals, by regenerating their lives and implanting pure motives of action. Vice must now be attacked in detail rather than in the mass. The public sentiment, however unsound at heart, had adopted the standard of the cross. The impression made upon the world by this religious conquest was great. Christendom resounded with the triumph. It recalled the days of the primitive bishops, when Papal Rome in the infancy of her power sent forth her heralds throughout heathen Europe, and nations were born to her sway as in a day. This was the work of Protestantism in the nineteenth century, and its example has been the most active stimulant to modern missions. But while it had done so much for Hawaiians, it had left undone much equally as essential for their preservation as a nation. It had carried them to a certain height and bade them spread their wings and soar aloft. It was too soon. Christianity it is true had spread its healing balm over limbs lacerated with sin, and as with the touch of its author, the sick had risen and walked. But new evils had sprung up—new relations were now to be provided for—and new foes to be fought. Much as the Hawaiians had acquired in

the art of self-government, they were ignorant of political government considered in its foreign relations. Exposed as they were to the machinations of malcontent foreigners exciting treason among subjects—becoming more known yearly to the civilized world and incurring the responsibilities incident to national existence,—aiming at carrying out to an advanced civilization the experiment which Christianity had commenced, and desirous of appearing among the family of nations, it became requisite that they should lay the foundations of their new polity on sure and enlightened grounds. Ignorant themselves, they were obliged to look to others for knowledge. Versed in theology, with sacred history on their tongues' ends, they were as yet unacquainted with the practical science of international government and the axioms of political economy. Who should instruct them? The missionaries were debarred by their patrons in the United States from incurring the charge of moving in political matters—from following the example of the Jesuits and creating at once a church and state. This was a good rule so far as the clergymen were concerned, for excellence in religious polemics or single-heartedness in faith, by no means argued skill in the management of a state, or a practical knowledge of men. But having been instrumental in bringing the nation to a position where a new order of talents was as necessary for it to advance in its career as that of the past had been to save it from destruction by its own weight of vices, it was due it to provide the necessary pilots for the new sea on which it had been launched. Roman Catholicism never hesitates, when opportunity offers, to merge the church and state into one power; but she provides agents skilled for the work. Not so modern Protestantism. Its policy has been to convert; to make spiritual conquests, and leave the state to its own resources. This is right where talent and knowledge exist. But where the entire overthrowing of the past is necessary for the welfare of the future, it is indispensable that instruction and influence should be felt throughout, if the work is to be completed. In 1836, the chiefs were as much children in the science of government, as understood among civilized states, as in 1820, they were blind to the morality of the sermon on the mount. Troubles were thickening around them. They turned instinctively to the missionaries for advice. This was rather implied than given; no one could be found in the face of the principles professed sufficiently bold or confident in his own ability to meet the emergency, and proclaim himself at once the steward of souls and the adviser of the state. Had such an one appeared, if his talents and experience had been equal to the case, however great the outcry which would have followed from those interested in continuing the chiefs in darkness and from those who saw evils in such a junction, it cannot now be doubted but that great and serious evils would have been saved the nation. But an Ximenes or a Cromwell did not exist on Hawaii. Providence destined the nation to run its career through feebler agencies.

The chiefs, fully sensible of their political wants, sent by Mr. Richards, in 1836, to the United States to procure a suitable person to fill the situation of legal adviser and teacher in the new policy circumstances were forcing upon them. In this they were backed by the opinion of the mission, who desirous of preserving themselves from the responsibility, would gladly have seen it in able and disinterested hands. The wants of the chiefs were fully appreciated by the American Board, but nothing was effected. Individuals of talent, by the time they have acquired the experience suitable for such a post, which in its real effect, would have been equivalent to the supreme direction of public affairs, generally have fixed themselves in permanent relations at home. With all the modern fervor in the cause of missions, and the very many excellent discourses yearly uttered from pulpits, we rarely see entire disinterestedness manifested in the middle-aged—those who have known the world and tasted its goods, however prepared they may be by these very qualifications for the posts they so industriously urge upon others. The path of novelty, sacrifice, enterprise and benevolence is rarely filled by any ex-

cept the young and enthusiastic. That the chiefs relying on the philanthropy of any experienced public man to have complied with their request should have failed, is what might reasonably have been anticipated. A young man, ambitious of the influence if not of the actual power of a Peter the Great or an Alfred, on a petty scale, might readily have been found, but the chiefs were suspicious of youth. Desiring age and experience, they should have offered a salary equivalent to some of the highest posts in the United States. On such a contingency few objections would have been found unanswerable. The path of duty would have been opened to many blind to all other considerations. This is human nature as we see it in the pulpit and on the bench. In every position it requires its motive power.

It is said that the Honorable Theo. L. Frelinghuysen was invited to become the adviser of the chiefs, but declined. At all events Mr. Richards was wholly unsuccessful. On his return, the position of the chiefs being none the less embarrassing, compelled them to apply to the mission for aid. Without any definite action of their body, then commenced that system which by the natural course of events has led to the direct employment of several of their number—having first been disconnected from their ranks—in the service of the government. Foreigners were required in public affairs. The chiefs chose those on whom they could most rely; and whatever may have been their errors of judgment, the result has shown that they were not mistaken in relying upon their zeal and fidelity; and it may well be doubted whether, at that time, the kingdom furnished men more suitable from knowledge and experience with the people and foreigners, to administer to its wants. The history of the policy they adopted will be traced to the period of its present development.

The mission and their seceders were united in their views to build up a nation of Hawaiians distinct from all foreign influence. The following resolutions, taken from the missionary minutes for 1838, show the just views entertained at this date: .

"1st. *Resolved*, That though the system of government in the Sandwich Islands has, since the commencement of the reign of Liholiho, been greatly improved through the influence of Christianity and the introduction of written and printed laws and the salutary agency of Christian chiefs, has proved a great blessing to the people; still, the system is so very imperfect for the management of the affairs of a civilized and virtuous nation, as to render it of great importance that correct views of the rights and duties of rulers and subjects, and of the principles of jurisprudence and political economy, should be held up before the king and the members of the national council.

2d. *Resolved*, That it is the duty of missionaries to teach the doctrine that rulers should be just, ruling in the fear of God, seeking the best good of their nation, demanding no more of subjects as such, than the various ends of the government may justly require; and if church members among them violate the commands of God, they should be admonished with the same faithfulness and tenderness as their dependants.

3d. *Resolved*, That rulers in power are so by the providence of God, and in an important sense by the will or consent of the people, and ought not to resign or shrink from the cares and responsibilities of their offices; therefore teachers of religion ought carefully to guard the subjects against contempt for the authority of their rulers, or any evasion or resistance of government orders, unless they plainly set at defiance the commands of God.

4th. *Resolved*, That the resources of the nation are at its own disposal for its defence, improvement and perfection, and subjects ought to be taught to feel that a portion of their time and services, their property or earnings, may rightfully be required by the sovereign or national council for the support of government, in all its branches and departments, and that it is a Christian duty to render honor, obedience, fear, custom and tribute to whom they are due, as taught in the 13th of Romans, and that the sin of disloyalty which tends to confusion, anarchy and ruin, deserves reproof as really and as promptly as that of injustice on the part of rulers or any other violation of the commands of God.

5th. *Resolved*, That while rulers should be allowed to do what they will with their own, or with what they have a right to demand, we ought to encourage the security of the right of subjects also to do what they will with their own, provided they render to Cæsar his due.

6th. *Resolved*, That rulers ought to be prompted to direct their efforts to the promotion of general *intelligence* and *virtue* as a grand means of removing the existing evils of the system, gradually defining and limiting by equitable laws the rights and duties of all classes, that thus by improving rather than revolutionizing the government, its administration may become abundantly salutary, and the hereditary rulers receive no detriment but corresponding advantage.

7th. *Resolved*, That to remove the improvidence and imbecility of the people, and promote the industry, wealth and happiness of the nation, it is the duty of the mission to urge mainly the motives to loyalty, patriotism, social kindness and general benevolence; but while on the one hand he should not condemn their artificial wants, ancient or modern, because they depend on fancy, or a taste not refined, he should on the other endeavor to encourage and multiply such as will enlist their energies, call forth ingenuity, enterprise and patient industry, and give scope for enlarged plans of profitable exertion, which, if well directed, would clothe the population in beautiful cottons, fine linen and silk, and their arable fields with rich and various productions suited to the climate; would adorn the land with numerous comfortable, substantial habitations, made pleasant by elegant furniture, cabinets and libraries; with permanent and well endowed school houses and seminaries; large, commodious and durable churches, and their seas and harbors with ships owned by natives, sufficient to export to other countries annually the surplus products of their soil, which may at no very distant period amount to millions.

8th. *Resolved*, That we deem it proper for members of this mission to devote a portion of their time to instructing the natives into the best method of cultivating their lands, and of raising flocks and herds, and of turning the various products of the country to the best advantage, for the maintenance of their families, the support of government and of schools, and the institutions of the Gospel and its ministers, at home and abroad."

Notwithstanding the banishment of the Jesuits, and the entire suppression of their partisans, as a political party, a powerful influence was at work to recall them. The mechanics left behind, acted as catechists and served to keep alive the embers of the faith among the few native converts. Charlton, still active in the cause, corresponded with the exiles. In 1835, the Pope sent them a brief, exhorting them to persevere in the attempt at Oahu. The party was strengthened by the arrival of a Mr. Robert Walsh, an Irish priest, educated at Paris. He landed at Honolulu the 30th of September, 1836. As soon as his clerical character was known, he was required to leave, but obtained permission to remain until the arrival of H. B. M. ship Acteon, Lord Edward Russell, commander, who was daily expected. On the 7th of October, Mr. Walsh was officially informed that he would not be allowed to remain permanently. The day succeeding, the French sloop-of-war Bonite, Captain Vaillant, arrived; and he was immediately waited upon to engage his influence in his favor. Seconded by the assertions of the English consul, who claimed the privilege of his being allowed to remain regardless of his profession, M. Vaillant procured permission for him, with the proviso that he should make no attempts to propagate his religion. This, Mr. Walsh confesses in his correspondence with his employers, he violated whenever it could be safely done. The Acteon arrived on the 23d, and the Bonite sailed the ensuing day. Captain Russell, prejudiced by the ex parte statements of the English consul, actively interfered in behalf of the Romish priests. Captain Jones, of the Peacock, in 1826, had first set the example of negotiating a treaty with the Hawaiian government, in which the rights of the subjects of both countries were generally defined. Defective as it was in some important points, it had been of eminent utility; though individual instances had occurred in which it had been held up to the native government as a bugbear, by which advantages or selfish interests, not contemplated in its spirit, might be secured. Violations of treaties, breaking the laws of nations, visits of avenging men-of-war, had been so often uttered, that they had lost their meaning; and it would not have been surprising if, in the constant efforts to entangle them, the native authorities should have given some occasion of complaint. The discussions which had arisen from time to time, on account of alleged grievances, particularly when Commodore Kennedy, of the United States East India squadron, was present, in 1836, had gradually enlarged their ideas of a national polity, and given them a better understanding of the laws of nations, though their knowledge was of an extent calculated to render them more timid than bold, or perhaps wavering in action though firm in policy. Those commanders who have acted with justice and moderation, and by impartial decisions gained the good will of the high minded of the foreigners, as well as that of the natives, have invariably been followed by the sneers and abuse of those who had sought their aid to prosecute unjust claims, or had endeavored to infuse their partial views into their minds. In Captain Russell, that party found a man accessible to their views. It was thought a favorable opportunity to secure a treaty, in which the most favorable terms should be inserted. The attempt was made; a definite period for its signature was insisted upon; and at the end of that time, if it were not received, the frigate was to coerce them by her guns. Whatever influence these threats may have had, the document which was finally signed, fully confirmed the government in all their legal rights, while it placed upon a firmer basis usages of English subjects which had heretofore been only tacitly admitted. It is probable that neither Lord Russell nor the consul dared risk the displeasure of their government by any act which, in its official bearing, should manifest gross injustice. The point on which the Hawaiian government would yield the least, was that on which the principle of their internal polity was based,—the unalienable tenure of the soil. Foreign wealth and property had greatly increased; much of it was in houses or farms, occupying lands which had been

the gifts of friendship from various chiefs, or the reward of services. In all such cases they argued that they were held on the same principle as those of their own subjects; and were incapable of transmission. The "Indian gift" was but for the occupancy or lifetime of the possessor or the will of the donor. Disputes had arisen in consequence, and innovations constantly occurred, by which some lands came to be held in perpetuity by foreigners, while all wished to obtain a like concession. Houses had been demolished and removed upon the departure of the occupants, and the lands reverted to the chiefs. A few leases had been obtained, but no representative value received; foreigners were desirous of obtaining tracts suitable for extended agricultural enterprises. The importance of developing the resources of the soil was fully acknowledged by the chiefs, but the fear of losing their legal control, by yielding the right of cultivation, was a stronger motive. It was a subject which had been already a source of much vexation, and at this time their ideas were not sufficiently enlightened to enable them to comprehend the distinction between deeding the right of soil, and retaining the sovereignty. Consequently, Lord Russell was only able to obtain the recognition of the privilege to sell or transfer, with the consent of the king. The important clause was also formally inserted, that English subjects should be permitted to reside on the islands only so long as they conformed to the laws.

Notwithstanding this provision, which was agreed to in full knowledge of the edict against Romanism, Walsh, supported by the consul, although detected in violating his agreement, refused to leave. He was forbidden to open the chapel. Information had been sent the priests at California that the moment for them to return was opportune; that the king had pledged himself to Captain Vaillant to protect them, and that the treaty made by Lord Russell would effectually cover the landing of Short. It appears they doubted of their success; for it was agreed that Short should land secretly, and after continuing for some time in concealment, claim the right of stopping under the provision of the treaty which allowed English subjects freely to land and remain, but contained, in the same paragraph, the sentence, "with the consent of the king," which the English consul in all cases studiously disguised. Bachelot was to attempt to land openly; if prevented, to hold intercourse with the natives from the vessels in the harbor, and if unable to effect this, to leave for the South Pacific.

They arrived at Honolulu on the 17th of April, 1837, in the brigantine Clementine, wearing English colors, though the property of Jules Dudoit, a Frenchman. She had been chartered by an American for the voyage to California. Upon their landing much excitement prevailed. Kekuanaoa, governor of Oahu, ordered the captain of the brig to receive them on board. He refused, saying he had no control over the vessel. The owner was next applied to; he declined to receive them, except by their own desire; in case they were forced on board, he said that he should abandon his vessel and look to his government for redress. He also stated that as the brigantine was chartered, he exercised no control over her movements. An order was sent the priests on the 19th to prepare to depart.* The king was absent at Maui, where he and Kinau had recently gone to deposit the remains of his sister, who died December 31, 1836, to the great grief of the nation. She was equally beloved by foreigners and subjects, to all of whom she had endeared herself by her sweetness of disposition. Leleiohoku, the son and heir of Kalaimoku, was her husband. One child had resulted from their union, which, if it had lived, would have been heir to the throne.

His majesty received a despatch from Kekuanaoa on the 26th, informing him of the recent events. The decision of the governor was confirmed, and on the 29th, a proclamation issued, declaring the perpetual banishment of the priests.* They were required to return to the Clementine, and Kinau arrived at Honolulu to enforce the edict. The priests resolutely refused to go. The Clementine had been made ready for another voyage. It was resolved to put the priests on board, and compel them to depart in her. Officers were deputed to see them off; on the 20th of May, two days before the appointed time of sailing, they waited upon them with the orders of government. Bachelot inquired if force would be used; they replied that they were to be compelled, if any resistance was experienced. The priests then drew up formal protests against the violence before the English consul, who had been active in urging them to this opposition. Endeavoring to excite the passions of the constables appointed to conduct them on board, to some act which should appear like outrage and implicate their rulers, he told them the vessel was taboo, and that any one who approached her would be shot; adding "come on, come on! you are cowards."† Several hours were consumed in preparation, and at three o'clock, P. M., the police informed the priests it was time to leave. They were conducted to the wharf. The priests, before stepping into the boat, induced the officer in charge to touch them, that the appearance of force might be made more apparent. Arriving at the Clementine, they were ordered off by the mate in charge. M. Dudoit then hurried on board, and the boat arriving the second

---

* Honolulu, Oahu, April 19, 1837.
This is what I have to say to *the Frenchmen :*
This is my opinion to both of you, who were sent away before from these islands, that you are forbidden by our chiefs to come here; this is the reason I asked you if you intended to live here. The answer you made was "no; we intend to stop here for a few days until we can obtain a vessel to carry us from here." I replied, "when you get a vessel go quickly." This is what I say to both of you, from this time prepare yourselves to depart in the same vessel in which you arrived; when the vessel is ready, both of you are to go without delay.   M. KEKUANAOA.

* Proclamation.—Ye strangers all from foreign lands who are in my dominions, both residents and those recently arrived, I make known my word to you all, that you may understand my orders.
The *men of France* whom Kaahumanu banished, are under the same unaltered order up to this period. The rejection of these men is perpetual, confirmed by me at the present time. I will not assent to their remaining in my dominions.
These are my orders to them, that they go back immediately on board the vessel on which they have come; that they stay on board her till that vessel on board which they came sails; that is to me clearly right, but their abiding here I do not wish.
I have no desire that the service of the missionaries who follow the Pope should be performed in my kingdom, not at all.
Wherefore, all who shall be encouraging the Papal missionaries, I shall regard as enemies to me, to my counsellors, to my chiefs, to my people, and to my kingdom.   (Signed,)   KAMEHAMEHA III.
† Tracy's History, p. 253.

time, thinking that sufficient opposition had been shown, hauled down his flag, and permitted the embarkation of the priests. He ordered the crew ashore, and carried the flag to Charlton, who, as a finale to this preconcerted farce of ineffectual resistance to the tyranny of the chiefs, publicly burned it, for fear, as he stated, the natives should tear it to pieces, of which there was not the slightest intimation. M. Dudoit then made a protest, stating that the Clementine had been forcibly seized by the Hawaiian government, claiming heavy damages. They had now secured the consummation so devoutly wished for, and so cunningly devised. With right and justice on their side, the chiefs had impolitically allowed themselves to be ensnared ; not that any act of which they had been guilty was a violation of the rights of others, for it was but a lawful enforcement of the supremacy of their own; but knowing the duplicity of those they had to deal with and their own weakness, it would have been better to have submitted for a while to their machinations, and appealed for justice to the good sense of their respective governments.

Three powers were now interested— the French, English and American ; for the property on board belonged to a citizen of the United States, who was anxious to secure an award sufficient to make a good sale of it. A great flourish was made by the consuls of the ready action of their governments, and the prompt vengeance which would ensue. A weekly paper,* which had been established the year before, under their control, from that period became an organ of virulent abuse of the government, missionaries, and their patrons, and strongly supported the measures of the priests. By its misstatements numbers of benevolent individuals abroad were led to suppose that a furious persecution of the Romanists existed, and that the government set at defiance all international law. Hence their sympathies were unintentionally enlisted against a much wronged people.

On the 7th of July the English surveying sloop Sulphur, Captain Belcher,

arrived. Influenced altogether by the English consul, the captain demanded the release of Mr. Short, and threatened, in case of refusal, to land him by force. Kinau urged him to investigate the matter, but he declared that he was obliged " to follow the statements of the consul." On the 10th, the French frigate Venus, commanded by Du Petit Thouars, anchored off the port. He united with Belcher in a demand for the instant liberation of the priests. This not being obtained, a body of marines from the Sulphur was sent to the Clementine ; thence, under their escort, the priests proceeded to the shore, the commanders of the men-of-war attending them to their former residence. The English flag was then re-hoisted on the Clementine, which, by the order of Captain Belcher, was despatched to Maui, for the king.

His majesty arrived on the 20th, and on the next day an audience took place. The two commanders refused to admit the interpretations of Mr. Bingham, who had been selected by the king for that purpose. Mr. Andrews, of the mission, was then chosen, with their approbation, and Mr. Bingham retired to the back part of the room. One of the foreign officers present crowded him back against the wall ; upon stepping aside to avoid this, he received a violent blow from a movement of the elbow of the individual who so determinedly insulted him. One of the council separated them, and a file of armed men was ordered in by the king. Another officer drew his sword partly from its scabbard, and stepping up to Mr. Bingham, said, menacingly, " do you see that ?" According to the testimony of Mr. Short, Captain Belcher threatened to hang Bingham to the yard-arm of his vessel ; though another authority relates that he merely said that if any of his men were injured in doing their duty, he would be the first man he should seize. These instances serve to show the virulence with which his enemies had been enabled to inspire acquaintances of but few days standing. Mr. Bingham enjoyed the confidence of the chiefs, and was devoted to the cause in which he had embarked. He had the reputation of a

---

much more active interference in political matters than he actually possessed. His opinions however given, undoubtedly carried with them great weight among the native population. The want of a responsible, intelligent adviser had never been more felt than at this juncture. From his long residence at Honolulu, Mr. Bingham had acquired a prominence in the affairs of the mission, which had drawn upon his head, in particular, the obloquy, calumnies and deepest hatred of the opposing party. On him was showered their wit, sarcasm, insinuations and falsities; his private and public character assailed, and all that detraction could effect, done to ruin him. He withstood the storm with a firmness, mingled with forbearance, that gained him the respect of the unprejudiced, while his warm affections and sincerity strongly attached him to those who knew him intimately. But it must be acknowledged, he possessed a tenacity of opinion and a sectarian zeal, which at times separated him in some degree from his friends, and marred his usefulness. The language and conduct of the English consul was in accordance with his character, supported by the presence of commanders pliable to his will. He bullied and stormed, and finally shook his fist in Kinau's face. After a weary discussion of eight hours, it was conceded that the priests should remain until an opportunity for their leaving offered; the respective commanders pledging themselves mutually for their countrymen, that they should conform to the laws while they remained.* By these documents, it is evident that they assented to the demand of the government, that they had a right to keep from their border individuals of any nation dangerous to the state. In every instance where the chiefs were enabled to obtain a hearing, even under the most unfavor-

able circumstances, this right was conceded.

On the 23d, the king consented to the following interpretation of the Russell treaty, which, although it justly modified, did not alter its general tenor:

HONOLULU, July 23, 1837.
BY KAMEHAMEHA III., King of the Sandwich Islands:
We consent to the interpretation you desire, on the first article of the treaty made with Lord Edward Russell, in "conformity with the laws of nations."
And, in the event of finding it necessary to exert the power "of refusal to admit a subject of Great Britain," we will grant a fair trial, and give satisfactory reasons for our act, of which due notice shall be given to the consul of his majesty the King of Great Britain.
(Signed,)   KAMEHAMEHA.

Captain Du Petit Thouars negotiated the following articles in behalf of his government:

HONOLULU, SANDWICH ISLES, July 24, 1837.
There shall be perpetual peace and amity between the French and the inhabitants of the Sandwich Isles.
The French shall go and come freely in all the states which compose the government of the Sandwich Isles. They shall be received and protected there, and shall enjoy the same advantages which the subjects of the most favored nations enjoy.
Subjects of the King of the Sandwich Isles shall equally come into France, shall be received and protected there as the most favored foreigners.
(Signed,)   KAMEHAMEHA III.
A. DU PETIT THOUARS,
Captain, Commander of the French frigate La Venus.

They are remarkable for their brevity, and may be called a compendium of previous treaties. It is important fully to understand the nature of this, as it is asserted that it gave the unqualified right for Frenchmen to reside within the kingdom; it is evident that they were to receive simply the same advantages as the most favored nation. England then stood in that light, and the right of expelling obnoxious persons, for "satisfactory reasons," had been fully conceded. Thouars had acknowledged, by his bond for the departure of Bachelot, that individuals of his profession were of the character described by the government, and their full authority to proscribe the teachings of Romanism. All other Frenchmen enjoyed the fullest protection and hospitality, yet for an alleged violation of their privileges, the vengeance of France was afterwards poured upon the devoted chiefs. M. Dudoit was appointed as French agent on the part of France, in which capacity he fulfilled the duties of consul, with the approbation of his government. On the 24th July, both vessels sailed without exchanging the usual national courtesies.

The 24th of September following, H.

* HONOLULU, July 21, 1837.
The undersigned, captain of the ship, commander of the French frigate La Venus, promises in the name of Mr. Bachelot, that he will seize the first favorable opportunity which offers to quit these islands, to go either to Manila, Lima, Valparaiso, or any civilized part of the world; and in case such an one is not presented, on the arrival of the first French man-of-war which visits these islands, he shall be received on board. In the meantime, Mr. Bachelot shall not preach.
A. DU PETIT THOUARS, Post Captain,
Commanding French Frigate La Venus.
Captain Belcher signed a similar one in behalf of Mr. Short.

B. M. frigate Imogene, Captain Bruce, arrived. Previous to leaving Valparaiso, some priests had applied to him for a passage to Oahu; this he refused, and advised them not to attempt to force themselves into the country. It was known that they were on their way, and M. Dudoit endeavored to induce Captain Bruce to interpose with the chiefs to allow them to land, which he declined. Desirous of not further involving themselves with France, the government sought his advice in regard to the interpretation of the treaty of Thouars. He frankly told them its true meaning, and of which not a doubt can exist. No nation has a right to force its creed, its laws or its language upon another. To be done at all it must be by conquest. The government of the Hawaiian Islands had received, after a close scrutiny, the forms of a faith which it found well adapted to its circumstances. Wisely or not, it had been voluntarily chosen, and was now warmly cherished. At this epoch, when through its instrumentality, the nation was rapidly advancing to a respectable footing, and its aggregate wealth, morals and civilization increasing, it desired simply "to be let alone." But France, deceived by the falsehoods of its internal foes, lent herself to a party which honest minds recoiled from in disgust; and her artillery was destined to effect what combined jesuitism, treachery and disloyalty had been unable to accomplish.

Mr. Short sailed for Valparaiso October 30th. Three days afterward the ship Europa arrived, with M. Maigret, pro-vicar of the Roman Catholic bishop of Nilopolis, who was the head of the newly-formed see of Oceanica. The native authorities, having received information of the presence of Maigret, gave orders to the pilot not to bring the ship to anchor. Permission was finally granted to bring her into the harbor; the owner being bound over by the sum of ten thousand dollars not to permit the landing of the priest.* Various subter-

fuges were employed to procure the desired object; the old story was repeated that he was to remain only transitorily, and had come to secure passage to the Marquesas group. This plea was the more inconsistent, as it was well known that he had just left Tahiti, where intercourse with those islands was common, while from Oahu it was of rare occurrence. M. Dudoit, who was active in his endeavors to secure his landing, would give no pecuniary security for his departure, or settle upon any definite period beyond which his stay should not be protracted. It was evident that it was only an attempt at the renewal of the scenes of the previous year, and the chiefs determined to nip the conspiracy in the bud. Captains Thouars and Vaillant had both assented to the justice of their exclusion; consequently the threats of M. Dudoit, in regard to a violation of the prerogatives of his countrymen, did not alter their intention. Finding it impossible to tamper longer with the government, Messrs. Bachelot and Maigret purchased a schooner, which they intended for the service of their stations in the South Pacific. The captain of the Europa received permission to embark his passenger on board their vessel; two thousand dollars fine and imprisonment were to be the penalties, should Maigret attempt to escape on shore. On the 23d of November, the priests sailed. Bachelot, who was in feeble health, died on the 4th of December, and was buried at Ascension.

Walsh was the only priest left; his outward conformation to the laws was, probably, the motive by which he was allowed to remain.

The chiefs desirous of bringing their complaints directly before the cabinets of London and Washington, addressed petitions to the King of Great Britain and the President of the United States,

---

* M. Maigret (Annals de la Propagation de la Foi, 1840,) says, Governor Kekuanaoa was surprised or entrapped (*surprit*) into granting permission to enter the port. It is amusing to see with what boldness the author of the supplement to the Sandwich Islands Mirror denies all attempts at evasion of their designs, and claims for his party throughout perfect ingenuousness, while the priests themselves, in their published accounts, unhesitatingly declare the various pretexts made use of for purposes of deception. It is unfortunate for their cause that so much discrepancy should have appeared between these witnesses in their behalf. Any one desirous of verifying this remark, need but to refer to the pamphlet in question, and the Annals above mentioned.

Maigret says, after Kekuanaoa had been "deceived" by others in relation to his profession, he asked him personally whether he was a priest. "I answered," he writes, "at once, and with a frankness which *displeased* some persons, but I could not betray my conscience to *please* them."

relative to the factious course of their consuls. The former was without avail—the latter had the effect to cause the removal of Jones, and the appointment of Mr. P. A. Brinsmade, a friendly merchant residing at Honolulu.

THE PETITION OF KAMEHAMEHA III. AND HIS CHIEFS TO THE PRESIDENT OF THE UNITED STATES OF AMERICA:
We the said chiefs of the Sandwich Islands salute you, desiring to confirm the good understanding in these islands with American citizens, when they come into this kingdom, in the same manner as with citizens of every other country. And we esteem and honor your people, because we have heard that our people are cherished there, dwelling under the laws and regulations of the country in peace. Likewise we protect people of your country, who are dwelling orderly, with obedience to the laws and regulations. Let us be regarded with favor, for we are a little nation, and ignorant also, like an infant amidst the continents, and we greatly desire to learn. Moreover, the teachers from your country are teaching us, and that the good understanding may be perpetual, we write to you with amity respecting a certain matter which we would not mention but because of our necessity and straightened circumstances, we think it proper to declare and make known to you as follows :
The dwelling of a certain man, Mr. J. C. Jones, at this place, Honolulu, Oahu, as American Consul.
We thought he was a good and just man when he was appointed to the office, but in the performance of its functions we have been disappointed, for he is a person who indulges an intriguing disposition and contempt of us, and we cannot depend upon his advice. He opposes us, and prejudices the minds of strangers and natives against us, by misrepresentation. He treats our laws with contempt, and violates some of them, and supports other persons in doing the same.
And these things which have been stated to you, and you have now seen, we declare with truth and amity to you. We are sorry to state these things, but we cannot suppress them that they be unknown ; therefore, we make them known respecting the said person. And if you can set aside this man, and place a good man in his stead, we shall be gratified.
Signed, Kamehameha III., Kaahumanu II., Hoapili, Honpiliwahine, Kekauluohi, Kekuanaoa, Paki.
Honolulu, November, 1837.

Kinau died April 4th, 1839, and was succeeded by her sister, Kekauluohi, acting for Victoria, infant daughter of Kinau, to whom her office and title, by custom, descended.

Effectually to forbid the introduction of the faith from which so much trouble had ensued, a severe ordinance, covering all grounds upon which it had been attempted, had been issued in December, 1837. The will of the chiefs in this respect, was the more confirmed as the opposition increased. A number of their subjects were arrested and confined for their adherence to the doctrines of the priests. They manifested a dogged obstinacy to the authorities, and a contumely which brought upon them unnecessary severities. They considered themselves of a separate party, and rigidly incorporated their religion with their politics, hoping for the final overthrow of the government. They were few, ignorant and powerless; the menials of the governor frequently apprehended them when they were detected in the exercise of their rites, and carried them before him. Whenever these cases were known to the American missionaries, they were made the subject of earnest and successful remonstrance; by their intercession many were released, and the folly and wickedness of persecution, for religious belief, so strongly represented to his majesty, that on the 17th of June, 1839, he issued orders that no more punishments should be inflicted; and that all who were then in confinement should be released. This was done at Lahaina. Previous to its promulgation at Oahu, sixty natives were driven from Waialae to Honolulu. Most of these were immediately released and returned to their homes. Some, however, were confined in the fort. On the 24th of June, two women were found there, ironed and suffering much from the painful posture in which they had been placed. The governor was absent, but, so states the author of the supplement to the Sandwich Islands Mirror, the foreign "gentlemen succeeded in liberating the prisoners." No inquiries were made of the proper authorities as to the nature of their offences, but they took upon themselves to set aside the municipal law ; an illegal procedure, but too common in Honolulu among the opposers of the chiefs. Inhumanity to the innocent or guilty, can never be justified. But benevolence, which is altogether one-sided, cannot be called praiseworthy; the principal of these meddlers had often been instrumental in confining seamen and natives, under circumstances of equal hardship, against whom they professed to have cause of complaint. Here there was an opportunity not to be lost, of proclaiming their charity, at the expense of their neighbors. Blind to the more judicious interposition of the American missionaries, they boldly charged upon them the authorship of a species of prison discipline, on which they had looked calmly, and had actively used when for their own advantage, for twenty years. As unblushingly they boasted of their unwarrantable efforts in effecting

the release of the women. One gentleman, who had been witness to their confinement, had, previous to this, hurried
to the governor to intercede on their account. On his way he met Mr. Bingham, to whom he related the facts, and
begged him to see for himself. Mr.
Bingham having heard of the edict of
the king, informed him that it was possible they were punished for some criminal act; religious toleration having been
proclaimed the week before. To satisfy
himself, he waited upon the governor
immediately, and informed him of the
circumstances. The governor promptly
ordered their release, " for their confinement was not by the order of the chiefs."
In the meanwhile, those who had been
so active at the fort, proceeded, taking
the women with them, to the house of
the governor. On their way, they met
him; surprised at such a cortege, he
remanded the prisoners to the fort, and
to the dictatorial tone with which he was
addressed, replied, " your business is to
take care of your stores ; there is the
road to them : mine is the government
of the island and the fort; and this is
my path." Upon receiving this well
merited rebuke, they dispersed. It was
afterwards charged upon the governor
that he was " *disposed to be insolent !* "
Whatever may be the secret of the
influence the agents of Romanism possess in the councils of France, it is
certain that, of late years, the French
Roman Catholic missions have received
efficient support from their government ;
and in the Pacific, political aggrandizement and religious proselytism have been
intimately connected. The priests appeared openly, under the patronage of
their nation. Ships of war carried them
from one post to another ; the military
paid deference to the spiritual ; the political consequence of their bishops was
enforced by arms, and warlike salutes
announced their rank. The seizure and
occupation of the Marquesan and Tahitian groups have now become matters
of history. That the Hawaiian did not
fall into the same hands was owing
solely to its superior importance and
the mutual jealousies of other powers.
Every effort was made by their agents
to compass a similar result.

The French frigate Artemise, C. Laplace, commander, arrived off Honolulu
July 10th, 1839. The purpose of this
visit was speedily made known to the
Hawaiian government by the following
manifesto, addressed to the king, by
Captain Laplace, in the name of his
government :

" His majesty the king of the French, having commanded me to come to Honolulu in order to put an end,
either by force or persuasion, to the ill treatment to
which the French have been victims at the Sandwich
Islands, I hasten, first, to employ this last means as the
most conformable to the political, noble and liberal system pursued by France against the powerless ; hoping
thereby that I shall make the principal chiefs of these
islands understand how fatal the conduct which they
pursue towards her will be to their interests, and, perhaps, cause disasters to them, and to their country,
should they be obstinate in their perseverance. Misled
by perfidious counselors, deceived by the excessive indulgence which the French government has extended toward them for several years, they are undoubtedly ignorant how potent it is, and that in the world there is not
a power which is capable of preventing it from punishing
its enemies ; otherwise they would have endeavored to
merit its favor, or not to incur its displeasure, as they
have done in ill treating the French ; they would have
faithfully put into execution the treaties, in place of violating them as soon as the fear disappeared, as well as
the ships of war which had caused it, whereby bad intentions had been constrained. In fine, they will comprehend that to persecute the Catholic religion, to tarnish it
with the name of idolatry, and to expel under this absurd
pretext, the French from this archipelago, was to offer
an insult to France and to its sovereign.
It is, without doubt, the formal intention of France
that the king of the Sandwich Islands be powerful, independent of every foreign power, and that he consider her
his ally ; but she also demands that he conforms to the
usages of civilized nations. Now, among the latter, there
is not even one which does not permit in its territory the
free toleration of all religions ; and yet, at the Sandwich
Islands, the French are not allowed, publicly, the exercise
of theirs, while Protestants enjoy therein the most extensive privileges ; for these, all favors—for those, the
most cruel persecution. Such a state of affairs being
contrary to the laws of nations, insulting to those of
Catholics, can no longer continue, and I am sent to put
an end to it. Consequently, I demand, in the name of
my government,
1st. That the Catholic worship be declared free
throughout all the dominions subject to the king of the
Sandwich Islands ; that the members of this religious
faith shall enjoy in them all the privileges granted to
Protestants.
2d. That a site for a Catholic church be given by the
government at Honolulu, a port frequented by the French,
and that this church be ministered by priests of their
nation.
3d. That all Catholics imprisoned, on account of religion, since the last persecutions extended to the French
missionaries, be immediately set at liberty.
4th. That the king of the Sandwich Islands deposit
in the hands of the captain of the Artemise, the sum of
twenty thousand dollars as a guarantee of his future conduct towards France, which sum the government will restore to him when it shall consider that the accompanying treaty will be faithfully complied with.
5th. That the treaty signed by the king of the Sandwich Islands, as well as the sum above mentioned, be
conveyed on board the frigate Artemise by one of the
principal chiefs of the country ; and also that the batteries of Honolulu do salute the French flag with twenty-
one guns, which will be returned by the frigate.
These are the equitable conditions, at the price of which
the king of the Sandwich Islands shall conserve friendship with France. I am induced to hope that, understanding better how necessary it is for the prosperity of
his people, and the preservation of his power, he will remain in peace with the whole world, and hasten to sub-
scribe to them, and thus imitate the laudable example
which the queen of Tahiti has given in permitting the

free toleration of the Catholic religion in her dominions; but, if contrary to my expectations, it should be otherwise, and the king and principal chiefs of the Sandwich Islands, led on by bad counselors, refuse to sign the treaty which I present, war will immediately commence, and all the devastations, all the calamities which may be the unhappy but necessary results, will be imputed to themselves alone; and they must also pay the losses which the aggrieved foreigners, in these circumstances, shall have a right to reclaim.

The 10th of July (9th, according to date here), 1839.

Captain of the French frigate Artemise,
(Signed,)   C. LAPLACE."

This document is a strange compound of error and falsehood. To declare that free toleration of all religions is permitted in the territories of all civilized nations, was untrue ; also that Frenchmen had been persecuted under the plea of their religion. Mr. Short, an English subject, had been sent away with the consent of his government ; two French priests, the departure of one of whom had been guaranteed by the highest official authority of their nation that had visited Oahu, had also been sent off. The few remaining Frenchmen who lived at these islands, of whom there were not above four, and the three whaleships which had for two years before alone represented their commerce, had been treated with all the respect and hospitality enjoyed by the most favored nation. The following letter was sent ashore at the same time :

MONSIEUR LE CONSUL:
Having been sent by my government to put an end to the ill treatment to which, under the false pretexts of Catholicity, the French have been subjected, for several years, in this archipelago, my intention is to commence hostilities on the 13th of July (which is the 12th of your date), at 12 M., against the king of the Sandwich Islands, should he refuse to accede immediately to the just conditions of the treaty presented by me, the clauses of which I explain in the Manifesto of which I have the honor of sending you a copy. Should this chief, contrary to my expectation, persist in his blindness, or, to express myself more plainly, to follow the advice of interested counsel ors, to deceive himself, I shall be constrained, in this case, to employ the strong means of force which I have at my disposition. I consider it my duty to inform you, Monsieur le Consul, that I offer asylum and protection, on board the frigate Artemise, to those of your compatriots who may apprehend danger, under these circumstances, on the part of the natives, either for their persons or property.
Receive, Monsieur le Consul, the assurances of the very distinguished considerations of your devoted servant.
Post Captain, commanding the ship Artemise,
C. LAPLACE.

A similar communication was also addressed to the American consul, with this addition :

" I do not, however, include in this class the individuals who, although born, it is said, in the United States, make a part of the Protestant clergy of the chief of this archipelago, direct his councils, influence his conduct, and are the true authors of the insults given by him to France. For me, they compose a part of the native population, and must undergo the unhappy consequences of a war which they shall have brought on this country."

By the tenor of the last, it is uncertain whether Captain Laplace intended to include in his denunciation Mr. Richards only, as being the sole official adviser of the chiefs, or the entire Protestant clergy, as exercising an influence hostile to his faith. They considered it as applying to their whole body, and were much alarmed, particularly as Laplace, in verbal communication with the American consul, had informed him that the American flag would prove no protection to the proscribed individuals; and that if a man of his vessel should be injured, it was to be a war of extermination.

The harbor was declared under blockade ; a vessel of the king's in attempting to reach Maui, with despatches for his majesty, was captured, but suffered to proceed ; Haalilio, his secretary, remaining on board the frigate as a hostage for his arrival. At the request of Kekauluohi, the date of commencing hostilities was postponed until the 15th, that sufficient time might be allowed for the arrival of the king. The excitement among all classes was great; many feared the natives would take advantage of the first confusion, fire the town and plunder the property of the residents. A number of the latter organized themselves into an armed force, to act in case of emergency. The native authorities took such active measures to insure tranquility, that the town remained perfectly quiet; guards were stationed at exposed points, and the people required to abide the orders of government. A disposition to a passive resistance to the demands of Laplace was at first manifested. It was proposed to abandon the town to the landing force, and strike the flag at the firing of the first gun from the frigate. Had Kinau been alive, it was thought more energetic councils would have prevailed; Kekauluohi was inferior to her in decision and intellectual capacity. Exaggerated stories were set afloat among the native population. It was said the French were to carry fire and sword through the island; their guns were able to reach the distance of ten miles, and to add to their horror, were loaded with the limbs of natives. The lowest class of whites, who had long writhed under the municipal regulations for the preservation of decency, rejoiced at the prospect of the approaching storm. The expected warfare was to be to them a jubilee of license and revenge. But the thinking part of the community freely expressed their opinion of the conduct of France toward her ill-matched opponent; their sympathies were warmly enlisted with the native rulers; and while they would have regretted the wanton destruction of lives or property, they would have rejoiced in any scheme by which the ill-disguised threats and triumph of the white allies of the Boki faction could have been defeated. In the fierceness of the zeal of these enemies of the nation, the most unwarrantable expressions were used; those whose professions had been the loudest for simply religious toleration, whose clamor had been, if their own accounts are to be credited, solely for the diffusion of equal rights, to infuse humanity into the acts of government, now lusted for revenge. The English consul was away during the first excitement; upon his arrival, he intrigued to defeat the designs of a party that had now become so formidable as to form a separate French interest, headed by M. Dudoit. French or American ascendency was equally obnoxious to him; a moral ascendency, more than either. The missionaries were alarmed. Hated and mocked at by some of their own countrymen, implicated in alleged criminality with the government, no explanation allowed from either, threats of pillage and bloodshed hourly borne to their trembling families, it argues no deficiency of courage, knowing from past experience the depth of the hostility that environed them, if they did fear the consequences for their wives and children. The friendly foreigners, engrossed by the shortness of the time for providing for their own safety, could only sympathize with them. Yet it should be recorded that the mission made no attempt to shift any responsibility which their influence with the government could legally have brought upon them. The fidelity of the native government to them, and the generous devotion of their converts, places the relationship of all parties in the highest light. It was decided to obtain peace

20

on the terms demanded. His Hawaiian Majesty not having arrived within the stipulated time, Governor Kekuanaoa, and the premier, Kekauluohi, in his behalf, signed the treaty, which, with the twenty thousand dollars, were carried on board the Artemise by the former. This money was raised with great difficulty; the government debts were yet unpaid, and much of this sum was borrowed at a high interest from foreign merchants. The tri-colored flag received the royal salute, which was promptly returned. The king arrived on the same day, Sunday, the 14th. Captain Laplace, escorted by two hundred seamen with fixed bayonets and a band of music, went on shore for the purpose of celebrating a military mass. To render this renewal of Romish rites more poignant, a straw palace of the king's was selected for the ceremony, which was performed by the Rev. Mr. Walsh.

The original design of Rives was now established so far as the formal introduction of Roman Catholicism was concerned.

Another purpose remained to be gained. In 1838, the king, yielding to the advice of his council, prohibited the introduction of ardent spirits into his kingdom, and laid a heavy duty on wines. These measures were popular, and had been strongly urged by many foreigners; through their influence the harbors became quiet resorts for shipping, instead of ports of noisy carousal. But the dealers were not disposed to quietly abandon their profits; the Sandwich Islands Gazette openly recommended resistance to the collection of the duties. Previous to the expected arrival of the Artemise, a plan was concocted by which the prohibition and duties should be removed, and forever prevented from renewal. Capt. Belcher, who had returned in the Sulphur, and sailed shortly before the arrival of the Artemise, witnessing the good results of the laws in question, wrote to the king, recommending a system of duties on liquors so high as virtually to amount to prohibition. But Laplace thought otherwise. Inimical to the nation, a stranger to its history, it was not to be supposed that he should be particularly anxious for the habits and health of the Hawaiians, when in competition with the tastes and pecuniary interests of his countrymen. So it proved. A treaty was drawn up, and offered to the king for his signature. Articles 4th and 6th received his objections; the first, because it was supposed to put too much authority into the hands of the consul, who would have it in his power to shield his countrymen to a considerable extent from the action of the civil law. The other, that it virtually repealed all their legislation for the promotion of temperance and shielding his subjects from a prolific source of evil and disease. It also took away from him the power of receiving a revenue from imports, greater than five per cent. ad valorem.

As no time was fixed for the termination of the treaty, it could be made always binding upon his government, however injurious in its operation. It was brought to him at 5 o'clock, P. M., on the 16th, and he was required to sign it by breakfast the next morning. No amendment of the objectionable features was allowed; it must be signed as received, or not at all. The king desired time to consult with his council; this was refused. Neither the consul nor Laplace dared openly to commit themselves, by saying to him, that if he refused war would ensue; but it was bandied about among his attendants, so as to reach his ears, that in such an event there would be no end to the trouble; that this frigate would be succeeded by a larger force, and ultimately his island would be taken possession of. It was a successful design to entrap the king through his fears; the treaty received his reluctant signature. The friendship of France was now secured, and everything was to go on swimmingly. But the unfortunate monarch felt ill at ease. In an interview with Laplace he repeated his objections, and pleaded his innocence of the charges for which his kingdom had suffered. But it was to no purpose. Fortified by prejudice and abused power, the representative of enlightened and chivalrous France argued for inundating a nation, against its will, with the poisonous products of his own; to the just and forcible arguments of a semi-civilized monarch,

pleading in broken English his own and his country's wrongs, replied with the threadbare calumnies of twenty years' growth; and to the picture of the evils which his acts would produce, in so youthful a stage of civilization, mockingly answered, "civilization eats up the savage." It is much to be regretted that those who had the confidence of the king at this date did not strenuously counsel him not to sign a document fraught with so much injustice to his kingdom. There is no reason to believe that any worse consequence would have ensued than the disappointment of its partisans. But the nation was yet too young to throw itself upon its rights. Much more untoward experience was in store for it, before it could claim a rank among independent kingdoms. After the treaty, the external courtesies of national intercourse were exchanged.

On the 20th of July the Artemise sailed; but previous to this, the residents opposed to the missionaries addressed a letter of thanks to Captain Laplace, in which, after much of similar character, occurs the following passage:

"We are willing to hope that the horrifying realities of persecution and torture for conscience sake will, by your firmness and *justice*, have been forever crushed—never again to show its hydra head; and that the simple and confiding children of nature in these islands—so long deluded by designing and interested counselors—will see the necessity of immediately retracing their steps, and taking a manly and nobly disinterested example you have set them for their guide, that the blessings of freedom, and peace and prosperity, may be henceforward the increasing portion of these hitherto deluded people."

The French consul was not slow to avail himself of the extorted privileges. A vessel belonging to him, the same Clementine which had already acquired an unenviable notoriety in the annals of Hawaii, returned from Valparaiso in the following May with a cargo of liquors. The bishop of Nicopolis, M. Maigret, and two other priests came passengers in her. The coincidence of ardent spirits with the cause of papacy, had been striking throughout; while Boki favored the priests, intemperance prevailed; the commander that had ensured them an entrance into the long coveted ground, provided for the accompaniment of liquors. Walsh encouraged their use, both by example and precept. And now a vessel arrived, well provided with both. No wonder then that the terms for brandy and Frenchmen, meaning Papists, became synonymous through the nation; to this day *palani* is the common term of both.

Previous to the arrival of the bishop and the priests, a disposition was manifested to renew the practices of Boki's misrule. Old songs and sports were indulged in by the party who had long favored them in secret, and forms of vice and error prevailed, which it would be unjust to suppose would have received the countenance of their present spiritual guides. But such facts serve emphatically to show the difference of opinion and desires among the native population, between those who favored the cause of Popery and the advocates of Protestantism. With the former, the disorganizers of society, the rude and reckless, embodied themselves, bringing with them the remains of their idolatry, and creating discredit to their cause; around the others, the rulers, scholars, and people generally, desirous of enforcing moral restraint and the supremacy of law. Kaikioewa died April 10th, 1839. Both he and Kinau were chiefs of well known Christian principles, and firm supporters of the American mission. Their bodies, after lying in state for several weeks, were committed to the tomb with the honors due their rank, but with a quietness of grief, and an order, consonant with the faith which they had embraced. The funeral ceremonies of Liliha, who had lived deprived of office until her death, which occurred on the 25th of August, 1839, gathered the partisans of heathenism from all quarters. An attempt was made to revive obsolete rites; wailing was heard night and day; the shouts of a former generation were renewed; but the guards of the king prevented any disturbances of the public order. With her were buried the last hopes of the faction she had so energetically headed.

Roman Catholicism was now fully tolerated, both as a creed and a system of proselytism. Introduced however under circumstances so repugnant to justice and the wishes of the people, it could not be expected to operate harmoniously with its rival faith, in the outset of its career. The sentiment of the nation was against it. Not a chief of importance attached himself to the cause, though numbers of the lower order, disaffected either with their rulers or coldly inclined towards their Protestant guides, enrolled themselves among its neophytes. Curiosity drew many to its rites; but their attendance or support were uncertain. Enough were found however to encourage the priests to persevere in their mission. The bishop returned to France in 1841, having first provided for the erection of a spacious stone church in Honolulu, to procure more laborers in his field, with a supply of church ornaments and the gaudy paraphernalia of their ritual, on which so much is relied to attract the multitude. On the passage back with a company of nuns and others and a cargo for their mission, the vessel foundered at sea and all perished. In the meanwhile, his brethren found much source of complaint against the government, particularly in regard to the school laws and the marriage contract, which was a civil institution. The priests at first presumed to separate and re-marry couples at their option, and their partisans declined contributing their quota of taxation for the public schools. The ill-blood arising from past sores was not yet purified. Both parties among the lower order were prone to collisions. The Roman Catholics were sustained in their seditious views by the belief that France would support them. The French consul protested against any restraint on the internal traffic in ardent spirits by way of licenses. Affairs were in this state, when on the 23d day of August, 1842, H. M. C. M.'s corvette Embuscade arrived. As she hove in sight, the native converts to the Roman creed raised the cry, "ko makou haku e," there is our master. Captain Mallet, without exchanging the customary salutes, immediately forwarded a letter to the king, in which he made several arbitrary demands.

A compliance with the demands of Captain Mallet would have been contrary to the laws, and rendered the Roman Catholic party independent of the king's sovereignty. The answer of the king was courteous and dignified. It so far satisfied Captain Mallet that he sailed without giving further trouble, assuring the king that he should deliver his letter to Admiral Du Petit Thouars, who might be expected the ensuing spring. Whatever designs the Admiral had upon the Hawaiian Islands can now only be conjectured. Providence so ordered events that the French from this period, sufficiently occupied in establishing themselves in their southern possessions, neglected the affairs of this kingdom until it was too late to frame a pretext for its occupancy. But other agents were at work for the same purpose. At this juncture it would seem as if each of the three great commercial nations, fortuitously through their naval agents rather than by any preconcerted policy at home, were bent upon seizing available ports in the Pacific to extend their power and curb that of their equally ambitious rivals. The United States, through Commodore Jones, made a sweep upon California; France, by Admiral Du Petit Thouars, took possession of the Marquesan and Society groups. England, not to be behind in the race, by Lord George Paulet pounced upon the Hawaiian Islands.

CHAPTER XII.

BEFORE proceeding further in the course of political events, it will be well to retrace our steps a little, and show to the reader the different stages through which the government became involved in those difficulties which led to the seizure of the islands by Lord George Paulet. Without doubt the French, encouraged by misrepresentations from interested individuals, desired at that period to do by them as they afterwards did by Tahiti. But too many national interests were involved and the islands were too valuable for them to succeed as quietly as they wished; so they turned their attention to fields of lesser note. England, with highly honorable policy, has ever been willing that these islands should rise and prosper under their native dynasty. This is more to her credit, from the fact that her representative, Mr. Charlton, had ever urged a contrary policy, indirectly if not directly, by representing the native rulers as wholly unfit for governing, and sedulously inculcating the sentiment that they were subjects of Great Britain. On many occasions, he treated them with indignity, threatening their lives and using language unpardonable for its violence and unreasonableness. In the early part of his career it has been seen how he, impolitically for the interests of his own countrymen, countenanced the introduction of French priests, which finally led to the creation of an adverse interest that well nigh gave the nation to a rival power. Perceiving when too late the direction of affairs from the impulse he had given them, he followed in their lead by raising grievances of his own which he confidently hoped would lead to the active interference of the British government, and ultimately to taking possession of the group. To have effected this, he must have deceived not only his own government, but blinded the rival interests of France and America. Had he been a dispassionate, shrewd man, possibly he could have effected greater injury than he did; but from 1833, when his natural character was so forcibly disclosed by leading the king into vicious habits to the upsetting of order and morality, his influence had been on the wane. Disappointed by this very natural consequence, he zealously lent himself to the injury of the nation, opposing all that they favored, and nourishing every case which could generate discord or involve the rulers. His conduct was a pitiable illustration of passion without reason, and it is the more melancholy to refer to it as its effects were so pernicious for a time to the welfare of the nation and the moral tone of society. His official rank alone entitled him to consideration and gave him influence. Without it he would have been politically harmless.

Previous to the appointment of the Rev. Wm. Richards, July 3, 1838, as chaplain, teacher and translator of the government, it had been swayed alternately by missionary, mercantile and official influences brought to operate upon it. In the early stages of the influence the latter had often the advantage; but later, the former acquired a paramount influence, though Mr. Richards was the first who received an office and title, first dissevering himself from the mission by their advice and consent. Under these modest titles his influence on the foreign policy of the chiefs became considerable, and in it he was sustained by his late brethren. The sort of influence which the missionaries held has been much discussed. It is impossible to ascertain its full extent as it was so undefined. That it was great and legitimately acquired and sincerely used for the good of the people, no candid person who has made himself acquainted with their history will doubt. Each missionary was generally the friend of some chief living in his neighborhood, and over whom he imperceptibly acquired that influence which moral confidence is sure to engender, so that without knowing exactly how it was, he felt himself powerful in his little field. The missionaries being united in policy were thus enabled to affect the tone of the public councils through the voices of their individual friends. They mainly employed this influence to benefit the people, by indoctrinating them with more humane views towards their dependents and juster sentiments of their rights. In this way the national taxes, burdens and customs, the offspring of despotic heathenism, became vastly ameliorated, and the chiefs themselves advanced to some degree of knowledge and refinement. The missionaries could not however exercise even this wholesome influence without subjecting themselves to invidious charges. Hence arose the enmity developed in the political proceedings given in the previous chapters. Mr. Bingham was long known by the soubriquet of " King Hiram." But influence was not confined to the missionaries alone. It was acquired by those who differed widely from them on the same principle by securing the friendship and confidence of individual chiefs whose tastes were congenial with their white intimates. But these were greatly outnumbered by the more reflective and serious class with the all-powerful Kaahumanu at their head. Throughout their history it has been found that whenever the spirit of license came in conflict with the sense of right, the former, though often for a while ascendant, in the end invariably succumbed to the latter. The mission and high chiefs formed a moral bulwark to the nation that had never been wholly cut down, but has arisen firmer and higher after every assault.

It is not intended by this description to convey the impression that either side were wholly right or wholly wrong. So long as the missionaries confined their influences to purposes wholly within their legitimate sphere of action, and of which they were by profession and experience the best qualified to judge, all went well. But when, even though with the best intentions, they overstepped that line, they failed—failed through those very qualities which were their own passports to confidence. In honorable, practical business men, the chiefs would have found much more efficient advisers in purely business matters, and it is now much to be regretted that the agency of such had not been earlier called in, when they were in doubt. But the implicit faith they had in the intentions of their religious teachers led to an equal reliance on their judgments; these judgments were too often formed rather through the medium of a professed common faith or sanctity than through the exercise of sound reason and necessary caution. A plain answer from a practical business man of good principles, whether he was a brother communicant or not, would have been worth quires of sentimental essays on prospective good and benevolence, which were to find their dubious way to the nation by first lining the pockets of the projectors. The errors into which the advisers of the chiefs not unfrequently fell were very natural, but very lamentable. A more comprehensive view of the selfishness and deceitfulness of human nature would have saved them. At all events, it would have been a wise policy to have distrusted sanguine schemes whose fate depended upon profound secrecy even from those who were to be most affected by their success or failure, and it would have been wiser still to have offset one set of views, whether mercantile or political, by an appeal to others, and thus hit upon safety by a prudent medium.

In another sense the managing parties were right. Deceived they might be in the motives and character of their professed friends, yet so long as they believed them sincere, it was just that the countenance should have been mutual. The fault was not over-support but over-confidence.

However, governments, like men, acquire wisdom by dear bought experience. It has been thus with the Hawaiian. None of the numerous lessons from friends or foes have been lost on them, and the adversities of one year have added to the wisdom of the next. It is a small nation, but history will develop the fact that it is hardening its bones and sinews by a process analogous to that of the youth who leaves his father's house with but little in the outset to meet the rubs of active selfishness save an honest heart and a docile disposition. Sooner or later the faculties develop, and the incautious boy ripens into the experienced man.

Mr. Richards entered upon his official duties by delivering to the chiefs a course of lectures on Political Economy and the general science of government. From the ideas thus derived, based upon their old forms, a constitution was drawn up. Although greatly limiting their power, the chiefs passed it unanimously.

The laws of the kingdom were care-

fully revised and published. In comparison with the past, the progress of the nation was now rapid. The liberal policy of other nations, and whatever of their forms could with propriety be here transplanted, were embodied in the new statutes, but on a scale commensurate with the feebleness and youth of the people. The penal code was greatly improved; primary and courts of appeal established; the jury system adopted. Provision was made for the more regular enforcement of debt—transmission of property, property in trust, interest accounts, in short sufficient was done greatly to benefit the position of natives and foreigners. Taxation was rendered more equal and lighter. Encouragement was proffered to industry and to the increase of population. An enlightened public school system was organized. Their laws, imperfect as they may seem to the critical eyes of a superior civilization, were yet in advance of the people. But wherever they were allowed to operate fairly and systematically much good was effected, and they served to prepare the way for more important changes.

The people were thoroughly convinced that the immunity once claimed by chiefs for crimes of their own, was at an end by an impartial trial by jury of one of that class in 1840, for the murder of his wife. He with an accomplice were both brought in guilty, and suffered the full penalty of the law, death by hanging. The foreigners also began to see that there was some virtue in the courts, by a fine imposed upon the English consul for riotous conduct.

The results of the Laplace treaty in removing the prohibition of ardent spirits were not so pernicious to the nation as was first anticipated. The immediate effect was bad. Natives of both sexes were seen reeling through the streets. But so much moral sentiment was brought to operate, that the government prohibited the natives from manufacturing ardent spirits, and finally the king and chiefs, in the spring of 1842, destroyed what store they had on hand, and pledged themselves to total abstinence. Numerous temperance societies were formed and considerable enthusiasm awakened on the subject. The pledges have in general been kept. The king and court continued strictly temperate, and the rules of government visit prompt penalty and disgrace upon any of their officers found guilty of violating their pledge.

While the nation was thus advancing in moral improvement and respectability, the government experienced constant annoyance from the arrogance and pretensions of Mr. Charlton, who was evidently concerting a collision between it and his own. The most frivolous complaints were willingly received, judged upon and made subjects of threats, before they had been referred to the proper tribunals or one word elicited in reply. In effect, he centered in himself at once, prosecutor, witness, judge and sheriff.

The courts of the country were constituted upon the best basis its means allowed. In ordinary mercantile cases, with the aid of foreign juries, where no national prejudices were involved or party interests at stake, they gave satisfaction. But in the struggle that was constantly going on between the rival interests of England and America—the one represented by Mr. Charlton, and virulently opposed to the government, and the other by the United States consul, Mr. Brinsmade, who willingly, with most of his countrymen, lent it efficient moral aid by complying with the laws, and treating its feeble endeavors to sustain order and promote civilization with respect—the nation through its courts suffered repeated assaults.

Mr. Brinsmade's predecessor, J. C. Jones, had been in the habit when offended of applying the epithets cheat, liar and other equally indecorous terms to the chiefs.

Complicated law suits arose, in which the principals were American and English. The decision of the governor of Oahu, its constitutional judge, being adverse to the English party, greatly embittered them. The involved estate of French and Greenway became another bone of contention, two Englishmen claiming to act as assignees, neither of whom were recognized by one of the principals, the other being insane, nor by the other creditors. The parties brought their cases into the court, where they were decided unfavorably to the claims of the self-styled assignees. These cases are merely referred to as having given rise to questions of jurisdiction, and being some of many others which after having led to the seizure of the group by Lord George Paulet, were decided upon in England by the law adviser of the crown in favor of the king.

In the spring of 1842, Sir George Simpson and Dr. McLaughlin, governors in the service of the Hudson Bay Company, arrived at the islands. Having extensive mercantile relations on them, they naturally felt interested in the stability of the government and its institutions. After a careful and candid examination into the merits of the existing controversies between their own countrymen and the native government, they came to the full determination of sustaining the latter with their powerful influence. Their agents were instructed accordingly. The king fearing the effect of the false representations of Charlton and his partisans, sought the counsel of Sir George Simpson, by whose advice and pecuniary assistance in a loan of £10,000, it was decided to send commissioners to Europe and the United States, with full powers to negotiate for an acknowledgment of the independence of the islands, and a guarantee against their usurpation by any of the great powers. Recognized as an independent nation, they would be freed from many vexatious interferences in their domestic polity, and questions of jurisdiction, which served no other end than to gratify evil passions and postpone justice. Mr. Brinsmade, the American consul, had left some months previous, on business of his firm—Ladd & Co.—carrying with him an extensive contract for grants and leases of lands under certain conditions, entered into with them, in November, 1840, by the king. On the strength of this he proposed to get up a joint stock company, which should develop the resources of the islands. Unless however the governments of Great Britain, France and the United States "acknowledged the sovereignty of the Sandwich Islands government and accord to it all the rights, powers and privileges and immunities of an independent state," the said contract was to be "null and void." Mr. Brinsmade thus bound himself to see this object secured previous to selling his contract. The after history of this agency in Europe proved a lesson to the government not to involve itself under any pretences or hopes with the private schemes or speculations of mercantile firms. Ladd & Co. had been serviceable to the islands in being the first to introduce agricultural enterprises on an enlarged and systematic scale, by which the industry of the inhabitants was awakened and the resources of the country developed. Their sugar plantation at Koloa, Kauai, was creditable to their enterprise, and had been the means of giving a start to the production of sugar at several other points. Perceiving the real advantages derived to the country from this enterprise, and feeling desirous of sustaining and enlarging it, the government put Ladd & Co. at their solicitation, based upon the idea that their views were philanthropic, into possession of the contract before mentioned. They also advanced them large sums without a sufficient examination into their credit; a neglect arising from over-weening confidence, and which afterwards, failing to get their pay when due, proved very vexatious in the results. But previous to the contract, other sums had been loaned them. The knowledge of these facts naturally excited the jealousy of the English opposition.

Sir George Simpson, Rev. William Richards and Timoteo Haalilio, a native chief, were appointed joint commissioners to proceed to the United States and Europe. Sir George Simpson left immediately. The other two sailed in July, 1842, for Mazatlan, whence they proceeded direct to the United States. G. P. Judd, physician to the American Mission, long and intimately acquainted with the chiefs, was invited by them to supply Mr. Richards' place, acting as recorder and translator. Upon this occasion the mission passed the following vote:

"That as Dr. Judd has resigned his connection with the mission, we therefore express to him our high estimation of his past services, and affectionately request him to co-operate with us in furthering all the grand objects of the mission, so far as he can consistently with his new engagements."

Mr. Judd was further appointed President of the Treasury Board, and to correspond with the commissioners abroad. Upon assuming the duties of the treasury, he immediately introduced a system of reform, which by husbanding the financial resources redeemed the credit of the government. Previous to his advent into office, the sums collected were received by the governors, tax-officers and chiefs, and expended very much at their option without accountability of any kind. It was a system useless to the nation and expensive in its results. Under it any amount of peculation prevailed, though with the ideas of the chiefs it could scarcely be called by that term, as they all claimed the right to help themselves from the public crib. In its stead a rigid economy was exacted. Books were opened; revenues collected and deposited in the treasury; accounts kept with all public officers; useless mouths cut off; services alone were paid for; salaries established; the public debts made up; national property distinguished from individual; in short, a system admirably calculated to gain the confidence of the community and to benefit the nation arose out of the confusion and bankruptcy that prevailed before. This was not done without murmuring or discontent from those whose sinecure offices were now at an end. But the perseverance of Mr. Judd triumphed over all obstacles, and the statistics of the treasury since have told a flattering story.

In September, 1842, Mr. Charlton, fearing the results of the embassy of Messrs. Haalilio and Richards upon his own office, left his consulate surreptitiously for London via Mexico, to lay his complaints before the British government. Mr. Alexander Simpson, his friend and appointed successor, says of him in his history of these events, "he did not possess the qualifications necessary for a diplomatist—coolness, discretion and an abstinence from party heats and personal animosities."

Mr. Charlton's career was terminated by his own act. He had no sooner arrived in London than he was removed from his situation under circumstances of disgrace. The Earl of Aberdeen considered the finale of his diplomacy as intemperate, improper and ill-judged, calculated to do great mischief and to produce in the minds of the king and his advisers, whether *natives* or *foreigners*, a resentful feeling not only against Mr. Charlton, but against the British government and their subjects. These sentiments are authentic, and clearly show that it was no part of the policy of England that her commissioned officers should insult even Hawaiian majesty.

The king declined receiving Alexander Simpson as vice-consul. The grounds of his refusal, in the words of his officer addressed to him, "were because you despise the authorities of the kingdom and say you are going to make disturbance in the kingdom." Mr. Simpson fully justifies the king in believing him to be a seditious character in his own work, where he states, "From the period of my first visit to the Sandwich Islands, I became convinced of their value and importance, and, therefore, desirous that *they should form a British possession.*"

Mr. Simpson immediately called a meeting of the favorers of his views, who passed a resolution favorable to his exercising the duties of consul, which he continued to do, unnoticed by other consuls and unsanctioned by the king.

His ambition being to make the islands an appendage of the British crown, he industriously fomented difficulties and devised means to effect this favorite project. Through his influence, memorials purporting to come from British residents, but notoriously signed by individuals of no note, were forwarded to his government.

At this time, Mr. Pelly, agent of the Hudson's Bay Company, instituted a suit for nearly £3,000 against Mr. Charlton, for a debt due parties in Valparaiso since 1832. The case was brought before a foreign jury and a verdict given against Mr. Charlton, whose property was attached by order of the court for payment.

On his way to England, Mr. Charlton had fallen in with Lord George Paulet, commanding H. B. M. frigate Carysfort, and by his representations interested his

lordship in his views. Simpson had also sent despatches to the coast of Mexico, which induced Rear Admiral Thomas to order the Carysfort to Honolulu, for the purpose of inquiring into the matter. She arrived on the 10th of February, 1843, before the sale of Charlton's property had taken place. Simpson immediately went on board to concert measures with Lord George, who, from his entire acquiescence in his plans, appears to have been wholly won over at this interview to sustain them. The authorities on shore suspected there was no friendly feeling, from the withholding the usual salutes. Mr. Judd, on behalf of the government, made an official call on board, but was informed he could not be received. Visits from the French and United States consuls were similarly declined. Captain Paulet addressed the governor, informing him that he wished to confer with the king, who was then absent.

The king arrived from Maui on the 16th, and on the next day received the following letter and demands from Lord George Paulet:

H. B. M.'s Ship Carysfort,
Oahu, 17th February, 1843.

Sir:—In answer to your letter of this day's date—which I have too good an opinion of your Majesty to allow me to believe ever emanated from yourself, but from your ill-advisers—I have to state that I shall hold no communication whatever with Dr. G. P. Judd, who it has been satisfactorily proved to me has been the punic mover in the unlawful proceedings of your government against British subjects.

As you have refused me a personal interview, I enclose you the demands which I consider it my duty to make upon your government; with which I demand a compliance at or before 4 o'clock, P. M., to-morrow—Saturday—otherwise I shall be obliged to take immediate coercive steps to obtain these measures for my countrymen.

I have the honor to be your Majesty's most obedient, humble servant,

George Paulet, Captain.

His Majesty, Kamehameha III.

Demands made by the Right Honorable Lord George Paulet, Captain Royal Navy, commanding H. B. M.'s Ship Carysfort, upon the King of the Sandwich Islands.

First. The immediate removal, by public advertisement, written in the native and English languages, and signed by the governor of this island and F. W. Thompson, of the attachment placed upon Mr. Charlton's property; the restoration of the land taken by government for its own use, and really appertaining to Mr. Charlton; and reparation for the heavy loss to which Mr. Charlton's representatives have been exposed by the oppressive and unjust proceedings of the Sandwich Islands government.

Second. The immediate acknowledgment of the right of Mr. Simpson to perform the functions delegated to him by Mr. Charlton; namely, those of Her Britannic Majesty's acting consul, until Her Majesty's pleasure be known upon the reasonableness of your objections to him. The acknowledgment of that right and the reparation for the insult offered to Her Majesty through her acting representative, to be made by

21

a public reception of his commission and the saluting the British flag with twenty-one guns, which number will be returned by Her Britannic Majesty's ship under my command.

Third. A guarantee that no British subject shall in future be subjected to imprisonment in fetters, unless he is accused of a crime which by the laws of England would be considered felony.

Fourth. The compliance with a written promise given by King Kamehameha to Captain Jones, of Her Britannic Majesty's ship Curacoa, that a new and fair trial would be granted in a case brought by Henry Skinner, which promise has been evaded.

Fifth. The immediate adoption of firm steps to arrange the matters in dispute between British subjects and natives of the country, or others residing here, by referring these cases to juries. One-half of whom shall be British subjects, approved by the consul, and all of whom shall declare on oath, their freedom from prejudgment upon, or interest in the cases brought before them.

Sixth. A direct communication between His Majesty Kamehameha and Her Britannic Majesty, acting consul, for the immediate settlement of all cases of grievances and complaint on the part of British subjects against the Sandwich Island Government.

Dated on board H. B. M.'s ship Carysfort, at Oahu, this 17th day of February, 1843.

GEORGE PAULET, Captain.

Captain Long, of the United States ship Boston, then in port, was informed, by letter, at midnight, of the anticipated attack of the British commander. In the morning the Carysfort was cleared for action, springs put on her cables, and her battery brought to bear upon the town. The English families embarked for security on board a brig in the outer roads. The Americans and other foreigners having but short notice, placed their funds and papers on board the Boston and other vessels, intending to retreat to them with their families in case of actual hostilities. The town was in a state of great excitement. The dispositions of the chiefs were uncertain, and it was feared that the rabble, taking advantage of the confusion, might pillage the place. Excited by the gross injustice of the demands, the first impulses of the king and his council, in which they were sustained by the indignant feeling of the entire foreign population, excepting the few who sided with Simpson, were for energetic measures. Arms were procured, and bodies of men began to assemble. The common natives, unconscious of the fatal effects of disciplined gunnery, ardently desired to fight the ship. Some supposed they might overpower her crew by numbers in boarding. But peaceful councils at last prevailed. It is in such emergencies that the real influence of the missionaries becomes apparent. The natural desire of chiefs and foreigners was to resist at all hazards; but the entire

indoctrination of the mission, animated by the peaceful principles of the Gospel, had been of that nature that depends more upon the sword of the spirit than the arm of flesh. Desirous of avoiding the unhappy consequences of strife and bloodshed, and relying, through Providence, on the justice of the nation's cause and the magnanimity of the Queen of Great Britain, they counseled peace. Shortly before the hour of commencing hostilities had arrived, the king dispatched a letter to the Carysfort, informing Lord George Paulet that he yielded to his demands, under protest, and had appointed Sir George Simpson and William Richards as his commissioners to the court of Great Britain to settle the pending difficulties.

His majesty appointed February 20th, at eleven o'clock, A. M., to receive Lord George and the vice-consul. On the same day that the king notified Lord George of his acquiescence in his demands, in conjunction with the premier he protested against his acts in these words :

WE, KAMEHAMEHA III., King of all the Sandwich Islands, and KEKAULUOHI, Premier thereof, in accordance with the laws of nations, and the rights of all aggrieved Sovereigns and individuals, do hereby enter our solemn act of protest before God, the world, and before the Government of Her Most Gracious Majesty, Victoria, Queen of the United Kingdoms of Great Britain and Ireland :

Against the Right Hon. Lord George Paulet, Captain of H. B. M.'s ship Carysfort, now lying in the harbor of Honolulu, for all losses and damages which may accrue to us, and to the citizens of other countries residing under our dominion and sovereignty, in consequence of the unjust demands made upon us this day, by the said Right Hon. Lord George Paulet, enforced by a threat of coercive measures, and an attack upon our town of Honolulu, in case of a non-compliance with the same within a period of nineteen hours; thereby interfering with our laws, endangering the good order of society, and requiring of us what no power has a right to exact of another with whom they are on terms of peace and amity:

And we do solemnly protest and declare, that we, the Sovereign authority of these our islands, are injured, grieved, abused and damaged, by this act of the said Right Hon. Lord George Paulet, and we hereby enter our solemn appeal unto the Government of Her Most Gracious Majesty, represented by him, for redress, for justification, and for repayment of all said losses, damages and payments which may in consequence accrue unto us, or unto the citizens of other countries living under our jurisdiction

On the 20th, the king and premier visited the Carysfort and were received with royal honors. This courtesy, however, was but a prelude to a further series of demands rendered necessary to accomplish Simpson's aim, by the unexpected compliance of the king with the first. These were brought forward at an interview on the following day. The total amount demanded in money was $117,330.89. The character of these claims, and the object of the parties, may be gathered from a brief notice of the first brought forward. This was in favor of a Mr. Skinner, a connexion of Mr. Charlton's. Indemnification to the amount of $3,000 was demanded for him on the alleged ground of having lost the interest and profits on $10,000 unemployed for four months, which he had reserved to purchase the property of Mr. Charlton, if sold on execution. The arrival of the Carysfort had stopped the sale, and he had lost the opportunity of thus employing his funds.

The peculiar nature of the official intercourse of the British officers with the king, is best illustrated by extracts from a journal of the interviews kept at the time on behalf of the native government. "*February* 22d.—Simpson insisted the Dominis case should be re-tried. No plea that it had been done, and that the parties had settled and passed receipts, was to be admitted. The government must plead the case, and pay all that a jury should bring in over the $10,000 which had been paid by Captain Dominis to Mr. Skinner.

"Next, a claim of $400 for a chronometer, alleged to have been detained by the harbor master, an American, (which he denied,) and in consequence Mr. Skinner had to purchase another. The king said he was not acquainted with the facts. This was considered an acknowledgment of his incompetence to be sovereign.

"A demand that either Kekuanaoa or Dr. Judd be set aside as the author of a falsehood."

"Next, a detailed account of the legal proceedings against Simpson and Skinner, and the blame thrown on the governor and the courts." The king said he was not acquainted with the facts in the case. This was denounced as a strange neglect, and no statement to the contrary could be admitted. "Insisted on the immediate reversal of the decision of the courts. The king must do it. He ought to know the merits of the case. He must pay damages." The object of Simpson, to drive the king to despair by the magnitude and unreasonableness of

his demands, was fast gaining ground. Still it was acknowledged, and is on record, that previous to the last act in this semi-tragical drama, it was necessary to obtain the official acknowledgment of the king to all the pecuniary claims he brought forward in his own behalf and those of his interested supporters. Should the government be transferred previous to this, they would be as valueless as they were unjust, which afterwards proved to be the case, as all previous complaints were quashed, and no British subject allowed to bring a grievance against the new government. By this course Simpson was converting what under any circumstances would have been an unjustifiable robbery, into contemptible swindling. In his eagerness he overshot the mark, though not before he had intimidated the king into ratifying a claim which Charlton had set up on the strength of an alleged deed from Kalaimoku, in 1826, to a valuable portion of the town of Honolulu, near the water side, then covered with native houses, and partially owned and built upon by foreigners. This pretended deed had been kept in abeyance for more than twenty years, unheard of by chiefs, and not brought forward until long after the alleged signer and witnesses were dead. By the unanimous testimony of natives and foreigners, Charlton was never considered as having owned one foot of this land. The adjoining property, separated by a street, although given to the English government, by the order of Kaahumanu, in 1826, was still in his undisturbed possession. The land to which he now laid claim belonged, by the most undoubted testimony and by continuous possession, to Kaahumanu and her heirs. Kalaimoku, the alleged granter, had never owned it. More than one hundred natives had lived on it ever since Charlton came to the islands. Yet in face of these well-known facts, Lord George sustained this claim, and through fear of an attack upon his town, induced the king to sign the more than doubtful paper. For even those who conjectured that the signatures might be genuine, were far from supposing that the deed was valid, as it pretended to no consideration, its boundaries were dubious, the circumstances under which it appeared were suspicious, and none believed that Kalaimoku ever signed such a document with a knowledge of its contents. It was contrary both to his habits and power. The weakness of the king in consenting to a ratification of such a fraud upon his territory is lamentable; being wrong in itself, no considerations of force or threats should have availed. But it was done, and a most fruitful diplomatic sore has it since proved between England and this country. The journal of this period, kept by Mr. Judd, so fully illustrates the policy which brought the country into the hands of England, that I quote largely from it, as the most authentic record extant of the actual feelings and dispositions of the king and chiefs, and the various motives operating upon their minds. It is a humiliating confession of weakness, and cannot fail to enlist the sympathies of readers. Sufficient firmness was wanting to give a decided refusal to the treacherous demands of Simpson. Whether force would then have been used is doubtful. If it had, the unauthorized acts of Lord Paulet would have been purely piratical; and on whomsoever the evil might have fallen, the disgrace would have been solely his. Expediency, and the fear of the consequences were English blood shed and the rabble let loose upon the town, decided the question. Aided by the advice they most confided in, which was of a missionary nature, the chiefs chose what they considered the more prudent measure. It savored somewhat of impotent despair on the part of the king and premier, that if they would avoid Sylla they must rush upon Charybdis—save themselves from France by giving themselves to England.

"*24th.*—A meeting having been arranged for 10 o'clock, A. M., the king requested me to visit Lord George, and say to him that he could bear this course no longer; he would give up and let them do as they pleased, etc., etc. I accordingly met Lord George and Simpson in the street, coming to the meeting; said I had a message from the king, that he was sick. I went with them to the consular office, where I was left alone

with Simpson. I said, the king feels himself oppressed, broken down, ruined, and, to use his own expression, a dead man; that he had been up all night, and was sick; that he had determined to give up; that if he, Simpson, persisted in his present course, ruin would follow; that the king could not undo by his own act the action of the courts, and enforce these claims without time to modify the laws. I begged him to desist, and give time to modify the laws and act with consistency. He would allow juries to be composed of half Englishmen in case their interests were concerned. The Dominis case had been disposed of according to the king's written promise to Captain Jones. Moreover, since that time, the parties had settled by amicable arbitration. That to require all the late decisions of the legally organized courts to be set aside by the act of the king, would be illegal and oppressive on the part of Mr. Simpson, and decidedly oppressive on the part of the king, and would justly involve him both with Americans and French, etc., etc. Simpson replied that the English had been treated harshly, and consequently the government must suffer. His course could not be altered.

" Went with Lord George and Simpson to the council; acted as spokesman; reiterated the above, and added, the king was determined to hold out no longer; do what you like, take the islands, but do not force him to acts of injustice; it would be cruel in the extreme, better take all. Lord George replied, that his demands were not unjust, he acted on the best information and testimony. I said, I know that you think so, but I assure you that such is not the opinion of the government. The king remarked that he did not think that his government had done wrong. I said, we must be heard; your information is incorrect; we appeal to Great Britain; take the islands, we will yet have justice. Lord George replied that he did not come to take the islands. I said, you had better do it than pursue these subjects further in this manner. He or Simpson said that they could only act on a request of the king, and it must be in writing. Said I, let all proceedings be stopped; let the government have time to reflect, and I think they will come to the conclusion that it is better for you to take the government of the islands than to go on any further. But we must have time; you drive the king to distraction, and I fear that he will cede the islands to France, as he has been invited to do. Simpson said he would not allow much delay. Lord George said, two or three days and no more. Simpson said, to-morrow noon, and if it was not done, he should expect the Dominis case to be tried on Saturday. I observed that the time was too short. Monday then at the furthest. We went into certain explanations as to the manner of doing the thing, and I wrote down in pencil the following:

"'In consequence of the difficulties in which the Sandwich Islands are involved, and the impossibility of complying with the demands made by Her Britannic Majesty's representative, we cede [the government of] our islands to Lord George Paulet, etc., etc., for the time being, subject to any arrangements that may have been entered into with the government of Great Britain, and until intelligence shall have been received, and in case no arrangement shall have been made previous to date, subject to the decision of Her Majesty's government on conference with the ministers of the Sandwich Islands government, after a full report of our affairs shall have been represented to Great Britain; and in case the ministers are rejected by Her Britannic Majesty, then subject to any arrangements which may be entered into.'

"Simpson took the paper and walked in the verandah with Lord George, and returning, said that would do; he would make a copy with a very few verbal alterations.

"It was arranged that the chiefs should have an opportunity to consider these things, and an answer to be given to-morrow noon. Lord George and Simpson left. King and Auhea sat with astonishment and misery. Discussed awhile in council, when I left them in order to take some refreshment. When I returned, I found them anxious to gain further information. The subject of ceding to France and the United States was a ray of hope which seemed to gleam across their dark path, but they foresaw that under such circumstances they would still have this fury—Simpson—to deal with until the French took possession, and he would doubtless involve them in more trouble, and their cause become too bad to admit of justification. France is still acting a hostile part towards them. Charlton and Simpson are their enemies, but England is their friend. To England they look up with the most filial affections. France is picking a quarrel with them now, and complaints are now in existence which will make more trouble. If the claims of Simpson are allowed, the laws will suffer, and the nation be weakened so much that France will leave them nothing. England can defend them from France, and to cede to France would be to say England had no right here, which is to the government more than doubtful, reckoning right as the nations do. This might be considered an act of treachery.

"May be that their independence is secured already; if so, a forcible possession on the part of either would annul it. A cession would not, if made with provisos.

"In the evening I went for Lord George, who, together with Simpson and Dr. Rooke, came. Regulated a few points respecting the course he should pursue in case he took possession. Informed them that we should take every possible step to justify the government and get back the islands, and demanded a pledge that such exertions be not considered an act of hostility to them.

"It was agreed that a decision should be made by 12 o'clock on the 25th. Lord George went away. Every possible view of the case was taken up by the council, and the result seemed to be to give up the islands on the terms proposed.

"*25th.*—The king sent for me before breakfast. Wished to know what I thought of the old proposition of ceding to France and the United States. I said I feared it would involve the government in great trouble. The French admiral would soon be here and take possession, which would excite hostility between Catholics and Protestants; meanwhile Simpson would continue his course of conduct, and the difficulties would become inextricable. Give yourself into the arms of Great Britain, trust to the generosity of that great and good nation, you may have the benefit of the intervention of France for the adjustment of difficulties and the security of your independence. Let them take possession, and then you can represent your case in full. Lord George called. I informed him that the matter was nearly decided. One of the propositions that came from me was waived, viz : that a commission be appointed to adjust the claims of British subjects. "Dudoit called, and many others. Every argument used to induce the king to cede to France and the United States. Sat down to put the documents into form. The king proposed to make a speech. I said they could make that out among themselves, which they did. Deed of cession being ready, the chiefs came in and it was read. Sorrow and distress marked every countenance. I was asked to pray. During prayer, sighs suppressed were often heard. I committed the case to God, imploring His blessing on the step about to be taken as the only peaceful alternative for the nation, etc., etc. When I rose, not an individual left his knees for a full minute, and then I saw that tears had come to their relief. They sat in silence for a moment, when the king arose, and with a firm step seized a pen and subscribed his name. 'Let it go,' said he ; 'if I get help I get it, if not, let it go. I can do no more.' The premier then added her signature."

Having decided upon a provisional cession of his dominions to Great Britain, the king announced the event to his subjects in a touching proclamation :

Where are you, chiefs, people and commons from my ancestors, and people from foreign lands!

Hear ye! I make known to you that I am in perplexity by reason of difficulties into which I have been brought without cause ; therefore, I have given away the life of our land, hear ye! But my rule over you, my people, and your privileges, will continue, for I have hope that the life of the land will be restored when my conduct is justified.

Done at Honolulu, Oahu, this twenty-fifth day of February, 1843.

(Signed,)   KAMEHAMEHA III.
                    KEKAULUOHI.

At the request of Lord George, Mr. Judd was appointed by the king as his deputy. Mr. Judd positively declined to undertake the responsibility, and the king then appointed William Paty, Esq., whom Lord George refused to receive. Upon the renewed solicitation of the king, that he could do much for the nation and his interests, and a written assurance from Lord George that his services were required in the new ad-

ministration, Mr. Judd consented to act, the king authorizing him to employ Mr. Paty in his other duties. The night of the cession the king went to Maui, and officers were sent the next day to hoist the British flag on the other islands.

Disturbances between the English soldiers and natives commenced immediately, but were quelled by prompt action on the part of the native authorities. The policy of the chiefs was to preserve order and await the decision of England. The foreign residents were, however, restless under the new rule. No respect was shown the British officers, and their conduct was loudly execrated. The French consul refusing to acknowledge the new government, his official functions were suspended.

The commission immediately issued a proclamation, levying an additional duty of one per cent. on the previous duty of three, ad valorem, on imported goods ; all lands held by whites were required to be registered previous to June 1st ; new registers were granted to vessels owned by foreign residents, putting them upon the same footing as British bottoms ; and some alterations were made in the municipal law. Mr. Judd refused assent to many of these measures, so that the new commission was far from acting harmoniously.

On the 11th of March, Mr. Simpson left Honolulu for England, in a vessel belonging to the king, with dispatches to the foreign office from Lord George Paulet. The king and chiefs, desirous of being represented at London on an occasion of such vital importance by an agent of their own, ordered Dr. Judd to look for one. Mr. J. F. B. Marshall, an American gentleman resident at Honolulu, was applied to. Having consented to go, secret instructions were given him ; his commission and papers were signed by the king at Waikiki, who came from Lahaina for that purpose, and stopped there to avoid meeting the British Commission. Without disclosing his agency to Simpson, Mr. Marshall was allowed passage in the same vessel, by which he carried the news of the cession, via Mexico, to the United States and England.

Notwithstanding the solemn stipulations on the part of Lord George Paulet to respect existing laws and engagements, repeated efforts were made to violate their spirit. The populace, impatient under the new rule, became less tractable daily. Great efforts were made to get up a native British party. Men were bought by promises and gifts. The loose practices of former times were partially winked at. The auction laws were altered, and heavy duties imposed. The wholesome regulations regarding lewdness and other common vices were repealed. Boat-loads of prostitutes were allowed to visit ships in the harbor as in the days of Liholiho. Indecorous and disgusting scenes were witnessed in the streets at noon-day.* Soldiers were enlisted under the name of the Queen's regiment, and officers commissioned. The king and his chiefs were repeatedly insulted. Every effort was made to seize the national treasury and records. Illegal orders on the former were presented. Mr. Judd was formally informed by Lord George, that unless he honored his drafts, he should be dismissed from office, and some one put in his place who would be more pliant. The authority of the courts was prostituted;—in short, anarchy and violence began to appear, and it was evident that the British officers, rioting in their brief and ill-gotten authority, respected no compacts and acknowledged no guides beyond their own wills. Mr. Judd, anxious to preserve the authority of the king as long as possible for the good of his people, held his office until the 10th of May, when entering a solemn protest against the acts of Lord George Paulet, he withdrew from the commission, absolving the king from all further responsibility or connection with its doings. This act was formally approved by the king and premier. On the 24th of June following they issued a proclamation, charging the commissioners with having maintained soldiers not called for by any exigencies of the country, " out of funds appropriated for the payment of our just debts," and " violating the laws which, by the treaty, were to be held sacred," and of other mal-practices, calling the world to witness that they had " broken faith

with us," protesting in the face of all men against all such proceedings both towards themselves and foreigners.

After this withdrawal of the king, affairs daily became more uneasy between the natives and resident foreigners and the British force. Mr. Judd fearing imprisonment and the seizure of the national records, withdrew them from the government house, and secretly placed them in the royal tomb. In this abode of death, surrounded by the sovereigns of Hawaii, using the coffin of Kaahumanu for a table, for many weeks he nightly found an unsuspected asylum for his own labors in behalf of the kingdom. It required no small degree of prudence on the part of one so influential and beloved among the natives to prevent an actual collision between the hostile parties. With unshaken reliance on the justice of England, the chiefs impatiently awaited her decision. On the 6th of July the United States ship Constellation, Commodore Kearney, arrived. He immediately issued a public protest against the seizure of the islands. The presence of a ship of war of a nation friendly to their sovereign rights was encouraging to the chiefs. Commodore Kearney on all occasions treated them as independent princes. This courtesy exasperated still further Lord George, who wrote the king that if he should suffer himself to be saluted under the Hawaiian flag, he would forfeit all consideration from Her Majesty's government. The king came from Maui on the 21st to hold communication with Commodore Kearney. So much irritation was now manifested on both sides, that a violent explosion must soon have occurred, when unexpectedly to all, on the 26th of July Rear Admiral Thomas, in the Dublin, frigate, arrived from Valparaiso, from which place he had made all possible speed on receiving the despatches of Lord George. The design of his visit was at first doubtful. He lost no time however in making known his intentions. In a few hours it was understood that he came to restore the islands. The joy of the natives and foreigners was unbounded, the mortification of the Simpson party extreme. The renegade natives feared for their heads.

* *Friend*, vol. 1, p. 37.

Negotiations were promptly opened with the king by the admiral, and at an interview on the 27th, the terms of the restoration were agreed upon. The 31st of July, a day ever memorable in Hawaiian annals, was the time appointed for the world to witness England in the person of her gallant and worthy officer, restoring to the petty sovereign of the Hawaiian Islands his prerogatives and his dominions. It was done in great good taste. The weather proved auspicious, and the entire population, white, and native, except the few who, sad and disappointed, sympathized with the commander of the Carysfort, poured forth en masse on to the plain east of the town to participate in the general joy and witness the ceremonies. On this occasion, the foreign residents who had stood by the king so warmly through all his distress, gave unbounded testimony of their sincere satisfaction of his restoration to authority. A tent was prepared for the ladies. At 10 o'clock, A. M., several companies of English marines were drawn up in line facing the sea, with an artillery corps on their right. The king came escorted by his own troops. As his royal standard was unfurled under a salute of twenty-one guns from the brass pieces of the Dublin's corps, the English ensigns at the forts were lowered and the Hawaiian colors re-hoisted. National salutes were then fired successively from the Dublin, Hazard, Carysfort and Constellation men-of-war, and the two forts and shipping in the harbor. After a review of the military, the king returned to his house, and ordered the native troops raised by Lord George to appear before him. They were required to salute the king's flag and to swear fealty to their lawful sovereign. Those officers who had received British commissions came forward and kissed the king's hand. At one o'clock the king attended divine service at the stone church, where he addressed his people, informing them that "the life of the land" had been restored to him. Mr. Ii followed his majesty in a spirited address, announcing in the name of the king a general amnesty, the release of all prisoners, and a festival of ten days for the people. During this period the residents manifested their satisfaction by balls and entertainments, attended by the chiefs and the officers of the numerous men-of-war in port. Before the festival was over, the United States ships United States, Commodore Jones, and the Cyane, Capt. Stribling, arrived. The last brought the news of the recognition of independence by England and France. Efforts were made to effect a general reconciliation among all parties, and all pending difficulties were left to the adjustment of the king's commissioners with the powers abroad.

Notwithstanding the handsome manner in which Admiral Thomas, before hearing from his government, undertook to restore the king to his sovereignty, in his diplomatic arrangements he required stipulations highly favorable to British interests and calculated to be embarrassing in execution to the king. As these however were to be but of temporary effect, the king gave them his assent, trusting for independence in reality as well as in name, from the exertions of his agents in Europe. The admiral, as if apprehensive that even his cautious policy might not be wholly acceptable to his government, moved his flag on shore, where he was received as the nation's guest, and awaited advices from England. His presence was favorable to harmonizing parties and to preserving the tranquility of the kingdom.

The policy of the provisional cession to Great Britain has been much questioned, but viewed as to its results and a cool examination of the alternative at the time as impressed upon the minds of the chiefs, it must now be allowed to have been a sagacious act. The natural impulse among all classes was to resist such aggravated injustice; but those who felt thus, reasoned that to have done so, would have played the part of Simpson, who ardently desired to drive matters to that crisis, that English blood having been shed, the kingdom should fall by conquest. Resistance or retaliation, however just, on the part of savage nations towards civilized, is always viewed as wanton aggression. England herself has given an instance of this in her late contest with the natives of New Zealand. The act which led to the vengeance exercised by Capt. Wilkes, of the United States Exploring Expedition, at the Fiji group, by which so many unhappy wretches were slaughtered, originated in the unjustifiable detention of a native against his will; the attack on the officers being the savage thirst for revenge on the part of the chief, the father of the captive, who in an attempt to escape was fired at, and supposed to have been killed. So Cook, in 1779, lost his life by the natives in defence of their chief. A country won under the specious glory of arms, arouses the pride of the conquerors, and the iniquity of the aggression is lost sight of in the self-satisfaction of the acquisition; or else lives and treasure having been lost in the undertaking and the notice of other nations attracted, it becomes a matter of honor to persevere. No nation willingly confesses itself in the wrong. The French at Tahiti illustrate this principle. Simpson was well aware of the force of an appeal written in blood to the pride of his nation. He says, "Indeed I cannot but regret now, seeing the undecided action of the British government, that *some act* on the part of Lord George Paulet had not left any other conclusion open, than that the dynasty of Kamehameha *must cease to reign.*"

Passive resistance it was feared would have been attended with evils scarcely less threatening to the rights of the king than active hostilities. The demands might have been wholly negatived and Lord George compelled to hostilities. Unopposed, one gun would have been sufficient to have given the character of force to the possession. But the chiefs felt that that gun would have been the signal that the native authority was at an end, and lawless whites inciting the rabble, stood ready to burn and plunder. In the melee, the town would have been consumed, property destroyed and lives lost; the responsibility of which acts, although the direct result of Lord George's aggression, would have been placed upon them. There was reason to fear that, winking as the English ministry did at the French usurpation at Tahiti, had their flag been raised here through bloodshed, it would never have come down.

22

The plan to evade the intention of Lord George by a joint cession to the United States and France was impracticable. Captain Long, to whom it was notified, confessed his inability to do anything beyond reporting the fact to his government. There was no French officer present to have availed himself of a possession his country coveted. Had there been, and the French flag raised, English blood would not have brooked the interference at such a crisis, and another subject matter for quarrel would have been added to the long catalogue between the two countries. Before any action on the part of the Congress of the United States could have occurred, either France or England would have forcibly possessed themselves of the islands, or both landing have engaged the natives in a civil war. The actual employment of force under any circumstances by any party, it was considered would inevitably have lost the king his crown; hence, with such views, the policy adopted, emphatically a peaceful one and appealing to the compassion of a brave nation without exciting its pride, was judicious. In the event of its failure to render justice, the Hawaiians would have preferred English to French rule, from the greater intimacy with that nation and the implied guardianship which since Vancouver, she had been supposed to exercise over them. Whatever credit then may be supposed to arise from the mode of the cession, by which so powerful an adversary was disarmed, it belongs in chief to Mr. Judd, with whom the form originated, and who, rather than countenance any of the other plans proposed, offered to resign his commission into the king's hands.

———

CHAPTER XIII.

Embassy to the United States and Europe—Acknowledgment of Independence at Washington—Diplomacy in London—Paris—Belgium—Independence acknowledged by England and France—Excitement in the United States—A. Simpson—Correspondence between Mr. Fox and Mr. Upshur—Claim of indemnification from England—Joint Guarantee of Great Britain and France—"Times" newspaper—Return to the United States—Death of Haalilio.

MESSRS. Haalilio and Richards entered upon the business of their mission at Washington, in December, 1842. They were favorably received, though the administration did not at first enter so fully into their views as they desired. After some negotiation, the President transmitted to Congress a message, dated December 31, 1842, in which he said :

" Just emerging from a state of barbarism, the government of the islands is as yet feeble ; but its dispositions app ar to be just and pacific, and it seems anxious to improve the condition of its people by the introduction of knowledge, of religious and moral institutions, means of education, and the arts of civilized life.

" It cannot but be in conformity with the interest and the wishes of the government and the people of the United States, that this community, thus existing in the midst of a vast expanse of ocean, should be respected, and all its rights strictly and conscientiously regarded. And this must also be the true interest of all other commercial States. Far remote from the dominions of European powers, its growth and prosperity, as an independent State, may yet be in a high degree useful to all, whose trade is extended to those regions; while its nearer approach to this continent, and the intercourse which American vessels have with it—such vessels constituting five-sixths of all which annually visit it—could not but create dissatisfaction on the part of the United States at any attempt, by another power, should such an attempt be threatened or feared, to take possession of the islands, colonize them, and subvert the native government. Considering, therefore, that the United States possess so very large a share of the intercourse with those islands, it is deemed not unfit to make the declaration that their government seeks, nevertheless, no peculiar advantages, no exclusive control over the Hawaiian government, but is content with its independent existence, and anxiously wishes for its security and prosperity. Its forbearance, in this respect, under the circumstances of the very large intercourse of their citizens with the islands, would justify this government, shou'd events hereafter arise to require it, in making a decided remonstrance against the adoption of an opposite policy by any other power."

These sentiments, with the act creating a commissioner to reside at the court of Hawaii, were considered tantamount to a formal recognition, and on March 3d, 1843, George Brown, Esq., was appointed to that office.

The king's commissioners arrived in London in February, 1843, where they were joined by Sir George Simpson, and entered into communication with the Foreign office. Lord Aberdeen declined receiving them as ministers from an independent nation, but consented to acknowledge them as authorized to " represent the government of the Sandwich Islands." Their first interview was on the 22d of February. Lord Aberdeen was unfavorable to the recognition of independence, saying " it would be ridiculous, for it cannot be supposed that the king governs himself ; he is influenced by others ; " and that the islands, through the exertions of the missionaries, were falling " exclusively under American influence, to the injury of British interests ; " but added, " that it was of no consequence to British interests whether the government were under the influence

of missionaries or whoever else, so long as justice were done."

On the 8th of March the commissioners left London for Paris, by way of Belgium, where they saw King Leopold, who pledged his influence to aid the great object of their mission. They arrived in Paris on the 15th, and on the 17th had an interview with M. Guizot, who received them with marked courtesy, and promptly gave a pledge to acknowledge the independence of the islands. They reached London again on the 20th, and in an interview with the British minister on the 25th, received " the full assurance that the independence of the islands would be virtually or really acknowledged, and that Mr. Charlton would be removed." On the 1st of April, the Earl of Aberdeen formally communicated the sentiments of his government to the king's commissioners, as follows :

" Her Majesty's government are willing and have determined to recognize the independence of the Sandwich Islands under their present Sovereign.

" I think it expedient to add that Her Majesty's government desire no special favor or immunity for British subjects ; on the contrary, they wish to see all foreigners residing on the Sandwich Islands treated on a footing of perfect equality before the law, and equal protection afforded by the government to all."

The commissioners had thus far been successful in their mission, when news arrived of the provisional cession of the islands to Lord George Paulet. Mr. Marshall had already carried it to the United States, where, added to other causes tending to influence the national mind against England, it created a prodigious excitement. Throughout the Union the public press echoed with denunciations of the rapacity of England. The Oregon and California questions were then beginning to awaken public interest. The act of Lord George Paulet was considered as the commencement of the denouement of a grand aggressive political drama, by which England intended to appropriate to herself the islands and the neighboring continent. The people of the United States felt the deepest interest in the independence and welfare of Kamehameha's dominion, both from self-interest, as a depot for their vast whaling trade and other commercial interests, and from jealousy of their great maritime rival, and also as being the petted object of their religious sympathies. They claimed its conversion to Christianity as a moral conquest altogether their own. More than half a million of money, the contributions of their piety, had been lavishly bestowed in redeeming it from heathenism. To prevent so important a post from passing into the hands of England, was an object worthy of national interference. Such was the general voice. Some presses, more moderate, regarding the matter in a truer light, believed that England would hesitate to avail herself of what they considered to be the unauthorized act of her officer. They were correct. Mr. Marshall after delivering his dispatches at Washington, hastened to London, where he arrived in July. The news had preceded him, as also had Alexander Simpson, who immediately repaired to the Foreign office to justify his conduct, and to induce the British ministry to retain the prize he had gratuitously placed in their hands. The British public and government were both astonished at an event so little anticipated. The latter had gone too far to retreat. Public opinion in Europe and America, whatever might have been their real desires, was too strong for them to openly face it in violation of the pledge already given. Alexander Simpson soon learned their decision. He says : "Instead of a prompt acceptance of the cession, which had public opinion been brought to bear on the subject, would undoubtedly have taken place, the ministers used such red-tapist language as—' It was quite unauthorized, quite unexpected. Everything connected with it is of a novel and peculiar character—it requires a more than usual deliberation on the part of Her Majesty's government to determine the line of conduct proper to be pursued in the matter.' " With some sharpness he adds : "The 'do nothing' spirit of the Peel cabinet could not be excited even by the gratuitous addition to British possessions of a valuable colony."*

From this time Mr. Simpson, disavowed by his own government, disappears. The boldness of his design, and the energy with which he carried it through, with his rational views of the

* Simpson's History, p. 92.

ultimate advantages to Great Britain of such an acquisition to her territory, present a striking contrast to the petty maneuvering and disgraceful intrigues of his inferiors in talents, whom he used at will as coadjutors or agents in his plan. Never for a moment does he appear to have faltered in his undertaking from any obligation of right, justice, or even humanity. Boldly and unflinchingly he persevered through all obstacles, and faithfully acted up to his threat of the 29th August, 1842, to Governor Kekuanaoa, made in the presence of witnesses and on official record, that "I will do everything in my power to bring this government into difficulty. I have both talents enough and influence enough to do it." Though the end recoiled upon himself, had the British ministry been less scrupulous his reward and fame would have been far different.

On the 13th of June, Lord Aberdeen informed Messrs. Haalilio and Richards that "Her Majesty's government had no desire to retain possession of the Sandwich Islands." This intention was communicated to France through their minister, and on the 25th of June, Mr. Fox, H. B. M.'s minister at Washington, addressed the Secretary of State to the same effect, adding, it "was an act entirely unauthorized by Her Majesty's government," and that—

"Instructions which, during the past year, were addressed by Her Majesty's government to the British Consul residing in the Sandwich Islands, and to the naval officers employed on the Pacific station, enjoined those officers to treat upon all occasions the native rulers of the Sandwich Islands with forbearance and courtesy ; and while affording due and efficient protection to aggrieved British su'jects, to avoid interfering harshly or unnecessarily with the laws and customs of the native government.

"It has been the desire of the British government, in regulating the intercourse of its public servants with the native authorities of the Sandwich Islands, rather to strengthen those authorities and to give them a sense of their independence by leaving the administration of justice in their own hands, than to make them feel their dependence upon foreign powers by the exercise of unnecessary interference. It has not been the purpose of Her Majesty's government to seek to establish a paramount influence in those islands for Great Britain at the expense of that enjoyed by other powers.

"All that has appeared requisite to Her Majesty's government has been, that other powers shall not exercise there a greater influence than that possessed by Great Britain.   H. S. FOX."

This prompt decision at once quieted the public mind. Mr. Marshall having become associated with Messrs. Haalilio and Richards in their mission, the three entered into correspondence with the Foreign office in London on the subject of complaints brought by Simpson against their government. In the course of this business, Mr. Addington, the under secretary, remarked that the British government "could not afford to risk their reputation by doing other than justice to a small nation which could not resist them;" thus confessing that innocence united to weakness had become a match for even the greatest power itself. The Earl of Aberdeen having been invited to pronounce judgment himself upon the charges brought forward by Simpson which led to the occupation of the islands by Lord George Paulet, after an examination of the papers submitted, with the aid of the principal law adviser to the crown, came to a decision favorable to the Hawaiian government. The decision in the immediate case of Skinner and Simpson, is worthy of quotation as bearing upon the jurisdiction of the courts, a point since frequently contested.

"After maturely weighing the arguments on both sides, Her Majesty's government are of the opinion that whatever motives Messrs. Skinner and Simpson may have entertained of the impossibility of having justice done them in the courts of the islands, they were bound, in the first instance, to submit their case to the judgment of those courts; and that having neglected or refused so to do, it is not competent in them now to get rid of the effect of a decision adverse to their views."

The minor cases of grievances the government abstained from entering upon, "as not requiring so formal a decision," thus implying their frivolousness.

Mr. Skinner's claim for $3,000 was pronounced unjust, and the government not liable for the sum demanded. Mr. Charlton was required to produce the original grant of the land which Lord George Paulet had put him in possession of, and show it *to be genuine.* Mr. Addington further assured Mr. Richards that, provided the lease was genuine, General William Miller, who had been appointed on the 25th of August H. B. M.'s "Consul General for the Sandwich, Society, Friendly and other islands in the Pacific," would be instructed not to deliver to Mr. Charlton "any ground which had been occupied by others, unless it was occupied against his *bona fide* remonstrance." If this had been acted upon it would have been tantamount to a judgment in favor of the Hawaiian government. In answer to a claim for indemnification for the damages accruing

to the treasury and national property by the illegal acts of Lord George Paulet, the Earl of Aberdeen, on the 16th of November, replied that "Her Majesty's government, although regretting the inconvenience and expense to which the Sandwich Islands government has been subjected by the cession of the islands to Lord George Paulet, do not consider themselves in any way answerable for the evils arising from it, or liable to make good any expense which may have resulted from the temporary occupation of the islands." This opinion is founded on the allegation that the cession was a "perfectly spontaneous deed" on the part of the king. In a letter of March 13th, 1844, the Earl of Aberdeen, in reply to the claim again presented, on the assurance that Lord George Paulet took *forcible* possession, says: "But it is obvious that there was no necessity on the part of the king to take so extreme a step. He might have refused compliance with the terms imposed upon him; and in declaring his intention to appeal to Great Britain, he might have left Lord George Paulet to take on his own responsibility whatever measures he might think proper. Had the king adopted this course, and had Lord George Paulet taken forcible possession of the country, then there might have been ground for the Sandwich Islands government to claim compensation; provided the grievances which led to the occupation should have been admitted by the British government to be unfounded, or even insufficient to justify so strong a measure." The doctrine which makes the aggressor the sole judge over his own illegal act, would most likely save his purse. The case would indeed have been clearer, and the damages greater, had the occupation been forcible; but would the British government have assumed the monetary responsibility growing out of the losses arising to all classes in case of a resistance, whether active or passive, which the peaceful policy of the king, relying upon their justice, alone prevented? If the Earl meant to imply that Lord George would not have taken that "responsibility," it was more than the king had any reason to believe, as he was then situated, an unrecognized semi-savage chief. History shows that acts of aggression on barbarous powers without the pale of nations pass unreproved and unnoticed, and there is reason to believe that whatever Lord George had done would have been no exception to the rule. On the contrary, there was great reason to fear that resistance would have led to the fulfillment of Simpson's ardent desire, the permanent acquisition of a valuable colony to the British crown. Under such circumstances, after a virtual condemnation of Lord George Paulet, it cannot but be viewed in a moral and equitable sense, however diplomacy may shuffle about it, as a small matter for England to refuse, to redress her own wrong when it comes to matters of dollars and cents.

On the 28th of November, the Hawaiian commissioners obtained from the governments of France and England a joint declaration to the effect that—

"Her Majesty, the Queen of the United Kingdom of Great Britain and Ireland, and His Majesty the King of the French, taking into consideration the existence in the Sandwich Islands of a government capable of providing for the regularity of its relations with foreign nations, have thought it right to engage reciprocally to consider the Sandwich Islands as an Independent State, and never to take possession, neither directly nor under the title of Protectorate, nor under any other form, of any part of the territory of which they are composed.

"The undersigned, Her Majesty's Principal Secretary of State for Foreign Affairs, and the Ambassador Extraordinary of His Majesty the King of the French, at the Court of London, being furnished with the necessary powers, hereby declare in consequence, that their said Majesties take reciprocally that engagement.

"In witness whereof the undersigned have signed the present declaration, and have affixed thereto the Seal of their Arms.

"Done in duplicate, at London, the 28th day of November, in the year of our Lord 1843."

(Signed,)   ABERDEEN. [L. S.]
     "   ST. AULAIRE. [L. S.]

This solemn engagement on the part of these two powers was the final act by which the kingdom of Hawaii was admitted within the pale of civilized nations. The London Times of August 20th the same year, in a semi-official leader, had thus announced the views of the British government in relation to the independence of the group :

"In their independent condition, the islands of the Pacific were useful to all nations, and dangerous to none ; and all that was needed to respect that independence, and to leave them alone. The British government, acting upon this principle, even after our neighbors had avowed their determination to hold the Marquesas and the Society groups, repudiated the sovereignty of the Sandwich Islands, and withheld its approval from the act of cession which had been concluded, subject to the final orders from the home government. That decision was taken, not from any want either of right or of power to defend that right, but simply because it was held to be inexpedient to found a colonial establishment, and to

awaken the jealousy of other countries for no purpose that cannot be equally secured by the maintenance of the independence of the country. But before the temporary connection is dissolved which has placed the sovereignty of the Sandwich Islands in our hands, it obviously becomes the duty of our government to secure by the most positive and formal pledges, both from France and from America, that independence which we now propose to restore to the native princes. We are perfectly well satisfied that the ports of these islands shall remain open, as harbors of refuge and supply, to the vessels of all nations, in time of war as well as in peace ; and the establishment of this neutral and independent character is an object not unworthy the policy of a high-minded statesman."

The commissioners returned to the United States in the spring of 1844. On the 6th of July, they received a communication from Calhoun, Secretary of State, confirming the "full recognition on the part of the United States, of the independence of the Hawaiian government." In November they took passage from Boston for Honolulu, in the ship Montreal, Capt. Snow. Haalilio, whose health had been very precarious during the latter period of his embassy, died at sea, 3d of December, 1844. His remains were taken to Honolulu, where they were deposited in the royal tomb with much ceremony and sincere mourning. His loss was severely felt ; for from his intelligence, and the ardor with which he stored his mind with knowledge derived from the intellectual circles he visited abroad, great hopes were entertained of his enlightening influence, especially in matters of internal polity, over his brother chiefs.

CHAPTER XIV.

Policy of the Government since their Independence—Appointment of Mr. Judd—Arrival of General Miller—Commissioner Brown—Treaty with England—Attorney General appointed—R. C. Wyllie, Minister of Foreign Relations—Rival parties formed—Polynesian—Political Events from 1843—1847—New Laws—Executive—Foreign officers—Royal School—Commercial Statistics—Revenue and Public Debt.

WHATEVER doubts may have existed, from the 28th of November, 1843, the Hawaiians were entitled to the full rights and immunities of an independent nation. The boon so ardently desired had been granted, and they were now fairly launched on the sea of international existence, to steer their little bark and trim its sails to catch every favorable puff to advance them in their new career. The rulers felt grateful for the aid and sympathy they had experienced in the disasters brought upon them by the reckless passions and intriguing dispositions of their unprincipled antagonists. They were now freed from the fear of lawless attacks or summary revenge. The great nations having admitted them to the nominal footing of equality, the least they could do now was to hear before they struck. Desirous of deserving the confidence shown, the king determined upon a policy, which while it should be protective to himself and his subjects, should be just to foreigners. Difficulties and dangers yet remained in the way. The former arose rather from the unpromising materials of his own kingdom, and the latter from the latent hostility still existing, which disappointment had rather disarmed than destroyed. His resources for forming an enlightened and influential government were few; the wants of his kingdom were many; the expectations of foreigners high; men of all races, embracing every variety of interest, mental culture and enterprise, existed within his small domains. To unite these into an harmonious whole, and build up a respectable nation, qualified to maintain with regularity its relations with foreign nations, was no easy task. This, however, the king and his advisers have undertaken. The fundamental principles of their policy are to develop a purely independent Hawaiian nation; to preserve the Kamehameha dynasty; to advance the young chiefs sufficiently to enable them to discharge the entire functions of government; in fact, to discover if there be life enough left in the dry bones of heathenism, touched by the revivifying spirit of civilization, to clothe them anew with flesh, and reanimate their sinews and muscles. To effect this it is necessary to maintain civil institutions commensurate with the wants of enlightened foreigners, but to avoid any paramount foreign influence; to develop new ideas of political economy among the natives; to nurture the germs of a national enterprise; and equally to allow reasonable scope for the more refined tastes and ambitious desires of whites. To meet the necessities of such a heterogeneous population, the government must necessarily be a mixture of barbarism and civilization, accommodating itself in its range of objects to all the diversified wants and intelligence of the mixed population. The one part are not to be blinded with too much light, nor the other left in total darkness. The events which have since followed are too recent and undetermined in their result for the historian to do more than pass them in rapid review.

In November, 1843, Mr. Judd received the appointment of Secretary of State for Foreign Affairs, an office created at the suggestion of Mr. Commissioner Brown, who arrived at Honolulu 16th October, and on the 30th presented his credentials and entered upon the duties of his post.

Consul-General Miller arrived the February following, bringing with him a convention drawn up in London to be signed by the king. It was based upon the terms of the irresponsible and unratified treaty of Laplace, requiring the admission of ardent spirits, the proposal of juries in criminal cases, by the consul, and the limitation of duties to 5 per cent. ad valorem. Each of these conditions was a restriction on the king's prerogatives, to which he gave unwilling assent, trusting that both the French and English governments would before long listen to his representations, and leave him wholly and virtually as independent as other sovereigns.

The want of a legal adviser to the government had long been felt. Mr. Judd had written to Mr. Richards with great earnestness on this subject, urging him before he left Europe to engage a lawyer qualified for this situation. Failing to do this, on the 9th of March the king appointed John Ricord, Esq., an American practitioner of talent, member of the bar of the State of New York, as Attorney General of the Hawaiian Islands, he having first taken the oath of allegiance. From this period, to avoid the charges of undue national bias, by the employment of officers from rival nations, which had already created great distrust on the part of Great Britain, all employed in the service of the government were required to become naturalized Hawaiians. This policy was extended also, after the system of the United States, to all who wished to avail themselves of the privileges of citizenship; it being considered to strengthen the king's independence, and to procure for him a useful and enterprising class of foreign born subjects, who by their superior enterprise and talents could materially advance the welfare of the natives, and raise up a counterpoise to any inimical external influence.

In March, 1845, Robert C. Wyllie, Esq., a Scotchman by birth, who had been appointed by Consul-General Miller, while he visited Tahiti, to act for him in the capacity of Pro-Consul, and had in a friendly and official intercourse of eight months won the confidence and respect of the chiefs as well as the residents, was invited by the king to accept the situation of Minister of Foreign Relations. This appointment was a judicious one in many respects. It relieved the king of the objection on the part of the English of having filled his cabinet entirely from Americans by birth, while it materially strengthened the government by bringing into its councils a gentleman of extensive acquaintance and enlarged views. Under his administration the business of the foreign office has been reduced to a simple and efficient system, greatly to the advantage of all who have to do with it, and his influence has been the means of promoting many useful reforms in the general management and policy.

The employment of whites in official stations gave a character to the government it had not previously possessed. In place of secret and embarrassing influences operating upon its councils, it openly announced its dependence upon white intellect to conduct its foreign relations. The main charge heretofore brought against the chiefs had been, in the words of the petitioners to the English government, that they were "quite unfit to perform any of the functions of government."

As every government that allows freedom of speech and press must have an active opposition, one soon arose against the new policy, denouncing the white advisers and advocating the idea that the chiefs themselves were adequate to perform all the functions of government, though it was generally admitted that some foreign assistance was necessary. Foreigners being invited to fill responsible posts, and received into the nation on the basis of citizenship, it was perfectly natural that an opposition should arise. In effect, there became two parties, struggling for pre-eminence. The officers of the king, taking stand on the broad ground of his independence, claimed for him, regardless of the differences in power and estate, all the rights and immunities of a sovereign. The opposition viewed these efforts as unwise and impolitic, thinking that a sovereign so little removed from barbarism was better provided for by a species of guardianship—not greatly removed from dictatorship—emanating from the consuls of the three great nations that had recognized their independence. The king's officers considered there was less danger and embarrassment in claiming a nation's rights in full, than in submitting to the dictation of agents of rival powers, who, however much they might desire the welfare of the Hawaiian people, were pledged by official oaths to advance the interests of their own, and whom it would be impossible to unite in full harmony upon any disinterested course relative to the nation. Such a system as they advocated, contrary to international rule, could not fail to embroil the chiefs with one power or the other, according as they might be charged with partiality, and the government thus proposed would soon terminate in no government at all, or in a foreign protectorate, as at Tahiti. From the stand which each party took arose a war of words, which unfortunately but unavoidably, from the complexity of interests and dispositions involved, and from the smallness of the political field, degenerated into much personal animosity, so that in little more than a year from the retro-cession of Admiral Thomas, the country was again distracted by conflicting opinions. M. Dudoit, the French consul, kept aloof from these controversies, and both he and his countrymen, from the time the policy of Guizot was made known in regard to the kingdom, treated it with all the courtesy and respect due even a great nation. Dudoit's policy was at once respectful, considerate and serviceable, affording a striking contrast to the embarrassing course previously pursued by him and other official gentlemen. By this means he rapidly acquired for France a position as high in the confidence of the government as it had before been low; and his kind offices in the preservation of order among his countrymen, the settlement of their disputes extra-judicially, and without annoyance to the authorities, his tact in the management of his consulate and in preserving harmonious relations among all parties, secured for him a well-merited esteem. His example was the more valuable, as it illustrated to the king with what facility a foreign consul could render real services conjointly to his countrymen and the native authorities, advancing equally the best interests of both, when a good disposition prevailed. All complaints on the part of the Roman Catholics ceased, and they formally professed themselves gratified with the entire toleration of religious beliefs that prevailed, and the perfect impartiality of government. This was high praise from the priests of Rome to a Protestant government. But the government soon met with much annoyance from the officials of the United States; and before long equally as much from Consul-General Miller. The government undoubtedly erred in taking too high a tone, and repelling with too much acrimony, what they considered invasions of their rights and unfair attempts upon their independence. Without enumerating cases of but temporary and local interest, it is sufficient to observe that the diplomatic intercourse which ensued was long, tedious, and ill-calculated to appease national pride or conserve public harmony. The disputes which arose originated chiefly from questions of national right— the one party zealous in their exaltation, the other carrying them to an extreme of intrigue and dictation offensive to justice and candor. The claim of Charlton to the land in Honolulu was the commencement of troubles with Consul-General Miller. The parties disagreed as to the meaning of the Earl of Aberdeen. The government claiming the interpretation in full of the requirement to produce the deed and show it to be

genuine; Mr. Miller limited it to an ascertainment, by comparison of hand-writings, of the genuineness of the signatures alone. The former considered the courts or arbitration as the proper source of the decision; the consul-general claimed it to emanate from him in concert with the king or his agent. In complex and dubious questions it is poor policy for a weak power to assume positions which can only be sustained by physical strength. In questions of moral right they cannot be too decided ;—expediency has then no vote. But when there is ground for a difference of opinion, without compromising principles, deference is due both from policy and respect to the superior party. The result in the Charlton claim was, that the land was taken possession of by order of the British government, and delivered over to the claimant in August, 1845; but upon further evidence presented to the British government by Mr. Barclay, the king's commissioner in London, has been again referred to the law adviser of the crown, under circumstances that induce the hope that England will do equal justice in this the last pending case growing out of the unauthorized acts of Lord Paulet, as in the others.

Mr. Brown, the United States Commissioner, early assumed a tone in his public and private intercourse which was considered overbearing and unbecoming. A question arose in August, 1844, under the jury clause of the British treaty, which brought matters to a crisis with him. An American had been fined $50 by one of the inferior courts for an offence which by the Hawaiian laws was punished as a misdemeanor, but which by English law would have been considered as a crime. The mulcted party appealed for a jury, which was accorded by the judge, under the Hawaiian statute providing six foreigners and six Hawaiians, the plaintiff in the case being a native female. An entire jury of foreigners selected by the consul was contended for and refused as not being within the meaning of the British treaty. The case was argued between Mr. Judd and Mr. Brown at great length, and terminated with so much heat that the king in September wrote to the President of the

United States desiring the recall of Mr. Brown.

It were an unthankful task to trace the spirit of contention through its varied phases until the appointment of new officers on the part of the United States. Much of the excitement of this period was the mere fumes of party violence, possessing no interest beyond its ephemeral existence. The courts of the country, themselves an epitome of the nation, as far removed from barbarism on the one part, as they were from intellectual equality with those of Europe or America on the other, were made the butts of abuse and attack. That they had other merit than honesty of purpose, and being the best the country could afford, was never claimed for them. The course in general pursued by them meeting the approval of judges abroad, strengthened them in public opinion at home. Amidst all the excitement and annoyance consequent upon ill-relations existing with Mr. Brown and Consul-General Miller, the government steadily pursued their policy of strengthening the power of the king, and consolidating the institutions of the country, as the most efficient course for promoting good morals and meriting the good will of other powers. Relying for support upon a correct public sentiment, and desirous of making their views known to the world, and justifying themselves against the prolific charges of their enemies, the government, in July, 1844, established the Polynesian newspaper as its public organ. In its columns will be found discussed their views, and a full relation of the exciting topics of the day. No surer index of the safety of the nation and its advancing civilization exists, than the fact that the press has become equally the weapon of the opposing parties, and both rely upon its use in maintaining their positions or enforcing their views. By its means the terrors of warlike threats, formerly so freely bandied, have lost their meaning, and public officers as well as public acts, have become equally as amenable to the bar of public opinion in Honolulu as in London or Washington.

The 20th of May, 1845, witnessed for the first time in Hawaiian annals, the regular opening of the legislative chambers by the king in person, in a short and pertinent speech. This was replied to in form by a committee of the nobles and representatives. The ceremonies were appropriate to the occasion and condition of the nation. On the succeeding day the several ministers read their official reports for the past year. Although the names and forms of official order and etiquette as they exist in more advanced countries are adopted in this, no one will suppose that nothing incongruous exists in comparison with those lands whence they are borrowed. The chiefs have ever been in advance of the people, and the foreign branch of government and its ideas must necessarily, springing as it does from civilized intellect, be in advance of both. It is the desire of the advisers of the king to prepare for the nation a polity of forms which shall be conservative of what it is expedient to preserve of the past; protective in what it is wise to borrow from abroad; and refining, organizing and elevating in its general effects upon the kingdom. Thus many forms and ideas are introduced, which although in the outset appear disjointed and crude, yet by practice conduce to useful results. By ceremonies like the foregoing, the nation becomes conversant with the legislative rules and conventional usages of enlightened countries. Acting on this principle, the king's birthday, 17th March; restoration day, 31st July; and independence day, 28th November, have been made national holidays.

On the 29th of March, 1846, H. M. C. Majesty's frigate Virginie, Admiral Hamelin, arrived at Honolulu for the purpose of restoring the $20,000 exacted by Captain Laplace in 1839. M. Perrin, special commissioner from the King of the French, came in the ship, entrusted with a treaty concerted between England and France, by which all previous conventions were abrogated, and the objectionable clauses regarding ardent spirits and juries modified so as to become more acceptable to the king. Juries in criminal cases were to be composed " of native or foreign residents, proposed by the British (or French) consul, and accepted by the government of the Sand-

23

wich Islands." Duties were allowed to be levied on wines and spirituous liquors, provided they did not amount to an absolute prohibition. The conditions of this treaty, although not acknowledging in full the king's complete independence, were the more readily acceded to, from an intimation on the part of the Earl of Aberdeen, that further modifications would be consented to by England as the condition of the Hawaiian nation might afterwards seem to justify.

The U. S. ship Congress, Commodore Stockton, arrived on the 9th of June, conveying A. Ten Eyck, Esq., the new commissioner appointed to succeed Mr. Brown, and Joel Turrill, Esq., United States consul for the Hawaiian Islands. Friendly diplomatic relations which had been so long interrupted with the officers of the United States, were resumed. Mr. Ten Eyck was the bearer of a letter from the President of the United States to the king, which, in connection with the friendly efforts of Commodore Stockton, and the widely different policy pursued by the successors of the late United States officials, went a great way to restore harmony, and to heal troubles kept alive more from the violence of partisan feeling and disappointed interests, than from any important principles at stake.

Capt. Steen Bille, of H. D. M.'s ship Galathea, on behalf of the King of Denmark, on the 19th of October, 1846, negotiated a treaty which is memorable for being the first convention entered into by the king with a foreign power which recognized in all their amplitude his rights as a sovereign prince. In this treaty, juries are allowed to take the course of the law of the land, and no limitation to the revenue of the kingdom by a maximum of duty is required. It is thus by piece-meal, even after the solemn recognition of his independence, has the king been obliged to secure, in practice, some of the most common rights of an independent nation, which had been unwisely yielded up while he was an unrecognized prince.

No measure tends more to consolidate and render a nation prosperous and respectable than a sound and judicious code of laws. The chiefs were early aware of their deficiency, and as soon

as their new legislative forms came into operation, proposed to execute the task; under any circumstances a difficult one; but in those of their kingdom doubly so, from the mixed population, foreign and native, that they were called to govern. The first volume of statute laws was issued in 1846.

The departments are subdivided into numerous bureaux, comprising the duties enumerated under their several heads. By this system the business of government and its machinery have become methodized on a simple and not expensive scale; for although the subdivisions are numerous, yet one clerk suffices for many. The judiciary act and the criminal code, on the new basis, are not yet completed. As in every other step forward which the Hawaiian nation has taken, unwarrantable abuse and unreasonable cavil has been showered upon it for this, chiefly upon the specious pretense that the system was too cumbersome and altogether beyond its growth. An impartial examination will doubtless detect points which can be amended with benefit; this is to be expected, and the intention of the legislature is rather experimentative than final; to feel their way as it were to a code simple and effective. But to do this experience must be acquired in legislation, and the practical operation of laws. In the transition of the nation, with its rapid growth from foreign sources, it has been found that there has been felt a want rather than an overplus of system. The machinery of government being of a liberal and constitutional character, provides in itself for checks on excess and remedies for evils. If "let alone" by foreign powers, there is ground for the belief that Hawaiian legislation will in no whit in character be behind that of numerous new countries, off-shoots of the old, now budding into existence on the shores of the Pacific.

The executive government was constructed as follows:

His Majesty, King Kamehameha III.	
His Highness, Keoni Ana,* Premier, and Minister of the Interior,	Cabinet
R. C. Wyllie, Minister For. Affairs,	Council,
G. P. Judd, " of Finance,	created Oct.
Wm. Richards, " Instruction,	29, 1845.
John Ricord, Attorney General,	

* Son of Mr. Young, Kamehameha's favorite.

NOBLES.

M. Kekauonohi.
A. Keliiahonui, Chamberlain.
Keoni Ana, Premier.
Alapai.
A. Paki, Judge of Supreme Court.
Konia.
I. Kaeo, Judge of Supreme Court.
Iona Kapena, Judge of Supreme Court.
Paulo Kanoa.
Namauu.
M. Kekuanaoa, Governor of Oahu.
W. P. Leleiohoku, Governor of Hawaii.
Ruta.
Keohokalole.
C. Kanaina, Judge of Supreme Court.
Ioane Ii, Guardian of Young Chiefs.
Iona Piikoi.
Beniki Namakeha.
K. Kapaakea.
James Young Kanehoa,* Governor of Maui.

Moses Kaikioewa, son of Kekuanaoa and Kinau, born July 20, 1829, Expectant Governor of Kauai.
Lota Kamehameha, son of Kekuanaoa and Kinau, born December 11, 1830, Expectant Governor of Maui.
Alexander Liholiho, son of Kekuanaoa and Kinau, born Feb. 9, 1834, heir apparent, by adoption, of the king.
Victoria Kamamalu, daughter of Kekuanaoa and Kinau, born November 1, 1838, Premier by birth.
William C. Lunalilo, son of Kanaina and Kekauluohi, born January 1, 1835.
Bernice Pauahi, daughter of Paki and Konia, born Dec. 19, 1831.
Jane Loeau, daughter of Kalaoiulumoku and Liliha, born 1828.
Elizabeth Kekaniau, daughter of Laanui, born September 11, 1834.
Emma Rooke, daughter of Fanny Young,* born January 2, 1836.
Peter Young Kaeo, son of Kaeo and Lahilahi,* born March 4, 1836.
James Kaliokalani, son of Paakea and Keohokalole, born May 29, 1835.
David Kalakaua, son of Paakea and Keohokalole, born November 16, 1836.
Lydia Makaeha, daughter of Paakea and Keohokalole, born September 2, 1838.
Mary Paaaina.
Kinau Pitt, son of W. Pitt Kalaimoku.

The governors are honorary members of the privy council.

Beside the four cabinet officers of foreign birth, there are five Americans and four Englishmen, naturalized subjects, commissioned as judges in foreign cases, collectors, director of government press, heads of bureaux, etc. In addition to these are a number of clerks transiently employed, and officers connected with the several departments, who depend upon fees for their recompense.

In no one respect have the government shown more laudable zeal than in educating the young chiefs, who by birth are destined to fill important posts. For the purpose of bestowing upon them a solid and practical education in the English language, embracing not only the usual studies pursued in the better class of seminaries in the United States, but to engraft in their minds the habits, thoughts, moral and domestic education which children of their age and circumstances receive in civilized countries, in 1839 they were taken from their native parents and out of the sphere of mere Hawaiian influences, and incorporated into a boarding-school under the charge of Mr. and Mrs. Cooke, teachers of the American mission. During the seven years the school has been established, their progress has been rapid, and they are now versed in the common branches of an English education, besides being practically acquainted with the tastes, household economy and habits of refined domestic life. The annual expense of the school is now about $5,000.. The number of scholars fifteen..

* Son of Kamehameha's favorite, Mr. Young, of the Eleaora, who landed in 1790, and died in 1835, at the advanced age of 93 years, highly respected by all classes.

The rapid progress of the Hawaiian group in commercial importance is best illustrated by their commercial statistics both before the organization of their present government and since, when under improved auspices their value has more rapidly developed. The facilities which they afforded the American vessels engaged in the lucrative North-West fur trade, to which was soon added the equally profitable one of sandal-wood, gave them such good repute, that previous to 1820 the hardy whale fishers resorted to them for recruits and men. As early as 1823, from forty to sixty whale-ships, mostly American, were to be seen in the harbor of Honolulu at one time.

From January, 1836, to December 31, 1841, three hundred and fifty-eight vessels belonging to the United States, of which four-fifths were whalers, touched at Honolulu; an average of seventy-one and three-fifths annually, besides seventeen men-of-war. Of English vessels during the same period there were eighty-two, and nine men-of-war. Those of France and other nations numbered not over twenty. The average annual imports for those years were to the value of $365,854, one-half of which were American goods, one-quarter Chinese and Californian, and the remainder from England, Mexico, Chile and other sources.

In 1842, there arrived at Honolulu 45 merchant vessels—17 English, 16 American, and 12 of other nations. The

* Daughters of John Young.

imports this year were valued at about $250,000.

During the same time there came 44 American, 16 English, 5 French and 1 Danish whale-ships.

In 1845, the imports from various nations ranged about as follows :

United States, ...	$245,681 40
China, ...	85,500 57
England and Sydney, .	75,303 04
Oregon, ...	34,807 48
California, ...	24,853 58
Chile, ...	16,589 12
Other countries (including product of whale-fishery and goods, mostly American, landed by whale-ships.)	64,206 53
Total, ...	$546,941 72

Beside merchandise, a considerable amount in specie is annually received from the Spanish American States.

1846.

United States, ...	$325,630 00
England, ...	116,929 00
China, ...	43,040 00
Valparaiso, ...	38,965 00
Columbia River, . . .	23,101 00
California, ...	17,040 00
Hamburg, ...	4,474 00
Bremen, ...	4,069 00
Sydney, ...	1,870 00
Kamtschatka, ...	1,087 00
Other countries (including oil, bone, etc.,)	22,186 00
Total, ...	$598,382 00

A proportion of the American cargoes —say about one-fifth—consists of English, French and German goods, but mostly of the first.

HAWAIIAN TONNAGE.

Year.	No vessels.	Tons.	Value.
1843, . . .	10	446	$27,400
1844, . . .	15	775	41,000
1846, . . .	29	1585	73,000

REVENUE.

1841 and '42.—The revenue as then collected was not worth more than $20,-000 per annum. 1843—$35,000.

Year.	Receipts.	Expenditures.
1844, . .	$64,045 55	$70,537 00
1845, . .	97,940 21	77,820 69
1846, . .	90,110 28	87,045 16

The receipts for 1845 include $20,000 restored by the French.

The expenditures for 1844 and '45 include large appropriations to discharge the public debts.

The financial years commence and terminate on April 1st. The year 1845 gives a period of but nine months. The entire receipts of the year 1846-7 are estimated at $110,000—expenditures at $100,000.

In 1842, when Mr. Judd came into the Treasury, the debts of the government, including £10,000 borrowed of the Hudson's Bay Company for the expenses of the embassy to Europe, amounted to $160,000. In 1846 this debt had been wholly extinguished.

Besides the custom house, the chief sources of revenue are the poll taxes, land tax, stamps, rents, etc.

CHAPTER XV.

The American Mission—History of—Progress—Policy—Expense—Character and results—Tone of society—Missionary Pastors—Destiny of the Mission—Moral condition of the Hawaiians—Crimes—Romanism—State of—Comparison with Protestantism.

THE American Mission is so interwoven with the history of the Hawaiian Islands, that although its progress has been succinctly noticed in the preceding pages, further mention is necessary clearly to understand its practical results both upon the people and its own members. Very much has been written upon this topic, but too frequently by those interested rather in confirming theoretic views than in portraying plain truth. As a well sustained experiment of religious philanthropy it deserves critical examination, for although founded upon the plain command, "Go ye and teach all nations," yet it is left to human wisdom to organize the means. Hence, to arrive at the soundest conclusion in a policy so ordained by heaven but left to man to execute, it is expedient to sift the results of the various methods employed and compare them one with another, that we may arrive at sound conclusions as to their practical effect in improving and elevating savage tribes. The Hawaiian Mission early obtained a powerful hold upon the sympathies of the religious public in the United States, and even arrested the attention of the world at large, in a much greater degree than that of any other modern mission. This arose from its isolated position, rapid success, and the exaggerated ideas that got abroad of the actual moral change of the islanders.

Rightly to appreciate what the mission in reality has effected, the original degraded character of the islanders should be kept constantly in view. Notwithstanding the favor of the rulers, the real progress of the mission in the actual conversion of the people was slow. In 1825, they numbered but ten native church members; in 1832, 577. In 1837, there had been received into the church 1,259. In 1840, their numbers had swelled to 20,120, in the short space of three years, and in 1843 had reached 23,804, about the present standard.

Under the present system of common schools, sustained by the government at an annual expense of between $20,000 and $30,000, partly money and partly by the labor tax, there are 15,393 scholars, instructed in the elementary branches of reading, writing, arithmetic and geography. Besides these schools the American Mission established, in 1831, a seminary for the higher branches at Lahainaluna; 368 pupils have been received and taught sacred and universal geography, sacred and profane history, grammar, algebra, geometry, trigonometry, navigation, mensuration, drawing, music, etc. Of its graduates 108 have become teachers of common schools, and 45 are variously employed by government; the remainder are serviceable to themselves and the people in various ways. The expense of this institution thus far, beside valuable gratuities bestowed by the government, has been $70,000. There is a boarding school for girls on Maui, under the charge of the missionaries, averaging 50 pupils, who are instructed in the common branches of education, and in sewing, knitting, spinning, etc., with particular reference to the inculcation of good domestic habits. $20,000 have been expended on this school.

On Hawaii, there is another on a smaller scale, containing 20 pupils, and one for boys with upwards of 50 scholars.

Exclusive of aid from government and individuals, the mission have expended on these $13,000.

Four newspapers in the Hawaiian tongue have been sustained by the missionaries; the first, "Lama Hawaii," was commenced in 1833; the present, "Ka Elele," besides much religious matter, gives a summary of general news, publishes government notices, and affords scope for the literary efforts of the natives themselves, some of whom manifest respectable powers of thought and composition.

It is computed that 70,000 of the population have learned to read, and 65,-444,000 printed pages have been issued from the mission press, embracing among other works two complete editions, of 10,000 each, of the Holy Scriptures, three of the New Testament, amounting to 30,000 copies, Worcester's Sacred Geography, Universal Geography, Geographical Questions, Scripture Chronology and History, Animals of the Earth, with a chart, History of Beasts, Hawaiian History, Church History, Mathematics, embracing Geometry, Trigonometry, Mensuration, Surveying and Navigation, Colburn's Algebra, Anatomy, Wayland's Moral Philosophy, Colburn's Intellectual Arithmetic, Tract on Astronomy, Maps of Universal Geography, and Bunyan's Pilgrim's Progress.

The works published have been altogether of a devotional or educational class. More interest would have been awakened could some others of a less grave and more historic character been included.

In enumerating the actual amount of service performed by the American Mission, there is much which, although not figuring in statistics, has had an important bearing upon the welfare of the people, and should not be overlooked. Some of the missionaries had acquired in youth a practical knowledge of agriculture, general business, or the mechanical trades. This information has been combined with religious instruction, and quite a number of natives through their auspices have become tolerable masons, printers, book-binders, tailors, painters, engravers and carpenters, and gained some little skill in various other arts, besides receiving much useful information in the culture of their farms and raising of stock. The efforts of the missionaries in these respects, though secondary to their grand object, have been indefatigable; and their wives also have exerted much influence in instructing the females and in improving their households. These facts are the more worthy of mention because a contrary policy has been charged upon them, and the results of their labors in these respects are not perceptible without an examination into their immediate fields of labor. So far as lay in their power they have repaid commerce the aid she afforded them, by a succession of well-directed individual efforts to induce systematic industry among the people, and to enlarge their usefulness by bestowing upon them the first fruits of civilization. Their conduct however in this, as towards the government, has been cautious and unsystematic, varying according to individual principle or temperament. They have ever leaned towards screening the nation from a general influx of whites upon their lands; and when leases have been obtained through their influence, it has been given rather in the belief that the leasor from his character for honest enterprise and moral worth would be of an advantage to the nation, than that they were doing him a service. So far as a tolerably intimate acquaintance with them goes, I am enabled to say, in contradiction of a charge often made, that although in their opinions they may have been too much swayed by sectarian bias, yet they have ever been favorable to seeing white men of good reputation enlist themselves among the nation, prepared to develop the resources of the soil, and to afford a suitable example of industrial enterprise to the people. The only "dog in manger" policy that can be charged home upon them, is the desire to prevent the permanent settlement of doubtful characters, and the introduction of distilleries.

The expenses of the American Mission swelled from $13,250, in 1819, to $63,521.09, in 1837, and since have averaged about $36,000 annually, making a total of nearly $700,000, including $50,000 from the American Bible Society, and $19,774.51 from the Tract Society. The amount expended shows the deep interest felt by the religious public of the United States in its support, and the scale on which it is now sustained is very different from that of the first year of its existence. Then the habitations of the missionaries were but slight improvements of those of the natives; their household furniture sparse and simple. The females were subjected to many discomforts, annoyances, and even privations affecting their health, when compared with what they had been accustomed to in their New England homes. This, however, did not last long. The benevolence that sent them to heathen ground was equal to providing them with all the necessaries and most of the comforts of life. Suitable habitations were furnished; stores were shipped from the United States, physicians and secular agents sent out, until their plan of operations has settled into a most efficient and well provided system, admirably adapted to the object in view, expensive in the gross though economic in detail. The American Board of Foreign Missions have now employed at their various stations on the islands, 25 clergymen, with their families, 2 physicians, 8 teachers, 3 secular agents, 1 printer and 1 book-binder, numbering in all 212; a few of the children however being in the United States. Forty permanent dwelling houses, two printing offices and a bindery have been erected, besides large outlays in school houses and churches. The dwelling houses are of wood, adobie or stone, costing from $1,000 to $3,000 each, and in general convenience and comfort are not inferior to any class on the islands. They compare favorably with the better style of farm houses in New England. These are furnished plainly though abundantly, and in a few there exists pretensions to something more assuming in the shape of pianos, cabinets of curiosities, and articles combining the decorative with the useful. Some of the families aspire to Yankee "Dearborns," or wagons, for a social drive, and are enabled either through the liberality of their friends or the friends of the mission, to have summer retreats in the valleys or mountains, or to journey, when enfeebled by labor, to other stations. The nominal expense of each family is from $400 to $700 per annum, but to this must be added house rent, physicians' bills, merchandise from the mission depository at cost, the use of herds of cattle and other means, which in Honolulu render a missionary living equivalent to from $1,500 to $2,000 per annum.* Most of the families have been provided with small tracts of land, from which they are enabled not only to add to their domestic comforts, but to be serviceable to the natives by supplying them with varieties of foreign fruits and vegetables, and encouraging them by example in practical agriculture or gardening. It cannot be questioned that the American Mission at the Hawaiian Islands, whatever might have been its earlier condition, is now sustained on a scale so liberal, with such ample provisions for all the ordinary emergencies of life, as to leave its members nothing to regret in external comfort in comparison with clergymen in the United States.

In attaining this outward prosperity, the mission has but kept pace with the growth of civilization about them. This happy result is in great measure attributable to their own energies, and to the moral stamp and intellectual refinement they have been instrumental in placing upon foreign society. Puritanical and arbitrary as both may appear, they have created a standard of public sentiment, which if it border upon ascetism, is still highly favorable to the purer amenities of social life, and equally happy in its reflex upon the growing national character. The Pacific elsewhere affords nothing in tone comparable with it. The natural effect of this change of position on the part of the mission, from the time when they were involved as it were in one continual struggle against immorality and contumely for an existence, to the present period, when prosperous in worldly circumstances, they have come off victors over vice and traduction, and now stand forth to the world eminent in philanthropy and the creators of a very

great degree of the ruling public sentiment, is that which inevitably attends human nature in a transition from adversity to prosperity. Their fruit budded and blossomed amid the frosts and snows of early spring; hardy in its origin and tenacious of life, it grew amid storm and sunshine; alternately chilled by the cold blast, and wilted by fierce heat, it flourished through a long and variable summer until ripened by the favoring autumnal sun into the mellow fruit, it is now ready to drop, and yielding up its seeds, give birth to new existence. Such seems to be the present position of the American Mission. They have baptized the nation into the fold of Christendom. All the outward signs and forms of revealed gospel are upon it. The Hawaiian Islands no longer remain heathen ground. The people have been in faith "born again." The labor remaining is to affect the individual. Hence the entire position of the mission is altered. In its primary object it has ceased to be missionary, and to be effective in the greater object of purifying the heart, it must assume a new feature. Heretofore it has been a machine apart from the people, controlled, directed and kept a going by foreign agency. Now, if it would perfect its work it should implant itself among them, become of them, self-sustained and self-controlled. In no other way can it be more productive of usefulness to the coming generation. To effect this, the parent society in the United States should allow to each family the ownership of the immediate property around them on condition of their ceasing to be missionaries and becoming pastors. To this the government could add grants of land for glebes, and in the present condition of the country there are but few parishes inadequate with these aids to support their clergymen. The present system is an unnecessary burden to the religious public in the United States, diverts funds from other fields, and dries up rather than stimulates the benevolent energies of the Hawaiians themselves, by making them the recipients of bounty when they are rapidly arriving at a condition to sustain institutions now properly their own. By identifying themselves with the nation, the

---

* That this expense may not be considered as extravagance or pretensious to a style inconsistent with an economy proper to their profession, it should be stated that the current expenses of living at the Hawaiian Islands are more than 100 per cent higher than in the United States.

missionaries will acquire a deeper hold upon the hearts of the people, as by embarking in the same vessel, and depending upon the same means, they make common cause with them. Additional motives are to be found in the provision thus secured for their families; the settlement of their children around them by fixing them permanently in the land of their nativity; the impetus to be given to civilization by the creation of some forty independent Protestant parishes, each of which would be a nucleus of morals and industry and a stimulant to enterprise and benevolence by making the actual good thus to be derived dependent upon the natives themselves. Under such circumstances, with scope for the natural desires of the human heart in receiving and accumulating the fruits of industry, in directing the moral and physical energies of their parishioners amenable only to them, in providing for their families, without the painful prospect of an early separation, with the sentiment of an honest self-interest that would arise in witnessing the labors of their own hands made their own by right of property, the missionaries would cease their longings for a return to their native land, their anxious forebodings for the future, and become in reality children of the soil. The importance of an arrangement by which so desirable a class of citizens may be permanently secured to the country is apparent from the fact, that should their children continue to increase in the same ratio as since the commencement of the mission, in 100 years their descendants would amount to 59,535.

One missionary has already seceded from the society and become a Hawaiian pastor, supported solely by his parish, and that one of the poorest on the group. Another has received the appointment of judge, while two others, Messrs. Judd and Richards, have for several years filled important positions in the government. These cases point to the destiny of the mission. In no other way can they so effectually complete their work.

The amount of contributions by the natives, under the present system, for objects connected with moral and religious improvement, is already very considerable. They have erected many churches costing from $1,000 to $33,000, as did the large stone church at Honolulu. From 1837 to 1844 their miscellaneous contributions amounted to $19,987.

The religious and educational statistics previously given, would, without explanation, mislead as to the actual character of the people, if the reader base his ideas upon the standard applicable in Europe and the United States.

Numerically, church members bear a larger proportion throughout the Hawaiian Islands to non-communicants, than in the United States; an equal outward attention is exhibited towards the observance of its ceremonies; but it would be as incorrect, from these facts, to place their moral and religious standard upon a level with that of the American people, as from the number of common schools, the pupils that attend them, and the studies nominally pursued among the same people, to estimate their elementary knowledge, and their system of education as highly as the American. Yet statistics by themselves would give that result, were the actual conditions and physiological differences between the two races kept from view. What were the Hawaiians originally, and what were the ancestors of the Anglo-Saxons? The one a branch of the Malay family of the human race, the third in point of intelligence, delighting in sensuality, falsehood, theft and treachery; with not even a fictitious code of honor, which, as with the Bedouins and American Indians, might afford some guarantee of personal security; their chief characteristic a love of maritime and warlike adventure, a warm, excitable imagination and feeble intellect, though not untractable disposition while their passions were not aroused. When otherwise, their tender mercies were in literal truth "cruelty." Added to these, a superstition skillfully concocted and strongly sustained by the few for the degradation and subservience of the many. The others, off-shoots of the Caucasian race; cruel heathens, but bold, free and intelligent; sacrificing human victims in obedience to their priests, but, in domestic relations, chaste and affectionate. If their animal passions were strong and conspicuous, their virtues also shone out brightly, and they proved themselves moral and intellectual. Christianity introduced into soils so widely different, must, humanly speaking, flourish in accordance with the relative fitness of either for its support and increase. And it has been so. In England and America, rooting itself in the superior sentiments and intelligence of the people, it now exhibits itself in its fairest and purest light; transported to the Hawaiian Islands by Anglo-Saxon minds, it is there sustained by the strength it brought with it. Institutions and improvements are all borrowed from their instructors; by them and their ancestors they were originated and perfected. The Anglo-Saxon race are capable of teaching; the Malay of being taught; the one by its own native energies can conquer and rule the world; the very existence and advancement of the latter is dependent upon the forbearance and benevolence of the former. Such are the natural differences between the two, and these must be borne in mind, if a just opinion of the capacity of the Hawaiians for civilization and christianity is to be formed. They should be judged by the standard applicable to their position in the human family, and not by our own.

There is but little doubt that, although a majority of the converted natives do not conform strictly to their vows, yet in consequence of them they are a better people. They furnish a restraint which nothing else could supply. The conduct which would bring censure upon an American Christian, should not upon a Hawaiian; their temperaments, knowledge and circumstances are widely different, and they are not to be balanced in the same scale. Of him to whom much is given, much will be required.

A moral sentiment, founded more upon a classification of certain actions either as evil or as good, and their attendant punishments or rewards, than upon any definite ideas of sin and virtue considered in their relations to moral purity, and the love of the Father, pervades the nation. With the more enlightened something superior to this prevails. Consequently, as in older christianized communities, a man enjoys respect in proportion to his moral qualifications. Vice is condemned and virtue applauded. Many, of course, are to be found more fond of a good name, than of the means necessary for its attainment. Publicly they are one being, privately another. The very fact of the necessity of the deception, shows a great advancement in moral sentiment since the days of Liholiho, and instead of being considered a reproach to the missionaries, should be hailed as a favorable symptom of their labors; the dawn of further improvement. In humanity, care for the sick and aged, their domestic relations, honesty, temperance and systematic industry, there has been great advancement. From a warlike, treacherous and cruel people, they have become mild, tractable, and desirous of knowledge. The intelligent observer will find much in their present character to gratify him, and more to surprise, when he contrasts them with what they were but a score of years since. But he who goes among them, his imagination picturing a nation changed from brutal savages, by the Spirit of God, to guileless Christians, worshiping Jehovah in all the innocency and strength of a first love, their family altars emblems of purity and happiness, their congregations simple and sincere, and their dispositions and deportment refined to the high standard of Christian excellence in his own country, will be sadly disappointed.

It is still difficult to make the natives understand the nature of truth. They have been so accustomed, from their earliest years, to habits of deception, that with very many, perhaps the majority, it may be doubted whether any other sensation arises from the detection of a falsehood than mortification at being discovered. In no other point are they more obtuse, but this moral bluntness is gradually wearing away. Licentiousness is a chief vice of the nation; not that they are much worse in this respect than nations generally residing within the tropics, but it continues to be their most prominent trait. A few years ago, in its Protean forms, it was common to all, and as undisguised as the light of day. Now it hides its head, and seeks a new garment to conceal its foul markings. The following table of crime for Oahu, will

24

serve to show the proportion of other offences to those of sensuality. It is taken
from the Kumu Hawaii, of January 16,
1839, a native paper, but the period embraced in the report is not given. And
it should be recollected that but a small
proportion of the latter offences are ever
detected or exposed. A number of foreigners are embraced in the list, chiefly
for riot, mutiny and desertion.

OFFENCES.

Manslaughter,	4
Theft,	48
Riot,	32
False witness,	48
Desertion,	30
Mutiny,	15
Seduction,	18
Lewdness,	81
Adultery,	246
Total,	522

Another table of purely native cases
for Honolulu, taken from the records of
the "Inferior Court" from January 1,
1846, to December 4 of the same year,
gives the following striking results:

OFFENCE.	MEN.	WOMEN.	TOT.
Adultery, fornication,	126	127	253
Theft,	43	3	46
Gambling,	35	3	38
Desecration of Sabbath,	20	8	38
Reviling language,	12	2	14
Heathenish practices,	3	1	4
Assault and battery,	7	1	8
Drunkenness,	6	..	6
Furious riding,	6	..	6
Rape,	2	..	2
Interference with police,	3	..	3
Street walking,	..	4	4
Slander,	1	..	1
Passing false coin,	1	..	1
Desertion of husbands,	..	3	3
Total,	275	152	427

The above table shows a conviction of
427 cases out of a population of about
9,000. To these should be added 121
others, tried before the police court,
making in all rather more than 600 cases
for 1846. Of the 121, 38 were for licentiousness and 43 for stealing. But few
occur for fighting, the Hawaiians being
a very peaceable people. A great deal
of petty thieving exists, particularly to-

wards foreigners, to steal from whom is
not viewed so disreputable as from themselves. The standard of morality, it will
be seen, is low, particularly among the
men ; but crimes are rare. There have
been but five executions for three murders for ten years.

It is incontrovertible that there yet
exists in the nation a large body of people who are equally disposed to religious
rites, or to acts of a different character,
as may be most accordant to the taste of
those whom they wish to gratify. Another generation must arise, with better
homes and more civil and religious advantages, before the habits of the old are
sufficiently eradicated. While evidence
for the more favorable view of missionary labor, to a partial investigator, appears conclusive, ample grounds for the
opposite opinion exist. The truth lies
in neither extreme. The friends of humanity have just cause to be grateful
that so much has been accomplished, and
should labor earnestly that the remaining dark spots may be wholly effaced.

Romanism has gained considerably in
numbers since its entire toleration, but
without affecting the Protestant churches
materially. The latter perhaps were
never more sound and flourishing than
at present, while the former have made
many converts among the class ever adverse to the principles and restraints of
their American teachers. Over these,
its influence has undoubtedly been use-
fully extended. The Protestants report
270 churches and school houses, used as
places of worship. The Romanists 104,
with a total population attending them,
or supposed to be under their influence,
of nearly 14,000. By a similar computation, more than 80,000 Protestants
would be found on the islands, but in
these gross computations great allowance
should be made for those alike indifferent to religious rites of any kind, and
who are equally fair subjects for the religious zeal of both. The national religion, as understood in the sense of that
received by the rulers, the most intelligent of the people and the vast majority
of all classes, is Protestantism in the
form of a mild Presbyterianism as practiced in New England churches. From
all that has yet appeared, although the

Romanists will undoubtedly become a respectable and even flourishing sect, yet the system and creed first implanted in the nation seems likely to continue and strengthen, subject only to such modifications as Protestantism itself is undergoing elsewhere.

The Romanists have shown a creditable zeal for education and have enrolled 2,800 pupils, besides 600 children who do not attend school. In 1846 they commenced a high school at Koolau, Oahu. The Rev. Abbe Maigret has a select school at Honolulu, embracing several hundred scholars, who manifest a tolerable proficiency in the common branches of education. The French priests in the commencement of their career pursue a widely different policy from the American missionaries in regard to the economy of their operations. Which is the better adapted for solely religious objects it would be difficult to determine. The Frenchman in his clerical celibacy can well afford to be economic; but he does more; rejecting the softening influences of domestic life, he equally disdains its comforts and refinements, and putting himself upon a par with the native whom he has come to instruct, partakes of his coarse fare, sleeps on his coarse mats, and in his philanthropic tours, makes himself, so far as the mere fellowship of life is concerned, one of them. It would appear to be his policy to gain his neophytes' confidence by descending to nearly their level. Hardship and frugality with him are essential to his cause, and he cheerfully submits to a mode of living and a solitary routine of services which would appall his Protestant brother, accustomed as he is from childhood to rely upon the amenities of the social circle, and whose faith embraces the promise of the things of this life as well as those of the life to come. The Romanist loses sight of himself in the one great object of aggrandizing the holy mother church and bringing the entire world under her ecclesiastical sway. He is but a unit in a vast body, whose centre lies elsewhere. Educated to passive intellectual obedience and physical self-denial, if to these he adds a holy zeal and perfect faith, he makes a most effective religious agent, and there is nothing surprising in his contempt of the common pursuits and desires of mankind. Neither is it strange that the Protestant missionary should cling to those ties which, by education and faith, with him constitute a part of his religion. The family he brings with him to his field of labor, serves to teach others to be faithful husbands and affectionate fathers. He desires to give a practical example to the heathen, of a well directed Christian household, as a manifestation of those blessings which here attend religion and virtue. His desire is not to go down to the native, but to raise the native up to him. To him there is more of true religion in practicing the duties and refinements of domestic life than in denying them. Thus by their very creeds the Romanist and Protestant commence their work at extremes. The one as it were without scrip or coat, without wife or child, inured to toil and educated to repress the natural emotions of the heart, throws himself boldly into the field of warfare without counting its cost; bound by no ties except those of his order, having no hopes except of ecclesiastical advancement here, or spiritual reward hereafter, he becomes an efficient, uncompromising soldier of the cross, to be deterred at no obstacles, to be appalled at no danger, and to shrink from no means of compassing his object. The other counting himself a disciple of Jesus, takes his instructions direct from His word; recognizes no medium between himself and heaven; esteems it gospel-wise to provide both scrip and coat, purse and wife; carries with him to combat with the principle of evil, all the aids to good that flow from the virtuous relations of life and intimate connection with his fellow-men. The Romanist brings an adoring multitude before the decorated altars of his church and enkindles emotion by appeals to their visible senses, directing their sympathies through the pictured sufferings of holy men to the cause for which they died. The Protestant sanctifies the domestic affections by lighting up an altar of purity in the heart. He desires to make the world within to correspond with the world without and both to perform their mission of love from the Father. Intellectually we may admire the stern, self-denying discipline of the disciple of Rome, but mind and soul unite in proclaiming that best suited for man which, while it leads him to a rational use of the gifts of this life, best prepares him for the enjoyments of that to come.

CHAPTER XVI.

" Belgian Contract "—Messrs. Richards and Brinsmade's transactions in Belgium—Mr. Richards' Commission— "Statutes of Royal Community "—Failure of Belgian scheme—Debts of Ladd & Co —Proposition and threats of Mr. Hooper—Return of Mr. Brinsmade to England— United States—Oahu—Suit vs. Hawaiian Government —Arbitration.

CONNECTED with the embassy of Messrs. Haalilio and Richards to Europe, was the so styled " Belgian Contract," growing out of the efforts of Mr. Brinsmade for the sale of his lease from the king, mentioned in chapter 12. This scheme was so intimately interwoven with the political affairs and prospects of the kingdom from the period of its inception in 1843 until its final termination in 1847, as, with the singular suit which sprung from it, to make an important chapter in Hawaiian history. Unfortunately, the labors of Messrs. Haalilio and Richards were not confined solely to their diplomatic agency, and the particular objects of their mission, as specified in a power of attorney from the king to Mr. Richards. They were persuaded by Mr. Brinsmade, who had preceded them to Europe with his contract of 1841 from the Hawaiian government, to meet him in Brussels, in May, 1843, and lend him their influence in negotiating a sale of the contract with all other properties of Ladd & Co., to the Belgian Company of Colonization. Based on this transfer of property was an involved, and considering the condition of the islands, an impolitic and hazardous scheme for the establishment of an extensive mercantile and agricultural community, formed by agents and employees sent out by the parent society in Belgium, who were to enjoy certain questionable monopolies and privileges. The king was to have been a partner and stockholder in this foreign stock-jobbing company, and to guarantee a minimum interest of four per cent. during six years.

Before the final arrangements were completed, and any solid consideration paid over to Mr. Brinsmade, news of the occupation of the islands by Lord George Paulet arrived, and as Ladd & Co. alleged, threw a damper over the whole proceedings. Negotiations with the company were afterwards resumed, and the statutes of the community signed. But Mr. Brinsmade becoming discouraged by the delays thrown in his way by the Belgian company, who either were not prepared to enter so fully into the plan as he desired, or had grown lukewarm and sceptical as to its final success, under date of October, 1844, wrote Mr. Richards that he was in correspondence with merchants in Ghent, who "were anxious to get the business, but will have nothing to do with the Belgian Company of Colonization, but will establish a purely commercial company on common sense principles." * * * "If my propositions are declined, there will be an end to all attempts in Belgium, and I am feeling in London my way to bring the business before some persons here if I cut from Ghent." Relying upon these assurances, Mr. Richards, who was then in America, believing all connection with the Belgian company was at an end through the acts of Mr. Brinsmade himself, and the non-ratification of the scheme by the council general of the Belgian company, paid no further attention to the subject. Although both of the king's commissioners gave their consent to Mr. Brinsmade's sale and contract in Belgium, yet Mr. Haalilio did so with great reluctance, and Mr. Richards was actuated by the desire of countenancing on the part of the king a project which he had been induced to believe gave indications of being adapted to foster industry, and develop the resources of the islands. But further examination into the practical working of such complicated chartered corporations, with the bearing of vast foreign capital and influence, sustained by monopolies of commercial and landed privileges, upon a small nation like that of the Hawaiian Islands, convinced him that it could not but prove unfavorable. In signing an instrument of the kind, he evidently had transcended the objects of his mission, as defined in his commission and power of attorney, trusting to the utility of the scheme, as he understood it, to recommend itself to the chiefs before going into operation. In this, however, he was mistaken; for as soon as the king and chiefs were made acquainted with the arrangement, they expressed both anxiety for the results and disapprobation of the act. Their sentiments were founded in part upon the private reports and letters of Haalilio, who, although his judgment had been overborne in lending his signature to the transaction, was fearful he had made a wrong step, and communicated his doubts to the chiefs. Previous to signing the contract, Mr. Richards exhibited to the Belgian agents such powers as he had, and they were of opinion that they were sufficiently broad for him to make the king a party to the transaction.

Fortunately, both for Belgium and Hawaii, it fell through. But the affair proved a prolific source of anxiety and trouble for the king, and developed in full the evils of that policy which, through unbounded reliance on alleged philanthropic motives, involved the government in the speculations of individuals.

Mr. Brinsmade having failed of raising funds in Europe on his contract, returned to the islands in 1846, protested against the right of his partners to give mortgages on their joint property, and instituted a claim of $378,000 against the Hawaiian government for alleged illegal acts in selling their properties, and in preventing the Belgian scheme from going into operation. The government, fully persuaded that they had treated Ladd & Co. throughout not only justly but liberally, and that this claim was but another instance like the many already adduced, of nefarious attempts to extort money from them under specious charges, aggravated in this case by ingratitude from men on whom they had showered favors, and whose misfortunes were the result solely of the failure of their own schemes and agent, and an amount of indebtedness incurred to sustain their ill-judged speculation, consented that the whole matter should be referred to the arbitration of Messrs. J. F. B. Marshall and S. H. Williams, American gentlemen resident on the islands, to be decided on legal and equitable principles.

CHAPTER XVII.

Standard of civilization in 1846—Population—Captain King's estimate, 1779—Why erroneous—Great mortality—Causes of—Census tables for years 1832 and 1836 —Statistics of the islands—Conclusion.

In Cook's voyages, the population of the group, in the year 1779, is estimated at 400,000, which, it is to be presumed, far exceeded the truth. Captain King, who arrived at this conclusion, based his opinions from the numbers that flocked to whichever point the vessels moved. They were sufficiently wonderful objects in the eyes of the simple islanders, to draw together the whole population, to gaze upon them, wherever they went; consequently, vast crowds continually appeared, but composed, to a great extent, of the same individuals. He likewise judged the populousness of Kealakeakua Bay to be a fair sample of the condition of the coasts of all the islands; a conclusion which a better acquaintance with their actual state would have shown him to have been erroneous.

Judging from such data, his estimate gave to the whole islands a population nearly equal to that which he beheld in certain points; a conclusion as incorrect as it was too hastily made. Later voyagers formed similar opinions, from the large tracts of land to be met with, now deserted, bearing marks of former cultivation, and enclosed by broken walls, or partially irrigated by half ruined ditches. When it is borne in mind that the custom of changing the location of their cultivated grounds was common among the natives, leaving the old to go to waste, and that no chief of great importance was allowed by the policy of Kamehameha I. to reside away from the person of his sovereign, his presence being a security for his allegiance, and that the supreme chief frequently migrated, drawing after him a vast train of greedy followers, whose path was as destructive as that of locusts, it is not matter of surprise that such fields are common. The country became deserted by those interested in its culture; consequently no correct inference in regard to the former population can be formed from this fact. But whatever was its amount, it was vastly greater than at present, and since the time of Cook a rapid decrease has occurred. Neither is this melancholy result of difficult solution. The population of the islands probably never amounted to what, with the aids of civilization, they could be made capable of supporting. During their heathen state, though divided into many hostile tribes, perpetually engaged in warfare, their battles, from the imperfection of their weapons, were comparatively bloodless. That very condition served to develop enterprise and a national spirit. Warlike exercises and manly games had each a favorable effect upon the mere physical growth. The boundless hospitality which every chief was obliged by the spirit of the race to exercise, and which prevailed even among the canaille, always found food and shelter for the oppressed. A man dissatisfied with one master had but to flee to another, and he was sheltered and welcomed. Taxes were heavy, and much labor required, but as it was generally for the support of the whole, an interested motive existed. The same work which would destroy the energies of a man who was to receive no reward for his toil, would produce health and cheerfulness in one who had an interest in the result. Every individual had that to some extent in the wealth and success of his chief; hence a patriarchal feeling was developed, which, with long used and uncontested despotic power, will sufficiently account for the deep reverence, fear, and canine-like attachment, with which the common people regarded their superiors. Exceptions to this no doubt prevailed, and much misery was the consequence; but as a general principle it was correct, and stands in strong contrast with the relative condition of the two classes, after a thirst for foreign wealth was developed by intercourse with the white race. A grasping, avaricious disposition succeeded; ends were to be attained regardless of the means used. The little natural humane feeling the chiefs possessed, was extinguished by avarice. Interested foreigners stimulated this passion; cargoes of rich goods were brought, luxuries displayed, and no means left untried to excite their cupidity. The unfortunate result is well known. The whole physical resources of the kingdom were overwrought, and men, women and children were taxed beyond their pow-

ers, to collect sandal-wood; mountains and valleys almost inaccessible, were penetrated, and heavy loads borne on bleeding shoulders to the sea-side. Like the children of Israel, their toil was doubled, and their sufferings found no consideration in the eyes of their cruel task masters. Cultivation was neglected, and famine ensued. Multitudes perished under their burdens; others left their homes and wandered, like wild animals, in the depths of forests, where they either slowly sunk under the horrors of want and starvation, or sustained a miserable existence on roots and wild fruits. Blind to the consequences, the chiefs continued the same policy. Debts were contracted, which the power of the whites required to be discharged, and increased taxes were imposed. Under the twofold pressure of the avarice of the chiefs and their fears, property was unsafe. A native could neither hold nor acquire—all was his chief's; even his children became a source of additional suffering, for every head was taxed!—infanticide greatly increased;—parents gave away their offspring, and the natural feelings of the nation were crushed beneath this iron despotism. Life became a wearisome burden; numbers of the most active sought safety and employment abroad. The first effects of christianity added to this already intolerable load. So long had this system been pursued, that no other plan for public works, than the compulsory labor of the whole population, seemed feasible. Regardless of the advice and instruction of their religious teachers, they added to their labors the toil of building churches, school houses, and other works, necessary in themselves, but erected by unholy means. This system prevailed in latter days, with mitigations, however, until 1838, when it began to give away before the combined influences of the mission and foreign residents, and the more enlightened efforts of the native population. Predial servitude in its old shape now no longer necessarily exists in Hawaii, although the spirit of extortion is not wholly extinguished. The wars of Kamehameha I. were also very destructive, and his power at first maintained by great sacrifice of human life.

Before Captain Cook's visit, diseases were few and simple. Subsequently they increased in number and virulence, while the remedies and knowledge necessary for arresting them remained unknown; the fatality attending novel illnesses, the progress of which they knew not how to arrest, produced a deep and often fatal spirit of despondency. Savages naturally have but little horror of death. However simple at first a disease, they frequently die from *want of exertion to live.* The beneficent services of the foreign physicians are doing much to counteract this destructive apathy, and also to extinguish the influence of native quacks, who annually destroy numbers. Alcohol and licentiousness have usually been considered the most aggravated causes of depopulation, but their influence has been exaggerated. The habits of the natives, in both respects, are now better than they were before their discovery, when drunkenness, produced by the use of *awa*, and promiscuous intercourse and incest, were almost parts of their natures. The former no doubt has destroyed many, and created a predisposition to disease in more; but the natives were never so completely addicted to it, as to make it a primary cause in their destruction. The diseases incident to the latter, have extensively run throughout the whole race, doing irreparable injury by poisoning the very fountains of life, and engendering upon offspring effete constitutions. In 1842, the virus had almost run out, but since, owing to the great influx of shipping from all quarters of the globe, it has again developed itself in new and horrible forms, with a virulence and fatality unequaled since the visit of Cook. A remarkable feature attending this disease is that it is now more severe upon the females than males. Prior to their discovery by Cook, these diseases were unknown. It cannot be doubted that they have been a powerful means, not so much of destroying the increase as preventing it, and the effects are melancholy in the extreme. The habits of both sexes are of such a nature, that fecundity with young people is, when compared with other countries, of rare occurrence. It is sufficient to be known that such is the fact, without enlarging upon the topic. A missionary has informed me that upon inquiring of a Bible class of 80 married women, how many had been mothers, he found but 39. More die in proportion to disease than in other countries, but still fewer are born, as the tables of population show. The great pestilence of 1803 destroyed multitudes, and has been supposed to have partaken of the character of the Asiatic cholera. Great numbers of healthy young Hawaiians have left in whale-ships and other vessels and never returned. The number annually afloat is computed at 3,000. At one time 400 were counted at Tahiti, 500 in Oregon, 50 at Paita, Peru, beside unknown numbers in Europe and America. Their wives and families, left to provide for themselves, fall into vicious habits, and both evils combined, tend to diminish the native population.

A powerful agent, though one the effects of which have been greatly overlooked, is the partial adoption of foreign clothing. This may seem paradoxical; but unfortunately it is too true. In their original state, their clothing was simple and uniform. Alterations soon occurred; in their desire to imitate the whites, their old was greatly thrown aside, and replaced by such articles of foreign manufacture as could be procured. The wealth of the chiefs enabled them to make a complete change, and appear well. With the common people, every article, from the cast-off dress of a sailor from the Arctic regions, to the thinnest fabrics from China, were put into requisition. Some days the whole population would appear decently clad; on others, a mixture of their old and new would predominate. Many would wear their clothes but part of the time, and then finding them inconvenient from extra heat or cold, throw them aside altogether. The utmost irregularity prevailed, not only from poverty, but from carelessness, and ignorance of the results. Warm dresses would be worn for weeks by some, and then the same party would appear for as long a period in almost a state of nudity. The warmer and finer the weather, the greater the desire for display. If it rained, those who but a few minutes previous paraded their finery with all the importance of civilized belles, would lay it aside lest it be spoiled, and expose their naked persons rather than their newly acquired fashions, to the peltings of the storm. In all work, the same plan prevailed. At those seasons when clothing was most required to preserve an even temperature of the system, it was laid aside, and when least needed, most worn. Their constitutions already enfeebled, from causes before mentioned, could ill bear such treatment. Colds and fevers greatly increased, and of a more fatal tendency. Trivial predispositions to disease were aggravated, and death the frequent result of attacks which the slightest prudence could have obviated.

A corresponding cause likewise exists in the partial adoption of new modes of building, such as adobie houses, and others, which in many cases appear externally more comfortable than the mere straw hut, but which internally from want of knowledge of domestic architecture, are obnoxious to damp and strong drafts, which not being guarded against lay the foundation of much disease. Frequent migrations and changes of climate from wet to dry, and dry and hot to wet and cold, combined with equal alterations in diet, contribute to swell the annual mortality. Formerly, fear of enemies or the orders of their chiefs, kept them closely confined to their native villages.

But no one cause has had a more fatal tendency, both in human life and morals, than the vicious land monopoly of the chiefs, augmented and made more weighty at the national council assembled at the visit of the Blonde to regulate the succession. The first Kamehameha had done somewhat to relieve this evil by centering all power in himself, by which the serfs found one comparatively kind master, not inattentive to their wants. Amid the boundless rapacity and taxation that ensued in Liholiho's reign, the entire kingdom became in great measure one vast field of license and cruelty. The old feudal lines of demarkation between serf, clan, chief and king were greatly broken in upon. The king managed to sequester many estates and much property for himself and favorites. In the want of general order and continual change, there was hope for the needy by some turn in the wheel of fortune to secure something. Even the highest chiefs

were insecure. This universal laxity could have been turned to a useful purpose upon the accession of a more orderly ruler, by securing to each individual of whatever rank, security of life and property, and bestowing on all some landed rights in the latter, that they might find a value in the former. But no such policy prevailed. With a selfishness, paralleled only by the recklessness of those beneath them, the chiefs partitioned the entire country among themselves, so that at this present time, notwithstanding the many fluctuations of property and the increase of knowledge, there are not over 600 owners of soil throughout the kingdom, and less than twelve persons hold the great bulk of it. This in itself would not have been so great an evil, had it not been conjoined with a system aggravated from the past, which in spirit declared that the chief was everything, the people nothing. Not content to spare their goose that they might receive a golden egg per day, they essayed to kill it, that they might get all at once. The native historians of this period, say, that from Liholiho's time the chiefs left caring for the people. Their attention was turned to themselves and their immediate aggrandizement. The people became more oppressed than even in ancient times. Novel taxes were inflicted and new crimes invented, which bore a fruitful crop of fines and confiscations. Beside the soil, the chiefs claimed the entire right to all that was on it; even the very stones were not spared if they could be made convertible to property; the fishing grounds were seized and even fruit trees, not with the purpose of fostering and preserving them for the common benefit of themselves and tenants, but to get from them and their people the greatest amount in the shortest time. The present was the only moment, the future entered not into their calculation. As far as could be, the very idea of property, particularly in lands, the true source of national industry, was extinguished. A common man had no "home." Under such circumstances, it is not surprising that depopulation was not stayed nor immorality decreased. The relation between tyrants and slaves is ever fruitful of crimes in the one and vice in the other. The serf unprotected by law, secure in no fruits of his own handicraft or industry, met the rapacity of his chief and his selfish claims to lands he had never tilled, by cunning, deceit or evasion. Hence the character for lying, theft and petty dishonesty which we find so prevalent among the present generation. They are the natural fruits of the wicked system of land monopoly with all its attendant crimes, which their chiefs so fully carried out. Not the least of the evils arising from this policy, was the unsettled character it gave the entire population. Possessing no permanent rights in the soil, or such as were not respected, they ceased to have permanent residences. Leaving their native homes, they flocked to whatever points offered the greatest inducements, chiefly seaports,—the women to sell their persons, and the men to pick up gain in any way that offered. In consequence, lands were left uncultivated, households were broken up, and the people became roving in their habits. It were vain, therefore, under these circumstances, to expect patriotism, morality and industry, the foundations of a people's prosperity, to flourish.

The filthy habits of the natives would of themselves be conducive to disease, and much else might be named which would cause the philanthropist less to wonder at the decrease, than that it should have been so slight in comparison to the many causes so actively at work to create it. I have stated only those which have come into operation since their first intercourse with the whites. Wars were more bloody, owing to the possession of improved weapons, and on a more extended scale, until the conquest of the group was completed. They were succeeded by diseases of the most destructive character, which raged unrested by medical art. As fatal as either were the severe labors imposed upon the conquered. Then the aggravation of the vicious land system and taxes, with alcohol, swelled the list, and ignorance of, or blindness to the most simple physical truths, added their hecatombs. It is to be remembered that these causes were all additional to those which existed prior to their discovery, and which were

of themselves sufficiently active to prevent any rapid increase.

At the first glance, it may appear that civilization is destructive in its tendency when in contact with the savage. A more extended view will show it otherwise. If it destroy, it likewise creates. Evil, as the most active principle, may for a while riot uncontrolled, yet counteracting and more powerful tendencies are at work, which must eventually neutralize and overcome the former. Civilized man can add nothing to the vices of the savage, though by the contact the fruits may be made more bitter. Like the first effects of a brilliant sun upon tender vegetation, it will shrink and wither, but the same light continued will cause it to revive and shoot forward in all the luxuriance of its legitimate growth. Such has been emphatically the case at these islands. Their depopulation was more rapid, as far as can be ascertained, in the reigns of Kamehameha I. and his successor, Liholiho, than at a more recent period. As christianity and civilization have advanced, in just that proportion has this mortality ceased.

In 1847 the scene has greatly changed. Religion has provided schools, medical science, churches and kindred institutions throughout the land. It is a living spring, gushing up freely in their households; watering their young plants and refreshing the parent stems. It sends to every hamlet a knowledge of letters, and furnishes the word of life, and a constant supply of healthful food for the inquiring mind. A moral stimulant is constantly at work to elevate and preserve, in the shape of associations, societies, religious meetings, after the system of New England. Philanthropy plants her agents by scores among them, active, resolute, and untiring in efforts for their temporal and eternal welfare.

Such are the agents at work to arrest the obliteration of the Hawaiian race from the earth and to give it a passport to futurity. To the notice already given of their present moral condition, it remains to briefly delineate their position in the scale of actual civilization in 1847—an epoch in which the generation that was born in heathenism is still alive. Experience declares Hawaiians to be

25

susceptible of civilization. Unlike the nomadic tribes of Asia and the predatory clans of America, their insular position compelled them to a stationary life and the character of their soil and climate to labor for subsistence. Consequently their governments became fixed and their habits agricultural, the first steps towards civilization. Like all branches of the Malay family, their perceptive and imitative faculties are more developed than their reflective, which however cannot be said to be very deficient, though talent in the European sense is rare among them. The mass thus far have manifested neither enterprise nor capacity to fit them for higher situations than laborers, servants and seamen. With proper instruction, they become tolerable mechanics, but without sufficient genius to originate or improve. In Honolulu we find but twelve native carpenters, four masons, nine shoemakers, nineteen tailors, six book-binders, four printers, and a few others who have some slight knowledge of other arts and trades. They have succeeded in engraving upon copper-plate with some skill. In trade none have risen above peddling or petty retailing. In agriculture, we find but few examples of cultivation on an extended and liberal scale, with an eye to prospective results. The farms are little patches, not badly laid out, but producing slightly in comparison with what a white farmer would raise. Their stock is raised more by chance than skill. As yet, although there are numerous openings for an extended and lucrative traffic in the raising of fruits, cattle, poultry on an extended and systematic scale, yet but very few are alive to these enterprises. Some, stimulated by the advice and example of whites, have laid out coffee and sugar plantations and entered into the business of grazing on a plan of some magnitude. In boating, the natives show the most spirit, and they own about twenty small craft engaged in coasting. As a people, they are indifferent to the future, careless of time, improvident in their habits, unsteady in their pursuits, and fond of finery and show. Yet when the obstacles of an early bad government and other bars to their progress are considered, which have been but partially

removed, it must be acknowledged that it is no matter of surprise that in so few years, their advance has been no greater. The chiefs and better class of people, whose advantages have been far superior to the mass, have acquired a degree of refinement and attained to a comfortable style of living, creditable to themselves and encouraging to the nation at large. Their houses, of stone, adobie, wood, or grass, are many of them large, well built and comfortably and to some degree, tastefully and expensively furnished, and surrounded with neat, well kept grounds. They dress well, and their manners are gentlemanly. The women have never acquired the ease and good taste of the men, although they have adopted the fashionable costumes of modern civilization. Intellectually, both appear to tolerable advantage, particularly those who, like the young chiefs, have been educated. Indeed in mathematics they are apt; and in other branches of study quite upon a par in general knowledge with the whites similarly situated about them, lacking however their superior moral discernment and capability of applying their knowledge to practical purposes. The educated native, without the stimulus of a diversified national literature, and a cultivated, aspiring society, is apt to degenerate upon leaving the immediate influences by which he was surrounded, for the common sphere of his countrymen. As yet, though partial experiments have been made, the missionaries have not been able to rear a class of native clergy, whom they could leave to act wholly independent of their surveillance. With school-teachers they have been somewhat more successful, that profession not requiring so high a standard of moral judgment.

Between the classes above referred to and the lowest, exists another, composed of petty officers, deacons, teachers, the higher church members and most intelligent of petty traders, farmers, vessel owners and mechanics, who form the connecting link in the scale of civilization. These are possessed of some property, say from a few hundred to a few thousand dollars each; are frugal and saving; tolerably intelligent in their immediate spheres, and possessed of some ambition and enterprise. Like those above them, they have some knowledge of English, and are provident for their families. Their habitations are as much removed in neatness and pretensions from the huts of the peasantry as from the superior edifices of their chiefs. They have imbibed some knowledge of the tastes and proprieties of civilization, and instead of herding in common, divide their houses into apartments; sleep on beds; possess tables, chairs and a considerable amount of plain and useful furniture; adhere to the national dishes of poi and fish, but vary it with bread and meat; in short, are a comfortable middle class, rising in fortunes and creditable to the country. They are favorably distinguished by the attention they bestow upon their children. Their numbers cannot be given, but though not large they are increasing.

The great bulk of the people live very much as did their ancestors, in filthy huts and on impure diet, raw fish and poi. They are in general provided with clothing, and all have, or can have more or less articles of foreign manufacture for their common wants. The annual *ad valorem* consumption of foreign goods per head to each inhabitant does not yet exceed three dollars; a very small ratio compared to their wants and abilities, if industrious. They are naturally averse to labor, prompt to take advantage, unreasonable in their expectations and with little or no enterprise.

Whether the poison has entered too deep into the nation to be eradicated, is a question at present unsolved. In the view of many, races like individuals, have their time and purpose, which they fulfill and perish. History shows that fact in the past. One after another of potent nations has dropped from time, leaving on its shores no greater wreck than a tradition, a few pages of history, or a mere name. But the fact is equally true, that in the proportion that Christian principles have had sway, in that degree have nations flourished. The rank, sudden growth of powers like Spain, which founded its power and pride for a while upon avarice and conquest, is no exception to this rule. Trusting to such support, it fell again as rapidly as it rose,

strangled by its vices. England, France, the United States and other nations, taking revelation for their guide, and incorporating into their legislation its sound maxims of justice and humanity, steadily prosper and increase. So long as they maintain those principles, and the nearer they approach the true intent of their author, so long are they sure of life and success. Thus will it be with the Hawaiians, if their physical and mental stock has enough of vigor still remaining to bud anew and bear fruit. No fairer opportunities than are now offered for the success of the experiment of raising a savage tribe into a civilized state will ever again be offered. Could the missionaries have enjoyed the advantages open to Cook or Vancouver on their arrivals, and like Mango Capac to the simple Peruvians, have appeared among the Hawaiians as heralds of a new faith and civilization, authenticating their mission to native minds by a belief in their divine inspiration, their precepts would have taken root under better auspices and with more complete success, than afterwards, when the national mind was distracted by its new impulses of gain and antagonistic foreign example, and the physical energies of the nation were fast perishing in the service of vice and avarice. But the renovating spirit of christianity has steadily worked its way, overthrowing all obstacles, creating for itself a moral capital in its progress, until it has placed the Hawaiian nation in a position which if they do not improve to their advantage, it will be because heathenism has left them effete and incapable of sustaining the vigorous growth of christianity, and Providence intends to supplant them by a more worthy people. The causes that have operated to depopulate and demoralize the race, and ultimately extinguish it, have been recapitulated. I shall now pass briefly in review those of a conservative and renewing tendency.

The government of the kingdom is essentially Christian. Founded upon missionary teaching, it derives its principles and objects from gospel ethics. Under its influence, the despotism of the chiefs over life and property has been abolished and the nation invited to lay hold of its rights in both. Laws favorable to virtue, industry and increase of population have been enacted. Families having three children of their own are freed from taxation; those having more are rewarded by gifts of lands. The natives are encouraged to secure allodial titles by a remission of all taxes on such for twenty years. Taxation is lightened and made stimulative to honest industry. The present laws are equitable and protective. Justice is fairly administered, and the soundest principles of classical and modern law have become the professed guides of the courts. Commerce has brought among the nation many foreigners in every way an advantage to the morals and enterprise of the natives. Scattered throughout the group, they provide them almost at the very doors of their huts with ample supplies of foreign goods of all descriptions at fair prices, receiving in return the avails of native labor. They have furnished them with cattle and the vegetable products of other countries, and introduced the arts, trades and professions of civilized life. The examples and encouragements of civilized households are thus brought to their very thresholds. They have given a value to the time of the native by creating a demand for his labor, and have equally bestowed a value to his hitherto unproductive lands, by practically developing the hidden wealth of the soil. The most indifferent industry is sure of ample reward. Vice as in other lands has no apology for an existence here, on the plea of a super-abundance of labor in the honest branches of livelihood. Not a man need be a thief from necessity, nor a woman unchaste from want. Lands everywhere lie groaning in wild luxuriance, crying out for hands to till them. The handicraft of women and even the services of children are in constant demand. Commerce has raised the remuneration of the former and the wages of the laborer to the highest rate of stimulative reward.

The policy of the government is essentially protective to the Hawaiian race, to the intent to fully solve the question of their capability of civilization. The white advisers of the king, having this end practically in view, fail to meet the more enlarged views and desires of white residents, who look upon the final extermination or loss of the native race and dynasty as their destiny, and consequently desire to see the fullest encouragement offered for the ingress and permanent settlement of a foreign population and capital. While these would urge the government on with a rapidity commensurate with Anglo-Saxon spirit and intelligence, the native race by their slowness of apprehension and fears for their security in case the full torrent of civilized emigration and enterprise is let in unrestrained upon them, hold them back. On the one hand the government are as unable fully to satisfy the cravings of the whites to advance, as they are to bring the native mind to a clear appreciation and faithful carrying out of the measures best adapted to benefit it and render it more capable of assimilating with the superior intelligence of Anglo-Saxon intellect. They steadily endeavor to preserve the Hawaiian race; to christianize and civilize them; and to this end they invite a limited co-operation of foreign aid; enough to innoculate the nation with courage and enterprise, without deluging it in a torrent which in their present condition they would inevitably fail to bear up against. In this way a just middle course is adopted, which it would seem from past experience tends to build up a mixed Hawaiian and foreign race, civilized, moral and industrious, and capable of taking an elevated position in the ranks of minor nations.

In a former edition of this work, I advanced the idea that notwithstanding the former extraordinary rates of decrease in the population, there were operating causes sufficiently cogent to diminish that decrease materially and to lead to a reasonable hope that it might be wholly checked, and an increase take place in the native population. The tables below will serve to show the fearful rate of decrease up to 1840. These data are not wholly to be depended on in numbers, though the general results are doubtless correct.

Cook's vague estimate in 1779, made the population of the islands 400,000, but 300,000 would have been nearer to the truth.

	LOOSE ESTIMATE FOR 1823.	CENSUS OF 1832.	CENSUS OF 1836.
Hawaii	85,000	45,792	39,364
Maui	20,000	35,062	24,199
Lanai	2,500	1,600	1,200
Molokai	3,500	6,000	6,000
Kahoolawe	50	80	80
Oahu	20,000	29,755	27,809
Kauai	10,000	10,977	8,934
Niihau	1,000	1,047	993
	142,050	130,313	108,579

No fact illustrates more strongly the superior influences of enlightened christianity in a physical point of view upon the human race than the remarkable discrepancy in numbers between the children of missionaries and those of the chiefs, who are the most civilized among the Hawaiian population. Nine of the mission families number 59 children—an average of 6 5-9 to a family. Twenty Hawaiian chiefs have but 19 children among them all. The mission families within less than one generation have increased 175 per cent. At the same ratio of increase, in 100 years their descendants would number 59,535.

With these statistics I take leave of the reader, with the assurance that I have endeavored to portray faithfully the Hawaiian nation through all their progressive stages from heathenism to their present transition state, when civilization is making such rapid progress among them. The reader who calmly and naturally reviews this progress cannot fail to become interested in a race occupying so important a field of philosophic and philanthropic inquiry. Whether they are destined to perpetuity or not, Providence alone can foresee—cold calculating theories will not operate with the benevolent to discourage efforts which now promise so well; if fail they must, those who have labored for them will have the comforting assurance of having obeyed the injunction, "Go ye therefore and teach *all* nations," and soon with those whose souls they have raised from the mire of heathenism, they will hear the welcome sound. "Well done, good and faithful servants; enter thou into the joy of thy Lord."

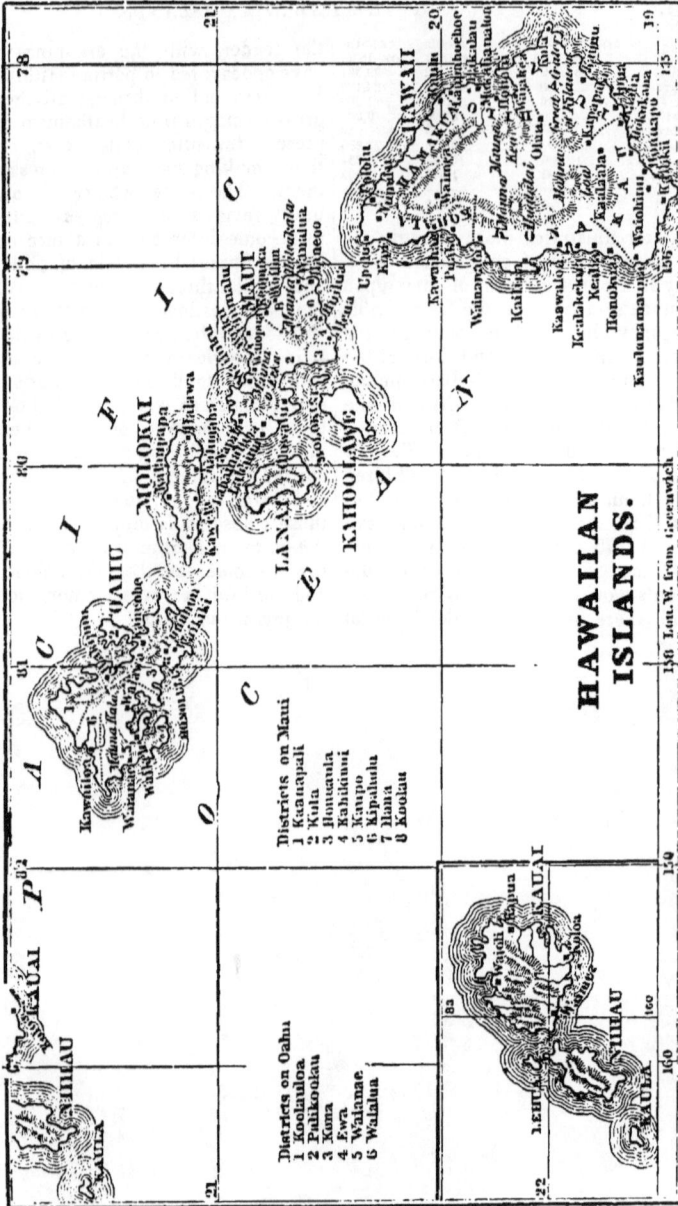

HAWAIIAN ISLANDS.

P A C I F I C   O C E A N

OAHU

MOLOKAI

MAUI

LANAI

KAHOOLAWE

HAWAII

NIIHAU

KAUAI

NIIHAU

Districts on Maui
1 Kaanapali
2 Kula
3 Honuaula
4 Kahikinui
5 Kaupo
6 Kipahulu
7 Hana
8 Koolau

Districts on Oahu
1 Koolauloa
2 Palikookau
3 Kona
4 Ewa
5 Waianae
6 Waialua

Lon. W. from Greenwich

156 157 158 159 160
19 20 21 22

APPENDIX,

COMMERCIAL AND AGRICULTURAL CONDITION

OF

THE HAWAIIAN ISLANDS.

BY HENRY M. WHITNEY.

1872.   .

APPENDIX.

THE valuable work of Mr. Jarves brings the history of this singularly interesting people down to the year 1847. To continue it to the present date would be a pleasant task to one identified so intimately with the Hawaiian people, as is the writer, who has watched their development and advancement with constant and increasing interest. It is less than a century since this group was discovered in 1778 by Capt. Cook—the story of whose untimely death was soon after published with more of the characteristics of a romance than a reality, attracting to this people the gaze of the Christian world, and exciting an interest in them which has never subsided. But little more than half a century has passed since the pioneer band of missionaries landed on Hawaii, and the Sun of righteousness rose to scatter the rays of truth and knowledge among a people even then restless to shake off despotic paganism, which had ground them down for ages, and thirsting for the freedom of civilization and christianity which they have so eagerly embraced that Hawaii is to-day as thoroughly Christianized as England or France. Scarcely one generation has passed since the first attempt was made to model a constitutional government, and the constitution of 1840 was proclaimed as the law of the land. Yet to-day Hawaii has its treaties with the principal nations of the old world and the new; and the statistics which follow will show that it has commercial intercourse with nearly every nation of the Pacific and Atlantic, and that its commerce is developing as rapidly in proportion to its population and area, as that of any other nation possessing like advantages. And all this, while the historian is compelled to record a continued extraordinary decrease in the aboriginal population.

Without attempting a continuation of the history of these islands from the period where Mr. Jarves left it, my purpose is simply to give a brief and necessarily imperfect outline of their present condition, including their population, commercial and agricultural resources, and other interesting data, closing with a sketch of the eruptions of the volcano.

POPULATION.

The estimate of the population of the group, as made by Capt. Cook, after a partial observation on each island, has been thought by some too large. The native traditions, however, as well as evidences still met with in every part of the group, go to confirm the opinion of this celebrated explorer. Certain it is that it was much larger at the time of the discovery of the islands than when the first missionaries arrived in 1820. The decrease, which must be in part attributed to the savage internecine wars existing at the time of Cook's visit, has been uninterrupted, and at times accelerated by the introduction of plagues from foreign countries, which have swept off the aborigines by tons of thousands. The table at the head of page 203 will show the population at various periods.

26

CENSUS OF THE HAWAIIAN ISLANDS, TAKEN DECEMBER 7TH, 1866.

	Hawaii—Hilo	Puna	Kau	South Kona	North Kona	South Kohala	North Kohala	Hamakua	Totals	Maui—Lahaina	Wailuku	Hana	Makawao	Totals	Molokai	Lanai	Oahu—Honolulu	Ewa & Waianae	Waialua	Koolauloa	Koolaupoko	Totals	Kauai—Waimea	Koloa	Puna	Koolau & Hanalei	Totals	Niihau	Grand totals
Total number natives in 1866	4,335	1,926	1,972	2,402	3,239	1,049	2,282	2,031	19,236	3,477	3,982	3,480	2,491	13,430	2,270	385	11,300	1,711	1,099	1,107	2,008	17,225	1,526	987	1,446	1,949	5,907	312	56,765
Total number natives in 1860	4,603	2,155	2,199	2,552	3,448	1,208	2,601	2,310	21,136	4,669	3,649	4,491	3,182	16,991	2,830	645	12,671	2,087	1,284	1,181	2,174	19,397	1,773	1,256	1,710	1,600	6,339	646	66,984
Total number foreigners, 1866	320	6	43	41	29	63	20		572	104	318	21	162	605	29	9	2221	73	37	56	181	2574	25	97	33	237	392	13	4104
Total number foreigners, 1860	139	3	28	31	40	63	53	20	346	217	40	18	128	409	34	1	1639	64	25	41		1778	88	28	41		148	1	2716
Laborers	910	2	90	402	65	81	301	43	1900	207	1207	78	391	1883	24	65	228	30	63	242		561	119	100	309		589	3	5026
Mechanics	106		22	14		111	30		283	137	3		100	240	5	10	477	13	3	50		543	12	13	39		64		1146
Agriculturists	781	626	10	960	166	535	535		3642	664	488	1038	422	2012	15	6	29	348	4	12		393	626	215	243	436	1419	119	8258
Professionalists	79		4		6	23	33	33	172	19	106	23	33	181	3	2	39		26	2	14	82	11	4	17	32	70	2	512
Freeholders	275	57	306	253	256	309	191	261	1756	481	631	545	263	1784	303	3	1440	300	223	202	393	2558	208	122	116	283	729	3	7164
Females over 40	631	308	306	286	419	148	148	331	2967	570	463	545	373	1988	454	60	1579	218	209	175	316	2465	241	136	169	251	837	61	8812
Males over 40	884	364	362	361	619	175	467	379	3,611	683	639	619	457	2,298	494	76	2,218	318	216	215	420	3,388	343	185	259	353	1,140	65	10,972
Females betw'n 15 and 40	793	231	309	406	566	188	360	385	3,380	650	873	631	462	2,616	353	61	2,964	400	197	222	409	4,193	361	166	294	420	1,141	52	11,795
Males between 15 and 40	1,419	328	408	461	654	247	401	392	4,200	784	1,144	603	585	3,115	416	73	3,717	426	209	258	574	4,184	288	336	373	662	1,658	54	14,702
Females under 15	429	290	308	409	549	170	340	266	2767	483	570	609	366	1948	290	65	1493	184	168	115	202	2162	198	145	156	224	723	38	7957
Males under 15	499	301	327	444	601	181	353	297	2983	511	594	594	389	2088	322	65	1550	238	177	177	274	2408	221	116	187	276	800	35	8721
Other foreigners, females	28	3	6	9		2	17		65	10	39	16	25	83	2		525	9	7	10	82	562	4	12	14	10	36	7	756
Other foreigners, males	141	3	40	30		28	29	17	316	59	115	16	66	246	25		1326	65	29	20	57	1515	14	28	21	57	120	0	2232
Chinese females	9					1	1		11	59	25	1	12	37			13				10	32		1	29		30		110
Chinese males	142		8	8	11	8	7	2	180	29	139		63	939	4	4	357	8	5	19	76	465	7	56	8	135	206		1090
Half-caste females	62	9	10	14	7	25	17	9	163	87	30	9	49	175	19	3	333	12	10	6	13	373	8	8	57		100		823
Half-caste males	57	4	13	29	16	41	28	14	202	61	57	14	50	162	13	4	386	14	16	4	28	347	4	16	40		64		817
Native females	1,754	927	907	1,170	1,587	478	1,089	973	8,835	1,600	1,629	1,673	1,335	6,237	1,046	176	5,165	787	525	490	885	7,852	686	401	653	793	2,535	144	26,875
Native males	2,462	986	1,042	1,189	1,587	505	1,148	1,036	9,996	1,729	2,066	1,784	1,257	8,836	1,181	202	5,516	898	832	605	1,082	8,350	825	537	1,059		3,208	108	30,250
Unmarried	2,265	854	892	1,591	1,487	516	1,040	895	9,340	1,872	2,254	1,542	1,307	6,975	1,118	211	7,532	895	644	664	1,080	10,615	756	544	750	1,201	3,251	162	31,672
Married	2,390	1,078	1,128	1,058	1,781	573	1,305	1,155	10,468	1,709	2,048	1,939	1,346	7,060	1,181	183	5,989	889	692	599	1,115	9,184	795	540	728	965	3,048	163	31,287
Tot. population	4,655	1,932	2,020	2,449	3,268	1,089	2,345	2,050	19,406	3,651	4,300	3,501	2,653	14,035	2,299	394	13,521	1,784	1,136	1,163	2,195	19,709	1,551	1,084	1,478	2,186	6,299	325	62,959
Females	1,863	939	923	1,193	1,594	506	1,124	982	9,114	1,703	1,923	1,685	1,221	6,532	1,067	180	6,036	802	642	512	927	8,819	700	447	659	695	2,701	153	28,564
Males	2,802	993	1,097	1,256	1,594	583	1,221	1,058	10,694	1,578	2,377	1,816	1,432	7,503	1,232	214	7,483	982	594	651	1,203	10,980	851	637	819	1,291	3,598	174	34,395

	Foreign.	Native.	Total.	Decrease.
1779 (estimated by Capt. Cook)............			400,000	
1828 (estimated by missionaries)..........			142,050	44 years 257,950
1832 (first official census)...................			130,315	9 " 11,735
1836 (official census).........................			108,579	4 " 24,414
1850 (official census).........................	1,962	82,203	84,165	14 " 24,414
1853 (official census)..........................	2,119	71,019	73,138	3 " 11,027
1860 (official census).........................	2,716	67,084	69,800	7 " 3,388
1866 (official census).........................	4,194	58,765	62,959	6 " 6,841

The census of 1866 is the last which has been taken, but it is probable that another will be taken the present year. The details of the census of 1866 are quite interesting, and are given on page 202. Some of them may be noticed here as compared with the returns for 1860 :

	1866.	1860.	Decrease.	Increase.
Total number of males........................34,395		35,379	985	....
Total number of females.....................28,564		31,705	3,141	....
Total population..............................62,959		69,800	6,741	....
Total number of married persons...............31,287		38,124	6,837	
Total number unmarried......................31,672		28,960	....	2,712
Total native population......................58,765		66,984	8,901	....
Total half-castes.............................. 1,640				
Total Chinese............................. 1,206				
Total other foreigners........................ 2,988		2,716	....	272
Total number of hired laborers................. 5,025				
Total number of agriculturists................. 8,358				
Total number of landholders................... 7,154				
Total number of mechanics or artizans.......... 1,146				

The number of males in the group has decreased but 984, while the females are 3,141 less than in 1860. This is perhaps the most disheartening fact developed by the census, as it shows the reproductive power of the nation to be lessening in an alarming degree. An examination of the table will show that the decrease has not been confined to any island or district, but preserves nearly the same ratio throughout the group. Honolulu and Lahaina might reasonably be supposed to show less decrease than the country districts, where medical aid is not so readily obtained, and the dwellings are less substantial. But they furnish no favorable exception, while in Lahaina the falling off in the population during six years amounts to twenty-five per cent., owing in part to migration to other districts. A table showing the population of each island, as compared with the two previous enumerations, will illustrate this better:

	1866.	1860:	1853:
Hawaii...19,808		21,481	24,450
Maui...14,035		16,400	17,574
Molokai... 2,299		2,864	3,607
Lanai... 394		646	600
Oahu....... 19,799		21,275	19,126
Kauai.. 6,299		6,487	6,991
Niihau... 325		647	790
Total...62,959		69,800	73,138

The annual decadence of the population between 1860 and 1866, was at the rate of 1,140; and it is probable that the next census, whenever taken, will show no great change in the rate of decrease. Were it not for the influx of foreigners, and especially of Chinese, with the rapid increase in the foreign element by births, and with the increase arising from inter-marriage, the population of the group would show a much greater falling off.

Official documents laid before the Legislative Assembly of 1872, show 4,961 more deaths than births during the four years from 1868 to 1871, or 1,250 per annum. Taking this average as a basis of estimate, the native population of this group, in 1873, will not exceed 50,000. During this period no epidemic has been reported, and the deaths have been from natural causes. Unless some means are devised to check it, the native race will continue to decrease in about the same ratio.

THE SUGAR INTEREST.

The first instance of the manufacture of sugar on these islands dates back previous to 1820, but the name of the pioneer planter is lost. Old residents speak of sugar and molasses of a coarse quality having been manufactured here in sufficient quantities for ordinary domestic consumption in 1828. In that year, extensive fields of cane were grown in and about Honolulu, and mills were erected in Nuuanu Valley and at Waikapu, Maui. At the latter place, a Portuguese, named Antonio Silva, is spoken of as the pioneer sugar planter. Some Chinamen also had a sugar mill near Hilo. These mills were all of wood, very primitive in their construction, and worked by oxen. The first attempt to cultivate sugar on a large scale was at Koloa, on Kauai, where Ladd & Co., a firm of Honolulu merchants, commenced what is known as the Koloa Plantation of Dr. R. W. Wood. This was about the year 1835, and the first breaking up of the soil for planting was done with a plow drawn by natives. From 1836 to 1841, sugar was exported from these islands to the value of $36,000, and molasses to the value of $17,130. In the " Hawaiian Spectator " for April, 1838, the late William Ladd contributed an article on " The Resources of the Sandwich Islands," in which he speaks thus prophetically of the manufacture of sugar, then in its infancy : " It is a very common opinion that sugar will become a leading article of export. That this will become a sugar country is quite evident, if we may judge from the varieties of sugar-cane now existing here, its adaptation to the soil, the price of labor, and a ready market. From experiments hitherto made, it is believed that sugar of a superior quality may be produced here. * * * It may not be amiss to state that there are now in operation, or soon to be erected, twenty mills for crushing cane, propelled by animal power, and two by water power."

The price of labor at that time, was indeed an argument in favor of making the islands a sugar producing country, which unfortunately does not exist now. Abundance of native labor could then be had, and the current rate of wages was from 12½ to 37½ cents per diem, or $2 to $5 per month.

In Wyllie's " Notes " on the islands, published in the " Friend," December, 1844, the export of sugar from the Island of Kauai is estimated at about 200 tons, and 20,000 gallons of molasses. Hilo in the same year exported 83,000 pounds of sugar. Maui at that time had two mills, but the amount of sugar produced is not reported. That was twenty-eight years ago. Since then, our sugar growing business has passed through many vicissitudes. As is generally the case in new pursuits, the pioneers have in many instances lost their time and money in their struggles for success, and those who have come after have learned to profit by their dear-bought experience. To-day, the total number of sugar plantations is thirty-two,—on Hawaii, nine; Maui, twelve; Oahu, seven; and Kauai, four.

The Custom House statistics have, during the past twenty years, given sugar the first place in our products and exports. The quantity exported in 1871 was 21,760,773 pounds, which added to the consumption in the group, gives a total of twenty-two millions of pounds. Not more than one-quarter of the area adapted to cane culture is at present under cultivation. Large tracts suited to cane are neglected, or devoted only to grazing, from want of capital and labor. As a general rule, droughts are rare, and rain sufficiently abundant, in all localities, both for grazing and agricultural purposes. On the four larger islands fine sugar plantations are established or in progress, varying from two hundred to several thousand acres in extent. On these are some of the largest, most complete and expensive sugar mills ever constructed in any country, driven by steam or water, and capable of manufacturing six to ten tons of sugar a day. No country can boast of finer mills or plantations, or more perfect arrangements for the manufacture of sugar and molasses. As a matter of interest abroad, a list is given of the plantations at present in operation in the group, with their average crop, and the capacity of their machinery :

	Average crop.	Capacity of mill.		Average crop.	Capacity of mill.
Kohala Plantation, Hawaii......	600 tons.	1,000 tons.	Haiku Plantation, Maui.........650 tons.		1,200 tons.
Onomea " "	500 "	1,000 "	Hana " " ....250 "		400 "
Kaupakuea " "	500 "	1,000 "	Union Mill " " ....300 "		600 "
Spencer " "	500 "	1,000 "	Hawaiian Mill (Wailuku).........300 "		400 "
Paukaa " "	300 "	530 "	Hobron (Makawao) Plantation...400 "		600 "
Kaiwiki " "	400 "	600 "	Kaneohe Plantation, Oahu.......100 "		250 "
Kona " "	100 "	200 "	Heeia " " ....200 "		400 "
Kau " "	150 "	200 "	Kaalaea " " ....400 "		1,000 "
Kaaiaha (Kohala) "	100 "	100 "	Kenahala " " .... 60 "		200 "
Ulupalakua Plantation, Maui....	800 "	1,200 "	Halawa " " .... 60 "		200 "
Pioneer " " ....1,000 "		1,200 "	Wainlua " " ....100 "		200 "
West Maui " " .... 600 "		1,200 "	Laie " " ....100 "		250 "
Waikapu " " .... 500 "		800 "	Lihue " Kauai.....400 "		1,000 "
Wailuku " " .... 800 "		1,200 "	Koloa " " ....250 "		500 "
Waihee " " ....1,000 "		1,200 "	Princeville " " ....400 "		1,000 "
East Maui " " .... 500 "		800 "	Waipa " " ....100 "		200 "

The plantations now in operation number thirty-two, producing less than half the sugar which they are capable of manufacturing. This is owing chiefly to the scarcity of laborers—a want which is each year more seriously felt. Next to Hawaiian laborers, who are considered the best and least expensive, Chinese are sought for. As they are always ready to leave their country and migrate to this group, it is probable that no difficulty will be encountered in obtaining all that may be needed.

The mode of manufacture is similar to that pursued in other sugar countries. The sugar is packed at the mills—the better grades in kegs, and the poorer in bags, and carted thence to the nearest port or anchorage, from which it is shipped to Honolulu by schooners or the steamer Kilauea, a vessel of four hundred tons burthen, owned by the Government, which makes regular weekly trips to Maui and Hawaii. It is estimated that the cost of manufacturing sugar here, on well-conducted plantations, is about five cents per pound, taking all grades into the estimate. At the present time San Francisco is the principal market for this as it is for most of our productions, though Oregon and Australia attract a portion of the sugar crop, the average net price realized for which is six cents a pound.

No attempt has been made to manufacture sugar from the beet root, which grows well in almost any part of the group. But it is not improbable that within a few years the sugar beet will be as extensively cultivated here as the cane now is, and that on the same plantations, and in the same factories, both will serve to furnish the juice for sugar manufacture. It is believed that the beet, when once introduced and its peculiarities studied and regarded, will be found a strong rival to the cane, and that it can be produced by native labor at a less expense than cane now is, with a correspondingly larger profit in the sugar manufactured from it.

OTHER AGRICULTURAL PRODUCTS.

Next to sugar, rice is extensively cultivated and exported. Hawaiian rice is in high favor in foreign markets, rating next to Carolina as a table rice. It is cultivated by both natives and Chinese in taro patches; and in localities where running water is abundant, the yield per acre is from 2,000 to 3,000 pounds of paddy (unhulled rice), which sells readily at two cents a pound. Rice and kalo may be seen growing side by side in nearly every valley in the group, the former supplying the Chinese with their staple food, and the latter the natives, who still prefer the kalo and its product *poi* to every other food. The quantity of paddy and rice exported in 1871 was 1,284,563 pounds. The cultivation of this grain could easily be extended to ten times what it now is, were the necessary labor obtainable.

PULU, which finds a place among our exports, is the product of the tree-fern, which grows abundantly on the mountain slopes of the principal islands, more particularly on Hawaii, and flourishes best in regions of perpetual moisture. It is a a silky substance enveloping the fronds of the plant, and when dried in the sun makes an excellent article for mattresses and for upholstering purposes. The quantity produced of late years has materially declined.

WOOL, HIDES and GOAT SKINS have been in active demand the past few years, and the quantity exported of each article shows a decided annual gain. The official census of 1866 gave the number of beef cattle on the islands at 59,913; sheep, 100,625; and goats, 56,980. But this amount is doubtless considerably below the actual numbers. It is estimated that the wild cattle alone on the different islands will number 40,000 head, and 100,000 cattle, 200,000 sheep and 100,000 goats are a more correct estimate. The finest of Merinos have been imported into these islands from time to time, and our breeds of sheep are now annually improving.

STEAM MAIL LINES.

The establishment of steam lines between the ports of Honolulu and San Francisco in one direction, and New Zealand and Australia in the opposite, has increased the foreign trade and travel with those countries, by furnishing more certain and comfortable means of crossing the ocean in either direction, in much less time than was formerly occupied. This is more especially the case with the route to New Zealand and Australia, whose industrious and thriving populations have a new avenue opened for their untiring industry in the steam line which now connects them with the Polynesian groups and the American coast. As these steam lines increase in number, and this port is brought in direct communication with Japan, China, Panama, Tahiti, South America, and the South Pacific island clusters, the advantages of its position will become more apparent. Easily approached by sail or steam, from every quarter of the compass, and lying advantageously between the great commercial marts of this ocean, it must, of necessity, become ere long an important coaling station, and perhaps a depot for the storage and transhipment of teas, coffee, sugar, rice, lumber, oil, coals, and other commercial products. Coal is now admitted free of duty, whether for consumption here, or for re-exportation. It will only be necessary to extend the same liberal legislation to the other staples named, in order to attract them hither. The accompanying table, prepared by Capt. Daniel Smith, giving the distances between Honolulu and the places named, will show its advantages as a central point:

Honolulu to San Francisco	2,100 miles.	Honolulu to Auckland, New Zealand	3,800 miles.
" Yokohama, Japan	3,400 "	" Sydney, N. S. W. (straight line)	4,480 "
" Hongkong, China	4,850 "	" Melbourne, Port Philip	4,960 "
" Papeete, Tahiti	2,400 "	" Callao, Peru	5,220 "
" Tutuila, Navigator Islands	2,290 "	" Valparaiso, Chile	6,000 "
" Levuka, Fiji	2,740 "	" Victoria, V. I. (straight line)	2,350 "

The steamers connecting this port with New Zealand and Australia are large and commodious vessels of about twenty-five hundred tons burthen, capable of averaging 250 miles a day, and 300 miles when necessary. They are better adapted to the tropical route over which they run than any other class of steamers. The mails have been carried through from London to Auckland, via San Francisco and Honolulu, in forty-two days, and to Sydney in forty-eight; and when the line is fully equipped and in operation, this time may be considerably lessened. At Honolulu the steamers are detained about twenty-four hours to coal and refit, and passengers can remain over one or more trips of the steamers, should they desire to travel in the group. The variety of scenery on this route—the fine and commodious vessels employed—the opportunity of touching at these islands—and the unrivaled diversity of scenery on the trans-continental trip, with the powerful and swift steamers plying between New York and England, present attractions such as no other route possesses, and which cannot fail to make it popular with tourists, whether seeking pleasure or on business.

The liberality of the Hawaiian Government and resident citizens has provided a first class hotel at this port, which is calculated to make the stay at Honolulu attractive and refreshing, whether it be for one day or longer. This building is constructed of stone, three stories in height, with fifty-eight sleeping rooms, and is fitted with parlors, dining, reading and billiard rooms, and with every modern convenience, not excepting gaslight. It is located in the pleasantest part of the town, and travelers cannot fail to find it worthy of their patronage.

The city of Honolulu (including a circuit of four miles in each direction from the Post Office) has a population, according to the census of 1866, of 13,521 persons, of whom 1,851 are Americans and Europeans, 370 Chinese, 619 half-whites, and 10,681 are pure Hawaiians. The number of foreigners and Chinese is now much larger. The number of dwellings is about 2,100, which are constructed mostly of wood, stone or brick, and from one to three stories high.

CLIMATE, ETC.

Some interesting data have been collected during the past few years relative to the climate and meteorology of the group. Though the amount of rain annually falling may be fully as great as a half century ago, it is believed to be less equally distributed through the year, owing to the destruction of the forests on the mountains and of the groves in the valleys and plains, which have unquestionably had some influence on the climate of these islands, as they have in other countries. This is more particularly noticed during the summer months, when the islands are more dependent on the trade winds for rain, than during the winter months, when the southerly storms spread the rain throughout their track, on land and sea alike, without regard to the amount of verdure on the land over which they pass. The destruction of the forests and groves has been caused in a great measure by the herds of cattle, sheep, goats and horses which of late years have been allowed to increase and roam unattended over the hills and mountains, tramping down and killing the young trees and stripping the bark and foliage from those of more mature growth. Forests and verdure assist in collecting the clouds which give the summer showers, so refreshing to the husbandman in the season when most needed, to ensure abundant crops, pasturage, and supplies of water for irrigation and manufacturing purposes.

But however much the rain fall may have been diminished by local causes, the trade winds, governed by laws which extend across hemispheres, have shown no change in their force nor in the invigorating, healthful influences which they carry with them, and which render life so attractive in this and other ocean groups where they prevail. Statistics show that they blow with regularity for three-fourths of the year. It is these winds which render navigation so safe and reliable around this group, and between it and the American mainland. With ordinary care and seamanship there is no safer ocean to navigate than this, nor one where losses are less frequent. This is attributable to the regularity of the trade winds, clear weather and atmosphere around the islands, (fogs being almost unknown, except occasionally during the southwest winter storms,) and to the employment of a steam tug at this harbor kept always ready for service, to tow vessels either in or out, or render assistance in case of necessity. To these may be added the admirable wharves in the harbor built by Government, which are probably not surpassed by those of any port of its size in the world, certainly by none in this ocean. Every vessel that can cross the bar can come up to the wharves, and discharge or load with as much dispatch as in London or New York.

The full and valuable meteorological tables which we publish on pages 208 and 209, prepared by Capt. Daniel Smith of the Harbor Master's office in this city, possess interest to those wishing to examine the details of our climate. They show the range of the thermometer at sunrise and at 2, P. M., and also the barometer, for every day of the year, with the direction of the winds. During the year 1869, the trade winds (varying from E. to E. N. E.) blew 290 days, southerly and variable winds and calms prevailing for the remainder of the year, and during five years reported by Capt. Smith, the trade winds averaged 273 days in each year.

The greatest range shown during the year 1869 by the thermometer is from 62 ° at sunrise in January to 80 ° at sunrise in August, and at 2, P. M., from 74 ° in January to 90 ° at the same hour in August. These are the extreme readings of the mercury during 1869. During a cold westerly storm the present year (1872) the thermometer dropped on the 24th of January to 56 ° at sunrise,

METEOROLOGICAL TABLES—1869. PREPARED AT HONOLULU, BY CAPT. DANIEL SMITH.

Place of observations, sea level. Thermometer noted at sunrise and at two o'clock, P. M.

DATE	JAN. WIND	BAR.	THER.	FEB. WIND	BAR.	THER.	MAR. WIND	BAR.	THER.	APR. WIND	BAR.	THER.	MAY WIND	BAR.	THER.	JUNE WIND	BAR.	THER.
1..	Northeast	30 10 68	82	N. N. E.	30 10 66	82	Southerly	30 00 72	82	Northeast	30 10 72	82	Northeast	30 10 73	82	Northeast	30 10 73	86
2..	"	30 10 68	82	Northeast	30 10 66	80	Northeast	30 10 70	82	"	30 05 72	82	"	30 05 72	86	"	30 10 73	86
3..	"	30 05 70	83	N. N. E.	30 10 66	80	Southerly	30 05 70	80	"	30 10 72	82	"	30 10 74	84	"	30 05 73	87
4..	Calm	30 00 68	84	"	30 10 66	80	"	30 00 70	82	"	30 10 72	82	"	30 10 72	85	"	30 10 73	87
5..	"	29 95 68	84	"	30 10 69	80	S. & S. W.	29 90 72	82	Southerly	30 05 69	82	"	30 10 73	85	"	30 10 73	86
6..	Baffling	29 95 68	84	"	30 10 69	80	South	30 00 70	82	"	30 05 69	82	"	30 10 73	86	"	30 10 73	86
7..	"	30 00 70	80	Northeast	30 12 68	80	"	29 95 70	81	"	30 05 70	82	"	30 10 73	86	"	30 05 73	87
8..	Northerly	30 10 69	74	"	30 12 69	82	Southerly	29 95 70	82	"	30 00 70	82	"	30 05 70	88	"	30 05 73	88
9..	N. N. E.	30 10 68	78	N. N. E.	30 12 69	82	"	30 00 70	82	"	30 05 71	82	"	30 10 72	86	"	30 05 75	88
10..	Northeast	30 10 68	80	Northeast	30 15 69	82	"	30 00 70	82	"	30 10 70	82	"	30 10 73	86	"	30 00 75	88
11..	"	30 10 72	84	"	30 15 69	82	Northeast	30 10 70	82	Northeast	30 10 70	82	N. N. E.	30 10 73	86	"	30 05 75	87
12..	"	30 10 70	82	E. and S.	30 10 70	82	"	30 10 70	82	"	30 10 71	82	N.E., S.E.	30 05 72	86	"	30 08 75	86
13..	"	30 05 70	82	Northeast	30 10 70	82	"	30 05 72	82	"	30 05 72	82	"	30 10 73	86	"	30 05 75	88
14..	"	30 05 70	82	"	30 05 70	82	"	30 05 72	82	"	30 05 71	82	"	30 10 73	86	"	30 00 74	86
15..	"	30 05 70	82	"	30 15 70	82	Light	30 05 72	82	"	30 05 71	82	"	30 12 73	86	"	30 05 75	88
16..	"	30 00 70	84	N. E. & S.	30 00 70	84	"	30 05 72	80	"	30 10 71	82	"	30 10 73	86	Variable	30 05 75	87
17..	Southerly	29 95 70	80	Easterly	29 95 70	80	Northeast	30 10 72	80	"	30 10 72	80	"	30 07 73	87	S. S. W.	30 00 75	87
18..	Northerly	30 00 70	82	"	30 00 70	82	Southerly	30 10 72	84	"	30 07 72	84	"	30 10 72	84	Sou'west	29 95 74	87
19..	"	30 05 68	88	Southerly	30 00 70	84	"	30 00 72	84	"	30 10 72	84	"	30 12 73	85	"	30 05 75	89
20..	Southerly	30 05 64	78	"	30 00 70	82	Sou'west	30 00 72	84	"	30 05 72	88	"	30 12 73	86	Southerly	30 00 74	89
21..	Easterly	30 00 62	80	"	30 05 70	80	Baffling	30 00 72	80	"	30 10 72	84	"	30 12 73	84	Northeast	30 05 75	88
22..	"	30 00 62	80	"	30 05 70	80	"	30 00 72	82	"	30 10 73	84	"	30 10 73	84	"	30 10 75	88
23..	Northeast	30 10 64	82	Northeast	30 10 70	82	Northeast	30 05 70	82	"	30 05 73	85	E. N. E.	30 05 73	85	"	30 05 75	88
24..	"	30 10 64	80	"	30 10 70	82	"	30 10 70	82	N. N. E.	30 05 73	86	N. N. E.	30 00 73	87	"	30 10 76	88
25..	"	30 05 66	82	"	30 05 70	82	"	30 10 70	82	"	30 00 74	86	Variable	30 00 73	85	Southerly	30 05 75	89
26..	"	30 00 66	82	"	30 00 70	82	"	30 10 72	82	N.E., S.E.	30 00 73	87	"	30 00 73	86	"	30 00 75	89
27..	"	30 00 66	82	Southerly	30 00 70	82	"	30 15 72	82	"	30 05 73	85	Northeast	30 05 73	86	Northeast	30 10 75	88
28..	"	30 00 66	82	"	30 05 72	80	"	30 15 72	82	"	30 00 73	86	"	30 05 73	85	"	30 10 74	88
29..	"	30 10 68	82				"	30 10 72	82	"	30 05 73	86	"	30 07 73	85	"	30 10 75	87
30..	Southerly	30 05 68	82				"	30 10 72	82	"	30 10 73	86	"	30 05 74	86	"	30 10 75	87
31..	"	30 10 68	82				"	30 10 72	82				"	30 10 74	86			

Mean temperature for 5 years (1860 to 1864) for months of January, February, March and April............Maximum, 82°; minimum, 70°; highest, 84°; lowest, 56°.

Mean temperature for 5 years (1860 to 1864) for months of May, June, July, August and September............Maximum, 84°; minimum, 84°; highest, 88°; lowest, 72°.

Mean temperature for 5 years (1860 to 1864) for months of October, November and December............Maximum, 85°; minimum, 74°. These three months, when the wind is southerly, have the greatest range of the thermometer,—say 66° to 68°.

METEOROLOGICAL TABLES—1869. PREPARED AT HONOLULU, BY CAPT. DANIEL SMITH.

Place of observations, sea level. Thermometer noted at sunrise and at two o'clock, P. M.

DATE	JULY WIND	BAR.	THER.	AUGUST WIND	BAR.	THER.	SEPTEMBER WIND	BAR.	THER.	OCTOBER WIND	BAR.	THER.	NOVEMBER WIND	BAR.	THER.	DECEMBER WIND	BAR.	THER.
1	Northeast	30 06	76 88	Northeast	30 06	76 87	Northeast	30 08	74 86	Northeast	30 10	76 88	N. N. E.	30 05	72 86	N. N. E.	30 06	74 84
2	"	30 08	75 88	"	30 06	77 88	"	30 05	75 86	"	30 10	76 86	Northeast	30 08	72 86	Northeast	30 05	74 85
3	"	30 10	74 88	"	30 05	77 88	"	30 10	75 87	"	30 10	76 88	"	30 10	72 85	"	30 10	72 84
4	"	30 06	74 88	"	30 06	77 87	"	30 10	76 86	"	30 08	72 86	"	30 08	72 85	"	30 10	72 84
5	"	30 10	75 88	"	30 08	77 88	"	30 15	78 88	"	30 10	72 86	"	30 10	72 86	"	30 10	72 84
6	"	30 05	75 88	"	30 05	77 88	"	30 08	76 88	South	30 10	76 86	Southerly	30 10	72 86	"	30 10	72 82
7	"	30 10	75 88	"	30 05	77 87	S. E. & S.	30 08	76 88	Northeast	30 05	75 87	"	30 05	75 86	"	30 10	72 82
8	"	30 10	75 88	"	30 05	76 88	"	30 08	76 88	Easterly	30 05	75 87	"	30 10	72 86	"	30 10	72 82
9	"	30 10	75 88	"	30 10	77 88	"	30 10	76 88	"	30 00	76 88	"	30 10	70 86	"	30 10	72 82
10	"	30 10	74 88	"	30 10	77 88	"	30 10	77 88	"	30 00	68 87	"	30 10	72 86	"	30 10	72 82
11	"	30 10	75 88	"	30 10	76 86	"	30 10	77 87	"	30 05	74 84	"	30 10	70 85	"	30 10	72 82
12	"	30 05	75 88	"	30 10	76 88	"	30 10	77 88	Northeast	30 00	74 86	"	30 12	72 82	"	30 15	72 82
13	"	30 05	75 88	"	30 05	76 88	Southerly	30 10	76 86	Southerly	30 05	67 86	"	30 10	72 82	"	30 15	72 82
14	"	30 05	75 88	Southerly	30 05	76 88	"	30 10	76 86	"	30 05	67 86	"	30 10	72 82	"	30 15	72 82
15	"	30 05	75 88	Northeast	30 05	75 88	"	30 10	76 87	Southerly	30 00	66 88	"	30 10	72 82	"	30 15	70 82
16	"	30 00	75 88	"	30 05	76 87	Southerly	30 08	77 86	Northeast	30 00	66 88	"	30 08	72 84	"	30 15	70 82
17	"	30 00	74 88	"	30 10	77 88	"	30 15	76 86	Southerly	30 00	68 87	"	30 10	68 85	"	30 00	64 82
18	"	30 05	75 88	"	30 10	77 88	Southerly	30 10	76 86	"	30 00	69 85	"	30 08	69 85	"	30 00	64 84
19	"	30 05	75 88	"	30 05	78 88	Easterly	30 10	76 86	"	29 90	74 84	Southerly	30 08	69 85	"	30 05	64 84
20	"	30 05	75 88	"	30 05	78 88	Southerly	30 10	76 87	Northeast	29 94	70 86	"	30 10	74 85	"	30 00	64 84
21	"	30 05	76 88	"	30 05	78 88	Northeast	30 08	76 86	"	30 00	72 88	"	30 10	72 84	"	30 00	64 82
22	"	30 05	76 88	"	30 02	80 90	"	30 07	76 88	"	29 94	74 86	"	30 10	72 84	"	30 08	64 88
23	"	30 10	75 88	"	30 05	79 90	"	30 10	76 86	"	30 08	72 88	Calm.....	30 00	74 82	"	30 10	64 84
24	"	30 10	75 88	"	30 00	78 88	"	30 08	76 87	"	30 10	72 85	"	30 00	74 82	"	30 10	64 84
25	"	30 00	76 88	"	30 00	78 88	"	30 10	76 86	Northeast	30 05	70 85	Northeast	30 07	72 84	"	30 25	70 82
26	"	30 00	76 89	"	30 00	78 89	"	30 10	76 86	"	30 06	72 86	"	30 08	73 85	"	30 20	72 82
27	"	30 00	76 88	"	30 10	78 88	N. N. E.	30 15	76 86	"	30 05	72 86	"	30 05	73 85	"	30 25	72 82
28	Southerly	30 75	76 88	"	30 10	78 88	Northeast	30 10	76 88	N. N. E.	30 05	71 86	E. N. E.	30 10	73 85	"	30 20	70 80
29	Northeast	30 75	76 88	"	30 10	78 88	"	30 12	76 88	Northeast	30 05	72 85	"	30 10	72 86	"	30 20	70 80
30	"	30 75	78 88	"	30 10	78 86	N. N. E.	30 05	76 88	"	30 05	72 86	Northeast	30 05	72 86	"	30 15	70 82
31	"	30 05	74 87	"	30 10	76 86				"	30 05	72 86				"	30 10	72 82

Average Number of Days of Trade Winds in Five Years (1860–64)—Mean for Five Years.............273 Days.
Average Number of Days of Southerly, Light and Variable Winds in Five Years (1860–64)—Mean for Five Years..... 92 Days.
Average Strength of our heaviest Kona Winds—No. 9.
Average Rain Fall, 38.04 inches for each of the Five Years noted (1860–64.)

and stood at 68° at 2, P. M. These cold spells are exceptional and rare, the average variation in the temperature from sunrise to 2, P. M., being about 12° Fahrenheit.

The climate of the islands is justly famed for its salubrity, possessing such a remarkable evenness of temperature that great changes, such as a severe storm with cold winds, or a long continuance of rainy weather, excite special notice. Though situated beneath a tropical sun, the heat is mitigated by the moist breezes which come to us over the wide expanse of ocean. By ascending or descending the mountains, the temperature gradually changes, and any desired degree can be obtained, from the perpetual summer of the sea-shore to the eternal winter of the tops of Mauna Kea and Mauna Loa. While at the sea-shore, wherever the trade winds blow, the ordinary range of the thermometer is 12° per diem, at an elevation of from three to four thousand feet the temperature varies from 48° to 75°, and the general average is about 64°.

The seasons at the islands may be divided into wet and dry, though they are not always well marked. The rain-fall varies very much between localities near the sea and near the central mountain ranges. For instance, at Captain Smith's residence, near the sea at Waikiki, it seldom exceeds 37 inches per annum; while at Dr. Judd's, one and a half miles inland, it averages 46.80. Still higher up the valley, where the showers at some seasons are very frequent, it amounts not infrequently to over 100 inches annually. Captain Smith has prepared the following average for eight years, which will serve to show the rain-fall in Honolulu, and the amount falling each month:

WET SEASON.	INCHES.	DRY SEASON.	INCHES.
October	5.47	April	2.00
November	6.15	May	1.25
December	5.03	June	0.50
January	5.30	July	0.74
February	5.02	August	1.20
March	4.05	September	1.67

Giving a yearly average of 38.38 inches.

IMPORTS AND EXPORTS.

To those residing abroad and not familiar with the statistics annually published in the local journals, the following table, prepared by the Collector General of Customs at the port of Honolulu, W. F. Allen, Esq., will give a better idea of the agricultural productions of this group than any other data that can be furnished. They are the exports for 1871:

Sugar, lbs	21,760,773	Ivory, lbs	592
Molasses, galls	271,291	Walrus hides, pcs	450
Paddy, lbs	867,452	Mules	7
Rice, lbs	417,011	Horses	10
Coffee, lbs	46,929	Cattle	202
Salt, tons	711½	Sheep	103
Poi, bbls	945	Hay, bales 94, tons	28½
Fungus, lbs	37,475	Shark fins, pkgs	4
Bananas, bnchs	3,876	Potatoes, bbls	68
Beef, bbls	817	Pumpkins	20
Hides, pcs	19,384	Tamarinds, bags	6
Calfskins, pkgs 40, pcs	649	Ginger, pkgs	15
Sheepskins, pkgs 304, pcs	2,028	Limes, bxs 14, and	2,000
Goatskins, pcs	68,900	Oranges	1,150
Tallow, lbs	195,240	Watermelons	50
Pulu, lbs	292,720	Plants and seeds, pkgs	5
Wool, lbs	471,706	Betel leaves, cs	22
Peanuts, lbs	68,151	Preserves, cs	1
Sperm oil, galls	4,867	Koa lumber, pcs	23
Whale oil, galls	140,319	Curios, pkgs	39
Whalebone, lbs	283		

The total value of the exports of this Kingdom for 1871 are given by the same authority at $1,802,069.45. The value of the imports for the same year were $1,512,697.20, showing a balance, in the export and import trade of 1871, of $289,462 in favor of the industry of the Kingdom—a result which very few older countries can present.

The following table, showing the import and export trade of this Kingdom for twenty-one years (from 1851 to 1871), together with other data relating to the commerce of the group, will be valuable for reference:

COMPARATIVE VIEW OF THE COMMERCE OF THE HAWAIIAN ISLANDS FOR 21 YEARS.

YEAR.	TOTAL IMPORTS.	TOTAL EXPORTS AND SUPPLIES.	DOMESTIC PRODUCE EXPORTED.	FOREIGN MERCHANDISE RE-EXPORTED.	TOTAL CUSTOM HOUSE RECEIPTS.
1871	$1,512,697 20	$1,802,069 45	$1,656,644 46	$158,974 99	$221,332 34
1870	1,930,227 42	2,144,942 62	1,403,025 06	630,517 56	223,815 75
1869	2,040,068 10	2,366,358 83	1,639,091 59	623,067 24	215,798 42
1868	1,935,790 72	1,898,215 63	1,340,469 26	447,946 37	210,076 30
1867	1,957,410 17	1,679,661 87	1,205,622 02	355,539 85	220,599 91
1866	1,993,821 56	1,934,576 76	1,396,621 61	428,755 15	215,047 08
1865	1,946,265 68	1,808,257 55	1,430,211 82	287,045 73	192,566 03
1864	1,712,241 61	1,662,181 47	1,113,328 81	548,852 66	159,116 72
1863	1,175,493 25	1,025,852 74	744,413 54	281,439 20	122,752 68
1862	998,239 67	838,424 61	586,541 87	251,882 74	107,490 42
1861	761,109 57	659,774 72	476,872 74	182,901 98	100,115 56
1860	1,223,749 05	807,459 20	480,526 54	326,932 66	117,302 57
1859	1,555,558 74	931,329 27	628,575 21	302,754 06	132,129 37
1858	1,089,660 60	787,082 08	529,966 11	257,115 97	116,138 23
1857	1,130,165 41	645,526 10	423,303 91	222,222 19	140,777 03
1856	1,151,422 99	670,824 67	466,278 79	204,545 88	123,171 75
1855	1,383,169 87	572,601 49	274,741 67	297,859 82	158,411 90
1854	1,590,837 71	585,122 67	274,029 70	311,092 97	152,125 58
1853	1,401,975 86	472,096 83	281,599 17	191,397 66	155,650 17
1852	759,868 54	638,395 20	257,251 69	381,142 51	113,001 93
1851	1,823,821 68	691,231 49	309,828 94	381,402 55	160,602 19

YEAR.	OIL AND BONE TRANSHIPPED.			NUMBER NATIONAL VESSELS.	MERCHANT VESSELS.		NUMBER ENTRIES WHALERS.	GALLONS SPIRITS CONSUMED.
	Galls. Sperm.	Galls. Whale.	Pounds Bone.		No.	Ton'ge.		
1871	63,310	283,055	29,362	9	171	105.993	47	18,823
1870	105,234	1,443,809	632,905	16	159	91,248	118*	19,948
1869	157,690	1,698,189	627,770	7	127	75,656	102*	17,016
1868	106,778	774,913	596,043	9	113	54,833	153*	16,030
1867	103,215	821,929	465,140	9	134	60,268	243*	15,144
1866	103,957	1,204,275	211,178	5	151	62,142	229*	13,135
1865	42,841	578,593	337,394	7	151	67,068	180*	11,745
1864	33,860	608,502	339,331	9	116	75,339	140*	10,237
1863	56,687	675,344	337,043	7	88	42,930	102*	7,862
1862	12,522	460,407	193,920	7	113	48,687	73*	8,940
1861	20,435	795,988	527,910	7	94	45,962	190*	9,676
1860	47,859	782,086	572,900	10	117	41,226	325*	14,295
1859	156,360	1,668,175	1,147,120	5	139	59,241	549*	14,158
1858	222,464	2,551.382	1,614,710	10	115	45,875	526*	14,637
1857	176,306	2,018,027	1,295,525	10	82	26,817	387*	16,144
1856	121,294	1,041,579	1,074,942	9	123	42,213	306*	14,779
1855	109,308	1,436,810	872,954	13	154	51,304	468*	18,318
1854	156,484	1,683,922	1,479,678	16	125	47,288	525*	17,537
1853	175,396	3,787,348	2,020,264	7	211	59,451	535*	18,123
1852	173,490	1,182,738	3,159,951	3	235	61,065	519*	14,150
1851	104,362	909,379	901,604	7	446	87,920	220*	9,500

*These figures give the Total Arrivals of Whalers at various ports—some of the vessels entering two or more during the year.

The following table, showing the kinds and value of the importations for 1871, will interest the reader:

DESCRIPTION.	VALUE OF GOODS PAYING DUTY.	VALUE GOODS IN BOND.	TOTAL.
Ale, Porter, Beer, Cider......................	$ 21,477 67	$ 5,441 12	$ 26,918 79
Animals and Birds..........................	1,286 50	....	1,236 50
Building Materials..........................	22,510 58	1,217 04	23,727 62
Clothing, Hats, Boots.......................	167,468 45	9,689 02	177,157 47
Crockery and Glassware.....................	12,330 13	315 46	12,645 59
Drugs···············	14,542 41	209 55	14,751 96
Dry Goods { Cottons......................	148,879 68	9,076 57	157,956 25
Linens.......:..................	13,319 64	585 04	13,904 68
Silks..........................	8,433 43	438 02	8,871 45
Woolens.........................	44,457 43	3,347 50	47,804 93
Mixtures......................	23,762 39	1,693 00	25,455 39
Fancy Goods, Millinery, etc.................	44,743 78	2,065 83	46,809 61
Fish (dry and salt).........................	19,782 07	12,657 44	32,439 51
Flour......................................	39,314 85	15,767 23	55,082 08
Fruits (fresh).............................	2,054 58	....	2,054 58
Furniture.................................	24,087 28	1,112 60	25,199 88
Furs and Ivory.............................	68 50	1,856 00	1,924 50
Grain and Feed.............................	14,918 30	853 98	15,772 28
Groceries and Provisions....................	76,525 54	41,025 50	117,551 04
Hardware, Agricultural Implements, Tools, &c..	91,410 88	2,555 89	93,966 77
Iron and Steel.............................	16,186 31	5,350 63	21,536 94
Jewelry, Plate, Clocks......................	19,044 26	215 10	19,259 36
Lumber....................................	77,714 34	326 63	78,040 97
Machinery................................	22,733 09	82 00	22,815 09
Matches..................................	7,345 70	....	7,345 70
Naval Stores..............................	30,640 08	45,202 49	75,842 43
Oils (Whale, Kerosene, Cocoanut, &c)........	11,292 70	38,827 27	50,119 97
Opium....................................	13,003 17	....	13,003 17
Paints and Paint Oils......................	11,622 65	56 87	11,679 52
Perfumery, Toilet Articles...................	5,088 07	1,281 75	6,319 82
Saddlery, Carriages, &c.....................	28,780 21	1,527 28	30,307 49
Shooks, Containers.........................	47,293 27	33,718 96	81,012 23
Spirits.......	2,686 67	31,390 43	34,077 10
Stationery, Books, &c......................	24,847 87	538 19	25,386 06
Tea.......................................	6,768 29	7 83	6,776 12
Tin, Tinware..............................	3,941 91	....	3,941 91
Tobacco, Cigars...........................	23,633 28	8,656 02	32,289 30
Whalebone...............................	10 00	....	10 00
Wines (light).............................	7,113 13	1,003 36	8,116 49
Sundry Merchandise not included in above......	34,711 27	7,177 74	41,889 01
Sundry Merchandise imported by Whalers......	1,334 63	....	1,334 63
Sundry Unspecified Merchandise..............	2,559 13	....	2,559 13
Charges on Invoices.......................	47,640 06	5,315 46	52,955 52
Twenty-five per ct. added on Uncertified Invoices.	7,627 00	2,100 62	9,727 62
	$1,244,941 13	$292,635 33	$1,537,576 46

THE TARIFF.—The import duties levied at the Custom House upon merchandise entered for consumption, is generally 10 per cent. *ad valorem* on the invoice cost; the following being the exceptions:

1. Such importations as are allowed free by law.

2. Tobacco and Opium, and all manufactures thereof, 15 per cent. ad valorem.

3. Alcohol, $10 per gallon.

4. Alcohol for medicinal, mechanical or scientific purposes, upon proper application, 50 per cent. ad valorem.

5. Spirits and Perfumery, when over 30 ° of alcoholic strength and under 55 °, $3 per gallon.

6. Wines, when over 18 ° and less than 30 ° of alcoholic strength, $1 50 per gallon.

7. Light Wines, Champagne, Rhine, etc., 15 per cent. ad valorem.
8. Sugar, the product of any country with which this Government has no existing treaty, 2 cents per pound.
9. Molasses, the product of any country with which this Government has no existing treaty, 10 cents per gallon.
10. Coffee, the product of any country with which this Government has no existing treaty, 3 cents per pound.
11. Rice, the product of any country with which this Government has no existing treaty, cleaned 1½ cents per pound—in the husk 1 cent per pound.

It is required that all invoices presented at the Custom House for entry, shall have attached the certificate of the Hawaiian Consul at the port or place of shipment, otherwise as a penalty 25 per cent. is added to the invoice value, and the usual duties levied upon the increase.

There are no transhipment or export duties or tonnage dues.

The usual port charges are : Pilotage—anchoring outside, $10 ; anchoring without pilot's services, when boarded by pilot as health officer, $5 ; entering or leaving harbor, per foot of vessel's draft, $1 ; buoys, $2 ; lighthouse, $3 ; harbor master's fees, mooring or unmooring, $3 ; wharfage, per ton, each day, 2 cents (Sundays not counted.)

Passengers arriving from foreign ports are taxed two dollars each, upon the granting of permits to land, which tax is collected at the Custom House, and is for the benefit of the Queen's Hospital. All passengers departing, after a residence of thirty days, are required to procure a passport; and any vessel taking a person away without such passport, is liable to a fine, as well as for all debts which such passenger may have left unsettled. This law does not apply to passengers arriving in transitu to or from the Colonies and America or Europe.

HISTORICAL SKETCH OF HAWAIIAN VOLCANOES.

The recent eruptions on Hawaii have excited a world-wide interest in Hawaiian volcanoes, which will render a sketch of them not inappropriate in a work of this kind. A portion of what follows appeared in supplements to the "Pacific Commercial Advertiser," issued March 26, 1859, and May 9, 1868 :

The only island of our group which has, within the memory of man, been known to be in a state of volcanic action, is Hawaii. All the others are of more ancient formation. It consists of four principal mountain divisions,—the Kohala range at the north, which is evidently of very old formation, Mauna Kea, an extinct volcano, Mauna Hualalai, on the western coast, which has not been in action since 1801, and Mauna Loa, which is now the only active volcano in the group. The height of these three mountain peaks, as measured by Captain Wilkes, are : Mauna Loa, 13,760 feet ; Mauna Kea, 13,950 feet ; and Hualalai, 10,000 feet.

Whether we view its height and immense size, the beauty and singularity of its dome-like summit, or the magnitude and length of its lava streams, the Volcano of Mauna Loa, on Hawaii, is one of the most remarkable in the world, rising from the sea to an elevation of nearly 14,000 feet. In height it is only exceeded by the active volcanoes of Cotopaxi, in Ecuador, (18,887 feet,) that of Popocatepetl, in Mexico, (17,700 feet,) and two or three others in Asia and America. All these, however, rise from elevated table lands, and consequently only show a height of

7 to 9,000 feet from their bases. Mauna Loa, on the contrary, rises in one stupendous mount directly from the sea, and, as seen by vessels passing it, forms one of the most beautiful sights in the world, its summit being apparently as symmetrical as the dome of a cathedral, and generally dotted or covered with snow.

On this vast mountain exist two craters, that of Mokuaweoweo on the summit, and Kilauea on the southern slope, both of which are seldom inactive. The summit crater is surpassed in extent only by that of Haleakala on Maui. It was first described by the lamented English traveler, Douglas, who visited it in 1834, and subsequently lost his life on the same mountain. Its size, as measured by Lieutenant Wilkes, is 11,000 feet long and 8000 feet wide, being about six miles in circumference. Its average depth is 800 feet. The bottom of this crater is rent by terrible chasms, which to all attempts yet made are unfathomable. It is divided into three lesser ones, the most northern of which is known as Mokuaweoweo.

The crater of Kilauea, being much more accessible than that of Mokuaweoweo, is the chief point of interest with tourists. It is approached either from Kau, (the most southern district of the island,) over a tolerably good road, or from Hilo, distant 29½ miles, over a rough and often muddy road, requiring from six to ten hours. to accomplish it, according to its condition. The "Volcano House," kept by an intelligent Hawaiian, is provided with the necessaries and food required by travelers. The government steamer makes monthly trips to Hilo, and weekly trips to Kealakeakua Bay, occasionally running to Kau. The cost of the round trip from Honolulu to the crater and back, by either route, is from sixty to one hundred dollars, according to the tastes of the traveler.

The crater of Kilauea, called by the natives "*Lua Pele*," or Pele's Pit, is simply a deep pit of oval form, about two by three miles in extent, its walls varying from five hundred to one thousand feet in height. Its bottom or floor is very uneven, and subject to frequent changes caused by eruptions. The level of this floor appears to have varied several hundred feet during the past forty years. It is seldom seen in action throughout its entire extent, the lava flow being generally confined to one or more lakes, which are sometimes connected by streams of lava flowing from one lake to another. The view of this crater given at the commencement of this Appendix, represents it as it appeared early in the present century, when there was more activity than now.

The eruptions of Mauna Loa are not confined, however, to these two craters, but occur on all sides of the mountain and at various heights, from 5,000 to 12,000 feet above the sea. It is only of the eruptions occurring during the present century that authentic data have been preserved, and of these we propose to give as full an account as our limits will permit, commencing with that of Mount Hualalai, which took place in 1801, and is the only one recorded on that mountain. The description is taken from Rev. William Ellis' "Tour Around Hawaii," as given by the English traveler Turnbull, who witnessed it:

THE ERUPTION OF 1801 ON MOUNT HUALALAI.

"In the afternoon, Messrs. Thurston and Bishop walked out in a northwest direction, till they reached the point that forms the northern boundary of the bay, on the eastern side of which Kailua is situated. It runs three or four miles into the sea, is composed entirely of lava, and was formed by an eruption from one of the large craters on the top of Mauna Hualalai, (Mount Hualalai,) which, about twenty-three years ago, inundated several villages, destroyed a number of plantations and extensive fish-ponds, filled up a deep bay twenty miles in length, and formed the present coast. An Englishman, who has resided thirty-eight years in the islands, and who witnessed the above eruption, has frequently told us he was astonished at the irresistible impetuosity of the torrent. Stone walls, trees, and houses, all gave way before it; even large masses or rocks of hard ancient lava, when surrounded by the fiery stream, soon split into small fragments, and falling into the burning mass, appeared to melt again, as borne by it down the mountain's side. Numerous offerings were presented, and many hogs thrown alive into the stream, to appease the anger of the gods, by whom they supposed it was directed, and to stay its devastating course. All seemed unavailing, until one day the king Kamehameha went, attended by a large retinue of chiefs and priests, and, as the most valuable offerings he could make, cut off part of his own hair, which was always considered sacred, and threw it into the torrent. A day or two after, the lava ceased to flow. The gods, it was thought, were satisfied; and the king acquired no small degree of influence over the minds of the people, who, from this circumstance, attributed their escape from threatened destruction to his supposed influence with the deities of the volcanoes."

OLD ERUPTIONS ON MAUNA LOA.

I. 1789.—"The first eruption of Kilauea, of which tradition gives any definite knowledge, occurred about the year 1789, during the wars and conquests of Kamehameha I. It took place between Kilauea and the sea, in a south-easterly direction. It is said to have been accompanied by violent earthquakes and rendings of the earth, and an eruption of stones and cinders from the open fissures. It was so violent and extensive that the heavens were completely darkened, and one hundred lives are supposed to have been lost. There are now, over a large area near Kilauea, a few miles distant to the south or southeast, great quantities of a light pumice-like scoria with stones and sand, which are believed to have been thrown out at this time." [This eruption is spoken of in Dibble's History, as having destroyed part of the army of Keoua, Kamehameha's rival.]

II. 1823.—"The outbreak of 1823, and the features of the crater after it, are described by Mr. Ellis. A large tract of country in Kau was flooded, and the stream, when it reached the sea, as I am informed by Mr. Coan, was five to eight miles wide. The earth is said to have been rent in several places, and the lavas were ejected through the fissures, commencing their course above ground some miles south of Kilauea. There was no visible communication with the lavas of the crater at the time, but the fact of their subsiding some hundreds of feet simultaneously with the eruption, is satisfactory evidence of a connection." [This overflow probably entered the sea at Kapapala. It is spoken of by Douglas, in the "Hawaiian Spectator," vol. ii, page 415.]

III. 1832.—"In June, 1832, an eruption took place both from Kilauea and the summit crater of Mauna Loa. The only ejection at this time of the lavas of Kilauea to the surface, of which we have definite account, occurred in the east wall from which streams flowed out, part back into Kilauea down the steep slope, and part across into the old crater, which at the time was overgrown with wood. * * *

"In September of 1832, when Rev. J. Goodrich visited Kilauea, the eruption had taken place. The lavas, which previously had increased so as to fill up to the black ledge and fifty feet above, had sunk down again nearly to the same depth, leaving, as usual, a boiling cauldron at the south end. The earthquake of January (June?) preceding had rent in twain the walls of the crater, on the east side, from top to bottom, producing seams from a few inches to several yards in width, from which the region between the *two craters* (Kilauea and the 'Old Crater') was deluged with lava. About half way up the precipice there was a vent a quarter of a mile in length, from which immense masses of lava boiled out directly under the hut occupied by Lord Byron's party." See "American Journal of Science," xxv, 199.

"From these accounts (Goodrich's, &c.,) it is probable that, in addition to the ejections from the east wall, which are insufficient to account for the subsidence in the lower pit, there must have been a *subterranean* outlet beneath the sea."

"An eruption is stated to have taken place in the summit crater of Mauna Loa on the 20th of June, 1832, and the mountain continued burning for two or three weeks. The lavas broke out in different places, and were discharged from so many vents, that the fires were seen on every side of the dome, and were visible as far as Lahaina." See "American Journal of Science and Arts, xxv, 201, in a communication from Rev. J. Goodrich, dated November 17th, 1832.

This eruption on the summit was doubtless connected with that in Kilauea, and should be considered as part of it, although not simultaneous with it.

IV.—THE ERUPTION OF 1840.

The best account published of this eruption of Kilauea is given by J. J. Jarves in his "Scenes and Scenery":

"On the 30th of May, (1840,) the inhabitants of the district detected a smoke and some fire rising in the direction of the volcano, (Kilauea.) As it proceeded from an uninhabited and desolate region, they gave themselves no further concern about it, attributing it to the burning of brush-wood. The next day, being Sunday, the several congregations at Hilo and its vicinity, were alarmed by the prodigious increase of the flames in that quarter. They increased so rapidly as to leave no doubt that the volcano was in motion; but in what manner it was discharging itself, was as yet conjecture. The fiery column, sending forth heavy masses of smoke and cinders, gave indication that it was no ordinary outbreak. Fear began to seize upon some. The burning torrent was four thousand feet above them, and if it turned in the direction of Hilo, the devastation would be dreadful. But on the 1st of June it began to move in a northeasterly direction, and in a little short of four days reached the sea, having flowed forty miles from its source. Owing to the inequalities of the country, the rapidity of its movement was not uniform. In some places it was stayed for a considerable time, until a valley had been filled up, or precipice overthrown. In such spots it spread itself into lakes many miles wide. On level ground it moved slowly and sluggishly, but when it met with a descent, it acquired a velocity of even five miles the hour, consuming everything before it. Its depth varied according to the nature of the soil, and is from twelve to two hundred feet and upwards. The average descent of the country in the direction it took, is about one hundred feet to the mile. Its general movement, owing to its great consistency, was in immense semicircular masses or waves. These would roll on, gradually accumulating, until the mass had become too heavy to hold itself together, while the exterior was partially cooled and solidified; then bursting, the liquified interior flowing out would join a new stream, and by its momentum cleave that asunder. By these accelerated progressive movements, the wave-like ridges were formed, which are everywhere observable on the older dykes. At times, it forced its way under the soil, presenting the singular appearance of earth, rocks, and trees in motion, like the swell of the ocean. It found its way into crevices and subterranean galleries, flowing on until it had filled them up, or met with some impediment, then bursting up the superincumbent soil, it bore off upon its livid surface, like rafts on a river, hillocks with trees still standing upon them; and so great was its viscidity, heavy rocks floated down with the stream. A white man, who was standing upon a small lime-hill, near the main stream, absorbed by the spectacle, felt the ground beneath him in motion, and, before he could retire, it had been raised ten to fifteen feet above its former height. He had barely left the spot before it burst open like a shell, and a torrent of fire issued rapidly forth. On the third day of the eruption, three new hills of a mile in length, and from six hundred to eight hundred feet high, were formed in the direction where the fire first appeared.

"To the windward, the running lava could be approached near enough for those who wished it to thrust long poles into the liquified rock, and draw forth specimens. On the leeward side, owing to the intensity of the heat, the noxious and deadly vapors and gases, with which the air was impregnated, and the showers of hot ashes, sand, and cinders, which were constantly descending, all vegetation for many miles was destroyed, and the inhabitants obliged to flee with the greatest expedition. Fortunately the stream flowed through two 'lands' only, according to the Hawaiian division of territory, those of Nanawale and Kanahikio, both sparsely populated and quite barren. Consequently, the warning being ample, although a number of small hamlets were overwhelmed, and a multitude of swine and poultry perished, no lives were lost among the people. The body of an old woman, who had just died, was consumed. The color of the viscid mass was, while flowing sluggishly, of the deepest crimson; when more active, it resembled gore and fresh blood violently stirred together. At Hilo, and places forty miles distant, such was the brilliancy of the light, that the finest print could be easily read at midnight. This noon-tide brightness, converting night into day, prevailed over all East-Hawaii for two weeks, and is represented, by eye-witnesses, to have been a spectacle of unsurpassed sublimity. It was like the glare of a blazing firmament, and was seen for upwards of a hundred miles at sea. It also rose and spread itself above the lofty mountain peaks, so as to be distinctly visible on the leeward side of the island, where the wind blew the smoke in dense and massy clouds."

V.—THE ERUPTION OF 1843.

An eruption took place in January, 1843, which is described by Messrs. Andrews and Coan, in the "Missionary Herald," vol. xxxix, pp. 381, 463, and vol. xl, p. 44. It broke out at the summit on the 10th of January, and ran down the slopes of Mauna Loa in two streams; one flowing to the westward towards Kona, the other northward to the foot of Mauna Kea, and then dividing, one stream continued on towards Waimea, north-eastward, and the other towards Hilo, eastward. The branch toward Mauna Kea is described as twenty-five or thirty miles long, and averaging one and a half miles in width. Mr. Coan, in his description, says of its origin : "On the morning of January 10th, before day, we discovered a small beacon-fire near the top of Mauna Loa. This was soon found to be a new eruption on the northeast slope of the mountain, at an elevation of near thirteen thousand feet.

"Subsequently," Mr. Coan continues, "the lava appeared to burst out at several points lower down the mountain, from whence it flowed off in the direction of Mauna Kea, filling the valley between the mountains with a sea of fire. Here the stream divided, part flowing toward Waimea, and the other eastward toward Hilo. Still another stream flowed along the base of Mauna Loa to Hualalai, in Kona. For about four weeks this scene continued without much abatement," &c. Ascending the mountain, Mr. Coan reached the stream of lava between Mauna Loa and Mauna Kea, about 7000 feet above the sea. On the evening of the third day, "as darkness gathered around us, the lurid fires of the volcano began to glow and to gleam upon us from the foot of Mauna Kea, over all the plain between the two mountains, and up the side of Mauna Loa and its snow-crowned summit, exhibiting the appearance of vast and innumerable furnaces burning with intense vehemence. On this plain we spent the day in traversing and surveying the immense streams of fresh scoria and slag which lay in wild confusion further than the eye could reach, some cooled, some half-cooled, and some still in fusion." On the ascent they passed fields of scoria, and regions that were at times steaming and hot, evincing igneous action beneath.

"Soon we came to an opening of twenty yards long and ten wide, through which we looked, and at the depth of fifty feet, we saw a vast tunnel or subterranean canal, lined with smooth, vitrified matter, forming the channel of a river of fire, which swept down the steep side of the mountain with amazing velocity. As we passed up the mountain we found several similar openings into this canal, into which we cast large stones; these, instead of sinking into the viscid mass, were borne instantly out of sight. Mounds, ridges and cones were thrown up along the line of the stream, from the latter of which steam, gases and hot stones were ejected. At three o'clock we reached the verge of the great crater where the erup-

28

tion first took place, near the highest point of the mountain.   Here we found two immense craters, close to each other, of vast depth and in terrific action."

VI.—THE ERUPTION OF 1852.

This occurred in February, 1852, and broke out on the north side of Mauna Loa, not a great distance from that of 1855.   An account of it, written by Mr. J. Fuller, and dated May 12th, we find in the "Friend" for May, 1852, and extract a few paragraphs describing the scene :

" During the first night, at the distance of forty miles, we heard the rumbling of the volcano, like the roar of the heavy surf breaking upon the shore, and saw the sky brilliantly illuminated above the crater and the flowing lava.   An immense column of vapor and smoke arose from the crater and formed a magnificent arc, reflecting the red and purple light of the fiery masses below.   Animated by sights and sounds so grand, we quickened our pace in order to gain a nearer view of the scene, believing that in this case distance did not lend enchantment to the view.

" On the second day, towards night, we came to a hut built by the party of the previous week.   Being wet with the rain, we concluded to spend the night here : we enlarged the house, built a fire in one part of it, put on dry clothes, wrapped ourselves in our blankets, and passed a comfortable night.   The morning was fine. We soon caught sight of the lava jets as they shot up above the distant mountain ridges, and passing the whitened bones of a mule lost by the King's party while crossing the mountains two or three years ago, snatching here and there a bunch of delicious ohelos, which grew by the path, we came, at about 10 A. M. of the third day, to the last ridge that separated us from the region of the eruption—ascended to the top of this, the whole scene, *wild, terrific, grand, magnificent*, burst upon our senses !

" It is impossible to give you a complete description of what we saw and heard, or to draw a picture which will produce the same impression on your mind that the original did upon mine.   Language, on such an occasion, is powerless, eloquence is dumb, and silence is the expression most congenial to the sentiments of the soul ; yet I will try to give you some facts and hints which will assist your imagination in its conceptions of the wildly interesting scenes we witnessed.

" Imagine yourself, then, just ascended to the top of the above mentioned eminence.   Before you, at a distance of two miles, arises the new formed crater in the midst of fields of black, smoking lava, while from its centre there jets a column of red-hot lava to an immense height, threatening instant annihilation to any presumptuous mortal who should come within reach of its scathing influence.   The crater may be a thousand feet in diameter and from one hundred to one hundred and fifty feet high.   The column of liquid lava which is constantly sustained in the air, is from two hundred to five hundred feet high, and perhaps the highest jets may reach as high as seven hundred feet !   There is a constant and rapid succession of jets one within another, and the masses falling outside and cooling as they fall, form a sort of dark veil, through which the new jets, darting up with every degree of force and every variety of form, render this *grand fire-fountain* one of the most magnificent objects that human imagination can conceive of.   From the top of the lava jets the current of heated air carries up a large mass of scoria and pumice, which falls again in constant showers for some miles around the crater."

VII.—THE ERUPTION OF 1855.

From an account published July 24th, 1855, in the "Pacific Commercial Advertiser," a weekly journal of Honolulu, we copy the following, respecting the origin of this remarkable eruption :

" On the evening of the 11th of August, about 10 o'clock, a small light, apparently of burning brushwood or grass, was seen near the top of Mauna Loa, which rapidly increased until the whole heaven reflected its brightness, and turned the night into day. So bright was it towards morning, that fine newspaper print could easily be read by the light. It was certain that some unusual eruption had begun. This light continued, varying in brightness, for weeks; sometimes a dense smoky atmosphere obscured it wholly, but when clear, the sight as seen by vessels at sea is represented to have been grand beyond description. The seat of this eruption, which is in the old traditional crater of Mokuaweoweo, is on the summit of Mauna Loa, some 14,000 feet above the level of the sea, in a region rarely visited by man."

Mr. Coan visited the source of this stream, and the following is from his report of the trip:

"Taking the channel of a stream which enters Hilo Bay as our path, we advanced with much toil through the dense jungle along its banks, and rested at night at the roots of an ancient tree—having made about twelve miles. The next day we made about twelve miles more, for the most part in the rocky bed of the stream, the water being low. Volcanic smoke filled the forest, and charred leaves came floating on the breeze and falling into the wild channel we were threading. At night, when the shades gathered over these deep solitudes, unbroken save by the bellowing of the mountain bull, the barking of the wild dog, the grunt of the forest boar, the wing and the note of the restless bird, the chirping of the insect, the falling of a time-worn tree, the gurgling of the rill, and the wild roar of the cataract, we made our little beds of ferns under the trunk of a prostrate tree, and here, for the first time, we found that the molten stream had passed us in the jungle on the left, and was now many miles below us on its way to Hilo. But we would not retreat, and as the jungle was nearly impenetrable in the direction of the stream, we pursued our upward way in the bed of the river until half-past one P. M. on the third day, when we found ourselves out of the forest, and on the high plateau at the base of the mountain. I cannot stop to describe the beautiful, the romantic, the wild, the wonderful, in the banks, the narrows, the widenings, the rocks, the rapids, the cascades, the basins, the caves and natural bridges of this solitary stream. Nor can I speak of the velvet mosses, the modest creepers, the rich festoons, the sweet wild flowers, the gigantic ferns, the ancient forests, and all the tropical glories which are mirrored in its limpid waters. We needed an artist and a naturalist to fix the glowing panorama, to paint the flora and catch the fauna of these romantic solitudes.

"When we emerged from the upper skirts of the woods, a dense fog obstructed our view of all distant objects, so that we could not see the summit-fires nor trace the molten stream down the slope of the mountain. We encamped early in a vast cave; but during the night the stars came out, and the volcanic fires played brilliantly from their high source down the mountain sides, over the scorified plains, and far down in the forest over Hilo.

"Early in the morning (Friday, the 5th,) we left our cavern, and at 7½ A. M. were on that black and smoldering stream, for which we had been searching for more than three days. Almost as far as the eye could reach, these regions had been flooded with seas of fusion—now, for the most part, hardened, but smoking and crackling with heat and escaping gases.

"We passed several miles up the left verge of the stream, and finding a narrow, well-solidified place, we crossed over to the right verge—our passage occupying an hour and a quarter. We now ascended rapidly along the right bank of the stream, sometimes upon it and again skirting it, according to the facility for traveling or the directness of its course. The stream is very tortuous, making ample detours and sudden zigzags, so that we saved much by cutting off bends or following the bases of the triangles described in its course.

"All this day we came to no open fire. The first overflowing had stiffened and solidified in contact with the atmosphere, forming a broad open pall. Under this self-made counterpane the continuous stream had formed a vast duct; and in this subterranean pyroduct it now flows like oil, at the depth of from twenty to one hundred feet, unexposed to the stiffening action of the air.

"At night we slept on the higher regions of the mountains, beyond the line of vegetation, with the slag for our pillow, the heavens for our canopy, the stars for our watch-fires, and Israel's Shepherd for our guardian.

"We were astir early on Saturday morning, climbing over indescribable hills, cones, ridges, and masses of hot and smoking debris and scoria, scattered wild and wide over those Plutonic regions. We soon came to a line of jagged cones with open orifices of from twenty to one hundred feet in diameter, standing over the molten river and furnishing vents for its steam and gases. We approached the vents with awe, and, looking down their fiery throats, we heard the infernal surgings and saw the mad rushings of the great molten stream, fused to a white heat. The angle of descent was from 3 ° to 25 °, and we judged the velocity to be *forty miles an hour!*

"The maddening stream seemed to be hurrying on, as if on swift commission from the Eternal to execute a work of wrath and desolation in the realms below. Upward and onward we went—climbing ridge after ridge, parched with thirst, panting in a rare atmosphere, blinded by smoke, almost scathed by heat and excoriated by sulphurous gases.

"All the rest of the way we saw frequent openings into the fiery canal, upon whose arched ceiling we walked for miles, with the fearful stream rushing madly beneath our feet. At one P. M. we found ourselves at the terminal crater and standing on its craggy and smoking crest.

"This was the high fountain of eruption—the great chimney which goes down immeasurable depths into those fearful realms where man's eye never penetrated, and where he cannot look and live. For nearly five days we had struggled to gain this point; and now we were here—specks, atoms in creation—obscured by smoke, startled by infernal hissings, amid these wild wonders, these awful displays of power which had scattered such a tempest of fiery hail and raised such a raging sea of molten rocks on these everlasting hills.

"The grandeur, the sublimity, the terror of the scene were unutterable. A vast chasm had opened horizontally on the top of the mountain, and along this yawning fissure stood a series of elongated, jagged and burning cones, about one hundred feet high, rent through their larger diameter, and throwing up dense columns of blue and white smoke, which, covering the mountain's summit, rolled in fleecy masses down its sides and spread out like the wings of chaos over unmeasured regions. Still no fire could be seen in this fountain-crater. We could feel it everywhere, and we could see and hear its escaping gasses, but the throats of the cones were clogged with cinders, pumice and ashes, with cracks, crevices, &c., for the escaping smoke. The fusion had long since found vent in a lateral, subterranean duct, several hundred feet below the rim of the crater, and in this covered way it flows off until it makes its appearance, as described, some two miles down the side of the mountain."

This eruption, which, in the quantity of lava thrown out, has probably never been surpassed during the residence of foreigners on these islands, continued for about thirteen months, and stopped when within six or seven miles of Hilo. The stream was more than sixty miles long, and the area covered by the eruption probably exceeded three hundred square miles, or about one-thirteenth of the area of the Island of Hawaii. It finally ceased and became quiet during September or October, 1856.

VIII.—THE ERUPTION OF JANUARY, 1859.

The commencement of this great eruption is described by Rev. Mr. Lyons, of Waimea, Hawaii, in a letter to us, dated February 4th. Mr. Lyons' dwelling was in full view of the crater from its commencement, and, seated on his verandah, so bright was the light of the eruption, that he could read a newspaper without difficulty, and during its height candles were unnecessary in the evenings. This will give the reader some idea of the splendor of the scene. Mr. Lyons says:

"Had I the ability, I should like to give a description of the present volcanic eruption; but I am fearful of a failure, should the attempt be made. When one has seen the real thing itself, there is no room for the play of the imagination or poetry. You may exhaust language of its most impressive and descriptive terms, and yet fail to reach the reality. I shall attempt to give no more than a few facts.

"On Sabbath, January 23d, volcanic smoke was seen gathering on Mauna Loa. In the evening the mountain presented a grand yet fearful spectacle. Two streams of fire were issuing from two different sources, and flowing, apparently, in two different directions. The whole region, earth and heaven, were lighted up, and even the interior of our houses received the lurid volcanic light direct from its source. In the morning of the second day we could discern where the eruptions were. One appeared to be very near the top of the mountain, but its stream and smoke soon disappeared. The other was on the north side, further below the top, and was sending out its fires in a north-westerly direction. On the second and third nights the dense smoke prevented us from having a fair view of Pele's doings; but on the four following nights we had a view—and such a scene! It seemed as though the eye could never weary in gazing at it. The burning crater seemed to be constantly enlarging and throwing up its volumes of liquid fire above the mouth of the crater—I will not venture to say how high—and the fiery stream rolled onward and onward, still adding grandeur and terror as it proceeded, till on the morning of the 31st, about sunrise, the stream was compelled, though reluctantly, to stop, by meeting the waters of the ocean. Even then its resistless and opposing energy carried it on some distance into the sea."

Immediately after the fact of a new volcanic eruption was known in Honolulu, the writer of this appendix took passage in the first packet for the scene, and from the account of his visit, which appeared in the "Advertiser" of the 17th of February, then published and edited by him, the following is taken:

"Our camping ground is located on the elevated table-land lying between the three great mountains of Hualalai, Mauna Kea and Mauna Loa, sixteen miles from Kailua, and some ten miles in an air line from the crater, which lies over against us on the side of Mauna Loa, distinctly in view. This plain is about 5000 feet above the sea, and is covered with small shrubs and trees, growing from ten to twenty feet high. In some places it is level and covered with a coarse black sand, similar to that found on the sides of Punchbowl, only much coarser, while the shrubs are so sparsely scattered as to allow a horse to travel across it on a full gallop; in others it consists of a dense jungle with numerous pits or caves, concealed by overgrowing shrubs. This part of the plain is almost impenetrable. In still other localities it is covered with coarse lava stones or "clinkers," over which traveling is next to impossible. The nights are extremely cold, frost covering the ground every morning. The days are, however, warm and pleasant, and the air, both night and day, is cool and invigorating.

"During the day-time the light of the crater and the lava streams is hardly perceptible. The night is the best time for observation. Soon after the sun had set, the molten streams began to show their courses, while the spouting of the lava from the crater became more and more distinct. The reflection of the numerous fiery streams rolling rapidly down the side of the mountain and across the plain, lit up the overhanging clouds, making it as bright as moonlight for many miles around. As night advanced, and every little stream and light became brilliant, the scene was grand.

"This new crater is located on the northern slope of Mauna Loa, at an elevation of, say 8500 feet above the sea. It is some ten or more miles westward and about 4000 feet lower than the last eruption of 1855, known as that of Mokuaweoweo. The course of the stream, from its course to the sea, we judge to be nearly northwest by north. The crater bears due east from Kailua by the compass, and is about twenty-four miles from that harbor in a straight line. Its latitude, as near as we are able to determine without instruments, is 19° 37', long. 155° 49'. By referring to a map or chart, its position on the island can readily be noted. Our figures are only estimates, and accurate observations may prove that we are in error in some of them.

" The actual size and form of the crater can only be determined by visiting its immediate vicinity, which we were not prepared to do. From the distance at which we observed it, about ten miles, and from various points of observation, it *appeared* to be circular, its width being about equal to its breadth, and over two hundred feet across the mouth. Its rim is surrounded or made up of cones formed from the stones and scoria thrown out, these cones constantly varying in extent, now growing in size and again all tumbling down. The lava does not simply run out from the side of the crater like water from the side of a bowl, but is thrown up in continuous columns, very much like the geyser springs, as represented in school geographies.

" A dense, heavy column of smoke continually poured out from the crater, but always on the north side, and took a north-easterly direction, rising in one continuous column far above the mountain, to a height of perhaps 10,000 feet above the crater. This smoke hovers over that island, and indeed all the group, and must at times, when the trade-wind lulls, obstruct the view. During our stay, however, it passed off from the mountain, leaving the lower atmosphere quite clear. We watched closely to observe whether any *steam* could be seen issuing, either from the crater or from any of the streams of lava, but could not see anything that could be called steam or vapor, unless occasionally very slight indications along some of the lava streams. Considerable smoke rose along the streams, as the molten lava came in contact with trees and vegetable products, but the mass of smoke came from the crater itself. Steam was noticed in various places on the plain, issuing from the rocks, and near one of the camps the heat was so intense that a teakettle could be boiled over it. But this steam was undoubtedly caused by the heat of the flowing lava coming in contact with pools of water in caves or pits.

" At times the spouting appeared to be feeble, rising but little above the rim of the crater, but generally, as if eager to escape from the pent-up bowels of the earth, it rose to a height nearly equal to the base of the crater. But the columns and masses of lava thrown out were ever varying in form and height. Sometimes, when very active, a spire or cone of lava would shoot up like a rocket, or in the form of a huge pyramid, to a height nearly double the base of the crater. The mouth of the crater being about 250 feet across, the perpendicular column must be 500 feet in height! Then, by watching it with a spyglass, the columns could be seen to diverge and fall in all manner of shapes, like a beautiful fountain.

" This part of the scene was one of true grandeur—no words can convey a full idea of it to the reader. The molten fiery-redness, ever varying, ever changing its form, from the simple gurgling of a spring to the hugest fountain conceivable—like a vast natural kaleidoscope—is a picture too grand to be described, but when seen will remain painted on the observer's memory till death. Large boulders of red-hot lava stone, weighing hundreds of tons, thrown up with inconceivable power high into the air, could be occasionally seen falling outside or on the rim of the crater, tumbling down the cones and rolling over the precipice, remaining brilliant for a few moments, then becoming cold and black, were lost among the surrounding lava. So awfully grand, so beautiful, was this ever-varying scene, that the spectator cannot help watching it with intense delight and increasing excitement for hours together; the only drawback being the severe cold of the night, against which travelers should be provided.

" On leaving the crater, the lava stream does not appear for some distance, say an eighth of a mile, as it has cut its way through a deep ravine or gulch, eighty or or one hundred feet deep, which hides it from view. The first, then, that we see of the lava, after being thrown up in the crater, it is branching out into streams some distance below the fountain-head. Instead of running in one large stream, it divides into a great number—perhaps as many as fifty—spreading out over a tract of five or six miles in width. For the first six miles from the crater the descent is rapid, and the flow of the lava varies from four to five miles an hour; but after it reaches the plain, where it is level, it moves slower. Here the streams are not so numerous as higher up, there being a principal one, which varies and is very tortuous, from an eighth to a quarter of a mile in width, with frequent branches running off from it.

" Some of the finest scenes of the flow were the cascades or falls formed as it flowed down the steep declivities below the crater, and before it reached the plain. There were several of them, and they appeared to be changing and new ones formed in different localities as new streams were made. One, however, which appeared without change for two days, was eighty or one hundred feet in height. First there was a fall, then below were cascades or rapids. To watch this during the night, when the bright cherry-red stream of lava was tumbling over it at the rate of ten miles an hour, like water, was a scene not often witnessed and never to be forgotten. In fact, the lava near its source had all the characteristics of a river of water flowing rapidly along, and gurgling with cascades, rapids and falls.

" On reaching the plain, where it is more level, the lava stream of course moves along more slowly and in one general stream, less divided than above. The stream which had run into the sea had apparently ceased flowing and was cooled over, so that we crossed and recrossed it in many places, and through the fissures the molten lava could be seen, with its red-hot glow and intense heat, issuing out from them. In many places the surface was so hot that the soles of our shoes would have been burned had we not kept in rapid motion. The length of the lava stream from the crater to where it enters the sea at Wainanalii, is estimated to be forty miles.

" On the afternoon of our arrival at the camping-ground, a new stream started some few miles below the crater, which had evidently been dammed up by some obstruction, and came rushing down with tremendous noise and fury through the thick jungle which lay in its track, burning the trees, and sending up a thick smoke almost as dense as that from the crater. This stream, from the time it broke away from the embankment, moved along several miles an hour till it reached the vicinity of our camp, when its progress was checked, and it moved not more than a quarter of a mile an hour. But it formed a magnificent sight. Here was a stream of lava rolling over the plain, twenty to twenty-five feet in height, and an eighth of a mile in width, though its width varied a great deal, sometimes broader, sometimes narrower. It was, in fact, a mass or pile of red-hot stones, resembling a heap of coals on fire, borne along by the more liquid lava underneath. As it moved slowly along, large red boulders would roll down the sides, breaking into a thousand small stones, crushing and burning the trees, melting the rocks, and destroying everything which lay in the track. It is impossible to give a true conception of the immense force of this lava stream, bearing along as it does an almost inconceivable mass. It reminds one most vividly of the breaking up of the ice in a large river, only the imagination must stretch the comparison and suppose the ice piled up twenty-five feet, and thus borne along by the current beneath, the whole width of the river moving at the same time, crashing and breaking and piling up cones and irregular masses on top. But even this comparison is far below the reality—to be conceived it must be seen.

" We visited the lava stream four or five times, both in the day and night, though in the day-time it appeared robbed of its peculiar beauty. Owing to the intense heat, it could not be approached comfortably within a hundred feet, yet some of our party, anxious to outdo the rest, ventured to the stream itself, and with long sticks raked out small specimens of red-hot lava stones, which were brought away as mementoes. This stream is made up for the most part of the dross of the lava, called *aa*, which as it becomes cooled crumbles into stones and rocks, and is thus piled up to a height of twenty or twenty-five feet, and carried along by the more liquid lava beneath it. This clinker lava, when moving along, is of a dark-reddish color, while the purer lava, called *pahoehoe*, is of a more brilliant cherry hue, and when it cools becomes very glossy, porous and lighter than *aa*. It also forms the best specimens for cabinets.

"About three o'clock, A. M., we visited the new stream which had been rushing down during the night and was glowing with intense heat. It moved slowly over the plain within fifteen minutes' walk of our camp. On reaching it, we stood sheltered by a small tree a hundred feet distant, and as it advanced were forced to retreat before it. In fifteen minutes the tree was reached, burned, and the spot where we were covered by the irresistible stream. Once, while standing on a rock with several others, perhaps two hundred feet from the stream, a loud ringing noise was heard as if the rock had been struck by an immense sledge-hammer. We started, not knowing but *Pele* herself was under and after us, but soon found our alarm groundless, though the noise was probably caused by the liquid lava running under ground and suddenly filling up a cave beneath. A little while after, a singular scene presented itself—the appearance of a man sitting on a rock and riding along on the top of the fiery lava stream. So deceptive was this illusion, that several of the party, when it was first observed, looked around to see if one of their number had not by accident got on to the stream. The life-like image moved slowly along, till suddenly its head tumbled off, and the whole soon disappeared.

"The tract over which the lava is now flowing is a barren waste, uninhabited except by wild hogs. Formerly cattle roamed over it, but they have been driven to the side of Mauna Kea, which furnishes better food. We are not aware that any valuable land has been overrun, unless it be near the village of Wainanalii."

After running a distance of about forty miles from its source, the lava stream entered the sea at a small fishing village called Wainanalii, south of the port of Kawaihae, on the morning of January 31st. The eruption having commenced on the 23d of January, it was consequently eight days in running over that distance. Of this, Rev. Mr. Lyons writes:

"The poor inhabitants of Wainanalii, the name of the village where the fire reached the ocean, were aroused at the midnight hour by the hissing and roaring of the approaching fire, and had just time to save themselves. Some of the houses of the inland portion of the village were partly surrounded before the inmates were aware of their danger. Wainanalii is near the northern boundary of North Kona, and about fourteen miles from Kawaihae. It is of course all destroyed, and its pleasant little harbor all filled up with lava. The volcanic stream was one mile wide, or more in some places and much less in others. It crossed the Kona road, and interrupted the mail communication. The whole distance of the flow from the crater to the sea is some forty miles."

The schooner Kekauluohi was passing this village at the time the stream reached the sea, and several foreigners on board have described the scene of the lava rushing into the sea as one of terrific grandeur. Perhaps we cannot give a better account of it than to insert the description given of the meeting of the lava stream with the sea in the eruption of 1840:

"When the torrent of fire precipitated itself into the ocean, the scene assumed a character of terrific and indescribable grandeur. The magnificence of destruction was never more perceptibly displayed than when these antagonistic elements met in deadly strife. The mightiest of earth's magazines of fire poured forth its burning billows to meet the mightiest of oceans. For two-score miles it came rolling, tumbling, swelling forward, an awful agent of death. Rocks melted like wax in its path; forests crackled and blazed before its fervent heat; the very hills were lifted from their primeval beds and sank beneath its tide, or were borne onward by its waves; the works of man were to it but as a scroll in the flames; Nature shriveled and trembled before the irresistible flow. Imagine Niagara's stream, above the brink of the falls, with its dashing, whirling, madly raging waters hurrying on to their plunge, instantaneously converted into fire, a gory-hued river of fused minerals; the wrecks of creative matter blazing and disappearing beneath its surface; volumes of hissing steam arising; smoke curling upwards from ten thousand vents, which give utterance to as many deep-toned mutterings, and sullen, confined and ominous clamorings, as if the spirits of fallen demons were struggling against their final doom ; gases detonating and shrieking as they burst from their hot prison-house ; the heavens lurid with flame ; the atmosphere dark, turgid and oppressive ; the horizon murky with vapors, and gleaming with the reflected contest ; while cave and hollow, as the hot air swept along their heated walls, threw back the unearthly sounds in a myriad of prolonged echoes. Such was the scene as the fiery cataract, leaping a precipice of fifty feet, poured its flood upon the ocean. The old line of coast, a mass of compact indurated lava, whitened, cracked and fell. The waters recoiled and sent forth a tempest of spray ; they foamed and lashed around and over the melted rock ; they boiled with the heat, and the roar of the conflict-ing agencies grew fiercer and louder. The reports of the exploding gases were distinctly heard twenty-five miles distant. They were likened to discharges of whole broadsides of heavy artillery. Streaks of the intensest light glanced like lightning in all directions ; the outskirts of the burning lava as it fell, cooled by the shock, was shivered into millions of fragments, and, borne aloft by strong breezes blowing towards the land, were scattered in scintillant showers far into the country. For three successive weeks the volcano disgorged an uninterrupted burn-ing tide, with scarcely any diminution, into the ocean. On either side, for twenty miles, the sea became heated, and with such rapidity that on the second day of the junction fishes came ashore dead in great numbers at Keau, fifteen miles distant. Six weeks later, at the base of the hills, the water continued scalding hot, and sent forth steam at every wash of the waves."

President W. Alexander, of Punahou College, subsequently visited the eruption on Mauna Loa, and furnished an interesting report, which is given in full :

" At a time when all information relating to the eruption is eagerly received, a brief sketch of what the company to which I belonged saw and did, may be interest-ing to your readers, particularly as we reached the source by a route different from that taken by any other party, excepting perhaps Mr. Vaudry. Our party sailed from Honolulu in the Kinoole, on Tuesday, February 1st, 1859, and landed at Kealakekua on Thursday noon. During the preceding night we had a distant view of the eruption, like a star, two-thirds up the mountain, with streaks of light branching out from below. Friday was spent in preparations for the jaunt, and on Saturday morning we set out for the crater, from Kuapehu, in a direction nearly east.

" As we began to emerge from the woods we had a fine view of the jet, playing at a distance of perhaps twenty-five miles, to a height, as we afterwards estimated, of three hundred feet. It was of a deep-red color, in form and movement exactly like a fountain, and was accompanied by immense columns of steam. It was soon concealed from our view, however, by the flanks of Mauna Loa. About twelve miles from the coast road we reached a watering-place called Waiio, which we found nearly dry.

" Here we were obliged to send back our horses and pack-oxen and proceed on foot. Our guide then led us in a direction about E.S.E. across a rugged tract of clinkers to a cave, about eight miles from Waiio, where we encamped for the night. This cave had formed part of the channel of a subterranean stream, which left a series of deep caverns, fissures and pits to mark its course.

" During the afternoon the party, being in want of water, pushed on six or eight miles S.S.E. to a well known watering-place called Puapuawai, where they encamped. At this point the cold was so intense at night, that a crust of ice half an inch thick was formed in our calabashes, and the berries around our camp were frozen hard. As far as we could judge by the horizon, we were about a thousand feet lower than the summit of Hualalai, and accordingly about 8000 feet above the sea. On account of the failure of this spring, as well as for other reasons, it was thought expedient to divide the party : half of them, headed by Pres. Beckwith, returned to Kaawaloa, and went out to the lava flow by Gov. Adams' road.

" The advance party started again directly for the crater on Wednesday morn-
29

ing, consisting of twelve white men and thirty kanakas, with a week's provisions. During this day's march the rarity of the atmosphere affected us all more or less, but especially our natives, who seemed unable to carry their usual loads. We were slowly ascending nearly all day. The vegetation became more and more scanty, till it almost entirely disappeared.

"About noon we crossed a recent flow, perhaps that of 1847, and at 4 P. M., (February 9th,) after a march of about twenty miles northeast, we suddenly found the two active craters, and the lava stream in its whole extent immediately below us. We encamped a mile and a half southwest of the larger cone, on an eminence commanding a fine view of the whole eruption. Large banks of snow and ice were found within a quarter of a mile from our camp, so that all anxiety on the score of water was soon dissipated.

"The sight which we enjoyed that night will not be forgotten by any of the party. The jet had ceased to play, but the two craters were blowing off enormous columns of steam and showers of red-hot scoria with a noise like that of heavy surf, or occasionally like discharges of artillery. Half a mile below the lower crater appeared a cataract of fire, continued for several miles in a winding river of light, which then divided into a net-work of branches, enclosing numerous islands. The branch towards Kawaihae still gave a dull-red light in a few spots, but the force of the stream seemed to be directed west, towards Kona.

"The new streams seemed to be running a race, as it were, in that direction, and we could see the forest blazing before them. The next day (19th) was rainy, and the fog so dense that we could not travel. We moved down a couple of miles and encamped on the fresh lava stream, half a mile south of the principal cone. By the heat of the steam-cracks we boiled our coffee, roasted meat and potatoes, and melted the snow, which our natives had brought down in sacks, till we filled all our water containers. During the day parties explored the craters.

"The two principal cones are about a quarter of a mile apart, the upper one bearing southeast from the other. They are about one hundred and fifty feet high, and are composed entirely of pumice and small fragments of lava which were thrown out in a liquid state. The upper cone was a closed crater, enclosing two red-hot vent holes or furnaces, several feet in diameter, from which it was emitting steam and sulphurous gas, and now and then showers of light pumice. The suffocating gases rendered it impossible to approach it except on the windward side. The lower crater, from which the great jet had been playing two days before, was somewhat larger, and a great gap was left open on the lower side, through which a torrent of lava had flowed down the slope.

"We found a third crater, above the two we have mentioned, which was still smoking, and in fact we could trace a line of fresh lava and scoria cones two or three miles farther up the mountain. The larger cones were in the centre of a still smoking stream, a mile wide, which must have flowed from a source considerably higher up.

"It was a subject of regret to the party that they did not have a barometer to measure the elevation of the source, but, taking all things into account, we think it cannot be less than 8000 feet, and is probably nearer 10,000 feet, above the sea. The elevation of the 'Heiau of Umi' is given by Wilkes at 5000 feet, and we think the source of the eruption is certainly 3000 or 4000 feet higher.

"We slept on the warm lava that night, and early next morning revisited the lower crater, and followed the central flow for half a mile, passing two or three small cones, till we reached the present outlet, to which the stream has evidently found its way from the crater by a subterranean channel. It was in appearance a pool of blood, a few rods in width, boiling up like a spring, and spouting up thick, clotted masses to the height of ten or twenty feet. One of our party approached near enough to run his pole into it. On the lower side it poured, in a cataract of molten metal at a white heat, down a descent of about fifty feet, with a roar like that of heavy surf. A strong south wind was blowing, which enabled us, by holding our hats before our faces, to get within a few feet of the brink. The lava appeared almost as fluid as water, and ran with a velocity which the eye could scarcely follow. The solid fragments which now and then fell in, disappeared almost instantly. For several miles the fiery river was a continuous series of rapids and cataracts. At length we reluctantly returned to our camp, a distance of two or three miles across the fresh lava, which in several places was hot enough to burn our sandals.

" After taking our breakfast, and starting our natives over the old *pahoehoe* along the south bank of the stream, we returned to the great cataract. The action had greatly increased during the last three hours; the pool had become a fountain, playing to a height of thirty feet, and the falling pieces were fast forming a crater around it, the rim of which was already ten feet high, but open on the lower side to afford an outlet for the torrent. Two smaller jets were playing above it, which will probably unite with it to form one crater. The upper one threw up light pieces of pumice to the hight of sixty feet, and was forming a very regular cone.

" It was fortunately a clear day on the mountain, and a strong wind was blowing from the southwest, so that we traveled for three or four hours along the very brink of the stream without inconvenience. It had worn for itself a deep, well-defined channel, so that there was no danger of any sudden change in its course. The canal in which it ran varied from twenty to fifty feet in width, and was ten or fifteen feet deep. But the stream was in reality much wider than this, for the banks on either side were undermined to considerable extent. Often we met with openings in the crust, through which we could see the rushing torrent a few feet, or even inches, below our feet.

" To describe the scene is impossible. No epithets in the English language are adequate to the task. For the first time we saw actual *waves* and actual *spray* of liquid lava. As its surges rolled back from the enclosing walls of rock, they curled over and broke like combers on the reef. Its forms, however, were bolder and more picturesque than those of running water, on account of its being a heavier and more tenacious fluid. There was, besides, an endless variety in its forms. Now we passed a cascade, then a whirlpool, then a smooth and majestic river, then a series of rapids, tossing their waves like a stormy sea; now rolling into lurid caverns, the roofs of which were hung with red-hot stalactites, and then under arches which it had thrown over itself in sportive triumph. The safety with which it could be approached, was matter of astonishment to us all.

" After following it six or eight miles we halted for dinner on an island, about a quarter of a mile from the largest fall, and then proceeded ·down the stream till 4 P. M. As the descent became more gradual the torrent changed its color, first to rose-color, then to a dark blood-red; its surface began to gather a greyish scum, and large drifting masses became frequent. It now began to separate into numerous branches, and it became more unsafe to follow the central stream, as changes were constantly taking place, and our retreat was liable to be cut off at any moment. We therefore kept nearer the edge of the flow, and at length encamped on an island in the woods. During the night the craters were very active, and the whole plain seemed to be on fire below and above us.

" The party was called out by four o'clock the next morning, and went up a short distance to observe a new stream which was pouring down through the woods to our camp. It was a shallow flow in a high state of fusion, and was forming smooth *pahoehoe.* Its mode of advance through the woods, girdling and slowly consuming the trees, the surface constantly cooling over and breaking up by turns, was exactly the same as that observed at Hilo, and needs no description. Here we were able to take out as many specimens in a liquid state as we wished, to insert coins into them, and if we had carried moulds with us, we might have forced the liquid into almost any required shape. We spent the forenoon in following the stream to the plain, partly crossing it in some places to reach the scene of a new overflow. We had been particularly curious to see how clinkers are formed, and our curiosity was now gratified. The difference between *pahoehoe* or smooth lava, and *aa* or clinkers, seems to be due more to a difference in their mode of cooling than to any other cause. The streams which form the *pahoehoe* are comparatively shallow, in a state of complete fusion, and cool suddenly in a mass. The *aa* streams, on the other hand, are deep, sometimes moving along in a mass twenty feet high, with solid walls; they are less fluid, being full of solid points or centres of cooling, as they may be called, and advance very slowly; that is, in cooling, the *aa* stream *grains* like sugar. At a distance it looks like an immense mass of half red-hot cinders and slag from a foundry, rolling along over and over itself, impelled by an irresistible power from behind and beneath. That power is the liquid stream, almost concealed by the pile of cinders, which has been formed from itself in cooling. We heard frequent explosions, caused by the lava penetrating caves and blowing them up. The principal stream of running lava which we saw on the plain, was three or four miles southeast of the extremity of the Judd Road, and was moving west by north. At this we left the lava stream, and descended to Umi's Temple by a short cut, through an open forest of *pahoehoe*. We reached the heiau about 3 P. M., and arrived at Mr. Johnson's about 8 o'clock the same evening. The other division of our party had already visited the flow by way of Gov. Adams' Road, and had returned. We sailed again from Keauhou the following Tuesday, and arrived in Honolulu on Sunday morning."

IX.—ERUPTION OF 1868.

The last eruption on Hawaii, (up to this date,) and the ninth on record, occurred in April, 1868. A full account of it was published in the " Pacific Commercial Advertiser " of May 9th, 1868, by the writer of this appendix, who was an eye-witness of it. This account is given below, with some omissions :

" The first symptoms of any unusual commotion on Mauna Loa were noticed on the morning of March 27th, about half-past 5 o'clock, when from the whaleships at anchor in Kawaihae harbor, a dense column of smoke was observed to rise in one massive pillar to the height of several miles, directly over Mauna Loa, accompanied with a bright reflection, showing that fires were again active in the great crater of Mokuaweoweo. In a few hours this pillar-cloud dispersed and passed off, and no light was seen on the following night.

" At about 10 A. M., on the 28th, a series of earthquakes began, which continued at intervals with varied severity for over a month. At Kona, as many as fifty or sixty distinct shocks were felt in one day ; at Kau, over *three hundred* in the same time, and near the great crater of Kilauea the earth is represented as having been in a constant quiver for days together, with frequent vigorous shocks that would send crockery, chairs, lamps, &c., spinning around in not a very pleasant way. Mr. J. J. Porter, the proprietor of the Volcano House, says he endured this for several days, as long as he could, till one night, about 11 o'clock, ' Pele sent one of Rodman's twenty-inch shot, with a well-directed aim, that struck the ground directly under his bed, when he jumped up and ran, where or how he hardly knew, but he found himself after a while in the woods, safe and sound.'

" One can readily imagine the state of nervous excitement produced by the continual swaying of the ground, with an occasional shock like that produced by a heavy rock striking the crust beneath him. A lady, who spent two weeks in this shaky region, says that she put her ear down to the earth during one of the ' ground-swells,' and could distinctly hear the rushing and roaring of the lava waves beneath the surface, like the surging of waves in a storm. Residents of Kau state that over *two thousand* distinct shocks occurred there between the 28th of March and the 11th of April, averaging over one hundred and forty a day for two weeks.

" The earthquakes continued to increase in severity from March 28th till April 2d, when, about 4 o'clock in the afternoon, one took place that shook down every stone wall, and nearly every stone, frame and thatch house throughout Kau, and did more or less damage in every part of Hawaii, while it was felt very sensibly on Maui, Molokai, Oahu and Kauai, the latter island being three hundred miles distant from the crater. Every church in Kau district was destroyed, with perhaps a single exception. The shock was so severe that it threw persons from their feet, and even horses and other animals were served in the same way. A gentleman riding on horseback in Waiohinu, found his horse lying flat under him before he could imagine the cause. The effect of the shock was *instantaneous.* Before a person could think, he found himself prostrate on the ground. The large stone church of Waiohinu went down in the same way—a sudden jerk, the walls crumbled in and the roof fell flat—all the work of ten seconds. Judge F. S. Lyman describes this remarkable shock as follows : ' Thursday, (April 2d,) between 4 and 5 P. M., we experienced the *most fearful of earthquakes !* First, the earth swayed to and fro north and south, then east and west, round and round, then up and down and in every imaginable direction for several minutes, everything crashing around us, the trees thrashing about as if torn by a mighty rushing wind. It was impossible to stand ; we had to sit on the ground, bracing with hands and feet to keep from rolling over.' It left nothing but desolation and ruin throughout the district.

" Respecting the course or direction of the shocks, we have made many inquiries. Those felt on Oahu have mostly been undulating, with a wave-like motion. On Hawaii they had three distinct characteristics—the *undulating*, with the motion generally from the northwest to southeast ; second, the sudden short, sharp, *jerking shock*, occupying hardly two seconds ; and, third, a *thumping*, like a boulder or rock thrown suddenly against the crust of the earth, and as suddenly falling down. Each kind was frequently accompanied with a *rattling noise*, like distant thunder or artillery, more or less distinct. The lighter shocks generally had no accompanying noise. We experienced one of these ' thumping ' shocks, while sleeping near the crater on the night of April 10th. It sounded precisely as if a cannon-ball had struck the floor under us, and then rolled off on the verandah floor. It started us out of a sound sleep. Simultaneous with the heavy earthquake on the afternoon of April 2d, occurred

THE MUD ERUPTION AT KAPAPALA,

which is so singular, and so unlike anything that has heretofore occurred on the islands, that we give a minute description of it. Kapapala is the residence of Mr. Charles E. Richardson in Kau, about fifteen miles from Kilauea crater, and twenty-five from Waiohinu. About midway between Mr. R.'s residence and that of Judge Lyman at Keaiwa, six miles west, are two beautiful valleys, that extend from the road a couple of miles, which every observing traveler must have noticed. They were studded with groves of kukui and other trees, and covered with a rich carpet of the softest manienie grass. Herds of sleek cattle were constantly browsing or enjoying the shade of the cool groves. Native huts were scattered here and there, and horsemen were frequently seen crossing the valley.

" This was the scene of the ' mud-flow.' Just at the instant the earthquake occurred the sides of the valley were rent, and from the fissure burst out, with a terrific noise, a stream of red mud and water, which was driven by the explosion fully three miles. This stream was ejected simultaneously with the heavy earthquake from both sides of the valley. Immediately under and near the fissures are heaps of stones and boulders, which were evidently thrown out first, and beyond these a vacant space, in which a native thatch-house was left standing and the inmates unharmed, while the mud and stones flew over and beyond them. Eighteen hundred feet from the opening the pile of mud commences, and extends a distance of three miles from the opening, varying in width from half a mile to one mile, and from two feet at the outer edges to twenty and thirty feet deep in the centre. Where it crosses the road it is thirty feet deep and half a mile across.

" This mass of mud, covering an area of at least one thousand acres and weighing millions of tons, was thrown out as if discharged from two huge batteries of ten thousand twenty-inch Rodman guns, planted on each side of the valley. At its further extremity is a pile of large boulders and stones, that appear to have been driven before the powerful explosion. As it swept through the valley, with the most indescribable and unearthly noises, it buried and destroyed men, animals and trees alike. Thirty-one lives were lost, and between five hundred and a thousand head of cattle, horses, goats and sheep, some of which were just at the moment being driven across the valley to the farm-house. This mud, or now more properly dirt, as it has become dry, consists of finely pulverized red soil, such as is so often found in the group. In some places it is mixed with stones, trunks of trees, fern-leaves, &c. Trunks of trees are found standing, with their limbs shot off by the explosion. The force with which these streams were ejected from the hills, and the speed, is said by eye-witnesses to have been at the rate at least of a mile a minute. The rapidity was so great, even at the very edge of the flow, that numbers of goats, which were fleeing for life, were overtaken by it, and found a short time afterwards by Mr. Richardson, sticking by their hind legs in the mud.

"From where the mud was exploded now issues a stream of clear, cool mountain water, which it is hoped will continue to flow, as it is the only stream in the district. It will be all the more acceptable, as all Mr. Richardson's cisterns have been totally destroyed by the same earthquake which produced the rivulet. Some of the natives present at this eruption state that the mud thrown out was cold, others that it was hot, and that steam and smoke issued from the rent after the eruption. It is quite probable that the earthquake created a subterranean rent, which brought this confined body of water in contact with the lava fires below, and thus produced the explosion without heating the mass above. Mr. Richardson's loss in cattle, horses, cisterns and houses, has been estimated at fifteen thousand dollars, which is probably the largest sustained by any one party. In the valley adjoining there was also a small land-slide, but not on the scale noticed above. The soil thrown out is rich, and will soon be covered with dense vegetation, especially should the fine stream remain permanent.

THE EARTHQUAKE WAVE.

"Immediately following the above explosion and the earthquake, there occurred a tidal or earthquake wave, which caused great destruction of life and property along the southeast coast of Hawaii, from Keauhou to Kalae, the most southern point of the island. Judge Lyman, whose residence is six or eight miles from the sea, describes the first view of it as follows: 'Some one pointed to the shore, and we ran to where we could see it. After the hard shaking had ceased, all along the sea-shore, from directly below us to Punaluu, about three or four miles, the sea was boiling furiously, all red, for about an eighth of a mile from the shore, and the shore was covered by the sea.' "

Mr. Abm. Fornander, who passed through the district a day or two before the wave occurred, communicated the following to the "Hawaiian Gazette":

"At Keauhou, the following results of the earthquake on Thursday have been reported. Mr. Stackpole, who had charge of the place, had been up to the Volcano House during the day, and was returning in the afternoon. While descending the pali to Keauhou, the first shock occurred, precipitating an immense amount of earth, stones and boulders down the pali after him. Escaping these, he arrived on the plateau below the pali, and looked in the direction of the village of Apua, but not a house was to be seen! He then rode down to the edge of the plateau, from whence Keauhou ought to have been in sight, but nothing of it could be seen. Descending to Pahoehoe, he met the men working at Keauhou running up mauka, who reported that nothing was left of Keauhou; that immediately after the earthquake the sea had rushed in and swept off every dwelling and storehouse, and all their contents, and that they had barely escaped with their lives. There were some 167 bales of pulu in store, ready for shipment, all of which was swept away. They represent that the sea went up as far as the two basaltic columns indicating the road down to Keauhou—a depth of wave of at least forty to fifty feet.

" At Punaluu, at the moment of the shock, it seemed as if an immense quantity of lava had been discharged into the sea some distance from the shore, for almost instantly a terrible commotion arose, the water boiling and tossing furiously. Shortly afterwards a tremendous wave was sweeping up on the shore, and when it receded there was nothing left of Punaluu! Every house, the big stone church, even the cocoanut-trees—all but two—were washed away. The number of lives lost is not yet ascertained. All who were out fishing at the time perished, and many of those ashore. A big chasm opened, running from the sea up into the mountain, down which it is said lava, mud, trees, ferns, and rocks were rushing out into the sea.

" The same wave that swept away Punaluu, also destroyed the villages of Ni-nole, Kawaa and Honuapo. Not a house remains to mark the site of these places, except at Honuapo, where a small *hale halawai*, on the brow of the hill above the village, stood on Friday last. The large cocoanut grove at Honuapo was washed away, as well as that at Punaluu. A part of the big pali at Honuapo, on the road to Waiohinu, had tumbled into the sea, and people coming from thence are now obliged to take the mountain road through Hilea-uka.

" The sea swept Kaalualu on Thursday last, as it had swept Honuapo and the other places along the coast, washed away several houses, and killed a number of people—how many, is not yet known. The earth had been shaking almost constantly and severely every day and night. A large land-slide had occurred on the west side of Waiohinu valley, near where Swain's tannery was formerly situated. Fire had been seen in the mountains above, but none had come down on the low lands between Kahuku and Waiohinu when they left, on Monday morning. A large hole, sixty feet in diameter, had opened on the flat below Kahuku, with no bottom visible from the brink of it, and emitting quantities of sulphuric vapor.

" I have just been told an incident that occurred at Ninole, during the inundation at that place. At the time of the shock on Thursday, a man named Holoua, and his wife, ran out of the house and started for the hills above, but remembering the money he had in the house, the man left his wife and returned to bring it away. Just as he had entered the house the sea broke on the shore, and, enveloping the building, first washed it several yards inland, and then, as the wave receded, swept it off to sea, with him in it. Being a powerful man, and one of the most expert swimmers in that region, he succeeded in wrenching off a board or a rafter, and with this as a *papa hee-nalu*, (surf-board,) he boldly struck out for the shore, and landed safely with the return wave. When we consider the prodigious height of the breaker on which he rode to the shore, (fifty, perhaps sixty feet,) the feat seems almost incredible, were it not that he is now alive to attest it, as well as the people on the hill-side who saw him.

" Mr. George Jones met a heavy loss at Keauhou by the inundation. Besides the houses and fixtures that were swept away by the sea, he also lost some 167 bales of pulu that were ready for shipment. On Saturday last he chartered the schooner Odd Fellow, and started in her to see if he could not pick up some of the pulu that might have been washed along the shore between there and the south point.

" Hilo and Puna have suffered, so far, comparatively least, though the shocks were severe and frequent, and still continue, and the damage to houses and property is very large. But poor Kau is almost wholly destroyed. The sea washed away the coast villages, and the earthquake razed the inland places.

" The number of people now known to have perished between Ninole and Keaiwa, (Punaluu and Hionamoa included,) is 47; at Kawaa, 7; at Honuapo, 27; total, 81, besides a number of the pulu-pickers up in the mountains, back of Hilea; how many I am not yet advised, neither have I heard the number of those who perished at Kaalualu."

This was one of those sad catastrophes where " distance lends enchantment to the scene," and which few witnessed. From all we can gather from the above and other sources, the wave rolled in along the Kau coast from forty to sixty feet high, and receded five times, decreasing in force each successive time. It covered the tops of the lower cocoanut-trees, swept inland from five hundred to six hundred yards, and destroyed nearly everything movable, including the trees growing along the shore. The total number of lives lost during the earthquakes and tide-wave was about one hundred.

After these events on the 2d of March, earthquakes continued to be frequent and alarming, but nothing noteworthy occurred till the 7th, when a lava eruption took place above Kahuka, seven miles northwest of Waiohinu, in the district of Kau, which is the most southern district on the island.

A company of eight or ten, including the writer, left Honolulu in the steamer for Kona on the 6th of April, and arrived at Kahuku on the 10th, three days after the eruption broke out. We consequently had the first opportunity that could possibly have been sought for seeing what proved to be a most brilliant display.

On the passage to Hawaii in the steamer, on the night of the 7th, the whole island of Hawaii was brilliantly illuminated, the overhanging clouds reflecting the glare of the fires beneath, and a stream of lava was seen from the vessel, a distance of at lest one hundred miles.

We left Kealakeakua Bay on the morning of the 9th of April, and after a slow, tedious ride of twenty-seven miles, over lava clinkers, reached Kapua towards night, where we slept in a thatch-house, built by Mr. C. N. Spencer as an accommodation house, it being just half way between the bay and Waiohinu, and distant from the lava flow about thirteen miles. During the night we could hear the distant noise of the eruption—a peculiar rumbling, so different from the roar of the sea or any other noise, that, to wake up at night and listen to its unaccountable utterances, tended to create fear with those who for the first time heard it. In the morning several of the party decided to turn back to Kealakeakua, and returned without seeing the grand sight before us. The others, seven in number, not counting native attendants, mounted horses and proceeded on to the flow.

As we approached it, the rumbling noise became more and more distinct, and the evidences of approach to some great disturbance of nature more frequent. The ground was covered with what appeared to be cinders, but on examining them we found they were fragments of pumice-stone, which had been carried by the wind a distance of over ten miles. Mixed with these cinders was "Pele's hair," which we found floating in the air, and when it fell thick we had to hold our handkerchiefs to our nostrils to prevent inhaling it. Our clothes were frequently covered with it. On reaching an eminence five miles from the stream, we found a group of forty or fifty natives who were waiting to cross over to Kau, and had been here several days. From this point dense clouds of smoke could be seen rising all along the lava stream, from the mountain-side to the sea.

We hurried on and reached the flow shortly after noon, where, from a ridge to the west of it, the whole scene opened before us. Between us and the crater was a valley five hundred yards wide and ten miles long, which had recently been overflowed throughout the entire width and length from the mountain to the sea, where it widened to two or three miles. The lava was of the smooth *pahoehoe* variety, from ten to twenty feet deep, and partially cooled over, though flames, smoke and gas escaped from numerous crevices. We stood on it, though it was hot enough to burn the soles of our shoes. This lava stream originated some ten miles up the mountain, and came down early on the morning of the 7th. It had ceased flowing, the eruption having opened a vent lower down and further south.

Beyond this valley, about a quarter of a mile distant, was the pali of Mamalu, a steep precipice, which runs from the mountain to the south point of Hawaii, and forms the west boundary of the table-land of Kahuku, a beautiful level plateau, covered with tall grass, affording excellent pasturage for herds of cattle, horses, sheep and goats. About a mile above the road were the farm-houses of Captain Robert Brown, who lived there with his family. Near by were the dairy establishment of Mr. C. N. Spencer, and other dwellings. This plateau was several miles in extent, running as far as Waiohinu, sloping gently off to the sea, and dotted with hillocks.

On Tuesday afternoon, April 7th, at 5 o'clock, a new crater, several miles lower down than that referred to, and about two miles back of Captain Brown's residence, burst out. The lava stream commenced flowing down the beautiful grass-covered plateau towards and around the farm-house, and the inmates had barely time to escape with the clothes they had on, before the houses were all surrounded, burned and covered with streams of fiery lava, varying from five to fifty feet in depth. Fortunately, all the inmates escaped safely to Waiohinu, but how narrow the escape was, and how rapidly the stream flowed, may be inferred from the fact that the path by which they escaped was covered with lava *ten minutes* after they passed over it.

On ascending the ridge we found the eruption in full blast. Four enormous fountains, apparently distinct from each other, and yet forming a line a mile long, north and south, were continually spouting up from the opening. These jets were blood-red and yet as fluid as water, ever varying in size, bulk and height. Sometimes two would join together, and again the whole four would be united, making one continuous fountain a mile in length.

From the lower end of the crater a stream of very liquid, boiling lava flowed out and down the plateau, a distance of two or three miles, then following the track of the Government road, ran down the precipice at an angle of about thirty degrees, thence along the foot of the pali or precipice five miles to the sea, the stream being eight or ten miles in length, and in some places half a mile wide.

This was the magnificent scene, to see which we had hurriedly left Honolulu, and had fortunately arrived at the right moment to witness, as it opened before us in all its majestic grandeur and unrivalled beauty. At the left were those four great fountains, boiling up with most terrific fury, throwing crimson lava and enormous stones, weighing many tons, to a height varying constantly from five hundred to six hundred feet. At times these red-hot rocks completely filled the air, causing a great noise and roar, and flying in every direction, but generally towards the south. Sometimes the fountains would all subside for a few minutes, and then commence increasing till the stones and liquid lava reached a thousand feet in hight. The grandeur of this picture, ever varying like a panorama, painted in the richest crimson hues, no person can realize unless he has witnessed it.

From this great fountain to the sea flowed a rapid stream of red lava, rolling, rushing and tumbling like a swollen river, and bearing along in its current large rocks that almost made the lava foam, as it dashed down the precipice and through the valley into the sea, surging and roaring throughout its length like a cataract, with a power and fury perfectly indescribable. It was nothing else than a *river of fire*, from two hundred to eight hundred feet wide and twenty feet deep, with a speed varying from *ten to twenty-five miles an hour.* As a huge boulder floated down, we imagined what if it were the iron-clad Stonewall, which had just left our harbor—would she have floated on to the sea unscathed, or turned into molten lava, and vanished from sight?

Night soon came, and with it the scene became a thousand-fold more beautiful, the crimson of the fountains and the river doubly rich and brilliant, the lurid glare of the dense clouds of smoke that overhung us, and the roaring of the crater and the cataract were fearfully grand and awe-inspiring. It was like a conflagration of London or Paris, as the whole scene extended over a distance of ten miles. Add to this the flashes of lightning and the sharp, quick claps of thunder, and the reader can imagine that a scene was before us that well repaid us for our opportune visit.

Dr. William Hillebrand and others have visited the crater since it ceased flowing, and find that it consists simply of a *rent or fissure* in the earth, from ten to twenty feet wide. He traced it about three miles up the mountain, but it is quite probable that it extends several miles farther on, as the mountain continues smoking in a line ten miles above. There is, therefore, no large crater, properly speak-

30

ing, but the lava flow was confined to this rupture, which continued to open lower down as the molten lava acted on it.

The view which we obtained of the eruption from the Kona side, on the 10th of April, was therefore a side view, and probably the finest and nearest that could possibly have been had. One peculiarity of this spouting was, that the lava was ejected with a *rotary motion*, and as it ascended the air both the lava and stones rotated always in one direction, *towards the south*. In this respect it differed from that of 1859, which we were also among the first to witness. This rotary motion of the lava would appear to have originated below the surface, as it rolled along like waves, and corresponds with the surging sounds heard by the inhabitants of Kau during the heavy earthquake shocks.

Regarding the rapidity of the stream of lava, since reading accounts of former eruptions, in which it is claimed that the lava flowed *forty miles an hour*, we will add that it is hardly possible to conceive of a stream flowing with greater rapidity than the cataract and river we witnessed April 10th. It reminded us of the Connecticut river in a spring-flood, with the stream filled with ice and rushing over the rapids at an impetuous rate. The speed is more likely to have been twenty-five miles an hour than twelve. Where it ran down the precipice, at an angle of about thirty degrees, it was more narrow and rapid than lower down, where it spread out broader. This was the only stream that reached the sea, and flowed into it a little west of the south point of the island, at a place called Kailikii. It lasted only five days, the eruption ceasing entirely on the night of the 11th or morning of the 12th.

During its continuance the atmosphere was filled with smoke so dense that the sun appeared like a ball of fire, and the whole island was shrouded in darkness. This smoke came from the rent or crater, and was highly charged with sulphur. As it spread over the island, it carried a deadly blast to vegetation, and the leaves of the more tender plants and vegetables were withered and died. It did not kill the plants in any sections, that we could learn.

Opposite the point of coast where the lava reached the sea, a small conical island was thrown up in the sea, half a mile distant from the shore, consisting of mud and sand, and emitting steam from its summit. This island has become joined to the main land by the lava flowing from the new eruption. As the lava entered the sea, clouds of steam and smoke rose up, and flames of blueish fire were emitted, rising from the water to a height of from ten to twenty feet.

During the night we were at the volcano, the air was highly charged with sulphur gas and electricity, and frequent flashes of lightning were seen over the lava stream, accompanied with short claps of thunder. These flashes were also observed less frequently farther up the mountain.

Two kinds of lava were erupted during the flow. It commenced with a stream of smooth, glossy lava, known here as the *pahoehoe*, which was followed by the thick, dirty kind, called *aa*. Kahuku farm was nearly covered with the latter, which branched out into four wide streams, covering a space of four miles wide and long. This was followed again by the liquid or *pahoehoe*, which ran into the sea, and continued till the eruption ceased. About four thousand acres of good pasture land were destroyed, besides which the lava ran over an immense district of worthless land.

On the night of the 6th, prior to the eruption, there was a shower of ashes and pumice-stone, which came from this crater, and covered the country to the distance of ten or fifteen miles each way. Generally the ashes were not more than one or two inches in depth, but in some places were found to be fifteen. The pumice-stone was very light, and appears to have been carried by the wind a great distance. Pieces two and three inches in size floated ashore at Kealakeakua Bay, forty-five miles distant.

The roaring of the crater was a novel feature to those who had never visited an eruption before. It was caused by the rocks thrown out by the crater, and the crushing process of the *aa* as it moved along. This *aa* flow is composed of half-melted lava, and as it is pushed along piles up sometimes fifty or even a hundred feet high, presenting the appearance of a railroad embankment, the sides having an angle of about forty degrees, down which the lava stones keep rolling. This stream generally moves along slowly, but when the quantity of liquid lava, which floats and carries along the *aa*, is abundant, it moves from one to four miles an hour. What makes the difference between the dry *aa* lava and the liquid *pahoe-hoe*, which flows like water, is an interesting subject of inquiry that has never been settled. They both flow from the same craters, one giving place to the other in turns. Our own opinion is that the smooth liquid variety obtains its character by long fusion, while the *aa* variety (which appears like half-melted stones and dirt mixed together) consists of the interior surface of the earth torn off and thrown out during the eruption. An examination of the various *aa* streams tends to confirm this theory.

Besides the dwelling and premises, which were completely burned and covered up ten feet deep by the lava, Captain Brown lost one hundred head of cattle, and other parties about one hundred and fifty head. These cattle appeared to be paralyzed on the approach of the lava, and made no efforts to escape. It is difficult to estimate the loss of property on Kahuku, but it may be roughly set down at from ten to fifteen thousand dollars. The houses destroyed were not expensive, the main loss being in land and stock.

The lava thrown out during this eruption has been of a more porous nature than in most of the late ones. Some of the specimens we have seen are exceedingly light. The shower of yellowish pumice-stone, which preceded the lava flow, was also something unusual in Hawaiian eruptions, and showed the eruption to possess a new character, perhaps the existence of more than usual steam and gases in its composition. Some have wondered why the flow ceased so suddenly—continuing only five days. The cause is probably this: so soon as the steam, which has been the active agent in producing the earthquake shocks, and in raising the lava so near to the top of the summit crater that it lightened up the clouds above it, found vents lower down the mountain, the eruption lost much of its power, and allowed the lava to rapidly subside. It is probable also that the submarine eruptions noticed checked the eruptions on land.

The quantity of lava thrown out has not probably been one-tenth what was discharged in 1859, but the quantity of steam, gas and smoke emitted during one week, must have exceeded what escaped during ten weeks in 1859, when the volume of smoke was comparatively small. We judge so from its density over all the group and for a thousand miles off. This has not occurred in any late previous eruption to the same extent. The inference therefore may be drawn that when an unusual quantity of gases and smoke escapes, a less amount of lava will be discharged; and, vice versa, when the quantity of smoke is small, the amount of lava is increased.

Respecting the weather during March, it may be added that it was of the same stormy character as has prevailed all over the western hemisphere, including the North and South Pacific. The quantity of rain that has fallen on the mountains of Hawaii has also been large; but to what extent these have affected the internal fires, and produced the earthquakes and eruptions, must remain a matter of conjecture. The thermometer during the same month showed no unusual fluctuation, ranging from 68° to 70° at sunrise, and 83° to 84° at noon, with considerable regularity.

Dr. Hillebrand communicated to the "Gazette" an account of his visit to the crater, from which we take the following:

"As the principal interest was the discovery of the main source of the stream, we at once went to that part of it where, according to common report, the lava had issued. A very light, dark-brown, glistening pumice-stone lay scattered about long before the lava was seen. Near the flow it increased so much that the animals' feet sank deep into it at every step. We soon reached the ridge of a hill, from which we surveyed the place where, according to our guide's account, the fountain of lava had been seen. This upper portion of the lava stream fills a broad valley or depression, between two parallel low hills of not more than three hundred feet high, both running almost due north and south. From the western one of these hills Mr. Whitney had witnessed the eruption. From the eastern hill we in vain looked for a crater or cone. We did not make out any indication of the character of the eruption until we had crossed nearly three-fourths of the stream, which here is not far from a mile wide. Then our attention was attracted by an accumulation of scoria. Nearing this, we were struck by a current of hot air, and, a little further on, found ourselves on the brink of a deep gap in the lava, about twenty feet wide, but narrowing and continuing itself northward. We walked round the southern end of the gap and followed it up on the west or lee side. Before long we came to another enlargement of the fissure like the former, emitting hot air charged with acid gases, which drove us back. Still continuing our march on the west side of the fissure, as close as the hot gases would allow, we came in sight of a pretty miniature cone, built up most regularly of loose scoria to the height of twelve feet, and located right over the fissure. It encloses a chimney crater of about twelve feet in diameter, with perpendicular sides, the depth of which could not be ascertained. Hot gases issued in abundance. On account of the exhalation of the latter, we were obliged to cross the chasm, on the bridge formed by the cone, to the windward side, along which we followed up steadily.

CONCLUDING REMARKS.

The record of the eruptions on Mauna Loa shows that there have been nine during the last seventy-nine years, or one in about every nine years. It is not improbable that some took place between 1789 and 1823, of which no record has been preserved. The latter is the first which occurred after the arrival of the missionaries in 1820. If we take the date of 1823 as the more reliable one on which to base an estimate of the frequency of the eruptions on Hawaii, we find that there have been eight during forty-five years, or one in about every five and a half years.

These eruptions on Hawaii are evidently produced by no local causes, but are attributable to the agency which disturbs the internal fires of the earth, and produces eruptions wherever vents are found. The most careful observer is unable to detect in the atmosphere signs of an approaching eruption, and probably nothing but the frequency and force of the earthquakes which generally (though not always) precede them can be relied on as true indicators of the disturbance of the internal fires, and of an impending eruption.

The last eruption (in 1868) occurred about the same time, or soon after, the earthquakes, hurricanes and eruptions chronicled in South America, the East and West Indies, and about six months before the severe earthquake of October, 1868, in San Francisco. These facts indicate that volcanoes located in different countries, have a connection more or less intimate; but beyond this, little has been learned of the laws governing them, and so far as the history of Mauna Loa is known, it shows a sympathy with volcanoes located in other countries.

THE CRATER OF KILAUEA.

The following vivid description of the great Crater of Kilauea is from the pen of Mr. Jarves, and is taken from his "Scenes and Scenery," pp. 237 to 251, a work to which we have made frequent reference. As a description of the crater as it appeared thirty years ago, it will be found interesting :

"The expectations of those who have formed their ideas of volcanoes from the stereotyped representations of Vesuvius and Ætna, with their conical sides and narrowed top, lava red and liquid running like rivers down its sides, stones and rocks soaring like feathers in the air, and volumes of steam and smoke, larger than the mountains themselves, ascending yet higher, will not be realized. 'Lua Pele,' or Kilauea, is unlike anything of the kind, and stands by itself, an anomaly in nature ; the mightiest and most wonderful of earth's safety-valves. As we gazed, its immensity grew upon us. More and more we realized its vastness; the stupendous area of the whole became more apparent by analyzing its parts. Vesuvius might easily have lost itself in that pit. All was black, with occasional gleamings of red, like the forkings of lightning in a dense thunder-cloud. It looked like the ruins of some mighty conflagration, from which the smoke and flame still rose, and at any moment liable to break out again, fiercer than before. At the farther extremity, a bright light showed itself, like the flickering flame of half-extinguished embers, and all was silent except the occasional hissing of gases and steam. I thought of Sodom and Gomorrah, and the cities of the plain. They must have appeared like this, before the waters flowed in and buried them forever. After gazing until nightfall, we hastened to the hut, where we were to sleep, a mere shelter of roots and grass thrown upon a few sticks, and covered on the windward side only. It was but *three* feet from the brink of a perpendicular precipice of four hundred feet, a portion of which had lately slid down part way, and hung threateningly over the remainder. Back of it was a crack in the earth, through which the steam constantly escaped. So occupied were we with the scene before us, that the danger to which we were exposed in sleeping here did not occur to us until we were ready to leave the crater, and the excitement was over. A slight shock of earthquake, and we should have known nothing more. However, having supped, we spread our blankets, with our heads towards the abyss, to be prepared for any display which might occur during the night, which closed in with a cold, drizzling rain. The wind blew in furious squalls, threatening at every gust to drive our frail shelter into the pit below. In the chasm, along its walls, and through the numberless rents and galleries of the superincumbent rock, the blast howled dismally ; at times dying away like the moan of some wounded animal ; and then again giving a fitful shriek, as it whirled through some narrow pass, and echoed itself from a hundred others. The storm-spirit was abroad, and triumphantly careered over the habitation of the fierce goddess, daring her to the contest. Her response was sullen and ominous. The hitherto quiet crater at intervals threw up columns of hot steam, stones and ashes, accompanied with loud reports, resembling the discharges of heavy artillery in a confined place. Occasionally the fires at the farther extremity would gleam up with considerable brilliancy; excepting this, nothing was to be seen through the darkness but the outlines of the chasm before us, and the whirling mist and smoke, reflecting the glare of the fires.

" What with the rain and cold, it was an uncomfortable night ; the scene itself was too novel and exciting to allow either the body or imagination to slumber. Occasionally I fell into a doze, from which a gleam from some new fire, or a violent explosion, aroused me. On such occasions, straining my eyes to pierce the turmoil beneath, I ceased to wonder that native intellect had peopled a place like this with strange and fearful beings. It was a fit habitation for their malignant deities. If the Christian, in this scene, pictures to himself hell and its torments, and how often has it been thus likened, is the savage to be blamed, who sees in it strange shapes, and fiery halls, the lakes, the palaces, and dwelling-places of *his* devils ? Pele, the consuming goddess, insatiable as her element, the fire itself, ' the rain of night.' ' the king of vapor,' ' the thundering god,' ' heaven-dwelling cloud-holder,' ' fiery-eyed canoe-breaker,' these, and many others, with names alike expressive of the varied actions of the crater, here, according to Hawaiian mythology, hold their court. They have gone from the minds of men, but their abode remains unchanged. Their requiem was borne to our ears in the driving storm, the whistling wind, the fire and smoke, and all that was furious and destructive. The morning of the fifth broke as the previous evening had commenced, but the sun soon dispelled much of the mist, and left us a pleasant day for our researches. Thermometer, 58 degrees.

"The plain on the north is much split up by fissures, from which steam continually issues, hot enough to cook meat or vegetables. In a few places it condenses and forms excellent drinking water. Four species of very palatable berries grew here abundantly, commonly called 'huckleberries,' though they have little resemblance in flavor, and none in color, to that fruit. To the northeast of this plain, we find sulphur banks several hundred yards in extent, and about twenty feet high. The gases were not powerful, and by digging into the earth, which was hot, soft, and greasy, we obtained some beautiful specimens of sulphur, in all its different forms, the best of which, however, soon lost their beauty by exposure to the air. The efflorescences at the mouth of the crevices were exceedingly delicate and beautiful. These banks appear to be volcanic rock, decomposed by sulphuric acids, for it is to be seen in all its stages, from the hard rock to the soft paste. An hour's *steaming* here dissipated all the pain and soreness which we felt from our exposure to the weather.

"We estimated the circumference of the whole crater at five miles, the western side of which was the highest;.but in no place did the depth to the black ledge exceed five hundred feet. It is more oval than circular, its greatest breadth being from northeast to southwest, and is aptly termed by the natives 'Lua Pele,' (Pele's Pit,) for it is nothing but an immense hole, which the fire has *eaten* in the ground. The natives have no other tradition of its origin, than that it has been burning from the time 'of chaos' until now, gradually extending itself laterally and perpendicularly. Formerly, it overflowed its banks, and the reign of each of their kings has witnessed destructive eruptions.

"Count Strzelecki makes the north-northeast cliff four thousand one hundred and one feet above the level of the sea; Douglas, three thousand eight hundred and seventy-four. In descending to the black ledge, at the northeast extremity, the path winds round an old crater, small and steep on all sides; its bottom is covered with masses of large rocks, shaken down by earthquakes, and large trees are also growing in it, indicating a long repose.

"Following this path, we soon arrived on the ledge, which appeared like a field of ice breaking up in the spring. It varied from five hundred to two thousand feet in width, and then abruptly terminated in craggy and overhanging precipices, which had burst in every direction, from the action of the fire beneath. The main body of the crater had settled down from the black ledge, in some places gradually, until its own weight burst it violently from the edge, leaving gaping chasms, the sides of which were intensely heated; at others, it appeared to have sunk instantaneously, tearing away and undermining the ledge, and leaving precipices of two hundred feet in height. The greatest depth was about two hundred and fifty feet. The lakes, cones and forges remained, but were emptied of lava, and quiet, emitting nothing but smoke, excepting a lake at the southwestern extremity, of which a bend in the ledge hid from our view all but the rising flames. Evidently, a short time before, the ledge had been overflowed, as the lava was piled in masses twenty feet high or more, on its outer edge, gradually decreasing in height as it rolled in immense waves from it; and, without doubt, the whole mass had been raised, as we could now stand upon it and pluck ferns from the bank. We walked around the crater on the black ledge, endeavoring to find a place where it would be practicable to descend, but the banks were everywhere too much broken up to admit of it. Independently of that, they were so heated, that the brink could only be approached in a few places, and these only at great risk. It was cracked into great chasms, from a few feet to a rod in width, to which no bottom could be seen, and in places large masses had swollen up, and then tumbled in, like the bursting of an air-bubble or the falling in of a vast dome. The hollow, echoing sound beneath our feet, showed the insecurity of where we trod, and liability to give way, and precipitate us at any moment to instantaneous death; and I must confess that it was with fear that I walked along this path of destruction. On the surface of the ledge the rock was black and very vesicular, but as it descended it grew more compact, and became of a white or leadish color. From all these pits and chasms a white flickering flame ascended, so hot in one place that we attempted to cross as to singe the hair from our hands and scorch our clothing. Nothing but a precipitate retreat saved us from being enveloped in flames. The hot air would frequently flash up from the fissures without warning, and it required much caution and agility to escape from it. The thermometer, over one fissure, rose to one hundred and sixty-two degrees; on the ledge, five hundred feet from the brink, three feet above the ground, ninety-seven degrees; on the lava at the same place, one hundred and twenty-three degrees; two feet above a fissure, one hundred and forty-eight degrees; eighteen inches below the surface, it rose instantly to one hundred and sixty-six degrees. Continual heavy explosions were occurring on the sides, sounding like muffled artillery, throwing up stones, ashes and hot steam two hundred feet or more into the air, and rending away the banks, tumbled large masses of rock into the crater beneath. Indeed, the whole black ledge appeared like a mere crust, the igneous action beneath having eaten away its support, and which the slightest shock would precipitate into the gulf beneath, and thus restore the crater to its ancient limits.

" Small cones and diminutive piles of lava were scattered over its whole surface, where they had suddenly rose and as quickly cooled. They had assumed many fantastic and even beautiful shapes, and their hues were singularly brilliant and varied. On the southeast and south sides, lava had gushed laterally from the bank, and flowed down from the ledge. Near here are the sulphur hills, from which the finest specimens are obtained. They were prettily coated with fine white, blue and green salts, but owing to the intense heat and suffocating fumes of the gases, we were unable to secure many. A little farther on, we found the lava fissures incrusted with the most beautiful crystals and efflorescences, which had condensed into every variety of form and figure, but too delicate to bear exposure to the atmosphere. Having reached the southern extremity, we obtained our first view of the lake, the light of which had attracted our attention the previous night. It was several hundred yards in circumference, and in the most sunken part of the cauldron. The lava was twenty feet below its banks, a liquid body, boiling, bubbling, and thrashing in great fury. Occasionally it would become incrusted over, and then red streaks would shoot rapidly across its surface, leaving a momentary glimmer like meteors. In the centre, the lava was tossed high into the air, with a puffing, spluttering noise like the blast of a heavy bellows, mingled with the roar of the surf. Its color was livid, much resembling clotted blood, of which the whole might be taken for an immense hell-brewed cauldron, and the unearthly noises for the moans of agonized spirits, and the fiendish cries of their tormentors. The effect upon the imagination was powerful, and the reality horrible and *hellish*, beyond description. To the leeward the gases were strong, requiring much caution to avoid the stifling currents of heated air. On the northwest side, filamentose lava, commonly called ' Pele's hair,' was thickly strewed for many acres, like a field of mown grass.

" Mr. C. and myself, having performed the circuit until we were underneath where our hut stood, where the bank, having given way to a considerable height, formed a steep hill, which appeared quite practicable of ascent, we proposed to shorten the distance by climbing up at this spot. No sooner thought of than we made the attempt, and reached the first two hundred feet without any difficulty. Here, the summit being hid from us, we held a consultation whether to proceed or not. Upon looking down, we saw our natives gazing in astonishment at us, and urging us to return, saying that it was impossible for us to reach the top, and nothing but a bird could. However, like all obstinate personages, we did not like to retrace our steps, so we pushed ahead. A few rods more climbing brought us to the perpendicular face of the rock, or rather rocks, which were loosely imbedded in earth, and relieved only by some jutting points and a few roots, on which but little dependence could be placed. We were now so high that it was impossible to descend, as we could not see where to place our feet beneath us, and the slightest look downwards might make us loosen our hold and be dashed to pieces. Not the least danger was, that one of us might loosen a stone, which starting would draw down an avalanche of others, and ourselves with them. By looking up, zigzagging along the edge of the rocks, and bearing our weight equally as possible on all parts of our bodies, we drew ourselves slowly up, until we were within ten feet of the top. Here we met with the 'unkindest cut of all.' The rock was the smoothest, and just at the rising of the brink, hot steam issued from it, making the earth scalding and slippery. Mr. C. being ahead, and blessed with the longest legs, managed, by bearing his whole weight upon a projecting point of rock, not three inches in diameter, to make a spring, and at the same time clawing into the soft earth, he reached the summit with only burnt fingers. He then laid down upon his back, with his arms over his head, clinging to roots, and dangled his legs over the precipice to assist me. Following his steps, I hitched myself up, and making a grab at his toes, was safely *toed* to the bank. It was not until we were in perfect safety, that we realized the full extent of our danger, and our consummate folly in rushing into it. The slightest misstep, or want of presence of mind, would have hurried us to immediate death; and, while we felt grateful for our escape, we vowed another time 'to look before we climbed.'

"In the excitement of visiting this wonderful phenomenon, its real dangers are overlooked, and many unnecessary risks undergone. No accident has as yet happened, but some escapes have been little short of miraculous. Two gentlemen, a number of years since, were in the heart of the crater, examining the burning cauldron, when a rumbling noise was heard, and an earthquake felt. The rocks began to rattle down the sides of the chasm, and the ground beneath them was so unsteady, that they could not leave the spot where they were. Providentially it was slight, and soon over, and no eruption followed. In January, 1841, Dr. G. P. Judd descended the crater, for the purpose of procuring some of the liquid lava. Not being able to reach it at the great lake, he ventured into a smaller one, at the bottom of which there was a small stream. It appeared very quiet, the banks were steep, and he found some difficulty in reaching it. Having obtained a frying-pan full, he had returned to within a few feet of its brink, the steepest part, when a roar and a hissing noise alarmed him; a stream of lava in a narrow column was forced up into the air, far above his head, and descended in a shower all around. Much alarmed, he shouted for help. All of the natives near by ran away, except one, who threw himself upon his stomach, and grasping the Doctor's hand, assisted him out. But before this was accomplished, the lava rose so rapidly, that the heat of it burned his clothes, and blistered the face and hands of the native. They were no sooner on their feet, than the lava overflowed, and they were obliged to run with all speed to avoid being overtaken by the torrent. A narrower escape from a more horrible death, it is difficult to conceive.

"It is a common remark, that travelers visiting the volcano, even at short intervals, never see it under similar circumstances, and consequently are apt to discredit previous statements. A moment's reflection should convince them, that with such a mighty engine of nature, exercising in their highest degree the combined powers of fire, heated air, and steam, and continually in action, great changes are momentarily liable to occur; and that they do, these very discrepancies bear ample testimony. It would be an interesting point gained in geological science, if some observing man could reside in the neighborhood and note the various changes, at the periods of their occurrence.

"I have endeavored to present a faithful picture of it as it appeared at our visit, and it evidently differs much from all preceding descriptions. Douglas makes the depth of the crater, in 1834 one thousand one hundred and fifty-seven feet. At the present time it had filled up one half, and the black ledge, which had been gradually rising, was in some places within three hundred feet of the top, while former accounts state it at eight hundred. A few years since, the basin was much in its present state, like the inside of a bowl. A foreigner who visited it a week only before the late eruption, described it as resembling a dome, there being a gradual ascent from the sides to the centre ; the lava having overflowed the whole of the black ledge, the limits of which could not be traced. The whole surface was in violent action, thickly indented with fiery lakes, and crowned with puffing cones, and forges, whose bases were lashed by burning waves, and the whole accompanied with dreadful noises. Had not the liquid lava found a vent by pushing its way through subterranean galleries until it met with a weak spot, which its gravity soon forced through, and running out until the fiery mass in the crater subsided to a level with the outlet, it might have risen to the top, and overflowing, destroyed all that portion of the island. The immense lateral pressure which must exist, increasing as the crater fills up, will probably prevent any great and sudden disaster of this kind, by forcing an outlet toward the sea, as it did in this instance. Though so much has drained out, an immense body still remains in the volcano. On the second night of our stay, the fires were much more brilliant, and the reports more frequent.

" It is a remarkable fact, that on all the islands the general course of volcanic action is southeasterly, or rather, the craters form a chain from the northwest to the southeast. On Hawaii, Mauna Kea appears to have been extinguished first, then Hualalai. Mauna Loa has probably fire still beneath, though it has gradually cooled down by forming a series of lateral craters, extending from the great one on the summit to Kilauea, which is now the great fountain-head. Kilauea is pushing itself eastelry, as the late eruption bears witness, and the whole earth in that direction is doubtless pierced with galleries, which carry off the superabundant lava ; and when the ground becomes too weak to bear the pressure, it forces its way to the surface, and flows until it creates a common level at Kilauea. The several eruptions can easily be traced towards the sea ; and a series of lateral craters also, some of considerable extent, which have no doubt been fed from Kilauea. One, six miles to the east, is a mile in diameter, and emits smoke and sulphurous gases.

" It is a common remark that Kauai is the oldest island, and that the others have been successively thrown up from the ocean. In confirmation of this, we meet on that island a greater depth of soil, more vegetation, and far more arable land in proportion to its extent, than on the others, while at its southeastern extremity only, exist two small craters. Age has reduced others (if such there were) to the level of the surrounding soil, or clothed them with forests, so that their limits are undistinguishable. On Oahu, the traces of volcanic action become more numerous, and the craters larger, while on Maui the principal one forms a mountain of ten thousand feet elevation. But it is not until we reach Hawaii, that this terrible agency assumes its grandest and most sublime forms. Of the age of this island we can only conjecture ; it may have been coeval with the flood, or have been formed since the Christian era. Certainly, no one can view the mighty ruins of nature, and the process of creation and destruction, as it were in perpetual contest, without realizing the truth of the transitory existence of this earth, and that the day may be not far distant when indeed ' the elements shall melt with fervent heat.' Hawaii is fearful ground to tread upon. We are amazed at beholding the visible fires of Kilauea and their terrific action, but what are they but a mere speck in comparison with the immensity and power of the force required to raise up mountains of three miles perpendicular elevation, with bases of one thousand five hundred square leagues. Hawaii was formed by continual and repeated eruptions, depositing layer of rock upon layer, until it attained its present elevation ; and for aught we know the same action is still going on, at present quietly, but ready at any moment to burst out and overwhelm its unsuspecting inhabitants. There cannot be a doubt that to a great extent the interior of Hawaii is a vast globe of fire, against the sides of which the liquified rocks dash their fiery spray, and roll with unceasing noise ; and were it not for the number and magnitude of its vents, it would be shaken to pieces by successive earthquakes. Those who live amid these scenes, scarce be-

31

stow a thought upon the dangers which environ them.   But Vesuvius, after having
been dormant for a thousand years, revived, and buried several cities in its devastating streams; and the inhabitants of Catania, in Sicily, regarded as fables the historical accounts of previous eruptions of Ætna, until they were themselves overwhelmed in a sudden and instantaneous destruction.   In many places where
volcanoes have become overgrown with wood, and covered even with elegant villas,
they have with scarce a warning burst forth and laid waste whole districts, as in
1812, at St. Vincents, West Indies, where nearly all the plantations on that island
were destroyed, the lava flowing so rapidly as to reach the sea in four hours.
When this eruption took place, the earthquakes at Caracas, four hundred miles
distant, ceased, evidently showing that there was a connection between the two
places.   With such precedents, it would certainly not be astonishing if any of these
craters, which are at present quiescent, should at any moment burst forth, and
renew similar scenes of desolation ; and even Kauai may give vent, by some submarine communication, to the fires of Hawaii."

www.ingramcontent.com/pod-product-compliance
Lightning Source LLC
Chambersburg PA
CBHW020856270326
41928CB00006B/732